# The Triumvi

# The Ghost of the Unsaid

# Part One:

# The Panopticon

Brendan Thomas Marrett

# DEDICATION

This book is dedicated to the one million Irishmen and Irishwomen who died and the two and a half million who emigrated during the Great Silence (1845-1852).

"By a lonely prison wall, I heard a young man calling:
'Nothing matters, Mary, when you're free.
Against the famine and the crown,
I rebelled.
They cut me down.
Now you must raise our child with dignity'"
(Pete Saint John, "The Fields of Athenry").

# CONTENTS

ADDENDUM      7

PROLOGUE: DOLLHOUSE      9

PROLOGUE: FAREWELL, GER      21

PROLOGUE: THE INCIDENT      25

1    WHAT THE WATER GAVE ME      44

2    THE PROMISE      70

INTERLUDE: KILLADELPHIA, HERE I COME      92

3    RECRUDESCENCE      96

4    AVARICIOUS      111

5    FIGHT, FLIGHT OR FRIGHT      135

6    PRIDE AND PREJUDICE; OR FIRST IMPRESSIONS      154

7    THE TRIUMVIRATE      177

INTERLUDE: AURORA      205

8    COVENANT      219

INTERLUDE: THE MADNESS OF MEHKABIKIL      236

9    SOMETHING WICKED THIS WAY COMES      247

10    HAPPY BIRTHDAY      264

11    THE LAIR OF THE ELDER ELF      290

| | | |
|---|---|---|
| 12 | MAUSOLEUM | 317 |
| 13 | THE BANQUET | 334 |
| | INTERLUDE: RISE OF THE ELDER ELF | 356 |
| 14 | THE BALCONY SCENE | 359 |
| 15 | THE MIST-LURKER | 372 |
| 16 | BATTLE ROYALE | 393 |
| | INTERLUDE: DAVE WITHERSPOON | 415 |
| 17 | SCATHACH'S ISLE | 418 |
| | INTERLUDE: K'K'KO ZSET'S PROPHECY OF THE TRIUMVIRATE | 448 |
| 18 | ENTER THE JUNGLE | 451 |
| | INTERLUDE: SONG OF SONGS | 482 |
| 19 | REBELLION | 498 |
| 20 | HEADS WILL ROLL | 505 |
| 21 | DEAD THINGS | 511 |
| | INTERLUDE: THE LAST PETAL FALLS | 530 |
| 22 | ORC-GORGER | 541 |
| 23 | MONGRELS | 554 |
| 24 | NOTHIN' BUT MAMMALS | 564 |
| | TEASER: PARLAY | 583 |
| | ABOUT THE AUTHOR | 596 |

# ADDENDUM

BENJAMIN THOMAS COFFEY-WITHERSPOON is our primary narrator. A divisive figure, no two people who meet him form the same opinion. He is considered the Dark Lord by many, and the Chosen One by some.

The princess of Loux Laxciila has many titles, including Lady Eirianwen Brythonwen, the Lady of Light, Lodes Heddwen, and Lady Louxandria—an allusion to the chain of seven stars under which she was born, the brightest of which is the silver Gwawrddydd. Only the Elder Elf can reveal her true name, but to Benjamin, she is simply AURORA.

The Elder Wizard is Angoria's oldest created being. His true name has been lost to time, but he is most commonly known as MÓSANDRIRL, Wizard the First, the Red Wizard of the Flame, and Surtskvasír. He has fought in all previous Eleven Dual Cycle Wars, and now he leads the Resistance in a bid to destroy the Maze that his younger brothers created.

Born Qal-Shub, ZSESON MEHKABIKIL is the Elder Elf and current King of Loux Laxciila. After King Prim's death, the Queen Mother Ratsach assassinated the royal line in one foul swoop. Her grandson, the infant Qal-Shub survived only because of the bravery of counsellor Etsah, nurse Theodora, and Mósandrirl. Also known as the Laxciilian Lord Syaddon Metakiiria, he is unhappily married to Lucinda of Delhood, resentful towards his eldest son Alk'erion, and impassionedly loathing of Benjamin over some unspecified age-old grudge.

GIDEON has been the most frequent host for the Void—the ultimate evil power in Angoria. A Laxciilian citizen, Gideon was the first physical realm being to sin in Angoria, when he murdered a human who consequently became the First Wraith. Gideon and the Void created armies of orcs, goblins, and other horrid creatures to lay waste to the Free Peoples and their homelands in what came to be known as the First Great Dual War. Now he lies in a hidden pit, and his followers hope that the Void will find a home in him once more.

Green Coat is an ambiguous figure with a shadowy past drenched in blood, heartache, and vengeance. A time-lost anti-hero, Green Coat, also known as CILLIAN J. AXEBREAKER, was whisked away from planet Earth and has been bounced up and down the timestream wherever and whenever there was need of his deadly services.

THE TRIUNE is a group of rogue wizards—the telepathic Silas the Purple; Liriondas Exeter Liriondias the Silver (or Lear), metal-manipulator; and the frequently-forgotten alchemist, Merrick the Gold, manipulator of elements—who have trapped Angoria in a Maze dominated by Fear, Hybrids, and Sharmedes, a son of their own creation. As punishment for abusing the ancient magics, the Triune have lost their bodies and been trapped in an underground chamber in their dark tower, but three wizards this powerful won't be detained there forever...

# PROLOGUE
# DOLLHOUSE
# 2041

The first thing you must know about Nuala Coffey is that she was a moral woman who liked rules and was pleased when they were obeyed. As a child, Anna-Marie Ní Laithbheartaigh (as she was called back then) was advised never to let a man know what she was thinking. Back in her teenage years she was told never to act on her "worldly" feelings. When she was a fiancée, she was encouraged to respect her husband and instructed how to make their house a home. Yes, the ever-composed Nuala Coffey had spent her life following orders, even in the most disorderly of situations. Perhaps that was the reason she was so annoyed when others did not act similarly.

Her bewildered face stood frozen at the foot of the staircase. Her nine-year-old son, Benjamin-Joshua, sat upright on the armchair next to the television, and played half-heartedly with a wooden wizard called Mo-Mo who had been carved by Gerard Coffey long ago as per Nuala's instruction. Benjamin-Joshua had once been told not to listen in on adults' conversations so, of course, his ears pricked at the scent of scandal.

"I see you've replaced the armchair with a hamper." Her eyes nodded to his jacket; its arms clawed around the furniture like dripping paint. Anything remotely out of place in 124 Lincoln Lane was a disturbance to Nuala's polished lifestyle.

"Of course. I'll return the jacket to the closet presently."

"Don't bother. You can wear it on your way to the police station. When might that be exactly? I'm thinking of serving dinner at six."

Ger laughed, unconvinced, and folded the newspaper in his right hand. "Never." At this, Nuala dropped the laundry basket in shock, her countenance fiery as her hair. "You weren't serious about that?"

Before Ger took two steps, his wife's long bony fingers caged tightly around his one good arm. His left arm had been cut off at the elbow one day while sawing wood in the seldom-used garage-cum-workshop. Every time Ger looked at him, all he saw was a five-year-old Benjy, the brightly coloured ball coming out of nowhere, and a blank bloody space where his arm had been. Perhaps this explained why he now looked at Benjamin-Joshua so rarely.

"You ran over our friend with your car, and I'll be darned if I'm going to let that slide."

It was true. After a particularly tough day at the news station, *Universal News Network* (*UNN*), Ger came home to his doting wife and a cold beer (or five), and in a senseless rage, attacked his better half; then nearly eliminated pedestrian and off-duty local cop Paul Samson, husband to Nuala's best friend Allison. Paul was comatose for three months—just like the Coffey marriage was now, ever since last week when a tipsy Ger confessed his road rage to his wife during the newest filmic adaptation of *The Great Gatsby*.

"I said I was sorry."

"I know you did. And I know it hasn't been easy since… your accident. But it has been four years." Before he could interject with a redundant repetition, she continued, "You're upset that you did it and you're fearful of the consequences… but you're not sorry."

"Nuala, please, I'll be ruined. I'll lose my job and my reputation!

Think about what my arrest would do to this family. We'd be humiliated, and Benjy needs me!"

Benjamin-Joshua hated to be called that name. Ger had never called the child by his full name; not only because Ger detested double-barrelled names, but because of what, and *who*, 'Joshua' represented. Benjamin-Joshua did not know its significance but there was something in that name Nuala tried to hold onto or reclaim from a vanished past.

Ger's words struck a nerve with her. If there were two things she would have risked her life on, it was that appearance was reality, and the importance of a platinum reputation. She considered his words for a moment.

"Don't you see? *You* have already been shamed. You almost took a human life. You have serious issues you need to work through. Just imagine if one day you were to hit…"

*There are worst things I could do*, thought Ger, and he cocked his head in the direction of the boy. "But Nuala—"

"No *buts*, my love. A sacrifice must be made to atone for what you have done."

"Paul has forgiven me for trying to k—"

"Exactly! You couldn't even murder him right!"

Ger ignored the seriousness in his wife's voice in an utterance she did not possibly mean. "My point is, had you let me finish, I have nothing else to be sorry for. Paul won't tell anyone. Our secret is safe. Why should I pay for something he doesn't resent me for?"

"Because I know. I stood by you when all my friends said you were violent, that I would be better off without you. I told them you were good, caring, and honourable—a moral compass. I need you to be that man now. I need you to prove me right." She let go of his arm. He raised his right one and rubbed hers. His lips parted but before he could speak—

"Doesn't my opinion mean more to you than anyone else's?"

"Well, of course—"

"Ger, right now I am afraid of you, and I..." She drew a breath that filled her with self-assertion and confidence. "I cannot wear this wedding ring if I am ashamed to know you. It's time you took responsibility for what you did... to Paul." She picked up the laundry basket and noticed her youngest son's all-knowing stare. She smiled endearingly. It was a smile that said, "*the grown-ups are talking, honey, so you shouldn't really be listening*".

"Nuala," Ger began, aware that the punishment was the only means to win back her favour.

"No. If this marriage is to work, then I have to be able to look at you, and if that is to happen, then you have to turn yourself in." She strolled to the kitchen, stopped in the doorway, turned, and indicated with a nod to the cell phone on the small table next to the front door. "I have a number of chores to complete this afternoon, so I'll be out of your hair. That will give you time to make the much-delayed call without any *further* embarrassment. I expect that call to be made by the time dinner is ready."

She disappeared inside the kitchen, her face, a stretchy, malleable mask that with each step moulded from one of sternness to fear followed by grief. Her silent son read that her heart was breaking but went back to playing with Mo-Mo.

She spun around instantly, a new woman. "Amendment: soup will be served at five-thirty and paprika chicken upon the hour. Don't be late." Then her plastic smile and snowy top teeth disappeared.

Ger wondered why he had ever married such a cold, stoic do-gooder. He turned his head to the phone and a callous smile snaked across his face—no such call would be made. He sneered at the jacket on the couch and climbed the stairs, a retreat his hawkeyed wife observed.

Yes, Nuala Coffey had been given orders her entire life—orders she had been expected to follow. But what Ger did not realise was that she also expected her demands to be obeyed. She picked up the phone in the kitchen and dialled 9-1-1. "Hello, my name is Nuala C... Laverty. May I please speak to the police?"

The starter course was served promptly by the tall beehive-haired woman. Ger thought she looked classy, but unlike Benjamin-Joshua, he gave her no such compliment. He sat at the head of the dining-room table which Benjamin-Joshua thought ought to be reserved for Mother.

Ger made no attempt to converse with the child. This came as no surprise to the boy, since Ger only ever acknowledged him directly when the boy was watching his shows to offer him headphones to silence all traces of his existence. Benjamin-Joshua informed Mother that Josiah was dreadfully unwell and would not be joining them for dinner, to which she nodded and *mm-hmm*'d in agreement. Rather, Mo-Mo would occupy the fourth space at the table—but he wasn't hungry.

"Just this once," Nuala compromised, and as she took her seat, said she hoped to see Josiah back to full health the next day. Ger shook his head as if listening to a fifty-year-old woman talking about Santa Clause more passionately than a child does.

After what felt like the time it takes to wash a sink full of dishes, Nuala tried to initiate conversation with the grimacer. She would have preferred had he yelled "Stop staring at me, you prune" than sat there seething silently. Thinking self-ridicule was the way to go, she derided her soup saying it was too thick, and dropped her jaw in feigned shock. When this got no reaction, she quietly resigned for an admission of truth—that it was the best borscht she had ever made. At ten to the hour, she cleared away two empty bowls and licked spoons, plus Ger's full bowl, and whispered, "What a waste!"

Next, she brought out three plates of paprika chicken and rice. She poured Ger a glass of expensive blue-black wine for which she received no thanks. She noticed her son's eyes were fixated where Ger's left arm should have been.

"Darling," his mother intervened.

He averted his gaze and lied, "Sorry!" Though he had not the words to articulate it, he had always found Ger's mutilation a perversion in their otherwise pristine household.

"It's amazing, Mommy," he beamed, eyes and tongue on his dinner.

"Speak only when spoken to, Benjy."

"Yes, sir." Head bowed reverently, Benjamin-Joshua swung his legs under the table. Ger's right hand plummeted roughly on his thigh, ordering him to stop. The doll-child blinked and averted his gaze to his dinner. And he froze and starved.

"Eat up, my child," Nuala encouraged. He obeyed. "Oh, and tomorrow we have to clean that room of yours," she said gently.

*Never going to happen*, he smiled back cheekily.

She turned her attention towards her husband. "I wish you wouldn't be so harsh with him. He just gave me a compliment." *It's more than you do.*

"Children should know their place. So should—"

"I called the cops, Ger."

*I will knife you, chop you up, dissolve you in a bucket of vinegar, and pour you down the drain.*

"But then I hung up. Straight away," she apologised.

"You did what?" he barked, sprang to his feet, and dropped his saucy plate to the floor. The chair clattered behind him for long hollow seconds, each one ringing with a harsh cacophonous beating.

"I understand why you're angry, but now that I know I could bring myself to turn you in... Surely that means something?"

"It means you're a lousy wife. I knew you had troubles, *Anna-Marie*"—Benjamin-Joshua had never heard this name before— "but to do this, to me, your own husband..." Ger raised a fist. Nuala fell back in her chair, aware of the rough ball's weight and the prickle of its thistly hairs. He breathed fire and turned, his heavy footsteps thudding to the couch where he retrieved his jacket. Then the front door slammed.

Against the tense thick buzz of silence, Benjamin-Joshua sat silently and ate his dinner at his normal pace—slower than most people. He began again to kick his legs up and down, but it soon lost its fun.

The nonchalance was so forceful it felt like the moans of a hovering ghost vibrated over the table until at last, Nuala spoke, her stare fixed on Ger's glass of wine: "Finally!"

Eventually the boy finished eating. Nuala got to her feet, made her way to the sink, and armed with her favourite yellow gloves, scrubbed and rinsed and scrubbed and rinsed. Tears welled up but she shoved them back into the ducts from whence they came. She had dishes to clean, and she made them sparkle.

Alone at the kitchen sink, she caught sight of her equally lone reflection in the wide spotless mirror. She sighed with relief.

Then she put her cutlery, utensils, and dishes in their respective places—everything had a place—but perhaps, she considered, not everyone did.

She returned to the dining-room, squatted, and wiped away Ger's splatters on the polished floor, then rose as if in slow motion, her mounting eyes level with the wine glass. Her mouth suddenly became very dry, barren, and very sensual. She wondered for a second what it would be like to reintroduce her lips to an old friend; one that had been there for her after her exploits in a far-off land back when her name was Anna-Marie. She licked her scarlet lips with the tip of her tongue. She couldn't remember if she had ever craved anything so much in all her life.

*Oh, the smell of it!*

"What's for dessert, Mommy?"

Suddenly alert to the temptation, she sped into the kitchen, and emerged with a large bowl of trifle, topped with custard, cream, and chocolate flakes.

But she left the glass of wine on the table, simultaneously with every, yet no, intention of drinking it.

Tucked in darkness, Nuala stood over her seemingly sleeping darling under a blown bulb and low ceiling. The room had once been hers; Anna-Marie's family moved into 124 soon after she turned sixteen. They had just left their homeland, Ireland, their friends, everything! Nuala, as she had begun to call herself, had chosen this room simply because she adored the view from the upper window. One could see both ends of the street from up there, including the house of Ger's now-deceased aunt, the one who proudly introduced the two Gaelic exiles, both sixteen then. She gave a speech at their wedding the year after they graduated from college. She died last year.

A children's Bible Nuala had read from lay open in her palms. David and Goliath. David's face had been scribbled over; he was no longer a young shepherd boy, but a masked superhero delivering pizza. And Goliath's number one worry was a bag of stones big as tennis balls no more, but an X's and O's grid of tic-tac-toe that had magically appeared before him. Nuala placed it on a bookshelf on the other side of the room.

Struck suddenly by memory, her eyes spun round to the fading walls she had painted a lifetime ago. In the darkness, she could no longer see them, but in her mind's eye they were vivid. On the wall facing the door, a young knight wore simple baby blue armour and a helmet. A conical visor lifted upwards revealed hazel eyes. In his right hand was an excellently painted sword with a hawk design on the handle and an emerald for an eye. Alongside the door was a pink and red dragon. Gone were the razor-sharp teeth, the scorching flames, and point-tipped wings—this image was child-friendly and full of circular shapes. Closets on the left made that wall invisible.

Outside the window on the right next to Benjamin-Joshua's bed, a car door slammed. The front door swung uncertainly. Footsteps crashed into furniture. Heavy steps climbed half the staircase and called out for someone called Nora. *Great, he's drunk!*

Moments later, Ger stumbled into the room. Her eyes remained on her son as she asked, "Where were you? I was so worried." *That's what people are supposed to say, isn't it?*

"I just drove around town, thinking," he said, hoping his mouldy hiccups would not give him away. Looking at the child, he emotionlessly added, "He's getting so big."

"No, he isn't. He's Mommy's little man." The child stirred unnoticeably, very much alert. "We used to be so happy. There was a time when our lives were perfect. I'm sure of it. I just can't remember it right now."

Ger said nothing. He had always been aware that in this suburban picture, certain silences had been kept—what was unsaid ceased to exist—but it was only now that he began to consider that perhaps ignorance was not enough to sustain their idyll pretense. After a pause: "I will miss you when I'm gone." Nuala gave no indication that she had heard him. Benjamin-Joshua wondered if Ger would miss him too. When Ger inched closer, Nuala sprang to guard the bed and stared him right in the eye, focused and determined, not to be crossed. Ger's time in the plastic world of 124 was over.

Benjamin-Joshua wondered if Ronan belonged—he did live elsewhere, after all.

It ensued that an argument erupted, an attack on Nuala's virtues, her heart-palpitating repetition that *"Perfection is not a flaw,"* how she had not been a "nut-job nobody" when he first invited her to the cinema. That the child's slumber resumed through all this should have been evidence that he had not been asleep to begin with—but they had not had the wit to realise it.

Finally, defeated, Nuala turned away from Ger, plumped the pillows Benjamin-Joshua's head were not on, and released her anger with a gentle breath. She plastered a smile over her face, cheerfully bid her husband goodnight, and promised him cinnamon rolls and pastries for breakfast that she had no intention of baking.

But just as she was about to leave the room, something inside her snapped and she turned and faced the bed. "I'm not strong enough. I thought I was. I really did. But I'm not. I was depending on you to do the right thing and you let me down. I was depending on you to be the strong one and you failed miserably." She paused, words on her tongue, but said no more until long after Ger, thinking she was asleep, had crept into bed, when she spat, "Just go."

Nuala awoke not fifteen minutes after Ger's dusk exodus, her sheets (on Ger's side of the bed) yellow from the beer his pores had excreted. There had been many things she expected to wake up to:

limescale in the kettle; the morning newspaper on her lawn, drenched by the sprinklers; a bottle of chardonnay lingering in the refrigerator door, but a note written in Ger's excellent penmanship was not among them:

*My dearest Nuala,*

*You were correct, as always, when you said that a price had to be paid for my transgressions. That is why I have decided to turn myself in. Please do not come and visit me; the shame would be unbearable. Be happy, my dearest one, and raise Benjy to be a true gentleman, just like the man I will be upon my release from prison.*

*Truly, my darling, there will never be another one like you. Keep fighting the good fight and wait for me until I return. Please.*

*Yours sincerely,*

*Gerard Coffey.*

Not the most eloquently phrased apology, but it was a start. This was what she had wanted: breathing space, justice.

Just then, it hit her she had never realised how large the bed was, or how empty the closet was without Ger's clothes.

But she resented what he had done to their family. In disgust, she tore up the letter and lashed its shreds into the trash can by the bed on top of the five inkless pens he had tried to write with before he found one that worked.

By her bedside stood their favourite wedding photograph, and oh, how she admired the smiling gent who held her, for he was frozen in time, immortalised in blissful stasis, and would never know what lay in store: endless bills; over-the-phone frauds who request your bank details; treachery of the highest order; and exactly what he deserved.

# PROLOGUE
# FAREWELL, GER

At six o'clock that morning, Benjamin-Joshua woke with a startle. He had always slept heavily, but now the slightest noise was enough to wake him. He scanned the room to see if something had fallen. His inaccurate alarm clock was buried beneath a pile of dirty socks he did not remember wearing. Entertaining books he had only ever scribbled on piled in a pyramid. An upside down five-hundred-paged mammoth gobbled some *Jenga* blocks. Everything was exactly where it had been last night before Nuala left.

He rolled over onto his left-hand side and stretched his right arm down beneath the bed. Like a dog snooping for clues, his hand poked and prodded about the floor, shaking off used tissues, tough jigsaw puzzles, and a mushed half-eaten brown apple. His fingertips brushed off the cell phone he used predominantly as a watch.

He heard the *chink-chink* of a car trunk, then peaked out the window and witnessed something he did not fully understand but had been half-expecting. Employing much caution, he opened his window wide enough to aurally observe the man in his driveway mutter to himself about the witch upstairs, but subtly enough to go unnoticed.

But that was an easily discarded detail when compared to the crazed, orange, thirty-something crossing the street. She sported a pink dressing gown that clashed violently with a yellow woolly scarf. Her baggy pyjama bottoms sank below her thong and one kneecap. She resembled one who knocks on a stranger's door and creates a diversion while her friend goes around the back and steals the washing-machine. An army of striking pink bobbins gave her a Medusaic look. Her name was Allison 'Ally'

Samson and she was Copper Paul's wife, and one of the few people who knew the truth about the hit-and-run. Behind her back, Ger called her "the Duchess".

Ally had woken a couple of minutes before the youngest Coffey. The technologically illiterate dinosaur once accidentally set an alarm for "earlier-than-sane-people-wake-up-at-a.m." and had no idea how to turn it off. Too proud to ask her husband for assistance lest he joked about it with his mistress (who abandoned him the day after the hit-and-run incident) she confined herself to the fact she would never sleep through the night again until either she or her phone died. The former was the likelier. Ally had crept out of bed as inconspicuously as she could to avoid waking Paul and tiptoed down the staircase to avoid waking her son Rupert, Benjamin-Joshua's best friend and the only one who was not imaginary. Quietness, however, was not Madame Samson's strong point, and angry, exhausted groans and moans echoed from the bedrooms.

As she filled herself a glass of water in her kitchen, she saw Ger exit his house. Since they worked together, and she drank tea with his wife tri-weekly, Ally knew he had no prearranged out-of-town assignments for at least another week, and suspected Nuala may finally have called it quits on their marriage. Considering it her divine assignment to investigate, Ally crossed the sleeping street and tardily curtained her dressing-gown. Its uneven belt slithered to her feet and she nearly tripped. She was accustomed to making bizarre, unnecessary hand gestures, so it looked like she constantly swatted flies only she could see. She pelted the non-existent cretins so ferociously that her girly pink fingernails got tangled in her hair and swiped several bobbins onto the road. She melodramatically scooped them up again, having no tolerance for waste, hence the bathtub-cum-flowerbed in her back yard. Benjamin-Joshua pictured the giant lollypop stick as a large flower one might see in a far-off tropical island and beamed giddily.

Her reflection appeared in Ger's window. His gaze remained on his car, if it can even be called a gaze since his sore head forced his eyes to press down like slits. He hoped she would walk past the car, but her clown-sized slippers only neared. Though they both worked for *UNN*, they had barely engaged in any verbal exchanges since the day they met. They left for work at the same time, had the same hours off for lunch, and returned home shortly after one another, but carpooling was never discussed. Since it was abundantly clear that Ger was aware of her presence, feigning ignorance was futile. Physically pained at having to acknowledge her, he greeted Ally less than half-heartedly and asked what she was doing up, with a tone of unconcealed annoyance and of an aspiration that she would not answer.

"Oh, I couldn't sleep," Ally lied. "Ger," she whispered, "What's going on? Where are you headed at this hour?" (Perhaps it should be delineated that Ally's definition of whispering was to speak as loudly as a thunderstorm—hence, the boy hearing every word).

"I'm off to a conference in Chicago." He closed the trunk of his car and hoped she would take the hint to go home. A scorching spotlight scanned his back and he turned to find her face bobbing like a dog in a car window, encouraging elaboration on this imaginary trip.

"Philadelphia, huh? It's been a while since you were there, I imagine…"

"Oh, yes. Too long. There's nothing better than the fresh Philadelphian air on a beautiful morning such as this."

She was surprised to have caught him out so easily. Frankly, so was the eavesdropper. "Wow, you really have not had a cup of coffee yet, have you?" she asked, embarrassed for him, but proud too for having engaged in their longest conversation. He quietly walked toward the car door and insinuated that it was time for this untimely encounter to end.

"Ger, wait," she said and nearly tripped again. Much to his annoyance, she grabbed his stump for support. She told him she forgave him (she said this for she had made a bigger deal of his road rage than Paul had after waking up and returning to the Lane) and did not want their history to tear him away from his family, and interferingly added that he should just stay somewhere local until Nuala calmed down.

Benjamin-Joshua heard his mother stir slightly. He shut his window more loudly than intended, swiftly leapt back into bed, pulled the covers over his face, and pretended to be deep in slumber. He was so anxious to know what happened outside that, by the time he had finished day-dreaming of how their conversation went and ended, the full-grown morning sun had signalled it was time for all the Lane to rise and shine and greet the day with a smile.

However, had he known that only a few hours later his hands would be smeared in the blood of a Samson, he would have stayed in bed or shut the window on his neck.

# PROLOGUE
# THE INCIDENT

The aromatic scents of almond essence and vanilla extract had already begun perfuming the kitchen when Benjamin-Joshua snuck in. He tiptoed behind the open door, enjoying his free front-row ticket to the baking show, engrossed in the determination in his mother's eyes and how it shifted into a fake look of surprise when the dessert turned out perfectly. She usually sensed when he was there but was too absorbed in her grief and therapy this morning to notice him enter.

She sweated as she vigorously attacked the cake mixture with the full might of her until-then pent-up fury and agony. Though usually such a tidy baker, flour smeared her forehead like sleet on a window and creamy balls braided her unmade do.

The front door opened and closed. Footsteps. Her youngest son was surprised she noticed, given the intensity of her daggering the cake mixture. "Ger?" Her face lit like morning sunshine. She was surprised by how readied she was to pounce into his arms, so did not have time to assume a false demeanour when Ronan's face appeared. He noticed her disappointment.

"Hello to you, too, *Nuala*," he said, offended.

She welcomed him with all the cheer she could muster, and said she thought he was—

"In my mid-forties, beardless, and sporting a really strange haircut."

"Obviously."

"Sorry to disappoint," he said sarcastically.

Benjamin-Joshua adored his older brother and although he did not show it, was very upset the day Ronan left home.

"Where's B?"

"Upstairs, I imagine."

*Mwahahaha.*

"Good."

*Oh...*

"How much do you need?"

Ronan feigned offence, but deep down was impressed by her spot-on prediction, even if she portrayed him primarily as a mercenary. "Sixty bucks," he chimed.

"Take twenty less." She nodded to her purse. "What's it for?"

Certain that Lincoln Lane's most traditional homemaker would not approve of his future purchases, he ignored her question and responded with one of his own. "Where's himself?"

"Why is Ronan not answering Nuala's question?"

"Probably for the same reason Nuala's not answering Ronan's."

"Don't call me by my name. It's weird."

"So," he snooped around like a stranger, "Where is he?"

"So," she returned, void of any interest in conversing about her marital breakdown, "What's it for?"

"You don't want to know."

"It's my money, so if you want it—"

"A few cans and bottles."

"Shush! Not while your brother's in the house." Her glance attacked him. Although he knew it had been a struggle for her in the past, Ger had always drunk in the house, and Ronan's excessive liquor consumption had long been a source of contention with Nuala, mostly because of the reckless abandonment he infamously gave way to afterward, a cracked mirror of her own teenage frivolities. More than once, someone had ended up bloodied, in jail, or in a car wreck after Ronan downed the strong stuff.

Ronan smirked, "Told you so."

Resisting the urge to say *charming* disgustedly, she made him promise to be careful. Then she poured her cake mixture into a baking tray and placed it in the pre-set humming oven.

"So... Ger... Where is he?"

The phone rang: "There is a God!" Nuala praised with relief and made her closest ever gesture to a fist-pump.

"Hello," she greeted, composed and formal. "No, I am not he. I am his better half. To whom am I speaking?" Ronan sat on a stool and glared like a vulture sizing up a mouse, assessing its probability of survival, only to find that it is zero percent. "Ah, yes, of course. I am so sorry. I've been meaning to call you all morning, but Ger has left town. It was a last-minute thing. Israel. That country is just full of good news stories. .... Mm-hmm, it is just shocking how he ups and leaves at all hours. If you would like, I could ask Allison Samson if she's free. I know it's her day off, but she is so interested in this one world currency thing. .... Oh, worry not. I will call Ger as soon as I have a moment and give him a good telling off. How dare he leave you in the lurch! .... Yes, yes, goodbye now. Have a lovely day." She returned the electronic phone to its charger and kept her back to Ronan.

After all these years, Ronan knew when his mother was keeping something from him, and he now saw that her heart was breaking. He gazed at her, but not for information, but to offer support. Nuala wanted so much to tell him that Ger, who he had never got on with, had left, but she could not articulate the words or even face him. Ronan got up and walked towards her.

"I know you don't want to talk about it, but I am here for you." As he said this, he took slow small steps towards her. "You're a private person. You don't like to share your problems... or deal with them. You cover them up, and most times that works for you. But I don't work that way. I'm not going to ask you what's wrong, but I promise to be here for you when—or if—you need help in any way."

She looked up at the extraordinary young man who stood before her and found it hard to believe he was the same psychopath who had done everything in his power to drive her crazy in his teens. He and her husband had swapped roles. Her mouth curved with pride. She tried to speak, but to open her mouth would be to fall apart.

"I know demonstrations of emotion make you all robotic." She laughed. "However, I'm going to hug you and as soon as you're ready to

28

break, just pull away, okay?" She allowed him to wrap his arms around her and make her feel a little bit better.

He was so proud when she leaned into his embrace. Her tears fell freely, but she would not let Ronan see her cry. She caught the salty beads with her fingers to keep his shirt collar dry and she cried her fill. Benjamin-Joshua, on the other hand, felt disappointed—she had basically admitted she needed help, that she had been defeated. He would revise this scene later and Mother would be a conqueror who tells Ronan to sod off and get out of her kitchen.

Eventually she pulled away with haste. Ronan was surprised when the time came to separate, but backed away slowly, and beheld the perfectly dry face of the repressed mask who had raised him. It was an impersonal smile, a haunting one.

"You should go now. I should give the house a clean."

Ronan scanned the room; it was flawless but for a few splatters of cake mixture. He looked at her quizzically. His mouth opened wide as a washing-machine at his mother's unsettling transformation. She practically swept him to the front door, opened it fully, thanked him for stopping by, and wished him a happy day's shopping. He walked out speechlessly and left the money behind.

They had had their most intimate moment, but the very coldness that had led him to despise her back in his prepubescent years had brought it to an end. By the time he thought of something to say, she had closed the door in his face, and that was the last time he ever saw her.

A month later he died in a road traffic accident; the local papers claimed that it was his fault.

Early afternoon rolled away. There was an unexpected knock on the door. Nuala had barely opened it when her name was screamed by healthy lungs apparently more upset than her.

"Allison, darling, whatever is the matter?" she asked, and let her in.

"Oh, Nuala, I've just heard," she lied. The world's most sympathetic friend asked how her flame-haired bestie was doing and made such expressive arm gestures she looked to be lifting dumbbells.

"I am perfectly delightful, thank you, dear. But what is this story you heard? Come now, don't be selfish." Her tone gave nothing away about inkless pens, empty closets, and prison bars.

Ally faked a smile and bit her lip at her neighbour's diffidence, and, as though some carnal vermin sniffing for meat-threads from a thrown-out fishbone, the scents of chocolate-chip cookies, cake, and banana bread carried her towards the kitchen. Nuala usually hated such forwardness but allowed Ally away with a surprisingly expansive array of offences in the decorum handbook.

Just then Nuala saw a car drive past her house. Inside were potential buyers of the Holden house in which a family of five had lived until recently. They moved some time after two of the children had vanished without a trace. It was all anyone talked about for months. She said a short prayer for them and shut the door tightly.

"I do hope my darling boy is behaving himself over in your place," Nuala called out as she walked through the sitting-room and into the adjoining dining-room, where Ally was.

"He and Rooper the Trooper are watching a movie, and he is as polite as ever," she replied, which Nuala had already guessed. The closed book scooted in front and led her into the spotless dining-room. Ally quickly felt embarrassed her house was never as tidy and rejected the offer of a glass of water. She pulled out a seat and sat unsteadily, waving her upper body, fidgeting with her hands, and flicking her fingers like blinking traffic lights. "Where's Ger?"

"Chasing down a story on new age dentistry."

Ally's follow-up questions quickly became intrusive. When asked why so interested, she shrugged, "I just have something to ask him."

*Buzz…*

"Doorbell."

Directly across the street, Benjamin-Joshua and Rupert Gabriel Samson stared at the Coffey house from the kitchen. Rather, Roop gawked while his friend's head bobbed above the cutlery drawer, so he could see the discoloured fishbowl and a whole lot of sky, but he knew what he was supposed to be looking at.

"So, what do you think of the movie, Thomas?" Thomas was Benjamin-Joshua's middle name. They had played a game once in which they were characters in a fantasy world and adopted different personas— "You can't let the goblins know your real name, or they'll find out where you live and eat the man of the house and run off with the woman," Roop had explained to his wide-eyed neighbour who smiled every time he thought of Ger on a goblin's dinner plate. The name Thomas had just stuck after that.

"I don't like it. I don't think my mom would, either..."

Roop followed with a petulant *"My house, my rules"*-type remark, then, parched, loudly downed a glass of lemonade. Thomas eyed it for a few seconds, but quickly accepted that Roop had no intention of offering him one. The unnecessarily turned-on lights flickered, and the upstairs shower whirred.

In their most homo-social moment to date, during the movie, Roop had informed the blissfully ignorant and firmly disbelieving Thomas of anatomical things that Thomas asserted could not possibly be true. They then shared with one another their secret crushes. After fifteen minutes of blushing and shyly saying, "Naw, it doesn't matter, it's silly," and "It'll never happen, we're just nine," Thomas named Paige Shauna Andrews, a pretty girl their age who was moving to Ireland soon. Roop mentioned half the girls in town, and over half a dozen women. And in unison: Poison Ivy of 135.

Thomas stood on his tiptoes, head tilted towards the window like a seal balancing a ball on its nose, because he was so short. His eyes locked on a man he had never seen before standing outside a house the local teenagers had begun breaking into every weekend; for what purpose, Mother had never said. Quietly and very dramatically he asked, "Do you think he'll buy *that* house?" and with a terrified tone, "The haunted one?"

Roop stared at him omnisciently, "It wasn't the house that ate Cassie and Peter, stupid. It was the Lights."

"Uh-huh. You expect me to believe that a streetlamp ate two teenagers?"

"Are you a moron, or do you just like people to think you are? And wipe that look off your face. It fattens your cheeks. No, don't smile. You have an ugly smile. It's all just... too much. ... Better... Better... Now, where was I? Oh, yeah, they were outside lights, on the street, in the air, between the trees, within and outside of reality... Cassie told me about them—twice, actually. She said they called to her, like a whisper, saying nothin' but her name." Then he proceeded to imitate the wind calling Cassie and appeared to swim in the air. "Before she died! And Peter, too." He dived at Thomas who seemed unmoved by Roop's theatrics, and more interested in the lemonade glass he knocked over and smashed.

"What are you talking about?"

"Do you know nothin'? Like, are you for serious? The Lights called to Cassie one night when she was outside, and it was dark, and she couldn't see nothin'. So, she ran inside, like, into her house, and the noises stopped. The next day, as she was leavin' for school, the Lights gobbled her up and took her and Petey away for hours, no days, months even, then spat them back to that very same moment. Petey couldn't handle the transition, so he jumped off that bridge; the one that's closed now. At least, that's what Dad says. Not that he'd know, since he slept through all of it. But they never found Petey's body, so I think the Lights got him again. And as for Cassie, well, she went cray-cray. Men in white coats came to take her in the middle of the night, but they couldn't find her. It was the Lights again. I'm sure of it."

"And she told you all of this?" Benjamin-Joshua replied, utterly unconvinced; even more so when Roop relayed the Holdens' adventures, a mere summary of *The Lion, the Witch, and the Wardrobe*, minus the Beavers.

Roop continued to spy out the window. "Oh, look, Mister Man has children. Wait here." Exeunt: Roop.

For two hours, Thomas stood on the spot and waited for his friend to come back. And when, finally, Roop did return with an ice-cream cone, triumphant expression, and slobbery-kissed cheek, he regarded Thomas with more irritation than if he was a fly. "Are you still here?"

"You told me to wait."

"Right," he remembered, then walked past, plopped himself on the couch, and resumed the movie. "Idiot," he mumbled under his breath.

Benjamin-Joshua looked up at the still-whirring ceiling. "Is he okay? He's been in the shower for a long time."

"Sometimes he forgets how to walk, the poor sap," Roop shrugged, much in the manner of his mother.

"I think I'll go home now. Do you want to play tomorrow?" Roop only licked his ice-cream. "So, I'm going now. Bye."

"Beejie-Weejie, do you wan' play out back? I've got a really great game for us to play."

"Sure!" Thomas exclaimed. At this, Roop smiled in the knowledge that the puppet was under his power and when it truly mattered, would do whatever he asked. Tugging tightly on his strings, Roop led him out to the back yard.

Benjamin-Joshua crept from Roop's yard and snuck into 124, hoping that his friend's mother wouldn't notice him. He closed the front door even more quietly than he had opened it, tiptoed into the kitchen, and saw that the double doors to the dining-room were open. Like an adventurer hiding from cannibals in a jungle, he slunk down low, and crawled silently to the opening. He stared at the women and hoped his mother would see him.

But he went completely unnoticed.

Ever since the headscarf-donned Rita moved into 128, the ladies of Lincoln Lane had met once a month to play a card or board game. A talented player and game maker, Rita was well-versed in just about every card game that existed. As a direct result of her knowledge, passion and commitment, the games table quickly became the ladies' sanctuary, their homo-social space where purses emptied, stories on the... joys of parenting were exchanged, and where the women learned the unvarnished truth about the lives of their nearest and dearest. Yes, these gaming events marked the knocking down of the white picket fences, and the establishment of community and friendship. However, for one of these women, the table was primarily a place for listening as opposed to sharing—much to the annoyance of her friends.

Nuala dealt the cards delicately and distributed them soundlessly. "It's so odd having more cards in the deck now that Henrietta's gone."

"Five more cards... the weight of it," Rita laughed wryly.

"Don't poke fun. Her children vanished without a trace. Children from our street, gone, just like that. Perhaps we should replace her with Georgia," she suggested, considering how much it would mean to the Lane's oldest resident to be included.

"But she doesn't even like you," Ivy Bird, the Governor's lady friend, retorted thoughtlessly. Sexy, fun-loving, and armed with a crassly acidic tongue, the regal young resident of 134 always had a bad word to say about someone. "Remember that time someone threw trash all over your front lawn, and painted *PRISSY-PRISSY-PRISS-PRISS* on your garage door? I'm pretty sure that was her." Rita nodded in agreement and gave Nuala a warm, pitiable smile.

The moment was cut short by the Duchess' unsubtle and continuous queries regarding Ger. This struck Nuala as odd given that Ally's relationship with him had always been congenially amicable at best, and cold at that. Thus, the host decided to change the subject.

"Oh, come on, surely someone has something juicy up their sleeve," Nuala encouraged. This confused her son, who always thought his mother favoured more constructive forms of verbal recreation, yet he also knew she was one pragmatic woman—she did what needed to be done. "Ivy, you're an egoist. You must have something to say; if not about others, yourself then. Come now, sharing is caring."

Ivy denied having any such tale to tell. When she returned the invite, Nuala's response was the same. Ally nudged Ivy, who was just as eager to get the scoop on the Coffeys' marriage problems, and whispered, "You're the only one who can salvage this." In that second, Benjamin-Joshua distrusted his mother's friends. Ivy shot Ally a look so dirty it might as well have been a gun and revealed something she had had no intention of broadcasting. "I'm pregnant."

Chorus: "Wonderful! That's great news! Congratulations! Good for you! I didn't even know you were trying."

"Oh, I assure you, it wasn't planned."

Chorus: "You will be an amazing mother. Little Miss Christmas Belles beauty pageant has an upcoming sure winner."

Ivy *uh-huh*'d unconvinced and denigrated it as nothing more than an invasion of an organ that proved to Benjamin-Joshua that Roop's recent icky words had been true.

Roop. Benjamin's heart broke at the thought of him. As if he had thought of anything else during the last hour.

"We're done congratulating you, right?"

"Oh, yeah," Ivy scowled, unimpressed.

Cards were thrown down, distributed, and picked up. No one wanted to tell Rita, who was supposedly teaching them a new game she invented, just how like Poker this was. She had not quite been herself since her last surgery.

"So, Nuala, where's Ger?" Ivy asked with a snakelike rattle to her voice, eyes black. The initial response was a pair of raised eyebrows.

"Dear," Nuala began, noticing a pattern in the day's conversations, "Not all of our men are fortunate enough to make a living running around telling people what they think they want to hear. Some actually have to work."

She had never liked Ivy's muse, and not just because he looked fifteen years older than her. She had not liked him when he was just the local politician, and especially now that he was running for presidency. She feared his policies were too dictatorial, his personage too shady, and that anyone whose climb up the political ladder was as fast as his had to be riddled with bribery, manipulation, and poison.

"Ouch, Red, I was only asking. What's up with you anyway?"

"Nothing, just having a bit of banter is all."

Rita eyed her. She considered putting her dark hand on her friend's to let her know she was there for her, but knew she would not appreciate it. Rita asked Ivy how the election was going. Ivy was pleased to say the outcome, as always, looked to be in her favour: "Our favour." Then she soliloquised about her *Innamorato*'s efforts to appeal to his Jewish "brothers." By November, the world would be at his feet, she prophesied with pride. Ally and Rita laughed gently. Ivy was not joking.

"So, what is new with you, Nuala?" Rita asked. She hated putting her friend under pressure, but interpreted her reluctance to share as an underestimation of the strength of their friendship.

"None."

"Really, hon? No gossip?"

"Rita, you know me; I don't believe in the public parading of one's misdemeanour. The guilt, shame, and punishment that follow their actions are humiliating enough without me being privy to the tittle-tattle of their deeds." Ivy wondered if Nuala prepared these longwinded sentences in advance.

*MOTHER, LOOK AT ME!*

Ally's ears twitched. She thought she heard Rupert's name being shouted from the street by Paul. She excused herself and walked outside slowly, with a horrified look on her face, pretending she feared the worst. Like a Duchess. An attention-seeking, belongs-on-TV-because-reality's-not-good-enough Duchess. She left her bag, so Ivy stuck her hand into it and stole $20 and lip balm. Ally's cell phone rang.

Benjamin-Joshua wanted to die.

Ivy answered it, but Paul must have seen Ally, for he hung up.

Benjamin-Joshua wished he could exchange places with Roop. As silent as a lowering coffin, he ran upstairs to his room and took his cell phone from his drawer. He opened the contacts' list and dialled the downstairs home phone. Immediately, Nuala sprung to her feet, grasping the attention of all present, like a guest at a wedding about to make a speech. Then the feeling of happiness came.

"He gets one phone call," she whispered clearly to herself. Her neighbours gasped at each other. Indirect as it was, she had finally admitted Ger had turned himself over to the authorities. "Out," she ordered quietly, then demanded with a scream that they leave.

They darted in the direction of the front door. Ally was just about to re-enter when the other two hurried into her. She screamed so loudly it hurt her vocal chords. The thief flung Ally's purse behind her, up in the air—she did not even try to catch it before it crash-landed in Nuala's flowerbed. Ivy called back, "My house—coffee—now!" But Ally just paced in circles and moved her arms bewilderedly like a crazed woman.

The Coffey phone kept ringing.

Nuala sat in a kind of trance, frozen on the spot like a mourning widow, afraid to move lest time move on and leave her behind. The phone still rang. Slowly, she made her way across the floor. Everything was familiar, but blurry too, as though between the caller I.D. and her eyes there hung a veil made of gossamer or a thin sheet of gauze. The second she answered the phone, the hopeless caller hung up. Benjamin-Joshua crawled beneath his bed and tunnelled his way through clothes and apple cores and wrappers, his thoughts fixated on the punishments distributed to his kind: abandonment, disappointment, juvie, prison, death. He looked for safety in the darkness.

Downstairs, the recipient heard only a long stretch of silence. "Why didn't I answer it sooner?" Her hand sprang open, or became suddenly weak, and the cell phone fell to the floor with a crash. "Well... That's that then."

"Where are they?!"

"Allison, what are you—?"

"Where are they?"

"They left just now, actually. I got a—"

"Not those two! Where are our sons?"

"What are you talking about? They were in your house."

"Paul showered. He said he forgot I was here, so like always, he just lay on the wet floor whimpering about he'll never walk again, expecting me to show him love, compassion, and all that stuff. He's a—Agh! He shouldn't have done that. I know that. You know that. He knows that. We all know that. But where are our sons?"

Despite the pain she knew she should have experienced, Nuala felt nothing. Like when a dentist numbs one's mouth, and they accidentally bite their chewy jaw, and spend hours spitting blood, all the while wishing they could dine on something fleshy again. All understanding of time and reason evaded. All that remained was a cold broken machine. She looked down at the floor at the shattered cell. She knelt slowly and like a fragile twiddling-fingered thing, terrified of touching its remains, delicately pieced together the scraps. *Bleep!* It was in working order again.

"Did you not hear me? My husband has lost our boys! Nuala!"

"And you're sure they're not in your house or playing hide-and-seek?" she rose and asked calmly and assertively.

"Yes!"

And although they both thought it, neither mentioned Henrietta's teenagers.

"You go right. I'll go left. Tell Paul to check the park."

"Paul's looked everywhere!"

"By himself. Simultaneously, we'll cover more ground. Keep your cell on. It's in your purse, which I assume is the miscellaneous object that thumped my rosebush. Be a dear and take it out."

Ally ran out of the house and met Paul outside. She intentionally left her cell in Nuala's garden: there's nothing more dramatic than going to it alone, coming face-to-face with danger, and having no means of communication. Paul's face was as white as Nuala's bed sheets; his entire countenance reeked of guilt and humiliation, then determination.

To the tune of the door slamming shut, Benjamin-Joshua glided silently down the stairwell and appeared like a phantom in the kitchen doorway.

"Sweetheart," Nuala breathed, overwhelmed, and wrapped her arms around him so tightly his little arms nearly cracked. "I was so worried.

Where were you?"

"Mom…"

"Yes, my darling? What is it?"

"Roop…" His body froze, but in his eyes, there was a story—and a sort of madness. They narrowed like slits, leapt, pounced, and sank back to the chorus of chattered, vibrating teeth. "There was an accident." Then he breathed deeply through his nostrils. "I mean, an incident." It took him a long time to tell her what happened.

"No one has… is… to know, my son. Absolutely no one. Not one word."

Like a thief, she snuck into her own house, handbag bulging. She had not told Benjamin-Joshua where she was going, only that she had it under control, and to stay away from the windows.

Despite having put her traumatised son to bed before departing, she looked up to find him sitting on the staircase like a crooked child from a horror movie. She left him there, knowing full well that he'd eventually find his way back to his bed and out of her sight. She locked the front door, blanketed the windows with curtains, switched off every phone. There was no communication with the outside world that night, despite Ally's continued hammerings and screams barely a minute after Nuala's return.

She scrubbed the inside of the oven clean. She spent fifty minutes removing the stains from a teapot she had used virtually every day since her honeymoon ended. She attacked minute dust mice on her stairs. She held a brush down the toilet and scrubbed so intensely the apparatus's head broke.

She wiped away the streaks on the shower door. She went downstairs and sat on her favourite seat in the dining-room and wished either to reverse time or die. She heard the clock tick thousands of times.

By the time the sun rose, all she thought about was the mistake she had made giving up alcohol. Finally, she disappeared into her room and imagined sobbing, screaming as she suffocated on her pillow, and smashing things, but only sat on her bed imagining.

Her son got out of bed the next morning un-rested, though with a clearer mind. No one could sleep through Ally Samson's whines and bangs and the sirens. He poured a bowl of cereal and sat at the table. From through the double doors, he saw Nuala storm into the kitchen and fling open the refrigerator door, and tear from its door Ger's drink. And she wrestled with downing it for several minutes before coming to her senses, smashing it against the wall, and sinking to the floor as the tiles became drenched in glassy grape-smelling sand dunes. Her exhausted head collapsed in raw, overworked hands and she wept tearlessly, knowing the next time she opened the refrigerator she would down the first bottle she saw. "It hasn't even been forty-eight hours. How did I lose it all?" She curled up in a ball like a racoon freezing to death on the side of the road.

The boy accepted all of this as part of his reality, just as he accepted her next utterance: "We need to move." The only thing he did not accept was responsibility.

# 1
# WHAT THE WATER GAVE ME
# CHRISTMAS DAY 2046

[The kitchen is modern but unimpressive. It overflows with microwaves, fridges, freezers, ovens, and Tupperware. Badly hung lights slouch and twinkle lazily along the ceiling, destined to plummet atop the kitchen table. The few Christmas ornaments that maiden house-owner Molly Laverty bothered to take down from the attic just add to the clutter and exude no holiday cheer. The short dusty grey tree she inherited from her late mother is pushed awkwardly against the back door, its gold star lopsided, its tinsel coiled over a pile of dog hairs on the tiles. The Witherspoons and Lavertys sit around the rectangular table under the pretence of visiting the ailed elderly Grandpa Laverty who has returned home from a retirement facility to die. Since their arrival, Grandpa got up once to watch his soaps, then returned to his deathbed without so much as a Merry Christmas. Benjamin Witherspoon's back is to a cupboard. To his right, Dave Witherspoon takes up a great deal of oxygen. To his left juts Nuala's spiteful bottom lip; she has just said something silly (that the Revenue's newly given ability to monitor all transactions over one hundred Harps was a good thing) and people laughed. Across from Benjamin sit Lucas Witherspoon and his two cousins. Next sits Nuala's brother Raymond Laverty in a suit and tie, the price of which he has unsubtly referred to three times in the last hour. He believes he is entitled to wear a sneer though Benjamin has his doubts. Raymond is why third-level academics hate capitalism. To his right, and Dave's left, sits Andrea Watson-Laverty, Raymond's wife].

ALL: [Pause. Nuala's mood is bringing everyone down].

ANDREA: Did you just put three teabags in that pot?

BENJAMIN: That's the difference between tea and coloured water.

RAYMOND: That is too many.

BENJAMIN: It's a big pot.

LUCAS: Ben's th' tea-master in th' family. [It's a quote he picked up from somewhere, not a sentence he strung together himself].

DAVE: The kettle is on ev'ry forty-five minutes, so it is. ... He only ever makes enough for 'mself.

INNER: You do not deserve one ... for your rudeness.

NUALA: That'll be as thick as tar, so it will. And your teeth will be rotten.

INNER: I brush thrice daily. I floss.

NUALA: Anyone who wants tea, make it now before it gets too strong. It'll be as thick as tar. Thick as tar.

RAYMOND: That's too strong. Three's too strong. You couldn't drink that.

BENJAMIN: [Swirls the spoon around the inside of the large pot, presses the teabags against its sides. He lifts one bag out and throws it into his cup. He keeps his mouth closed, not allowing anyone to see his sparkling teeth, lest any naysayers feel foolish].

NUALA: This is every forty-five minutes. Without fail. 'S no wonder the water bill's always so high, so it's not. It's him. And as for the length of time he spends in the bath each night. I don't know what he does be at.

DAVE: It's not your money tha' pays it so I don't know wha' you're givin' out abou'.

RAYMOND: How many spoons of sugar was that?

INNER: Two half-spoons. I know, right? It's quirky. Two, as per my reputation, but I shave half off each spoon to avoid activating my diabetes gene. But it gives my brain the placebo effect of thinking I still take two. Clever, huh?

BENJAMIN: Two half-spoons.

ANDREA: Isn't that the same as just one spoon?

BENJAMIN: No.

ALL: [Pause].

ANDREA: [To Nuala and Dave] So, are you going out foreign next year?

NUALA: I don't have a penny t' my name, so I don't. Not a penny do I have. I can't go anywhere. I couldn't even afford the bingo this week. Not a penny do I have.

DAVE: Spain.

NUALA: Yeah, it should be lovely. [Nods to Benjamin] He's not comin'.

ANDREA: Oh, why's that?

NUALA: He was asked. Again and again. Said he's not coming. So that's that.

BENJAMIN: I have sensitive eyes. I don't like the sun.

INNER: Not to mention, you cry poverty on a daily basis. At least this way you'll have a little something-something left over to buy yourself something pretty.

NUALA: Oh, would you shut up about your eyes.

RAYMOND: Before my boys finish their studies, I am sending them out foreign.

INNER: That's nice.

RAYMOND: You need to go out foreign. You must get life experience.

BENJAMIN: I have plenty of experience.

ANDREA: So, Benjamin, how is this famous novel coming along?

LUCAS: His time would be be'er spent learnin' how t' drive. [Obviously, a remark he picked up from Nuala and Dave—who must not know much about fourteen-year-olds].

BENJAMIN: Good, thank you.

INNER: Excellent. I wrote the entire first draft during the summer holidays. It requires heavy editing, but it will get there.

NUALA: I hope it's not a religious novel.

RAYMOND: Going out foreign will help you get experience to write.

BENJAMIN: My novel is one of inscapes, not landscapes.

NUALA: You have no life experience. You know nothing about how the world works. You know nothin' about strivin' an' strugglin' an' scrapin' every coin together t' try and buy a loaf o' bread. So, don't you go pretendin' you know anything about *experience* and how the world operates. You know nothin'. Not a thing d' you know.

INNER: [Considers all the black experiences Benjamin has never shared and decides for now to wear it as a badge of merit that he's kept it so secret all this time].

BENJAMIN: [To Nuala] I do.

NUALA: No, you don't!

BENJAMIN: [To Andrea] I wrote the f–... the entire first draft during the s–... summer holidays. Sixty-six thousand words... so I did.

RAYMOND: That's too long.

ANDREA: What is it about again?

NUALA: You should be out there workin' like all th' other boys your age. Get you out from under my feet, so it will.

RAYMOND: No one's going to read that.

LUCAS: Yeah, y' shou' be learnin' how t' drive, shouldn' 'e, Mam?

BENJAMIN: Fantasy. A boy who is broken. [Sees Andrea turn her nose up, so he stops speaking].

INNER: A teenage boy who has enemies crawling out of the woodwork in every area of his life... so one day he decides to destroy them all. I analyse the fine line between destiny, self-preservation and revenge.

DAVE: What novel?

BENJAMIN: I wrote a novel.

INNER: You know this. You went on a rant about how expensive it was that I plug my laptop into your plug sockets. … Seconds before you ran my hand into said plug socket. … Which hurt by the way.

ANDREA: So, you want to be an author?

INNER: I already am. Unpublished, but a date has been divinely appointed.

BENJAMIN: And a teacher. A [wets mouth] secondary [coughs] school [wets mouth longer than before] teacher [coughs again].

RAYMOND: There's no money in teaching.

INNER: [To Andrea] I'm good at it. I took an extracurricular course that prepared me to teach primary school and First Year classes about the harmful effects of peer pressure, smoking, alcohol misuse, and drug abuse. I start teaching first week in February.

DAVE: You should spend less time thinkin' about the future and get a part-time job now. Help your mother and me pay th' bills. [It is not clear if he realises he's just contradicted his earlier snipe at his wife].

NUALA: A part-time job. All the boys his age have one.

BENJAMIN: [To Nuala] Why invest time in something that is of no consequence to me when I can work on my novel series, the long-term plan?

INNER: [To Nuala] Sure, the benefits of my work will not reap for some time, but oh, when it materialises, when it all comes together, it will be glorious. It will be everything.

RAYMOND: You do know that publishers get hundreds of manuscripts a week? They read the bare minimum of them past chapter three.

INNER: The publishing process, Sherlock, is not beyond my comprehension.

BENJAMIN: I believe I can make it.

RAYMOND: Yours will not be good enough. You should aspire to be a doctor or something. Maybe a road-sweeper.

INNER: [To everyone] God put this vision on my heart; that I was going to help and heal people by giving them a voice in my work. I have a destiny. I'm going to change the world. And no one, and nothing, least of all ye band of one-another-hating-pirates is going to stand in my way.

NUALA: You should be out there doin' real work and pay'n' me back for all those school books, so you should. Cost me a fortune, they did [expletives omitted].

INNER: [To everyone] She'd have the money if she didn't squander it on drink and trashy magazines but, shush, don't tell her!

DAVE: You don't think he can make it?

NUALA: No.

DAVE: Have you no faith in him at all?

NUALA: No, I don't.

DAVE: [Sneers]. Neither do I.

INNER: Not to sound prideful, but I have won more literary awards and recognitions than all of you combined, and probably more than anyone you know combined.

RAYMOND: There was a recession when I was in university. I had to balance class, study, bartend during the weekdays, and work my father's farm from sunup to sundown at the weekends.

INNER: Well, boo-fricking-hoo! I honestly could not care less.

BENJAMIN: [To Raymond] I am working. ... I just don't get paid for it yet.

DAVE: "Microwave generation". "*McDonald's* generation".

INNER: Excuse me, Mr. I-Own-Three-Laptops, but I not once advocated for that lifestyle. ... Nor was it my generation that created it.

DAVE: The *McDonald's* generation. He wants everything handed to him on a platter. Has no respect for money, no appreciation.

BENJAMIN: [Winces, then says to a knife on the table] I've given up collecting comic books [literally the only thing he has spent money on since he was ten other than blue shirts] to save money.

NUALA: Comic books? What about all the sacrifices I've made? There's no word about the things I do have to give up, is there? Oh, no, you're quick to forget them, so you are. I haven't bought a new jumper for myself in three months, but that means nothing to you, does it? No, I didn't think so. Tell a lie, I haven't bought myself new clothes all year! But that doesn't bother you, does it?

LUCAS: Yeah!

NUALA: Oh, no. You come in from school and there's food on the table.

[Bless her heart, but Nuala momentarily forgets that Benjamin cooks his own food the night beforehand]. No word about who buys the food. Oh, no. No word about who pays the bills and makes sure you have clothes on your back. Or who pays the mortgage. Oh, no, that would be beneath you, so it would. Real life doesn't measure up to your notions of yourself.

INNER: You would have the money had you not slot-machined away literally thousands of Harps of our life savings.

RAYMOND: You need a real job. I know you—

INNER: Don't you dare speak those words again.

RAYMOND: …think you're too good for it, but you need to make a proper investment in your future. [He looks well-chuffed with himself for that comment, so he does. Nods his head and all. Is he expecting a medal?].

BENJAMIN: [To the knife which seems pretty blunt right now next to the seven pairs of eyes] Writing is a real job.

DAVE: [Trying to score brownie points with Raymond, die-hard agnostic] Or you'll fall to the wayside, just like the [he realises he's not up-to-date on his Old Earth beasties] ape.

NUALA: There's no money in it.

BENJAMIN: I'll be the exception.

NUALA: You're not exceptional.

DAVE: You're not even special.

NUALA: Well, all's I can say is, I hope you remember your mother when your name's in the limelight.

INNER: I'll remember not to invite you to my book launch, alright.

RAYMOND: We mean this for your own good.

INNER: Hardly.

RAYMOND: Your efforts would be better put into something you can make money from.

INNER: Money is not the most important thing to me. It is to [glares at Dave, then turns away, repulsed] … himself, and there's no way in Hell I'm turning out like him. It is to [Nuala] her, and all she does is complain that it must be spent. [To Nuala and Dave] You satisfy your son's greed [points to Lucas] at every turn as well as your own lusts and drives, and somehow, *I'm* the villain? Offspring cost money: deal with it.

BENJAMIN: Money is not the most important thing to me.

NUALA: [Sneers] Oh, it wouldn't be, would it? Sure, you spend every penny I own. Every single Harp.

DAVE: Do you hear the state of that? Money *is* important.

RAYMOND: You don't appreciate the value of money. But it is *the* most important thing. Without it you can do nothing.

NUALA: Sure, he does nothing as it is 'cept spend his life in front of his laptop in bed, watchin' his podcasts an' 'is Holographic Box shows, an' whatever else.

INNER: Hold! The phone! I watch eight H.B. shows religiously. I write fanfiction on them. I study history and write fictitious accounts of the more outstanding events I read about. I wrote a novel—who at my age can say that?! I read novels. One a week, at least! I got a black belt in karate at the beginning of this month. I assist Sunday school teaching for the Under Tens. I'm on the school's Newsletter committee. I'm on the Healthy Foods Initiative. I'm on Student Council. I'm a founding member of the Green Schools committee. I maintain an A1 average across the board.

BENJAMIN: I do...

NUALA: You have no life!

INNER: Yes, I do.

BENJAMIN: ... I do.

NUALA: No. You don't.

ANDREA: Are you doing anything for your birthday?

INNER: Goodness no, silly. *I have no life.*

DAVE: When's that? End of February? Another expense.

INNER: Early January.

NUALA: Sure, what would 'e be doin'? He has no friends. Never leaves his bedroom from one end of the day to the next. Just plugs in his laptop and raises the bills.

DAVE: Except to up the electricity bill with all that tea he drinks. Or eating every scrap of food in the house. Or fillin' his water bottle three times a day. Like, what's up with that? It's not normal, like. For a guy, I mean. Like, is it?

LUCAS: Yeah! You [Benjamin] need to lose weight! [Another stolen insult.

One that only now hurts Benjamin having come from Lucas's mouth].

RAYMOND: You should watch your weight. My sons swim three nights a week, climb a mountain every second weekend, and go for jogs every morning at six o'clock. You really should exercise.

NUALA: An' 'e uses th' ba'room for 'n hour a day. Wha'ever 'e does be a' I'll never know.

BENJAMIN: [To Andrea] No.

ANDREA: They've lowered the driving age here again, haven't they? You can do it at fifteen now, so long as there's someone twenty-one or older in the passenger seat. Are you going to start learning how to drive soon?

INNER: I see no need. School is the furthest I ever have to travel. What would be the point in taking time away from my novel to study the theory test book, sit the exam, learn how to drive, pay for lessons, do the practical exam, buy a car, pay outrageous insurance just because a percentage of my fellow male peers are reckless, and balance two or three jobs to pay for all the above? Plus, I have schoolwork. School's the furthest I have to travel.

BENJAMIN: No.

NUALA: He'll learn how to drive the second he turns fifteen. I'm makin' him. Oh, you can sneer all you want. We'll see who's sneerin' when I hand you the book.

BENJAMIN: I'm not sneering.

NUALA: Yes, you are. You have your nose up in the air like you always do!

RAYMOND: You think arduous work and effort are beneath you.

NUALA: He does think arduous work and effort are beneath him! ... Well, we'll see who is sneering. Just you wait 'n' see. You won't be so high an' mighty then. Oh, no. You're in for a hard lesson.

RAYMOND: You need to learn how to drive.

DAVE: It'll put an end to you askin' lifts from us all the time, every night of the week, whatever y' d' be at.

INNER: I thought I didn't leave the house in view of my, you know, not having a life...? "'Curiouser, and curiouser,' said Alice'. But seriously, when do you take me anywhere? When do I ask you to? I don't even talk to you!

ANDREA: Do you drink?

BENJAMIN: No.

RAYMOND: You are not a pioneer, are you? [Turns his nose up in the air like his wife did earlier].

BENJAMIN: I don't see the need... to drink.

INNER: Not that it is any of your business, but I am merely implementing my right to make a decision, and an informed one, at that. And who knows? There may indeed come a day when I take a drink. But rest assured: if or when I do, I will not be in the presence of those I do not like. I would hate for a loose tongue to unhouse any secrets or true feelings. ... Alternatively, one might consider the law. I am fourteen.

NUALA: Sure, he has no life.

ANDREA: I allow my boys [sitting uncomfortably, eyes fixed on Benjamin, embarrassed to be witnessing this attack on him] half a glass. I found I never had fun without alcohol.

BENJAMIN: … [To himself]. I do have a li…

DAVE: No, y' don't. Now would y' shu' up with y'r cheek or I'll take the jaw off y'.

RAYMOND: Do you still aspire to be an Egyptologist?

BENJAMIN: No.

NUALA: Y' used t' be mad abou' tha'. Wha' was tha' other thing? Acting. D' y'—?

BENJAMIN: No.

ANDREA: Oh, the tea will be very thick by this stage. Do you want to have it now?

BENJAMIN: No.


26 March 2047: Oh, how I live for days such as these when Dave randomly packs his suitcase and drives off to wherever the heck he goes, leaving the banshee in the doorway. It is a sound my ears could do without hearing, her wail, that is, but Dave's absence compensates for the poignancy. I feel my lungs fill with air in a way they cannot when he is around. He never liked me for reasons I dared never ask. Experience of his hand, larger than Ireland, has taught me the authenticity of the old-adage that "silence is golden".

I try to recall the last time I spoke to him. It's been three months, at least.

Before leaving the bathroom, I rub my shaved face; my fingers tell me I missed a few spots and my stubble feels like wood before it's been sanded. I've been shaving since I was nine. "Mustachio" and "Hitler" my classmates called me back then. Even at fifteen, I have yet to master the art of manscaping, but this will have to do. I pull the plug from the sink socket, fasten my grey shirt's top button, and noose my tie. I step into the narrow strip of hallway, hemmed in by nugget-sized rooms on all sides.

*Mother*, I almost address formally. *Are you alright?* It seems like the right thing to say but is pathetically patronising. Not to mention no one here in house 87 much cares about each other's feelings. Relationship has become something of a rarity since "The Incident".

She gets to her feet with poise. Hot bubbles of tears cake her eyelids shut. But I have no words of comfort for her.

"Go wake your brother." With a messy wipe of her face, her teary mascara smears to a mucky slush from her eyes to her chin. She ties her lustful red robe and walks into the kitchen where she makes Little Luke a fry, pancakes, or whatever he requested for breakfast last night.

Across the road, an elderly couple stare in our front door and judge—how very Irish of them. I want to arch my arm like a T-Square, wave, and smile like a villain, before asking them what the Hell they are looking at. But I neither wave nor smile. Instead, I close the door and separate the outside world from this sham-of-a-family or "*shamily*". With one step, I am outside Little Luke's bedroom door and knock on it three times.

*Time to rise, Little Luke.*

He moans some sort of abuse at me, so I return to my room and shut the door though this does little to block out the faux-cheery hum from the kitchen, occasionally broken with raspy chokes.

It's the start of another day, and all I wish is that I could cry or scream or run away or die. But it seems everyone has beaten me to it.

I throw on my jumper, read my morning devotion, and give the bedsheets a final smooth-over, stare in the mirror for a while, and leave. I prepare my breakfast and sit at the head of the dining-room table before anyone else gets to it. My head tilts to the flashing mirror splints Dave falsely accused me of shattering, then to the marble-cold tiles, lastly to my blood. I'm surprised I haven't cleaned that up yet.

As I drink my morning tea, Luke's heavy eyelids zombie-trudge in. Tiredness threatens to drag him to the floor. He has surfer blond hair like mine used to be before it turned brown. Three adorable freckles form a pyramid on each pale cheek. Whenever he enters the kitchen, his pointy nose sniffs at scents only he has the keenness to detect. His nose consists of a smaller helping of flesh than mine; his could not satisfy the hunger of a baby tiger. The only thing he has in common with Ronan is inactive genes.

For white noise's sake, he switches on the Holographic Box or H.B., the new addition to the television family. They make H.B.s in technicolour now.

I swear Nuala deliberately sets this thing on the American news-station, *Coffey and Chats*, or *C&C* to induce herself with soul-skewering knives. Gone are the female reporter's melodramatic hand-gestures. What remains is an unrecognisable doll. Her face is pulled back so tightly she has no skin cells in reserve. Her shoulder-length hair is blonde now. Even her eye colour has changed, and with them the doe-eyed sense of warmth.

Hawk-like, they give the impression that she judges me for what I did to her son, what I got away with. The harlotry Duchess chats away like a lady to her dismembered husband whose face is now bleached teeth-white and stretched like sheets, giving him the look of an effeminate corpse. They speak about how the President (who they boast drank tea with them a month ago) will soon be on Irish soil, and what this could mean for international relations and Gaelic-American compatibility. And, as they do every time Ireland comes up in conversation, they give a special shout out to the One-Armed Man's ex.

Why does she torture herself by keeping this station?

All finished, I clear the table and rinse, wash and dry everything I've used. I store them according to my routine—nothing has a place in this hellhole of disorder unless I give it one. My system is based on logic, convenience, and segregation. I shudder to see spoons mixed with forks in drawers, and dirty bowls on the pile of saucers in the press.

Monday to Friday mornings, I am in too great a rush to have a conversation with Luke, but our awkward housemate relationship suits us both grand. I depart without saying a word.

After another successful school day of taunts, slander, and spending lunchtime alone, I squat into my box of a room and sit on my bed. At sixteen metres squared, the rows of wardrobes and double-sized bed leave almost no wall or floor.

I keep my room tidy, exceptionally so. Everything has its place: from chronologically ordered comic books to my weapon collection to the six feet tall cardboard model of Michael Collins that seemed like a good idea to sneak out of the History Museum at the time.

In a secret lift-up drawer no one knows about, I house my illustrations. Most are fantastical in nature; others have a flare of the Renaissance about them. I haven't drawn a still life in three months since what was supposed to be a self-portrait became a postmodern distortion, a collage of random images torn from dozens of magazines. I wanted to tear it up, pull out a canvas, squeeze paint tubes on said canvas, and get messy and crazed with artistic fervour, but instead I put it in my drawer. Neither tarnishing nor smearing would remove it from existence. Among my more recent muses is Paige Andrews, who moved to Ireland shortly after my exodus from Lincoln Lane. We attend the same school, but never speak.

I root around under my bed and pull out a wooden box of my stories and my "Feelings Journal", documents of more importance to me than anything I could ever draw.

Compelled into misery, I flick through it, then re-read a poem I wrote yesterday at lunch time:

> *When all this is over,*
> *I will be free to wake—without wishing I was asleep.*
> *I will be free to smile—without being told it's ugly.*
> *I will be free to laugh—without it being thought odd.*
> *I will be free to joke—without being taken seriously.*
> *I will be free to walk—without being ambushed.*
> *I will be free to play—without being called gay.*
> *I will be free to achieve—without being wished dead.*
> *I will be free to excel—without being told I have no worth.*
> *I will be free to live—without dreaming that I'm drowning.*

Feeling strangely better already, I turn back the pages until my finger spies the first page of a memoir from two months ago:

*While dusting my bookshelf this afternoon, my photo album nosedived to the floorboards with a small thud. On the page on which it opened, I had pasted a photograph of Nuala's mother and myself from my ninth birthday party.*

*Mother Laverty—or Nanna L-ve, as she creepily asked us to call her, under threat of not receiving Christmas presents (yes, I wrote 'Christmas'. To Hell with the government's political correctness crud)—died several weeks ago. We weren't close. One day she was admitted to the hospital, next her bowel perforated, unleashed poison, and she croaked.*

*Before leaving to visit her, Nuala, Dave, and I were finishing a cup of tea. They drank theirs in the dining-room. I drank mine in my room. I remember looking at a number of books spread out on my bed (originally in order of how I hoped to reference them, then alphabetically). I felt quite overwhelmed to be deferring valuable time to non-academic matters. Every dedicated student knows this feeling: the sheer guilt that accompanies engaging in any activity that does not involve studying, other than watching one's shows.*

*My mobile phone vibrated. My phone never vibrates. I'm one of those people who shouldn't have one. I don't even believe in such unnatural forms of communication as phoning. And next to no one has my number. But, switched on silent mode and cemented to my windowsill, it vibrated.*

*The screen said my aunt Molly was the caller.* She's dead. *I tried to allow myself to believe my aunt only wanted to know when we would arrive. I knew otherwise. I answered, and somewhere amongst the sounds of a driving vehicle, gulps and tears, I received the news I had tried not to let myself expect.*

*In that second, I felt one of the weirdest sensations of my life. Adjective: as-of-yet unknown.*

*My only response was, "Oh."*

*Then I hung up the phone.*

*As if hoping they would lend me some of their superhuman strength, I stared at my superhero figurine collection stationed beneath the window. I put my hands together, raised my head, stiffly straightened my back, put one foot in front of the other and walked into the kitchen looking as though I'd been raised in an emperor's palace.*

*I stared for a few seconds at Nuala and himself. As a gentleman who takes manners, politeness, and propriety very seriously, I get annoyed when people speak to me from another room. On that day, however, I stayed behind the bar table, safely out of the line of fire from all potential emotional outbursts. In a reserved voice, I asked, "When are* we leaving for the hospital?" Before this could be interpreted as impatience, I continued to Nuala, "I just got a call from your sister." I gave a small cough—every speech has one. "We're too late." And in her eyes were expectancy, disbelief. Himself seemed a tad upset too. I said I'd put the kettle on, and I did. Tea solves life's problems, and all that jazz...

Then, right on time, along came the dramatic one who had to arrive after everyone else had been informed. Every Duchess deserves their moment in the spotlight. Luke enquired what was wrong, something he habitually asked whenever the phone rang or someone came to the door. Coolly I repeated the message he had missed and, as anticipated, he had his moment of melodrama and attention. Would he steal her plot as quickly?

I carried my red Nanna-Dot-bought BENJEMIN mug of just-brewed tea (adverse to my otherwise perfectionist ways, its misspelling somehow causes me to adore it all the more) into my room, and I resumed my study. Forty minutes later, we left the house. About twenty minutes after that, we arrived at the only hospital still in operation in the bite-sized county. Nuala directed us to her mother's room where many grave faces had already assembled.

Choked amid their feelings, I reserved myself to a grief of polite silence. Despite the abuse that the too-teary-eyed spat, I am not an uncaring person. We all liked the woman whose corpse now lay on a bed; I simply could not feel what others expected. It is not wrong not to be sad. And wouldn't it have been dishonourable to pretend otherwise?

I sat uncomfortably on an armchair staring at the lifeless vessel, disturbed that her eyes had not been closed properly. Between her eyelids was an evil blackness that sent shivers through me. I could not bring myself to touch her for fear she'd spring to life. Anyway, it's not like she was still a person. She stopped being herself the second she stopped breathing. All that remained was a shell—like me.

It was in that room that I changed my views on the flippant ending of Robert Frost's "Out, Out—". I had previously thought of the infamous "they" as cold, cruel and callous, acknowledging the boy's death but moving on with their lives "since they were not the one dead". Yet there I was doing the very same thing. Frost was right: "Life goes on." We either keep up or we fall behind. We adapt or we disappear. It's that simple. Hard, but simple.

I tried to recall Seamus Heaney's "Mid-Term Break" but to little avail; I remembered only a few lines. Still, I continued in my efforts, as it gave me an excuse to divert my gaze from the grey-haired horror in the centre of us.

After a while, my pastor arrived. I hadn't expected he'd show when I texted him, and suddenly became worried about how the others might react, but they behaved.

*He greeted everyone and respectfully told us he would not overstay his welcome, as this was primarily a time for family. He shook hands with my uncle Raymond, home from... wherever he lives... but misheard this as "Séamie", and then proceeded to call him Séamie for the duration of the five-minute stay. I had to hold in the laughter.*

*As the week progressed, Raymond's priggish over-achieving twin sons really grew on me. We haven't spoken since.*

*I must have refrained from displaying my sanguinity around Mrs. Laverty's neighbours as they kept asking me, "Aw, you poor dear, you're probably heartbroken, aren't you?" As much I hate to lie, I believe the truth is unacceptable when the question has been answered for you. "Oh yes, as you can imagine, this has been a very difficult time for my sham... uh... family," I replied more than once that week.*

*I had anticipated a tidal wave of emotion to one day hit me spontaneously, resulting in uncontrolled weeping. That did not and will not happen. In fact, the closest I came to such a reaction occurred at the funeral, just before I read a Bible passage on comfort. Out of nowhere something remotely like sadness hit me. My chest felt heavy. My lungs pressed in on my heart. I felt a rock in my throat inhibit me from producing sound. I did not give myself time to articulate it though, so I puffed for breath, raised my head, greeted, "Hello, congregation. I do hope you are well," and began. Whether people were shocked to discover what my voice sounded like, or found something about my speech inappropriate, the pulpits' mouths dropped.*

That's enough of that. I close the journal, as boisterous cheers and munches boom from the sitting-room, where the monster, the shadow, and the only actual fan watch a football match. Well, Mr. Witherspoon didn't stay away for long. I hide the journal in the box under the bed, walk into the bathroom, and lock the door behind me.

Car horns beep.
All people gossip—all—
The world keeps turning, turning.
I disappeared and no one noticed.

The boy endured another hellish day at school and at home—
Not hellish in the painful sense;
His ache was of a desensitised nature;
Every second: stabbed, skewered with numbing needles that

Anaesthetised his soul and stripped him of sensation.
No, his life was far from hellish—it was art.
He had been created, yet did not live; only existed.
He was an image: a perpetually ignored frost-encased statue gathering dust.
He had been moulded, shaped, and disregarded like an unfashionable piece
of art.
It took all he had to keep his head above water.


Undressed he stared in the mirror.
Two large owl-like eyes returned the gaze,
Brown, the shade of a mushed autumn leaf—
The season when things die.
They appeared to quiver, as if to cry, but
His rather three large middle teeth bit down on his bottom lip as it foamed
with sad saliva:
He would never let that happen.
Though seemingly feeble, he was strong
Enough to suppress every emotion
That threatened to leak out of his body:
Happiness, melancholia, pain, terror, rage;
All contained, because this is the perfect state.
Emotions are dangerous things.
The Incident and the family unit had taught him that.
Repression: his speciality.
Admitting defeat: never an option.
Asking for help:
Talking is only a sign of strength
Until your words are used against you.


The white box filled with steaming water.
Bobbling bubbles oozed oily.
Empirical snowy mountains rose from the deep lake.
He looked back to the mirror.
As he breathed in the thick citric-scented steam
The large reflected nose risked poking the authentic boy in the eye.
When the bath was quite full,
Water scalded toes bold enough to dip in.
It was painful,
But at least it was a feeling.


Eyes again to the mirror,
He ran a hand through his hair, white with crust.
He had spent some time that morning meticulously

Combing buckets of dandruff from his scalp, a magnet for dead skin,
But sit in front of a sniggering fat ginger and a tiny twig armed with
correction fluid
And these things happen.

Before climbing in, he examined his masculinity
And saw what he felt most ashamed of.
It was everywhere.
It was natural, sure, but why did it have to grow on his body?
He was the shortest guy in his year group, yet his body was the most
developed
And horrid.
He wanted to peel away this life and emerge as someone new and past-free.

The closed bathroom window forced
Floods like horses to run down the tiled walls.
Blinding vapour encircled the entire room.
The door and neatly folded clothes resting atop his spotless runners
vanished.
Nothing left, but
A misted scene and mysterious mind.
The top of the bath had two metal handles opposite each other.
His arms bent like swan necks from the bubbly blanket and grasped tightly.
His body rested beneath the water that scorched his face
And scalded what remained of him.

He had always expected his life to flash before his eyes
Before he died,

But he found forcing his consciousness through the canals of his mind
harder than expected.
All he could think about was the world outside the window
—The one he had believed he'd been destined to change—
Which he'd never see again
If he faded away.

Beneath the effervesce surface he lay
Invisible to all but the eyes of God.
No one would see him if they tried.
After embarrassingly long, he realised
He had forgotten to take a deep breath—
He had just shut his mouth and
Disappeared

And lay
There.
The soles of his feet shrivelled.
His arms began to tire.
Their hold on the sides of the bath weakened.
He had already decided to let go
Of all that he was
And all he had been through
And all he would have been
And all he had had to put up with
And all the things he had never told
And would never get the chance to
When something happened that he had not expected:
A thought:


*Is this how it ends?*
*An exposed corpse hogging the only bath in the house,*
*The door locked?*
*This is it? This is a life?*
*Is this how I want to be remembered?*
*(What if I'm not remembered? What if no one cares?)*
*No.*


His hands slipped,
And he was offered up to the world without end.


And so it was:
He escaped the snowy sarcophagus, dried himself, and
Powdered so much he became the colour of the bath;
His ghostly body, a reflection of the near-death.
No one had the wit to know what happened,
Inert before the television
To the splashing
And the kicking
And the squeaking of fingertips
As he pushed against the walls of
An above-earth coffin.
No one knew and
No one was going to know.
That which haunted him
And protected his secrets
Would not want him to
Feel better.

He turned the key, turned off the light, and went to
His room.

But before this,
He opened the bathroom window.
The threatening, steamy shroud of the air within
Whirled close to the lintel,
Just for a moment, menacingly, reluctant to leave,
But then
Disappeared.

With a mighty splutter that probably causes me to look deathly infected, I walk normally as I can into the kitchen. I'd lain beneath the scorching water before, but I'd never lost my grip on the handles like that. That was too close for comfort. (I need a cup of tea after that!).

Under the dim lights, Nuala sits at the table, muttering something about Ger, Ally, Paul, Ronan, my childhood imaginary friends Mo-Mo and Josiah, Rupert, Joshua. She looks as bad as I feel. A large half-empty glass of something brown haunts her hands. She ignores my presence—well, two can play that game.

I pour water, colourless as my personality, from the filter into the kettle, enough for one cup of tea and steam. Against my better wishes and although she doesn't deserve it, I decide to offer her a cup. I need something to distinguish me from her. I turn, expecting I'll reaffirm she's a poor excuse for a human being, but instead, for the briefest moment, I see beyond the bitter wreck she's become, and her heart is revealed to me. Oh, how I yearn for the old her.

My mouth opens, but before I can speak, I feel a great discomfort inside. That will be the bubbles. A giant icky worm slithers in my body, making figure-eight movements all the way to my throat. I suspect I'll vomit, but I pull out a neatly folded square of kitchen paper from my pocket—I always store tissue in every pocket—and splutter warm oily water into it quietly. I flick the switch. The kettle glows blue.

I hear her twiddle a small wine glass in her fingers carelessly. Half the liquid spills over the side and onto this week's newspaper. I consider handing her a dishcloth, but last time I did, she blamed me for the spillage, so I decide not to.

She sheds a few tears and, in synch with the singing of the kettle, says, "He's back. He's in the bedroom unpacking his things." And I realise the only person more upset than me about Dave's return is her.

She wipes her tears and stands up straight, as opposed to her usual slouch. Her faded red hair flutters either side of her grey face and bounces off her shoulder blades, as her dark purple dressing-gown swings above her skeletal ankles. Her slippers kick their way across the tiles rather than walk; a coffee-booze smell follows her to the doorway. I instinctively reach out an arm to her. But I am not Ronan, so I drop it and turn back to the kettle.

"I know."

She continues walking but lingers. Against the sound of my tea-making, I think I hear her whisper that she thought she was finally free. Then her slippers creep to her bedroom door, and she disappears.

# 2

# THE PROMISE

On the stroke of midnight, I switch off the bedroom light, then lie like a dead fish for hours and try not to tear my face off in frustration.

Twelve-thirty...

Two past one...

One-twenty...

Thirty-five past two...

Ten past four...

It is the same every night.

My brain's long nervous nails scratch my mental faculties to take my mind off the itching awareness that sleep forever evades me. And so, as though in some crafty plot to lull myself into slumber, my mind fixates on a grand excursion I took once upon a dream, and tries with its claws to drag me back into those black cavernous imaginative depths. In that dream, I went on a grand adventure to a fantastical universe I named Pocket, because it was a pocket-sized universe, and what an exodus from normalcy it was!

But I find I can never return. That door has long been closed to me. So instead I muse of Queen Mab, and of the beginning of hollow age-old unions and their inevitable end, and of beginnings and their inevitable endings:

Ben's wedding day had arrived.
As he stood in the large room, alone,
On trial for his life,
Struggling to memorise his vows,
He awaited an enthrallment that never came.

Everything felt wrong.

A white-sheeted beauty with a statue-expression
Approached the church building from the graveyard.
The long plain of grass, peppered with pentagon-shaped stones dipped
And the cross atop the roof came into view.
The clouds huddled together like American football players
And blocked out the violent rays of the scorching, unmerciful ball.

Darkness descended
In that unholy hour of unsanctified unions.

As the lash of the hot whips
Of the Southern summer sun subsided,
The dim glimmer of the candles in the church too went out.
The black burnings on the walls
Blended with the darkness.
Sweat sprinted down the groom's face.
Shivers raced like predators down his spine.
Goose pimples grew on the back of his neck.
He wanted them to explode like a minefield and to take him with them.

This is wrong.

The scarecrow organist hurried into the room silently as
Ben succumbed to anxiety and let his legs fly.
He hated that he did not have the ability to control himself;
His own body; every man's most basic sphere of influence.
His torn heart physically pained, he continued for the exit when suddenly
The Bride arrived.

A hollow tune, appropriate for a funeral, sounded.
And the groom froze. He had waited for this moment
For so long
That he had wondered if their journey would ever reach completion.

The Bride silently, slowly moved down the aisle like a chess piece, like the
queen.
The tips of her gloves stained brown.
The veil enshrouded her face in a pyramid of bony whiteness.
The plain dress covered her feet and smothered the floor.
It had seen four weddings over three generations.
Ben had once thought its whiteness virginal, but
Now only lifeless.

He remembered the anticipation of this moment months ago:
And the crash that had brought an end to all celebrations.
Holding her hand...
His soul dying...
Her life-force ebbing away...
But with that memory,
The sun shone splendidly like a phoenix and the Bride lit so radiantly
That for a single, long moment she became transparent.

She must have entered the darker half of the room after that
For the subtle hovering belle came into view again;
Her countenance beneath the veil one of indifference.
"Ready, my l–?" she asked, then dropped off, airily, dreamlike, not entirely
there or with it.
He cut her off, said her name, and
Whispered his feelings for her.

The sun abandoned them.

The wedding ended twenty minutes later.

Neither had been surprised the sun did not bless their ceremony:
Dim day, darker deeds;
Black sky, cryptic minds.
Neither cared.

The sickly paleness of the moon reflected the Bride's wan complexion.
The groom took her blooded hand in his:
Cold as ice, not warm like life;
Nails chipped, tips hacked and damaged,
Six feet sunken.

He tugged her hand a little.
She did not know where he would lead her.

She nodded emotionlessly, agreeing to follow.
They walked without words to
A forest tucked behind a windmill near the church.
At an almost supersonic pace,
Ambushed by memories of a previous life,
She turned to look at him.
Her sallow, sunk-in cheekbones pained as she attempted
A smile.

This had been their favourite place;
Where they first met:
Ben, under a tree, musing, drawing the spectacle of
An elf or fairy dancing in the woods.
He remembered how rosy her cheeks had been,
How full of life.

Life had been a marriage between the fairy tale and mundane since—
But for one day.
They walked past a small shrine dedicated to a young woman,
Killed tragically. Amongst this shrine was a photograph of
Two smiling teenagers, so drowned in infatuation.
The sinister image-warping rain had disfigured their faces
So that they now looked like creatures of the deep.

A dusty path lay ahead of them. He directed her to follow it.
The entrance to the kingdom of trees was soon out of view.
Trees towered threateningly, tall as rockets. Dozens were twisted and
Marshy and coloured like frogs. Poisonous scarlet berries hung from
Bended arm-shaped branches tempting visitors. Concealed blackbirds spat
insults.
But ignorant of it all, ethereal and wraithlike, the Bride's skin glowed
hauntingly,
Taking full advantage of the sunless earth.

He ran his fingers through her hair and flicked out the wooden chips.
A centipede ran over his finger. He shook it off and squashed it under his
boot, then
Stepped towards her, breathed her in, locked lips, and drank the bitter
draught of death.
They had transcended all of existence
But its unnaturalness made him sick to his core
Though he craved it more than life.

In the way that a bridge makes cross-barrier communication possible,
So too this world and the next came together.
The youngsters stood there, gazed at one another
Until well after the moon went down.
And so, he thought, began their fairy tale marriage
And a step towards happily ever after.

But then the sun came up.

I am all spirit, all soul, bodiless, free, and, for the first time in forever, at peace. Anchored. My inner parts bathe in light. But how long can this contentment last? This rhythm of grace, this unity, this oneness of self before it, like everything, dies.

I jolt awake.

My skull pounds. In the distance, I hear a drum of heads collide, skulls thud, and boulders roll off mountainsides and shatter into pebbles. Thunder growls in ferocious angst. Nature screams. Were the rocks sharp teeth and not blunt pillows, I would probably be dead.

And for what could very well last hours, all I see are fragments: the unsentimental Dave's obsession with buying scented candles and taping to them the faces of dead people; Luke striking the neighbour's fur-ball in the eye with his cushion-cover comfort named Pillow; a balaclava-faced Roop terrorising an Indian family's store—just one of his many criminal enterprises during his all-too-short career.

And then I hear the *Boop-boop... boop-boop...* bell of the world's biggest failure of a social experiment: secondary school. A maze of wiry chewing-gummy carpet that's been there since the seventies; yards of scraggy threads soaked in *Coca-Cola* and testosterone; lidless footprint-branded plastic bottles that have been kicked from one corridor to the next;

the merciless chill as all the radiators' heat soar through the tileless ceiling.

The *boop-boop* signals lunchtime—my least favourite time of day. It is hard enough being lonely without having a mocking institutionalised hour designated to leisure and recreation thrown in your face.

Though I stay close to the flaking blue wall, I still manage to get pounded by floods of hormonal meat sacks. By the time I get to my locker, students who are not my friends have already stashed slops of mucky curry sauce through the slits in the locker door. It was dog food yesterday. Expired meat the day before that. I spend many minutes cleaning it out, which I'm used to by now. At least I don't have the added pressure of an audience to contend with. I must be the only over-fourteen-year-old in this joint who still packs cling-filmed sandwiches for lunch and doesn't go downtown.

As I cross to the bathroom, from around the corner appears Jonathan Harker Grey who, like a mafia lord, is surrounded by tall stocky henchmen with furrowed brows and beady dark eyes. They wear stiff-lipped, heavy-browed, wrinkled countenances that suggest perpetual displeasure. Well, this is an oddity, their being here. They must have been in detention.

I am shocked when Jonathan gives me the faintest hint of a smile, and nods "Ben." He's my next-door neighbour, but we have only spoken twice and never in detail. I gulp before saying, "Hello," but my locked cheekbones only permit the release of one syllable. I hear one of the henchmen make a nasty comment about me, which consequently conducts an orchestra of sniggers, guffaws, and howls from the other one. I don't let on that I hear them, but when the crunching of chocolate bar wrappers and the fizzing and overflowing of soft drinks down the corridor ceases, I know they are gone.

I hide myself in one of the bathroom stalls, and have my daily social phobia-inspired panic attack. Next, I overly wash my hands just to kill time so as to spend fewer minutes in the prepubescent-peopled canteen. Then I breathe on a cracked mirror, write *AODH* on the fogged glass ("The Children of Lír" is still fresh in my mind as I've just finished reading a book on Irish fairy tales), and then scrub the skin off my hands again.

I swing by my locker, grab my bacon-lettuce-and-tomato sandwiches, a bottle of water, and a book to study, and walk (like a hopping fairy, it has been remarked) to the canteen in the Yellow corridor. Wafts of oozy sausages wade out the door and through the few cracks in the windows that aren't wallpapered-over with faded *NI-QUIT-INE* posters. The grumpy fat dinner lady scowls at me as I walk in; she believes I once called her a "washed-up has-been" while I analysed Frost's Abishag aloud, and I hadn't the heart to tell her she was grievously mistaken.

I find a quiet empty table in the back corner spat out of the mouth of the intoxicatingly numerous segregated clubs, societies, sects, and castes; a nucleic mind of a hundred conversations, each believing itself more important than the others:

"*Ich mag cazz-eh essen.*"

"Umlaut! Pronounce your umlaut!"

"Aw, here now! I hate *Huck Finn* with a passion. 'By-and-by'! What a horrible expression! And he spells it differently on every page."

"Seriously girls, I burned water making macaroni cheese in Home Ec. yesterday!"

"Go back to Poland."

"*Ach*, girls!"

"Like, it's my birthday on the day of the referendum, like. Like, I get to vote on my birthday, like. Like, sweet sixteenth or what? I am so votin' Yes, like. Like, I feel so mature now, like. I'm like, running the country, like. The government are like, so sound, like, to be lettin' us, like, do this, like. Y' know wha' I mean, like?"

"Mascara-masked sluts."

"I think the aliens are monitoring my *YouTube* views…"

"Me ma's found her Romeo. I've got my Juliet. I'm a lucky guy."

"I think she heard you."

"'Write any scene from *Pride and Prejudice* as seen through the eyes of Mary.' Who, may I ask, is Mary?!"

"*We*, and I speak in the kingly plural because *all*… are… *culpable*, have allowed for a *censorial dictatorship*… to arise… from a *liberal… democratic… institution!*"

"I don' wan' anyone cu'in' op'n my body."

"You don't have a choice. It's the law. Everyone's corpse is hospital—*cough, cough,* government—property."

"It's all in the name of progress. Think of all the lives that will be saved instead of just burying all those perfectly healthy organs in the ground for worms to feed on. No one cares about funeral processions and visiting gravesites now anyway. Excuse the cliché, but life is for the living. And that mandatory magnetic chip thing is coming in, too."

"It'll be good for banking and tracking kids, ex-cons, and people with Alzheimer's. It's about time."

"We've never had a female Taoiseach. It's an all-boys club. What more proof do you need that Ireland is still patriarchal? It is the man versus us. It always has been."

"What did you think when she died?"

"I'm only on season one…"

"I wouldn't eat those rolls if I were you. They've been there since yesterday."

"I'm telling you: there were no other suspects. Mammy says his mother knew the Governor (your man who is now the President). That's the only reason he got away with it." This is the one that most catches my attention. Both because of the alarm bells it sets off in my brain, and because of the speaker:

Paige Andrews. Blonde with streaks of tan. Blue-eyed. A black heart coated beneath her gashing coal flesh. I still can't believe I spent so many years hung up on her. Thinking she liked me… Thinking she genuinely wanted to know how I felt every time she asked… Thinking she was the same girl who had lived on the outskirts of Lincoln Lane, the only girl in school I would have given my heart to if I'd had one.

But I see her now for what she really is: a two-faced bully and gossip who destroys people for a living because she sees H.B. characters do it and still get their happy ending. A ruthless force, she already has two unfairly fired teachers under her belt, and countless fellow student suspensions. Roop, Master of Villainy, would be so proud of his apprentice.

Adding to my increasing number of qualms with Paige is her alliance or romantic dalliance with broad-shouldered, square-jawed, yoghurt-carton-chinned Steve Lautner: a semi-smart full-time waster who reminds me of a six feet tall glass of semi-skimmed milk at room temperature.

Inwardly, I chant: *She knows nothing. It's just gossip.*

But gossip once drunk flows into a person's innermost parts; and seeds of death, once sown, can grow into something thistly, poisonous, and nasty.

A soaking balloon of sweat bursts from the pores on my neck. I rub each of my fingers in succession, beginning with my favourite hand, my right. I feel every eye on me. I feel dirty. I feel unclean. I need a bath. I need to go back to the bathroom and wash my hands again. I need to turn invisible and be swallowed up by the floor and die and be born again as someone new.

*She knows nothing. It's just gossip*, I continue chanting. I wring my hands uncontrollably beneath the table and my neck feels hot. My legs rise and fall as though charged with voltage.

Suddenly, my concentration is broken by someone pulling out a chair from my table. I don't look up. I can't. More eyes on me.

"So, is it true, Mister Witherspoon? Does the angel have a dark side?"

Jonathan. What is he still doing here? I try to lift my eyes, but I'm abashed by the question. He's a heavy breather, and when he opens his mouth, he pummels my nostrils with a stream of cigarette smoke only partly disguised by fresh mints. The smoke lashes my already sensitive eyes, and they tear up. "Don't tell me you're taking them seriously? They're just bored. No one will buy it. Everyone knows you couldn't kill anyone, even if you are a Kung-Fu ninja."

"Karate."

"Karting. Gotcha. I must've misheard."

Close enough. Silence descends at our table for one... two... three... minutes. He sits back, perfectly at ease, content with the silence, but it is clear he's waiting for me to say something. I like rain, but Irish people are allergic to it, so I decide to compliment the dry weather. It's one of those Irishisms that every conversation, no matter how short-lived, demands be addressed.

"What sunny weather we're having."

"It's actually very cold."

Oh.

"It's supposed to improve as the day goes on, though. You want to walk home together?"

"Pardon?"

"You. Me. Home. Walk."

It was the word "home" that threw me off. I usually refer to my house ever so neutrally as 87. Add to that my divided attention as Paige tattles on about how I sacrificed Roop to a Grim Reaper statue as an act of

Satanic worship and then ate his heart for luncheon. That is not *exactly* what happened. "That sounds very nice. Thank you." I reign king of hermits and introverts, but allowances must be made in the name of manners.

"Nice shirt," he smiles with his big mouth and overly white teeth. Nodding approvingly, he says, "It's just so you. Elegant, classy, formfitting, red, black, white…"

And blue. I bought it because it has blue. I genuinely only check out blue clothes in a store, then the price tag, and finally what I call the salesperson's Accost Factor. I do hate giving money to uncouth pigs. "Thank you. Madrid's best." I hope that didn't sound arrogant. "I bought it when I was twelve," I add, and then feel like a stupid, socially awkward dwarf.

I'm not used to friendliness, so not to sound ungrateful, but I want nothing more than for him to go away and leave me to my cage. Right now, I feel very exposed and vulnerable. Yet all he does is silently beam those brilliant white teeth. "Nice teeth. They're exceptionally shiny."

"It's a medical condition."

Of course it is. His response bugs me a little though. I don't give accolades freely. The least one can do is accept praise on the rare occasions on which I distribute it. What a waste…

He eyes Paige, and hers glow ever bluer the longer he does so. He tears his eyes away from her somehow, leans his spotless silky skin and cigarette breath across the table, and asks if I'd like to hear a joke he found online. I'm not really into jokes and I hate comedies, but I hunch my shoulders in non-committing vogue. Asker's choice.

"Wouldn't it be cool if someone's name was 'Gurt'? Because then you'd be like, "Yo, Gurt!" I give a short laugh. "As in, 'yoghurt!'" He has himself in hysterics and alludes very obviously to Steve's carton chin.

"Oh, I get it," I laugh for all of two seconds. It might even be genuine.

"What? Then what had you been laughing at?"

"...Saying 'Yo' to someone instead of 'Hello'..."

I think he's relieved when the bell goes *Boop-boop... boop-boop...* He reminds me to meet him after school—purple corridor.

I remember school ending. I remember not seeing him there. I remember Paige, Steve, and many more waiting for me with their fists, accusations, and their lies. I remember thinking I could kill every single one of them. I am a black belt in karate, after all. And, as they are apparently so sincerely convinced already, it is not like I haven't dealt with bullies before.

But none of this explains where, when, or how I am here now. What did those toe rags do to me?! Knock me out with gamma-hydroxybutyrate? Toss me in a boot and abandon me in the dump beside the graveyard? Did they record their ambush? Am I being live-streamed? Have I already been uploaded? And where were all the teachers when this was going on? Preoccupied? Disinterested? Privy to the attack?

Suddenly, I become all body and twist and vomit. My numb fingers paw and claw for something to clutch, to feel. The pain in my skull intensifies and spreads as my chest heaves and stomps on its organs. I feel like a bomb set to detonate, and I wonder if I am having heart palpations. In the blackness of the void, I claw and paw and scratch and scrape...

And then, for an indeterminate time, I am silent and at peace, free of the spoilage that is humanity, when a lethargic woman's voice yawns welcome through eternity: "A man I once knew purported that the initial sensation of disembodiment and nausea eases with every visit, here in the Land of Experience. Get up now. Eat fruit. Enjoy the trees. Admire the flowers. And find the rhythm of grace for your life, here in Liberty Garden."

I open my eyes. A small luminous orb hovers overhead, suspended in the air with sightless whizzing wings that sound like sprinkling glitter. Whenever it changes direction, which happens quite often, it makes an alien *whoosh*ing noise like a wet finger circling a glass. It descends with the grace of a butterfly on my Jew nose, reflects my unblinking owl eyes, and enlarges them beyond proportion. And I feel terrified.

The light teases me, bouncing on my nose and rolling along my fingers. It tickles. Still, I lie as though in a coffin. Not even a chortle.

Then I think I hear it say my name. Which is crazy. Because it is a ball of light. And I am… Am I dead? I'd better not be, because I don't have time for that. I have homework to do and shows to watch.

The top half of my body springs. The light eyes me, then smiles— not that it forms a happy curve, but… I don't know, I just… know. Feeling returns to my arms quickly after that: first strength, then the ache. I feel like I fell out of the sky. But that's crazy talk. All my bones would be broken. And they are not. I am badly bruised perhaps, but I am not squished and mushed and mashed and dead. Not certain of that, I touch my face just to make sure it is still there. My right cheek must salivate blood because my shaking fingers come back scarlet. Petrified, I reject the voice in my head that says I am back in the White Room looking out the small window again.

I sweep off the oat-like dust that clutches to my zigzag gashed elbows. I run my hand through my hair and grainy chips shower to my shoulders, then a few dry crackled leaves. Large as ape hands, they have the typical flame silhouette, but are variegated with multi-coloured patterns. The outer edges are brown and beneath this design is painted black skin like tar. A puddle of red splashes within the black outline, and a vivid yellow flower blooms in the centre like an all-observing evil eye. Disgusted and violated, I look around and see that I've landed on a forest bed of colours. As many as a hundred aureole eyes pierce me critically, telling me I do not belong here.

The orb knocks against my legs as though wrapping a door, and then a rejuvenating burst of energy shoots from my pelvis to my toes. After a few falls and stumbles, I climb to my feet, and the sphere beckons me to follow. I regard it with unconcealed suspicion, but adamant, it waits above an opening between two bushes, and tests my willpower or resistance. Unfortunately for the ball, stubbornness is one of my strongest traits—until I spy behind the opening in the hedges, that is.

All I see is blue: towering blue trees; the watery remnant of a blue sun that died long ago; blue fishlike creatures that swim mid-air; the vapoury shadow of a misty moon; blue fruit hangs off branches; and a collage of blue fantastical statues straight from a C. S. Lewis novel. Now I know I'm dreaming.

Cautiously, I step in line with the orb. Fearing the sensation of heat, electricity, or nothingness, I stretch out my right hand and slowly, slowly, my fingers clasp around it. Not tightly, as if trying to crush a biscuit for the base of a cheesecake, but securely, to protect and to cherish. Something I am not accustomed to—except in fiction. And the instant I touch it, I feel what can only be described as the unleashing of a miniature star's solar flare deep within me that bathes my innards with newness and life. It is like a transcendental surgeon charged a defibrillator to two-hundred and restarted a fistful of ice tucked inside my chest cavity that has been frozen since The Incident. The experience lasts only a second before I return to normal, but it is the one time in half a decade that I can admit I honestly felt safe.

A little more willing to follow the orb's navigation now, it leads me into a glowing trove of blue. The occasional light furry leaf brushes against my cheek. A living mist encircles the open space, and drenches the terrain, vegetation, and shrubbery with a sleek black lustre. Everything is so at peace, I feel like this is a walk through a well-maintained graveyard on a quiet, sunny day with not a funeral in sight.

I duck as often as needs be to avoid contact with the fish-things. Now that I'm up close, I see they don't have scales but flesh. Nor do they have wings for flying; their fins take care of that. Suds bubble around their keyhole mouths that look to be saying "ooh-ooh" in old men's voices. They leave a sweet-smelling trail behind them, signified with musical notes.

The ocean of blue upsets my already off sense of coordination—the only thing mediocre about me, other than social skills and my status as a twenty-first-century human being, more generally—so it's only at the last second that I realise there's an elephant-thick tree leg coming right for me. I spring back with my karate stealth, but my feet aren't used to jumping backwards on a soaked hill, so I stumble and land on my coccyx. And then the grass sings; its dew soars upwards like confused rain. The rocks stand in formation and roar victory over enemy lines like thunder. And the hidden Pegasuses above the thick whirling iodine clouds sing songs in vowels.

I rise, blackened in the shadow of the suspended tree limb. It croaks an ancient tired welcome and then, having descended diagonally, appears to bow. Before I can ponder this, the orb speeds ahead. I pull my sleeve over my hand and wipe the blood from my forehead and begin a steady jog to keep up. I'm almost upon the orb when the road dips and I catch my foot on a rainbow-shaped branch and trip, and it evades me.

I tune my ear and hear lapping and bubbling at the foot of my Prussian blue hill. At first, I tread circumspectly, but break into an inevitable downhill sprint before long. And I discover a fountain of breathtaking splendour that demands to be regarded with a sense of wonder. Just before I touch it, a melodious tune arises from seemingly everywhere and nowhere all at once. Hundreds, maybe thousands of fish-like creatures, at home in their oxygenised element, circle upwards, and form an endless spiral staircase of blue. Dark patches on the hill and plain, what I had assumed were tufts of grass, spring open, revealing hand-sized indigo petals. Upright stamens glorify the source of the music, and the trees sway their hands and bark tunes from their mouths. It is a song of dreams, heartbreak, death, and unconsummated, unrealised, unspoken affection. A relationship that never stood a chance.

A flash of whiteness bursts forth from the monument as it sends floods of blue striped with spectra down three tiers. Wisps of smoke like melting runny wax steam from the layered pools as spectres. Bolts jut from the bottom bowl at equal intervals. In between these are abstract designs, geometrically accurate and crafted with skill not found in the world today. Elsewhere, there are stylisations of swirls, triangles, lozenges, and cosmos, and flowers identical to those that shot up from the earth so sprightly to the supernatural harmony. The middle basin reflects the glory of what appear to be elves, given the triangular ears: their purity, their skill in crown-making, their elegance in the art of battle, their wisdom, culture, and literature. Images of shells decorate the top of this layer, and a rope of stars hangs beneath as though from a banister and coil throughout the pattern. From the top bowl emerge three figures: a wizard, elf, and dwarf, I think. A silver spine connects all three basins, and above its spike stands an egg. Cut into it, much like the perverse yellow buds on the leaves, is an eye.

"The water is beautiful, isn't it? Don't you just want to stick your head in it?" Roop tempts. For the first time ever, I try to block him out. He gives me a demo; it's no skin off his nose, he says, he's already dead.

"You have drunk from the forbidden pool! Now and forever, a curse be on you and your descendants!" The assertion rolls off a mighty and majestic tongue fierce as the elements.

*No, I didn't!* I yell internally and straighten regimentally, as though a superior in the army has just given me a command. And everything in the forest goes silent but for the thump of my heart, and then from behind me, a giggle. My mask shifts from one of contentment to one of unmitigated fear, yet I settle for a countenance of indifference before I turn around.

"That was a joke. Allow me to welcome you to the woodland called Melancholia." Her voice is simultaneously refined, saintly, and powerful. Sweet, temperate and authoritative. Enticing even, though I don't think I'm being entranced.

I take a small breath, and turn to see the most beautiful creature, an image so idealised she could be a Renaissance sculpture if she did not move, and this she does with elegance and grace, and caution. Mahogany brown tresses twirl down her back, and in front of her ears, down her shoulders like drapes. Her skin is healthy and clear but for a maul above her breast, nearly perfectly disguised by a dangling necklace of emeralds, crystal shards, and jewels, and her person emits a glow. Heavenly, mayhap, or haunting, I do not know. Ethereal, I suppose. She is a halo in human form. Her eyebrows are perfectly plucked; her eyes dark polished wood, her lashes long and black. The subtlest hint of a smile hides on the corners of her frosty blue lips which part ever so slightly at intervals as though she has something to say, but retracts. I hone in on her mouth and notice her sparkling teeth—dental hygiene is very important to me.

Everything about her sparkles. This stroke have I finally seen a lady!

The goddess's garment is tight-fitting, beaming, and has a vivid rippling effect. Decorating her front are tiny silver charms that form subtle spiral and floral designs like those on the fountain. And a sword tip peeps from under her flowing green cloak.

She stares at me for some time with those intense and pronounced eyes. The science-fiction addict within me cannot help but wonder if she tries to read my mind. It is an anxiety that leaves me at first astonished, then embarrassed, next ashamed, but lastly okay. Seconds turn to minutes. But then the melancholy beauty looks away. I could be wrong, but there looks to be a diamond teardrop in the corner of her eye. After a long while, in a young girl's voice, she turns to the fountain and weeps, "I am sorry for always dying on you." I don't think it minds, it being an inanimate object and all, but I leave her to her sob.

Uber-self-conscious, after she has had enough one-to-one time with the fountain, I introduce myself: "T-t-t-t... Thomas." I'm not sure why I used my boyhood nickname. Perhaps because this is a dream and therefore not real anyway, or maybe because I'm terrified that the opposite is true. I hate to be touched, but since it is the polite thing to do, I stretch out my hand. She neither shakes it nor tells me her name, but rather regards me as an unintelligible alien.

"Are you indeed? How lovely…"

Giving up, I lower my hand. I'm quite relieved she did no more than look at it: she is a beauty derived from one of Botticelli's Venus paintings, and I have insecurities of the opposite sex of Edvard Munch proportions.

Head bowed, my eyes fall to the grass and wait for this riveting discourse to end, and the great mist creeps along and soaks over us. Eventually, I raise my eyes to smile goodbye, but they lock with hers. They draw me in. Her eyes tell many stories: tales of betrayal; perseverance; striving; futility; immortality; the unsaid. Internally, I ask if I am dead. She does not answer. Her eyes' response is blank.

"How did I get here?"

"You followed the great white light, of course," she says matter-of-factly, as though I chase after random orbs daily. Alright, this has gone on long enough.

"W-w-where are t-the… cameras?"

"The last chimera died quite some time ago. Long before you were born."

I officially no longer trust her. This wench is off her rocker and her meds. "Why are you standing by the fountain?" I ask.

"I was waiting for you." Then she unwittingly exposes the hilt of a concealed sword. This makes me anxious.

"Why?"

"To encourage you to always keep fighting, because the Tapestry never stops weaving. The Triune of Warlocks, the Leviathan, the Two-Headed Dragon, the Abaddon Destruction, the Warriors Three, the Darkness… The battles just keep coming and evil is relentless. This world is so lost that even the stars have stopped shining and the skies plummeted into shadow. Yet even surrounded by ash and the absence of everything, this garden remains. Life will out. The Tapestry never stops weaving."

"Who are you?"

"My name…?" I don't know if she drops off her sentence out of boredom, lethargy, or because she finds finishing it too meaningless or non-utilitarian a task. Perhaps she genuinely forgets. "My name… Ah." She seems to remember, if I'm correct about her having forgotten it. "My name… My name is the Last Immortal. That is to say, there remains not one kind soul who remembers it."

"Is this the future? Are you the last person left? Are you alone?" Hardly. This doesn't marry very neatly with Revelation.

Sadly, she smiles, "Yes."

"That sounds peaceful."

"Not particularly. The silence can get pretty deafening."

"I'd kill to be the last one left," I cogitate to myself. Her frosty eyelids flicker at me and narrow. Her lips zip; a heated rebuke sizzles on her tongue. "I didn't mean to be insensitive. I would just like the adage to be proven true that good guys finish last."

"Finality is an illusion and immortality a curse. In the end, all that remains is Eternity, a long stretch of graveyard made of Time and tombstones. Life is sweet as strawberries, and it does Man's heart good to see the sun. Every day is a gift and should be appreciated so. But remember the days of darkness, for they will be many, and when they come, they render all else meaningless. The Tapestry never stops weaving."

"Why am I here?" Am I in a coma? Am I suffering brain swelling? Am I drugged up?

"I do not know," she says cryptically, "To right some wrong, perhaps. Or so I can tell you... that no matter what... happened... happens... will happen... there is a chance for... for you to prevail. You inspire peace, hope and joy. It may not feel like it now, but you change the atmosphere and the environment. You have no idea of the power in your blood or of what you are to become." She tilts her head to the ground, bites her lip, and then whispers against any possible desire to do so, "Or maybe you are here so I can... give you... this gift... this promise." There's a look of doubt in her eyes as to the claim's authenticity, but I sense she needs it to be true.

"I—"

There are flashes of light: white, silver, yellow, blue, red, lilac, deep purple, and a thundering sound of titanic rocks shattering rocks.

And then the world goes white.

# INTERLUDE
# KILLADELPHIA, HERE I COME

[The west wing of the Summer Palace in the Elven Kingdom of Loux Laxciila, in a dark chamber she has never consciously been down before: the ceiling is held up unbelievably high by pillars hoisted by figures of men with curled ram horns and ox heads which they hide behind thick muscular arms, too ashamed of their hybridity to be seen by the flawless motley elves. About the statues of men stand sculptures of mighty dragons, great lizards, and arrogant peacocks. Stuffed multi-headed dogs, phoenixes, snakes made of onyx, and a Minotaur form a train of conquered beasts, long forgotten under heaps of dust and spider nests. The princess enters a secret passage in the wall she unwittingly knows is there and is greeted to the euphonious sound of the King playing classical music on the piano. He knows she is there, but, lost in the music, the moment, or his wicked musings, he plays until the end of the song].

KING: A–?

PRINCESS: It is I, my liege. [There is a cold, faint look in her eyes like she's not really there. All she can see is the mission behind those hazy blue lacklustre eyes].

KING: [Turns and looks at her dully] I can see that.

PRINCESS: There has been a terrible storm, both here and everywhere else in the warren. All our seers—dreamers, visionaries, prophets, and revelators alike—say that the blue fork lightning has even levelled mountains and skyscrapers throughout the lands. They also say that in some regions, there have been earthquakes that have destroyed cities, and sinkholes have swallowed entire camps of Yetis, Salamanders, Manticores, orcs and Merrows.

KING: And what of you, fair lady? [He assumes a sweeter tone with her now. In all his years on that earth, she is the only person that this immortal monarch can say he has ever loved]. What do you see?

PRINCESS: Proof… that an end is truly near.

KING: The seer gift is a curse.

PRINCESS: It hurts my head. [She sounds like a little girl in agony, but only for a moment]. But nowhere near as much as the Dark One will hurt as he dies. [All traces of agony in her countenance give way to venom]. It is he who has done this, yes?

KING: Unwittingly, perhaps, but yes… He has arrived in our world. Take him out of it.

PRINCESS: My steed is ready, as am I. I await only your command.

KING: Militarily, you are ready, yes. Mentally, I am not sure. What do you feel, *ab ús?* [This is Old Elvish for "my daughter"].

PRINCESS: Nothing, my Lord.

KING: That is for the best; the ideal state. Emotions are dangerous things. They lead to desire, desire to passion, and passion once blossomed always inevitably to death. Better best avoided, methinks. [Eyes shut, he circles his head to the tune he had played]. I require a moment's patience so I may get to the Tower. Forthwith I will lower the force field. You will have three minutes.

PRINCESS: I shall not require the latter two, my Lord. Your people are more than preoccupied with the cage-fight between the Frost Giant and the Cyclops, and should that finish promptly, for dessert I have prepared a skirmish between a Nanaue and Peryton. The streets will be quite deserted.

KING: I have placed a hefty bet on the Cyclops.

PRINCESS: Maccan the commentator is acutely aware. He hid crushed foxglove leaves and *cerbera odollam* petals in the Frost Giant's soup. The poor wretch had no idea he was consuming poison. You will get your money back and more... so much more.

KING: [He rises and stands so many heads taller than her, he cannot but appear threatening, then walks to the corner of the torch-lit room and retrieves his metal rod from against the stone wall. He joins the rod to a four feet long wooden stake so that it forms a grand staff. He comes close to her, every step terrifying and resounding]. Your excursion is long, and you will be outside the reach of even my incredible telepathic power for much of it, despite the ability of my rod to enhance my gift. Do you think you need further encouragement?

PRINCESS: Most doubtful, my King. But do as you wish. [He holds out the rod and gives her further encouragement through the mind manipulating powers of the rod].

KING: Now then, the golden question: what, pray tell, is the overall objective?

PRINCESS: [Her hazy deadened blue eyes blacken]. What it always has been, my Lord, since I first began my training: to kill the Dark One.

KING: And should my old friend happen upon you before you accomplish this task, and enquire how you came to be there?

PRINCESS: The goblins are always believable culprits. [She recites the speech she has prepared]. "My Lord, the Elder Elf, temporarily let down the Laxciilian barrier so he could personally confer with and infiltrate the ranks of the Triune. Scarcely was he to know that the lecherous Goblin King Mordok had sent spies to take advantage of such an opening. Many nights after my abduction, I overheard the cretin King's true aspiration: to blackmail my Lord and sovereign—Loux Laxciila's wealth for my King's kin. Seizing a later fortuitous opportunity, I rained on their heads the judgement fitting for terrorists and fled. That is how I came to be here".

KING: Very good. Go! Be my eyes and ears.

PRINCESS: And your blade, your majesty, should the wizard not find the Darkly Anointed first.

KING: Oh, and Lady Eirianwen Brythonwen? Return here without the head of the Triumvir, and I will bury you.

PRINCESS: May your honour hold you to that, my Lord, as surely as I was born under the Star Gwawrddydd. Farewell!

# 3
# RECRUDESCENCE

After a while, I become aware of a chorus of teeth-gritting that may have been sounding for hours. It takes me longer than it should to realise it's me. I wake, curled in the foetal position beneath the deep black sky and extra white stars. My neck itches. Everything hurts.

At first, I think Dave has hit me, but… But what? My fingers press against the crinkly leaves and mossy bark, and I shakily clamber to my feet, head throbbing. My skull throbs like a drum. Before long, I vomit. Concussions and blinding migraines pull me under. And everyone who is anyone screams their fill from the canals of my memory: Ronan, Roop, Lucas, Dave, Nuala, the One-Armed Man, Jonathan, Paige, Steve, Raymond… All the ghosts come out of hiding tonight.

I awake again, drenched in sickly warthog bed sweat. I need a long scorching bath, or I might just claw away my skin. I sit up too quickly and feel woozy. Deadened and bested, my head sinks like a boulder into my hands, then my long watery fingers seize my soaked hair, and fight the temptation to tear it out.

"ABC 6-5-1-18 9-20-19-5-12-6," I say.

Then I say it again, and again, and again. Maybe I've always been saying it. It feels like I'll never stop.

And I rock back and forth for what could be hours, all the while listening to Inner sing Keats's "Ode to a Nightingale", embarrassed to find I'm unable to answer his question: "'Do I wake or do I sleep?'"

ABC 6-5-1-18 9-20-19-5-12-6.

My head, like a drum, beating... beating...

ABC 6-5-1-18 9-20-19-5-12-6.

My wooden box soul creaking, creaking...

ABC 6-5-1-18 9-20-19-5-12-6.

"'til it seemed/ That Sense was breaking through".

Dickinson.

Inner:

> "Little Miss Muffet, she sat on her tuffet, and
> The itsy, bitsy SPYDER came up the water spout.
> Along came a SPYDER who sat down beside her
> And frightened Miss Muffet away!
> Down came the rain
> And washed the SPYDER out!"

My eyes open and I'm back in Dreamworld. I haven't had a lucid dream in a few weeks. Maybe that never ended. Maybe I never woke up. Maybe I was always here. Everything is so confusing.

My insides churn and project vomit into a nearby ditch. I cough the acidic remnant of crumbled rasher and scrambled egg out of my drainage pipe. I flail my arms wildly and scamper my fingers like a digger until I find a leaf, and though everything's blurry, I see no yellow goon-faced flowers staring back. Hoping that nothing has used this leaf for anything, I scrape the residue off my tongue, and await a third hurl.

Despite the groggy vision, I soon see that my journal and pen have voyaged with me today. They landed just inches away, in-between cracks of rocks and tufts of grass. I reach out and grab them, but the suddenness of my movements causes an indelicate feeling, like my body is warping or materialising out of thin air. I gag like I've just munched down a tub of soft creamy butter. I sit up, shiver, and tuck my journal half under my jeans and cover the rest with my shirt. The pen, I put in my pocket.

A sixth sense warns that it is not safe to stay here.

When I try to move, electric spasms shoot through my body to my fingers and my toes like fork lightning. But this does not disable me. Rather the current, like it a battery and I a toy, provides me with power. Sure, my jelly legs are unable to support my weight the first few times I try to stand, and my first step is wobbly and uncertain, but it gets easier.

Gradually, the throb settles, and my vision fine-tunes and drinks in the scene around me. This is not the wood of Melancholia. This is a different forest entirely. A low white moon haunts the sky, its centre blue and suspicious like an all-seeing eye. Its spiderlike rays add grey to the black canvas and multiply the shadowy trees on the forest floor. Under these dark trees is no path, just normal leaves and twiggy claws. A river of ghostly fog like spirits streams along a bumpy mount of firm mud twenty metres from me. Branches from all around point forward like signposts. I keep an eye out for a lamppost, but no such luck.

Vermin run in front of me. In terror I leap, but slide down the sleek wet face of the leafy mount. Whatever it is my right sole hits on the way down, the pain is a white light. As I scamper to my feet, I find a muddy red runner, but I take no heed. I've dreamt of stranger things.

Using a long sturdy stick for a walking stick, I venture up and over hill; a barricade of twiggy debris trudges along my dead foot. After a while, I notice that living branches delineate for me a track. Intrigued by their proposal, I turn my head to investigate, and collapse: something, or someone, is out there.

Gaps in between thistles and hedgerows reveal a cloaked bright dead figure. His face is large and fleshy with ancient hollow eyes. Lashing living hair whips before, against, and behind his head. His glistening hands are those of an anatomy of death, armed with a black blade that seeks someone to devour. And he hums a low and enchanting tune, like a forgotten song to which no one remembers the words.

Mother deer abandon their young in his presence. Pitiful, redundant act of cowardice. With movements as quick as the snap of a thumb, they are all dead anyway... their hearts in his hand... then his mouth... I feel cold. And repulsed. And horrified.

Keeping low, I fling my stick to the far left where there appears to be a great drop. He races after it, as expected. And for countless minutes, I crawl about like a purgatorial simian beast upon whichever hill and dip look most dramatic while maintaining distance between that thing and myself.

Eventually, I arrive at a smooth round plain of earth that invites me up a staircase of age-old slabs. And if I have any doubt that I should ignore the beckon, a thin stake branch snakes through the fortress of brownish-green and even offers me a hand. My first response is to try to wake up, but nothing happens. That having failed, and since it doesn't look like I will get any study done tonight, I ascend to my coronation.

The steps are as hard to climb as cinema stairs, varied between short and wide. Static and unsteady, my hand clutches to the sentient branch as to a railing. The nearer I draw to the top, the stronger the pound of firecrackers, rocks shattering rocks, and long-winded bellows. My nose wrinkles at the smell of foul flesh, fetor, and smoky trees.

I begin a sprint, but my momentarily forgotten limp reminds me that it's there, and I trip over the final slab that juts out awkwardly. My chin dives upon a toothy stone that pierces it badly and sends my top row of teeth crashing down on my bottom. I picture them shatter.

"Poor Thomas, lost in the world of play, the irresistible incorrigible world of your imagination. You really are so little in here, so mad, so alone. Is Mommy going to have to send you back to the—?"

Whiter than white, a dazzling counterfeit sunshine nimbus behind his head, stands a sixteen-year-old Roop, saintly as the pre-incarnate Christ, the Angel of the Lord. His hair is messy yet cool. He sports black shades. He wears denim shorts and woolly socks, too. And he's dead as the day I saw last him.

"I wouldn't get involved in that if I were you," he says of the bellowing and gnarly noises from what is obviously a skirmish from over the hill. "I know how timid you are—and how violent. An out-and-out paradox you are, Beej; as great a work of fiction as these *episodes* of yours..." And then he spouts at me every vulgarity ever heard in *Baile Átha Fhirdhia* since the day Cú Chulainn impaled his bestie Ferdia by the River Dee.

The moment lasts a lifetime, as always, and I cannot move in his presence. Gradually, mumbles between a girl and a man become more audible only to be drowned out by roars, scurrying feet, and the titanic trample of a battle scene. But I keep my eyes fixed on Roop until he walks away and evaporates. Then I crawl to the top of the hill, body pressed tightly to the ground, and peer over the edge.

For obvious reasons, two nine feet tall, hideous trolls catch my attention. One of their noses twitches when his head faces my general direction. I have convinced myself that I am a goner when I realise he is too transfixed on something else to notice me. The larger troll, whose nose is not quite intact, shouts "BRAH!" I can only assume this means they are brothers.

With no trees towering tall enough to block out the low stellar rock's luminous light—for it is not the same moon that observed me in the woods—their muddy skin glows bright green. Their hair is black and untidy, knotted, and styled with rusty mustard bones, and tangles down their tree stump lower backs; hairless slabs caked in dirt and grime that shine with oozy streams of sweat. Above their beady eyes, their foreheads are as large as two man-sized hands. Arched over their horned bushy eyebrows, muck wedges between their wrinkles as glitter clogs the smallest of cracks.

Few details distinguish them: the taller (older?) troll has warthog teeth either side of his jaw while the docile one's teeth remain behind his lips. The taller troll's nose looks gnawed while the intoxicated behemoth's nostrils are pointy like the Grinch's. Furthermore, the older one is armed with a wooden spiked club and a twenty feet long whip with a dozen metre-long blades. His brother holds a longbow he has clearly never practiced with and an array of arrows that rattle in their quiver behind his back every time he moves. His determination to fire an arrow proves so strong that he has become oblivious to the surrounding battle. There's a squelch as he sits in filth in a corner some way away from the entrance of a cave everyone keeps glancing at, content in his solidarity but annoyed at the futility of his task.

An old man I can only assume is a wizard fires blasts of pink and purple energy that crunch through a tree. He mutters something about having lost his hat like he expects someone to laugh, as though unable to comprehend the severity of the situation he is in. Needless to say, he's a great deal shorter than the trolls, but from up here I estimate he achieves an admirable height of six feet plus nonetheless. (It certainly beats my five feet two—and that's when my hair is gelled). He focuses his stringy thin hands, ornamented with three rings, so that it looks like he carries the broken tree, which in his own magical way, I guess he does. He then makes a flinging motion with his hands at the older troll. The tree hurtles towards the troll but is splintered by the force of the hand with which the creature holds his whip.

Now I do not approve of witchcraft, but at this point I'd rather see the end of the trolls. But that's the wonderful thing about lucid trances: the dreamer dictates the outcome. Right?

The wizard is agile enough to dodge the swipes of the troll's arm, the lashes of his whip, and the beatings of his club which surprises me given his haggard appearance: bushy wild eyebrows; a long grey beard flecked with tired ginger flames; and brownish red robes, the sleeves of which are decorated with designs not dissimilar to those found on the fountain in Melancholia. A heavy cloak sprawls over his back while across his front belts a small bag that whips back and forth simultaneous to his sprightly movements.

Armed with a staff, he appears most confident in its power. At the top of it are four claws, one on each side, and in the middle of them a white orb glows blue when in use. At the neck of the staff is a cut-out circular shape that a ring could neatly fit into. The bottom of the staff has been sharpened into a stake, and all about it are roots. He spins his staff like helicopter wings above his head and directs his free hand at the older troll, his eyes on the cave as if expecting something to emerge. At this, a tree uproots and flies towards the enemy who actually poses a threat. The troll's whip wraps around the wood, but it is too late to stop it smacking across his front and into slumber. The wizard lets out a short laugh.

The second troll continues to embarrass himself with his ineffective talents at archery. The greater his frustration increases, the stronger his brow furrows and longer his thick tongue hangs like a dog's. His hands fidget past the point of insanity and I wonder when he'll snap. Then something catches my eye. I sink as deeply into the dirt as I can (which is not like me at all) and inch ever closer to the edge of the hill, and notice dust floating around him like midgets. The wizard pegs a few handfuls of this dust from his loosely strapped bag to many orcs also cursing this scene with their company, and they behave similarly. A distraction spell...

This host of orcs run around frantically and aimlessly, occasionally getting squished—these fearsome and repulsive creatures are no friends of the trolls. They are led by an orc who won't stop shouting "Zj'hakim" so I go ahead and decide that's his name. He has a bald head but for some stray white scraggy strands of hair. Zj'hakim's skin is pale brown, almost white under the low moon, while all the others' skin is marshy green. Four filthy yellow teeth lower like stalactites above an orange tongue in his foul mouth, and hoops, piercings and crude markings make him more piratic than the others. But they all look evil. Things like fish scales sag above their black eyes like brows, and their armour is smeared with the blood of whoever they have just pillaged and killed.

A horrific flourish of snot-coloured snarling mongrels closes in around the wizard. He waves his hand in a circle; heads explode and his sword flies from further down the road, past my vision, and slices off more heads. The orcs' screeches are ear-splittingly high-pitched and carry on for a few seconds post-decapitation.

As the magical midgets vanish, but for a few overworked stragglers, the unconscious troll begins to waken. His jaw droops, lifts, and wobbles from left to right. He puts his hand over his face and massages it until his eyes open. The wizard is too preoccupied battling seven orcs with a staff that suffers no scratches regardless of how sharp the orc blade, that he does not see Zj'hakim gaining on him. Before I can clap my hand to it, from my mouth leaps a cry.

"BEHIND YOU!" And with a quick *whoosh* movement, the wizard sends Zj'hakim flying.

I lie flat on the dirt and crawl beneath a dense thicket. It is worth every scratch to shield myself from view. There is no way only he heard my cry. Torpid, I remain glued here for a few minutes before I'm brave enough to examine the battlefield again.

When I next look, the old man magically drops a tree suspended in mid-air over the dopey troll's head, but he shatters it into splinters with his hulk hand. He stretches his body forward like a train on a track and roars more loudly than anything I've ever heard. The orcs' ears fold inwards to protect themselves from the deafening thud of his voice. Zj'hakim spits some horrid-sounding words, but the wizard challenges, "Not if I get it first."

"Ar'k! Ar'k," an apelike orc alerts like a crow—metres from me—pointing. How rude. The orc scuttles awkwardly (uncomfortable armour, I think) for me, but when he's less than ten steps away a tree shoots a branch like an arrow and guts him. Good riddance. Several fiends who heard my voice also charge at me, but since no one and nothing here cares much for orcs, the trees soon fatally puncture them, as well.

Zj'hakim's movements are stealthier than the wizard's insofar as the orc king crawls over the troll's legs like a spider and sinks daggers into his thick squidgy flesh, before profanely drinking his blood. In retaliation, the troll beats the clubs into Zj'hakim's humped back and flings him across the plain. Foreign black blood like oil rains from his gargling mouth. After a short while Zj'hakim, well-protected by the layers of mismatched armour I suspect he's scavenged from many previous battlegrounds, is back on his feet and leading a second battalion. They usher past him as he stops at the entrance of the cave. A wave of thirty or forty orcs sprint carelessly, even climbing and hopping over one another in the direction of the wizard and the troll who now fight alongside each other—temporary allies in the anarchistic confusion. It is just as well, since I am convinced the troll has picked up my scent by the weird way his nose twitches.

Arrows fire through the thistles all around me. I must not have been as discreet as I had thought. I pull back slightly and scuffle combat-style into bushes to my right near an abandoned tent, drenched by a pool of water filled with twigs and insects. They impair my vision that much more, but provide me with more cover too, so it's much of a muchness. Occupying this space also permits me a privileged view of the cave whose mouth opens directly across from me; stone cones like lion's teeth descend from the ceiling of the entrance, unwelcomingly greeting wanderers. Zj'hakim is the first I see who tries to scamper inside. The expanse resists him. He is persistent, I'll give him that much, until he punches the emptiness in frustration, and it unforgivingly devours his hand. He wails like a cat caught in a storm just as dozens of newcomers scoff troll flesh by the pound, and one of them falls with a clamorous crash.

That is when I see her.

From the inside corner of the cave peeps a veiled face in a dark green coat. Her blonde hair falls down the sides of her face, and a complexly patterned tail sits on her shoulder. In one hand, she holds something long and covered in cloth. It is obviously a sword and probably a magic one, but I don't think I am supposed to have guessed that on my first try, so I name it Miscellaneous Item. In her other hand, she holds a fabulous blade that I only make out clearly when she steps out from the cave and under a temporary beam of moonlight. Her sword's peen block is silver with a blend of indigo, as are its pommel and grip, inside of which is a crystal of pinkish-red. Its guard is thin and sturdy, laced with a superb sheen metal. Its fuller is gold and its blade is large, curved, stainless, and sharp, as the orcs soon learn.

As the sky progressively darkens and the girl becomes the sole focus of so many of the brutes, for the first time yet, the wizard's face shows deep concern. But before he can do anything, the beasts leap onto his back and claw onto his legs. His purple cloak drops from his shoulders to the ground, and he nearly trips over it.

"Ar'k! Ar'k!" The orcs are coming for me again. Let them. Finding a fresh jawbone of a donkey nearby, I grab it with my sleeve-covered hand (germs and all that jazz), and strike down ten of them. (Wow! I am really getting into this dream. If I'm not careful, I'm not going to want to wake up). The few who were halfway up the hill turn on their heels and flee.

Dodging arrows like she can hear them leave the string and predict exactly where they will go, I see the girl run towards the cloak, throw it over her shoulders, and just begin to vanish when, mid-teleportation, she's swiped to the ground by what must be the Mother troll. The girl falls with a crash onto a few sharp grits but does not appear too badly injured. Whatever she's claimed from the cave is released from her grasp and lands beyond her reach. The Mother troll further asserts her mastery over the girl by tearing in two the cloak and chewing on it. The girl's pointy ears redden with anger.

Just then, Zj'hakim's lengthy turtle-like neck edges towards the heavily wrapped miscellaneous object, retrieves it, and snarls victoriously at the girl. A blast of pink and purple launched from the cave the wizard must have snuck into undetected, whizz past Zj'hakim's ear, and the orc flees, followed by five others.

Nine of the orcs I struck wake up from their catnap and scatter—not that they make it very far what with trees spitting spikes, spell-casters casting spells, and trolls on the rampage—but, as the expression goes, there is always one: the haggard beast crawls toward me and then leaps. I shatter the jawbone across his mushed nose, and stamp-kick his shins. Then I quickly and quietly, without making much fuss, pick up a hammer and tent peg from the abandoned camping gear behind me. I drive the tent peg through his temple into the ground, and he dies.

Down below, the Mother troll plods over to her youngest son, Brah, who sweats by the litre and breathes aggressively enough to induce a heart attack, but still makes no progress with the missile. The last of the midget-like dust literally just disappears when his mother, who must assume he has been permanently bewitched and rendered redundant by troll standards, lets out a torturous wail and wallops Brah's head off. It squashes the lone-standing orc as a boulder would have done. The she-monster's brow wrinkles like asps in a snake charmer's basket. Her auburn hair stalks behind her as she speedily totters to the older son. She lifts the corpse and mourns loudly, and upon examining the bite marks on the body, she tempestuously decimates the remainder of the present orc clan. I think the wizard will let her live; she's lost enough today. I know I would.

Then she sniffs a particular scent amongst the bark and the filth. I had forgotten my blood-streaming chin. It has formed quite the stain on my shirt. Inner shows her no compassion and says to the wizard, "On second thought, kill the—"

The colossal shrew charges at me.

ABC 6-5-1-18 9-20-19-5-12-6.

Fear induces paralysis. Communications are down between my legs and brain. I try to move. I can't. She's too fast and I'm too afraid.

Wake up, wake up, wake up, wake up, wake up, wake up, wake up! WAKE UP!

That is when the girl leaps in front of me with three simple movements. Her languorous grace and beaming energy dazzle before me as the carnal fiend's neck slides down her blade. The girl kicks Big Momma's head with power I only wish my legs had, and she falls back in a swampy heap, dead.

I try to thank her—to say anything—but words do not come. I even try and recall if Jonathan Swift prepared gentlemen for situations like these in *A Project for the Advancement of Religion, and the Reformation of Manners,* but the construction of coherent thoughts is rather outside my capabilities right now.

Incredibly light-footed—which is remarkably impressive as this is one steep and dangerous hill—she dashes to the wizard just as he collapses and sprawls out on the bloodbath. She drops her blade to the ground and holds him, and whispers some inaudible words to comfort him. I have no idea what she says, but her affection for the old man is undeniable. And though it's petty, I feel a little jealous. I mean, I'm the one with the bloody chin. I tiptoe down to ground level but, awkward as anything, I keep my distance.

"They took the forgery," I overhear the wizard say, more for my benefit than hers, I think. Eyes closed, wheezy and breathless, the poor chap looks like he might just kick the bucket any second now. With his last remaining strength, he throws the real sword (I mean, Miscellaneous-Article-Concealed-In-Heavy-Folds) to the ground. He says that ought to keep the Triune at one another's throats for a while and congratulates her on a simplistic but wily strategy. She hunches her shoulders a little, as if to say it's no big deal, that she does this all the time, and looks away.

"Is it really him?" he asks, too pained to move or get a good look at me, absolutely diminished save for a toddler's strength. In response, she whispers something I do not catch. I begin to wonder if she even speaks English. It doesn't sound Irish, German, or Japanese either, though. Hell kind of a dream is this? Am I inventing languages in my sleep now?

Her crystal blue eyes come closer to me and search my brown owls. I jump a little when a gentle breath from her small pink lips touches my nose; a tiny piece of the leap is excitement, but most of it is terror. And I freeze when she rubs her soft hand over my face and down to my chin. I have not been touched innocently in a long time. It feels weird and wrong.

"Do not fear. Just trust," she says with concern and authority mixed with a note of caution, as if she is not entirely certain that those are the correct words.

I'm halfway through saying "I am not afraid" when I realise I'm lying. Therefore, I hold my tongue. Her eyes shut gently in meditation. I could be wrong, but I think she's trying to heal me.

Instead, we share a premonition. It lasts only a few seconds, but what we see is enough to sway her feet the opposite direction. She returns to the wizard and blocks his vision of me. Then again, she could be returning for her sword to cut me down.

She does not acknowledge the sound of my heavy breaths or thumping chest, or the scurry of my feet as I scramble back up the hill and down the uneven steps from whence I came.

I wonder if she'll chase me and kill me.

I hope she does.

She strikes me as more merciful than these goblins into whose hands I have just run. These bad boys look like they could have a lot of fun torturing me before delivering the final blow.

# 4
# AVARICIOUS

*"Last time, Thomas. I will not ask you again."* His face is an ugly snarl, his tone goading and gloating...

*"Why, Gabriel?"*

*"Seriously, that didn't stick. Call me 'Roop'."*

*"I prefer Ga—"*

*"You would, wouldn't you?"* he winks.

*"I don't feel comfortable doing this."*

*"Don't you want to be my friend? To be in the Inner Circle of Uber-villains?"*

*"I'm not so sure I do anymore..."* Of course, I do. Who else do I have?

*"What was that?"*

*"Of course, I do."*

*"Then complete your final challenge. No more sittin' on the side lines like y' did when I knifed all those dogs' throats and drowned all those Satan-spawn cats. No more turnin' a blind eye like all those times I robbed those kids blind at the park. No more causin' distractions like when I stole from Mahatma Ghandi's store."*

I make sure to tell him that's racist, but he ignores me. He always ignores me. Would he miss me if I died? If I just disappeared and ceased to exist anymore? Probably not. No one makes me feel as special and invisible as he does.

*"Be more proactive, much like you were the day you hacked away Ger's 'ppendage. Or like when you threw that boulder at Daniel for dissin' Mother Dearest and crushed his foot. Like when you broke Rory's toes, for no other reason than 'cause you wanted to win that fight. Those trials were all preparin' you for this moment."*

*"No. I didn't mean to do those things. I was just so angry. I can't do those things anymore. They're not right. They're wrong."*

*"The bomb, Thomas!"*

*"It's a firework, Roop."*

*"Do it now or mark my words: you will be worse off than you were before I scraped you off the bottom of Toni Fletcher's boot and made you into someone people at least notice."*

This is the first moment I actually fear him. Not that I haven't always known he was a psycho and badly in need of either electroconvulsive therapy or Jesus, but this signifies the first time that I know he'll one day snap and take me to my grave, just for the sheer fun of it. Integrity departs from me, and I reply like a wimp, *"But your dad's a cop. He'll find out."* For several minutes, I stand frozen as wave after wave of insults and threats crash into me. More furious than brave, I say, *"No."* Never have I said a word with a more masculine, husky voice. He looks offended, poor sap.

*"Oh, Thomas... Sad, sweet, not-so-innocent, little Thomas... I'm online ev'ry night 'til one or two in the little hours. I know stuff. Lots of stuff. Stuff that would hack*

*you at the knees and make you even shorter, you retarded-growth-inflicted dwarf." He stoops down and picks up a little spider. "Man, I already have in mind the perfect punishment should you stray." And pulling off a leg at a time, he says, "So, cross me, and I will destroy you."*

*And he means every word of it. What will he do? Tell my mother? Frame me for something and leave the evidence in Hansel and Gretel Breadcrumbs fashion for Officer Samson to find; a trail that ends at 124 Lincoln Lane? Physically harm me? All the above?*

*"Go to Hell."*

*"I will ruin you!" He charges at me with animal speed, kicks me to the ground, and chokes me. And chokes me. And chokes me… until I submit to his final challenge and need him more than oxygen.*


I wake to the polluted taste in my mouth of bile mixed with something rotten that recalls an unpleasant pink mouthwash I once used that tasted both medicinal and out-of-date. My head aches. Nothing is clear, but I think I see the blurry contours of four feet high snarling creatures. I arch my neck to vomit, and almost choke on it, and the world spins like a Saint Catherine's wheel. A black cloak *whoosh*es and I'm out cold.

I fade in and out of consciousness for who knows how long, but eventually I'm alert enough to notice the rough sackcloth roped around my neck, barely loose enough to permit inhalation. I flounder like a fish in a full net with nowhere to squirm for embarrassingly long before I realise my hands and feet are bound. Beyond the world of the sackcloth, I hear the incessant ticking of many clocks or watches in perfect unison. Then my knees and lifeless legs are dragged along a hill of burning dust.

Maybe an hour passes before my dehydrated mannequin is dumped on what feels like millions of tiny shards of scorching glass. My skin sizzles and splits and spits scarlet a thousand times through the holes in my shirt. Feet draw near, kicking sand on my neck with each step. The sackcloth is loosened and pulled off my head. And the sudden brightness blinds me.

Tick-tock. Tick-tock. Tick-tock.

Under interrogation, the light judges me. I think I'm dead. I had always thought I was saved, but I suppose concealment is not the same as innocence. I'm being punished for The Incident, aren't I?

Suddenly, a dark shadow blocks the light and hovers, as if not knowing what to do with me. I can almost hear blood pump through the shade's neck, but when he mouths something, his words get lost in translation from his sightless face to my deafened ears. I must be slipping out of consciousness again, because the shape demands that I stay awake with a kick that drill-bits somewhere to the left of my belly button and digs in deep. I writhe with pain and hunger and curl like a wounded animal on the side of the road. And whatever drug I've been jabbed with, for this sensation is one I know only too well, pulls me back under.

Tick-tock. Tick-tock. Tick-tock.

When I next awaken, I am hoodless and bruised. The next time I close my eyes, I don't know if it's the result of tiredness, or my way of escaping the threat of social interaction with my captor, or my attempt to shut up the tick-tock-tick-tock-tick-tock-tick-tock-tick-tock-tick...

And gradually I remember how I came to be here: I see myself run through the woods, stumble over cloud-shaped stones and tree tentacles, flap my arms wildly, and put as much distance between those *Dungeons and Dragons* knock-offs and myself. The wizard called for me—once by name, I think. The girl, however, remained silent, convinced in her reservations thanks to her witchy fortune-telling.

This forest was nothing like Melancholia. Crickets made their presence known. Things slithered that I refused to picture or acknowledge.

Little demons scampered on the branches. One tree's fingers fanned like bat wings and others bore the countenances of eyeballs and gargoyles, and one looked eerily like Genghis Kahn.

From one of these trees jungle-swung a creature that kicked me in the back and sent me hurtling against a tree. The goblin's triple-bent back clicked with every movement, and its ill-fitting, incorrectly worn metal plates (an assemblage of shoes, shields, and teapots) clinked most irritatingly. Its mouth would not stop gnawing, and with each swish of its jaws its marshy, stretchy skin pulled and retracted with great elasticity. Its massive yellow eyes were evil. I ducked with only a second to spare before it sprayed me with revolting vomitous goo. Marking its territory, maybe. Signalling its prey. I gave him a *Mae Geri* in the groin and he didn't spit at me again in a hurry.

And then I heard a *zip*—something small and thin as a toothpick zoomed through the air and sank into my neck. And then the lights went out.

The next image I remember shows the world upside down; dozens of simians crawling over trees, grass, themselves. My hands and feet outstretched and bound like clock hands, on display for the carnal fiends with their expired egg smell and Dracula pincers. I remember now having had the impression that they did not know what to do with me. Sure, they hooted in perverse mockery, their cackles shrill and wicked; yet there was a formality or air of contemplation amongst the indecency, and one of confusion. There looked to be a council of Bearded Goblin priests, arms folded inside the sleeves of ratty robes. They spoke little, but were clearly regarded with trepidation and reverence, and when they spoke, all keenly listened.

The debates over my future went on a little too long for one cheeky impatient gremlin's liking, and he strung an arrow on a manacled bowstring. I was his target. I didn't hesitate to point him out. Overcome with rage, the others fiercely rebuked the chancer, and he quickly met his end. They fancied just about every part of him, but for his nails, hair, and intestines for some reason.

Soon after, a cloaked and evil figure appeared and massacred them all, even the pygmies. Then Black Cloak turned to me. I could not see his hooded face, though I imagine it was terrible. His spine erect, he appeared to slither along the black-with-blood forest floor like a ghoul. He seemed interested in my face—at least, I think he was by the way he moved his head in sheer examination. Then he stretched forth his gloved hand...

That's when the waters fell and drowned him out and a giant impenetrable hedgerow like a sliding door cut us off.

"Chosae Waaan! Git ap. You bitta nat 'av' di'ad on me."

Not even realising I had fallen asleep, I awake to the kick of a boot and cannot tell if I'm dreaming, dead, or just mad.

Tick-tock.

There are three mercenaries around me. As a black belt in karate, I could easily mop the floor with them if only they'd stop injecting my veins with the piping-hot drug, sending canals of fire through my insides. For the rest of the day, my waking hours are spent picturing how to incapacitate them.

By day three of my being here, I've discovered... not a lot.

The dark one who likes to kick me is called Edgar, though a lanky mouse-faced one calls him "Ade." There is much to hate about Edgar, bless his heart: his rotten teeth; his arrogant eyes; the unsubtle way he wears my gold and silver watch on his filthy shirt as well as a couple dozen more he's robbed from his victims' corpses. Tick-tock.

Mousey seems harmless but strikes me as a timid coward who just got involved with the wrong crowd. He worships the sand Ade walks on which is pathetic, and I think I saw him literally kiss his BFF's boots clean in a plea for forgiveness for some wrongdoing during one of my woken intervals.

Neither of them looks as ferocious as the third man, a plump pirate with an egg-shaped head slopped with scraggy white hair. His disgruntled face is dotted with mismatched beady coin eyes. The other two call him Skull. I would hate to find out why, though I am sure he would take pleasure in educating me should I ask. Not particularly well dressed, his homeless man routine gives him that rough-and-ready mien.

We stop trekking so they can drink their ration of water, but it ultimately results in a vicious fight amongst themselves. As with the goblins, it is the small matter of keeping me alive that divides them. You see, they want to keep me alive, yet they didn't bring sufficient rations for a fourth companion—or slave—as it were. The entire thing perplexes me, as my well-being has seldom been anyone's focus. It would have been logical to have considered the sustenance issue before kidnapping me and setting out on this grand scenic meander, but as I know all too well, the gifts of foresight and wisdom are distributed to the few. Good thing they have the pig-headed Edgar to concoct a viable solution to their dilemma: I can't hunger or thirst if I am asleep. I breathe in before the knock-out punch comes. Tick-tock.

My left eye widens halfway and then squeezes into a squint. My right one is, I imagine, a purple plum. I don't even know where I am. And I'm so weak with malnourishment, I can't even lift my neck. I thirst so greatly my days-old sweat begins to sound appealing. And I suffer major tea withdrawals: hallucinations, twitchiness, restlessness.

I think we're deep in an oasis—at least, I hope those tall bendy shadows are trees. While I slept, my wrists and ankles were chained to one of the rough bark poles behind me with ice-cold shackles. These are new. I'm not sure what happened to the rope. To be honest, I wouldn't put it past the pirate to have eaten them; for a fat man, he carries a perpetual look of starvation and savagery—he'd eat me if he could. This brings me to wonder what they want with me, but I'm not comfortable asking them. So, to pass the time, malnourished and tied up and bloodied or no, I ponder the best way to end them.

Once I've figured that out, my present predicaments dominate my thoughts: small pointy screws pinch my flesh. Brown patches of dry blood heavy as muck. My tattered jeaned legs arch in front of me like I have rickets. Something like staples are jabbed irregularly into them. If they aren't already infected, they soon will be.

Tick-tock. Tick-tock. Tick-tock. A twig snaps. Tick-tock. Tick-tock. Tick-tock. Now might I do it, pat, now he is coming...

A filthy sandy hand squeezes my chin and I get a close-up of a tanned face. Deep but tidy eyebrows. A thin stringy moustache and beaded triangular black beard. It takes me as long as ten minutes to remain awake long enough to absorb even these minor details. "Dreenk," he demands, and shoves a cow skin of warm water down my throat. I almost choke, and the shock spits it out. "What a waste, Chosae Waaan!" the man bellows, and smacks the back of my head with a rock-hard palm.

"Ade!" Mousey intervenes. How long has he been there?

"Ma nim is Adeg'r, nat dat dat is any cons'lation t' y'."

"Ade, what you go do that fo'? The Waw'locks ain' gonna be happy wif that. 'Aloive, full o' blood and, unmu'ila'ed', they said. Or *he* said, ratha'. Whichever wan of the Twy-oon yo'r in cahoots wif."

"'Triune'?" I ask, though I go unheard, amidst Edgar and Mousey's bickering over how abductees should treat their prisoners. Meanwhile, the third devil-grinned mercenary spits into a fire by the bucket load, ever sharpening his dagger or making "hoot-hoot" noises like the uncle in that Robert Louis Stevenson novel, eyes forever on me. He considers himself hilarious and cracks evil smiles that show missing, rotten, and golden teeth. … Okay, well, I don't actually know if his mouth looks as contorted as that, in view of my ninety percent blindness at present, but that's how I picture him… before I am pulled back under. Tick-tock.

I do not like horror films. Not that they frighten me, but of all genres, I find it to be most lacking in gems. In fact, the only four things that tear my eyes from the screen are:

1. The plucking out of eyes;
2. The yanking off of fingernails via whatever metal apparatus happens to be around;
3. The shooting of toes; and:
4. Sunburnt lips.

Even as I think of these things now, my eyes squirm and hide, my toes curl, and my fingers dig into the wormy sand beneath me as Edgar rants and raves about all the horrific things he's going to do to me. Tick-tock.

Surprisingly, the lanky one tells him off, and reminds Ade of the mission and the reward. The cover of the dark trees apparently provides Rodent Face with the courage he otherwise lacks. Edgar steps up close to him, his eyes in line with Lanky's chest. In Edgar's eyes is murder, and every threat he made to me transfers. After a taciturn lengthy stare, he grunts and gaits away slowly, every step heavier than the last. The tick-tocks fade more and more quietly.

Suddenly, there is a booming quietness against the deathly stillness. Then feet flap, leaves rustle, and through the branches comes the ragged breathing of a mutt struck with rabies—the pirate.

"Lear's men. Dey've gat spears, to'ches, kinetic exploseeves, and"—he smiles perversely as I see all too clearly, even with only half an eye— "women."

You sick, twisted…

"How many marauders?" Lanky whispers with a mix of curiosity and guilt.

Eight men, four *gersha*.

"Go," demands Lanky, then hops behind me on his springy legs and pulls out a knife. He barricades my mouth with his manure-smelling pan-sized hands and holds the cold blade to my throat. I struggle a little, but it is malnourishment more than anything that restrains me. To have gone from at least three meals a day to the occasional gulp of warm water has not been to the better. Still, if he thinks I'll make this easy for him, he has another thing coming.

Skull scuttles off after Edgar. The two rapscallions arrogantly believe they can beat a dozen or so other men, and they're probably right. Immediately, Lanky removes his hand and, as though we're friends, sits next to me. There's a slight crunch of foliage as he flattens a few dry leaves and a small bounce of cold sand. Because I do not want his cohorts, the marauders, coming this way, I choose not to scream.

"Hey, little buddy." I hear howls, fire crackles, terror, hyena laughter, and slaughter from beyond the trees. "You didn't think much of th' warm water, eh? Yeah, it's kinda gross." *So is kidnapping and torture, but what you gonna do?* "Y' know, we're from Earth, too." This I find disappointing. Being the only one made me special. "You like your sleep," he quietly laughs like an early twentieth-century car horn. *No, I do not.*

He tries to get a conversation up and running, but his attempts result in awkward silences as unpleasant as a seedy mandarin. After a while, he goes on to say that his master had sent an army of orcs to reclaim something precious (why won't these people just come out and say it's a sword?) while that same master, or 'Waw'lock, the one Ade's in constan' conf'rence wif' sent them the One's coordinates. I'm guessing 'the One' is me. He yammers on about some rhyming prophecy he cannot recite properly that predicted when and where the Chosen One would arrive, and that the Weapon would be near him. Of course, the time and place were quite vague, so the Master sent many scouts to the five likeliest destinations. When, half a week ago, a great thunderstorm of blue and white hailed above the Aegan Caves and Woods (which I was probably too out of it to notice), Lanky's triad of employers knew exactly where to send the Collectors.

"He said, 'Follow the...' Well, I dunno what 'e said, axually. Like I tol' y', Ade does all the talkin'. Or list'n'n', rath'a. I fink you came here in a storm, bu' didn' corporealise properly fer a li'il while. The wizard open'd some kinda portal, or somethin'. And there you have it: forest one second, desert the next, with the occasional woodland or oasis poppin' up. I still don't understan' this place, really. Never bin much good at geography, me, and this place only serves to complicate ma'ers, what wif places bein' there one secon' and then disappearin' or enlargin' or shrinkin' or breakin' and appearin' elfswhere the next."

Listening to him is harder than reading Joseph's lines in *Wuthering Heights*. "Wh... m... I...?" The carnage increases from the other side of the oasis. Lanky pretends that he is unmoved, but I see his bottom lip quiver before he dons a tight-lipped smile of blissful ignorance.

"Oh, you're in the Oasis in the Black Desert. Or Dead Desert. Or summit. But we 'aven't reached the Black Sands yet. ... At least, I 'ope we're in the right desert. I 'aven't been 'ere too long myself, though it feels like I've bin 'ere all my life. I suppose that happens when yo' in a wo'ld where ev'ryone's trapped, where places jump about all willy-nilly, and the cosmos make even less sense, eh?"

I don't care too much about what he says. I just want to know my part in all this.

"Look, I can' speak for th' others, but... I am sorry that we have t' do this."

"Wh...?"

"Hand you ova'... t' be ki'ed..."

Had I the energy to laugh at how Lanky can speak so intrinsically wrong a sentence and not unlock my shackles here and now, I imagine I would die doing so.

"I wan' t' go home. I wan' t' see my wife and daughta 'gain. And Ade's las' memory was of fixin' a car. And Skull, I'm guessin', though hist'ry's not my strong point, was taken from a piwate ship a few hundred years ago. We just wan' fo' this nightmare to be over. An' the Masters Three, they say they have the power t' do i', to send us back to our proper time in Earth's hist'ry. T' our families."

He pulls out a feather and a small jar of ink from his pocket, picks up a leaf, and begins writing something. I couldn't care less what he's penning, and huff in annoyance. He appears to mistake this for a question to which he answers: "Because yo'r the Chosen One, our Master believes. And if we hand y' ova' to 'im, he'll send us back."

He pauses, and his downcast eyes tell me he's failed to convince himself that that's true or justifiable. He freezes for a while, but then we both become so terrified of the boisterous butchery taking place on the other side of the trees that we depend on each other's sounds to serve as a buffer. Lanky carries on writing, and I muster the word "Mouthwash...?"

"Ha-ha, yay, I guess *Bolta* does taste like tha', don' i'? A really yucky pink one I tried a few years back."

"He... ca... me... "Chosae" ...?"

He crosses something off the leaf and writes again. "Oh, that's jus' his accent."

*No way! Well, clap-clap, Sherlock. And the Oscar for Stating the Obvious goes to...!*

"Our Master Silas suspects yo'r th' Chosen One… The one whose gonna bring an end t' th' Thwee Waw'locks, who are keepin' th' evil throne warm fo' th' nex' Dark Lord, thus destroyin' th' Maze an' all evil, an' stuff, or summit, I fink. Keep up! What'd you think you were 'ere fo'?" His buckteeth mouth breathes heavily on the leaf, and he buries his feather and ink deep in his pocket.

Between sore splutters and dry coughs, I say I've just gotten here. Lanky sighs deeply and summarises badly:

1. Three dark and powerful wizards have come to power in this world, Angoria. Collectively known as the Three Warlocks of the Triune, their names are Liriondias and Silas, and he cannot remember the third guy's name;
2. The Triune joined their powers to create a mighty maze that quarantines each race, kingdom, tribe, and village of Angoria, and shuffled them throughout a geometrically accurate map with a one-to-one ratio of the real Angoria. Traps have been laid everywhere, and floods of nasties murder, maim, and manage the captives in each territory. Unless killed by one of these warlock-instigated mechanisms, fiends, hunger or happenstance, however, death does not come to the inhabitants of Angoria. Rather, time stopped the day the warlocks cast the spell that birthed the Maze. Technically three hundred years have passed, but no one has aged;
3. Thought to have been impenetrable, a few prisoners have managed to escape their Zones, though this has thus far proven only to occur in accordance with a greater scheme predestined long ago by the warlocks, Lanky thinks;
4. It has been foretold since the earliest of days that the Chosen One, a conglomerate of mystical energy and Goodness personified, would come and bring an end to the Oldest Line (the wizards) and then stand against the Twelfth Dark Lord in the Final Age of this world; and:
5. According to drunken bar talk with the wizards' minions, the spell-casters have lost their corporeal forms. They exist now only as spirits trapped in an impassable mystical cage deep beneath the wreckage of their once pristine and ornate palace. Lanky speculates that killing me both ends the prophecy and somehow results in the Warlocks returning to their bodies. I wrestle with the urge to tell him I am not mythic, but

human, and that ghosts are not real, but he seems so convinced of his hogwash that I decide to leave him in his comfortable naïve darkness. "The power is in the blood," he says, and I am the saviour, the redeemer, the transformer, and the life-giver, and the only one who can reverse the big baddies' misfortune, if they bleed me dry.

He apologises for what he and his comrades are doing to me and throws his mouse-snout to the trees beyond before he cries pitiably, as though he has any reason to weep. It is only now that I notice the silence beyond the trees, and I realise just how loudly he had been speaking.

Tick. With horrific timing, a grim-faced Edgar appears from behind the bushes just as Lanky slips the leaf he scrawled on down the back of my trousers. Tock. Tick-tock. "Are you makin' smo' talk weet de Trium–?"

"No!" His tone admits his guilt.

"I tat so." Tick-tock. "Git ap." Tick-tock. "And follow me." Tick-tock.

Edgar disappears behind the black shrubbery.

"Don't go," I beg.

"I have to," he guffaws, and chokes back tears. Neither of us are in any doubt regarding what comes next. I repeat myself and so does he.

"Thanks…"

"Fo' what?"

"Talking to me…"

"I'm sorry, kid," he sniffles. "I'm so sorry."

"Now!" barks Edgar, unseen and perhaps for that reason more

terrifying.

"Kid—"

"Thomas," I say, not knowing why. His lips form to say something, and I never find out what, because Edgar's red headscarf leaps from the bushes and stabs him through the back with a branch. Tick-tock.

Scared to death, I feign sleep, though no one in their right mind would buy it. Acutely aware of my deception, Edgar's deep breath contaminates the air for a minute—and I know it was a minute for I counted the tick-tocks—and then he struts off. Tick-tock.

The living Skull, only a few metres off, cackles mockery and hee-haws like a donkey. They walk off and revel in their militant success. The women or *gersha* make no noise, so I can only assume not even they were spared. That may be in their best interests.

But Lanky is not dead. He paws my leg. I cannot look. I hate myself for it, but I cannot look. And he slips his knife into my pocket. "It ends tomorrow," he says. "Kill them both. Before they kill you. And they will kill you."

He vomits a hideous choky breath, then surrenders his spirit to the world without end where the Tapestry never stops weaving.

There. Now he's dead.

Tick-tock.


Until maybe an hour before dawn, I shiver with fear as Skull's unblinking eyes fixate on me from a nearby rock, and minus zero temperatures chill my insides. I give in to exhaustion just as the smithereens of sky through the branches above glow a rich sea blue. Conveniently, this is also the moment Skull protrudes forward and shoves an unwashed hand into my mouth and forces me to swallow something like stale bread, a layer of onion, and brown flakes glued with warm water.

"Ah look fo'wahd to dem weezahds schkinnin' yah 'live, preety boy." Is it bad that that's the nicest thing he's said to me in five days?

Edgar storms over, unchains me, and throws me to the ground. Before he can deliver my morning beating, I cover my vital organs, but he's not as tense as usual, so he keeps his feet to himself. He released some excess energy during his spree last night. For being such a model hostage through it all, he even treats my head to a sackcloth-free day, which means he wants to savour every look on my face as we cross the finish line to their Master's lair, or Masters' lair, whichever it is.

He pulls me out from the trees and the morning sun hits me with unexpected intensity. It's like the sky went from "Could Rain" to "Heat Wave" in a matter of seconds, and my bursting plum eye's vision is a total blur. In fact, the only thing I think I make out are a couple of horses, the only survivors from last night's massacre perhaps, not that they neigh.

That makes perfect sense, because, I soon discover, these are not horses. The black creatures stand on four stick camel legs; a fifth, reserve leg curls underneath their stomachs. Their feet are clawed and massive. Their bodies are shaped like ships. Skull's has two humps; Edgar's (the one he ropes me to) has one. Small batwings stem from their sides and, behind, a cow tail. Their necks are skeletal and ooze an entire physique's worth of green poisonous sweat. Their necks rattle toothily. Their skinless heads are long as horses'. Their ears are pointy as orcs' and their eyes pale as death.

They wheeze with pain.

Skull hyenas, "Pass me th' bottle" or "th' *Bolta*" and Edgar tosses him a dark vial. Skull dips his dagger into the glass and turns towards the beasts. Sensing that I'm watching, he flashes an evil grin, revealing just how few brown teeth he has left. And then he butchers the hybrids' hinds with his blade. They writhe, squeal, and gallop their feet on the spot as he injects them; either bewitchment or experience teaches them not to attempt flight. Their eyes burn rich red; they are mastered and tamed. Edgar spies me observing. "Eet's when dar ahs are yeller dat dey ought t' bay fayred."

He looks down on the ten hapless warped creatures he slew last night and demands that his steed dine. Every chomp of its buck teeth and slurp of its gloop tongue intoxicates the air with the stench of coal. Skull struggles to climb atop his, so he flogs it as punishment and tells it to eat too, in the hope that no one notices his shortness, obesity, and incapability. In a moment of perverse comedy, Edgar and I watch him scale between the hunched beast's black oily humps like a madman trying to climb air whilst maiming one of the creature's front legs and snapping off its fifth. Now I hate animals, but even I am disgusted by his carnal effrontery.

Not too far off, four heads gradually bob over the far side of a dune that cannot decide if it is white, orange, or brown. Likewise, these men ride on the backs of the hideous monstrosities. Their steeds have longer wings, curled in, but that probably extend about twelve feet. And maybe it is just tropic illusion, but their lifeless stares (not that I can see them from this far back) rebound like holograms on a projector above and beyond them. The travellers turn wordlessly in what Edgar understands to be a beckon whilst Skull pouts at having to tear his dirty gaze from the animalistic feast.

Ahead stretch miles of desiccated desert beneath a magnesium white sky. A stroke of rich blue washes in on my far right, while to my left an evening sky of pinks and reds appears to curve spherically around three suns. A mirage brought on by dehydration, maybe. My half-an-eye needs a rest, but I peal it open anyway as I am dragged along like a toddler's ragdoll lump after lump. The sands look like millions of beds of roots lined up from here to world's end. As we come to the steep edge of the tan brown snaky sands, a precipitous drop awaits us. An orangey-yellow perpendicular wall tasks us next. It's a good thing these creatures can fly. Not that I want my captors to reach their destination, I remind myself. As we descend the opposite side of that hill, my half-good eye sees the living shadow of the accurately named Black Sands, where this entire abduction has been leading all along—I should probably get to work on my escape plan right about now.

One of the four mindless puppets turns around on his beast—which I hereby call 'Warper' because, no offence to the creature, but nothing that grotesque is natural. I would sooner go as far as to say that it's a conglomeration of animals, science, sorcery, and one sick, sick, mind.

"Your task has ended. Your time is up. Only two may cross the Forbidden Sands," the cloaked puppet mouths: "My host and the Chosen One."

"Wat about ma fraydam?" barks Edgar. He catches the mongrel's eye. "*Arr* fraydam?"

"My master reserves the right to renege that contract, and he chooses now to do so," the man says matter-of-factly, though it is plain to us all that his is not the voice that we hear. Edgar loses the plot, and before I know it, he hysterically screams expletives or other boisterous exclamations in his native tongue. Finally, he returns to English, or at least his version of English:

"Way had a deal, Silas." Silas? One of the wizards? Lanky said they were trapped; he must have telepathic abilities, and this is his host body.

"Poor simpleton," the man—or rather, the commanding voice—goads him. "Have you paid no attention during your time here? Only the Fates may decide who returns to your world and when."

"Een all ma years here, I have seen no evidance tha' de' Fates exist! Bat you I have seen wark wondahs! Great and evil! I have slaved for you. I have keeled fo' you. I have lied and cheated and skinned all sortsa people fram da bone!" Skull must eye him again, because Edgar corrects himself, "We both 'ave!" And then he pleads with the apparition by drawing on examples of his kills this month.

"Vile and disgusting though you have been, mortal, only one thing was truly needed from you: the Triumvir. These four"—he gesticulates towards himself and his company— "brought to us the other voyager to arrive on the Night of the Low Moon." Suddenly, I remember the runners I saw in the forest before I climbed the staircase across from the cave. "These halfwits have chosen what is better, and the glory will not be taken from them. At least, not from all of them. Now hand the boy over to this body."

I recoil, bringing my sand-eaten legs in close to me, the bottom half of my jeans long since lost somewhere in the desert. I'd choose these two rapscallions over that possessed man any day. As I cower, my upper thigh hits off my elbow, pressed tightly to my side. And I feel something stiff... The knife!

"No!" Edgar objects.

"Very well," he compromises, which surprises us all. That is when the three silent riders kill themselves and collapse to the sand. Their steeds curl their upper lips, make a deformed grin, and laugh; a blue mist hovers unsteadily above them for a while, then darts into the lone rider that remains. "Nominate one of yourselves. I personally favour you, Edgar." Through Blank Face, the Unseen urges Edgar to accept the honour of serving, even temporarily, as a vessel for his master. Edgar's name, the host promises, will be immortalised for all generations. Statues of him will be erected. His name will mean 'exalt'. And in dying upon arrival (for no ordinary Man may gaze upon the Triune and live), Edgar will escape the purge of the race of Men in the new world that is coming.

"Bat ah'll b' daid!"

"Take it from one who has walked the land since before grass grew: mortality is a blessing and immortality a curse," replies Blank Face, for the first time with a hint of emotion.

"Lord Silas, please, ah want t' go 'ome…" I find it both pitiful and repulsive to see so cruel a man beg for mercy.

"The only fate that remains for you, Edgar," speaks the parasite, "is to serve as my temporal host or as food for your steed. Go on, Edgar." I shudder at his unctuous repetition of my captor's name. Eyes fixed on Edgar, the host nods in Skull's general direction whom he has not looked at once. "Kill him." I don't know what thought passes from his brain to his feet, but Edgar lunges at the blob on the beast next to him who is either too dumbfounded, drunk, or dizzy with sunstroke to comprehend what is happening.

130

I can't look.

One knocks the other to the sand; their beasts stand frozen, awaiting audible commands. I imagine it is a brief but vicious encounter. Meanwhile, I have cut my hands free and run for my life.

Adrenaline pushes me over the scorching sands, despite thirst, tiredness, and fiery micro rocks eating two layers of skin on the ball of my right foot and crawling inside my flesh. The sand is piping hot and I cannot keep my foot on the same spot for longer than a second. I have no idea where my shoe and sock have gone, though I wouldn't put it past either Skull or Edgar to have fed them to the Warpers after my morning dose of *Bolta*. That would explain the gash on my leg that has been closed over by jagged folds of skin held in place by staples.

I hear the screeches of the Warpers and flaps of wings as they slice and bite one another. *Left-right-ouch, left-right-ouch*, I recite, until my bare smoked foot somehow tumbles forward over my crown so awkwardly I'm blessed not to have suffered a neck injury. And I roll down the dune at rollercoaster pace. My body hurls into the air and twirls at intervals. The thrill is incredible but I'm much too afraid to have fun. I can't say I'm unhappy when the tumbling and rolling come to a stop midway down a slope, but then the searing pain from the baked paper-thin sheet that is my foot sets my brain on fire.

Just then, my eyes register the fluttering treetops of the oasis. What was it Lanky said about this world's geography? That it isn't fixed or static, but that it changes? I get to my feet, putting aside all fatigue and fear, and dash as fast as I can behind its leaves. It looks different than it did before. There's a fortress ringed around it for one thing, inside of which is a pool, and in this an island of trees. I would be open to the possibility that this is a different oasis altogether if it wasn't for Lanky's remains sprawled out on a bush.

I want to cover or bury the body; not because I necessarily agree with the notion of funerals, but because we Irish exonerate our martyrs, and this man died giving me the means to live. But I'm under attack, so I run into the thick of the trees.

One branch slits my right cheek. A pile of rocks I climb turns out to be a crossbreed of turtles and gnomes that nearly throw me into a pool of still water that looks like a dark diamond. And after a hundred of them jump me, I spend ten minutes knifing spiders off my clothes. Stress of Life.

The sound of heavy boots treading on the ringed outskirts of the oasis, and the incessant tick-tock, tick-tock, tick-tock tells me that Edgar was indeed the victor and has come to finish me off. I'm not too sure what happened to the Warpers. Maybe they're flying overhead to cover more ground.

My back tight against a tree, I visualise the knife twisting into his flesh and out again. Easy. (As if!). Killing the orc with that peg was easy. It was inhuman. But this is a man; flesh and blood; body, soul, and spirit.

Tick-tock. I hear the heavy wheezes before I glimpse the sweat-saturated savage, a dagger in his furious mouth and in each of his bloody fists. Tick-tock. His eyes glare in my direction, but I can't tell if he sees me behind those silent but gushing tears. But the malicious slime ball just murdered the only man he could possibly have called friend—he gets no sympathy. Not that he's looking for it: he smiles like a shark and a second later, two daggers whizz past my ears. Oh, yes, he saw me. Tick-tock.

I lose myself under a marquee of trees and dodge his endless supply of missiles. I duck as the daggers shave hairs from my head and bite bark. I creep but maintain a sprint, bury myself in shrubbery, pull back a thick stretchy branch, let go when Edgar's nose comes close enough, and cover more ground while his bone snaps.

In a small patch where trees clump together, I see a shrunken cave that sinks under the earth like a large wormhole. I stoop down to make sure no vermin scurry about inside, and then scrunch my body as far back as I can.

If he was hoping for the element of surprise, the tick-tock betrays him. His tiger-eyes jump to their hunkers at the burrow's mouth. Hunchbacked, he inches ever closer.

"You war my ticket out 'a here, Chosae Waaan. Ah wass goin' 'ome. Bat ah caan't. You stole dat fram m'. Fa'n, you didn' steal it, but it was stolen from me b'cas a' you! Well, if I can' trade you for freedam, then no Mage gonna get y' taday. Without you, they got no baddy. Dey de ghosts foreva! Spireets. Powerless, excep' when dey take over a baddy in de desert. An' all dees ha' bin for nateen. Heh-heh-heh-heh. Goo'bye, Chosea Waaan."

I bury my hand in my pocket and wonder if I can indeed do this. Kill him. That is what Chosen Ones do, after all. It's a no-brainer really. It's the only thing that will save me from his Pidgin English!

Of course, I can't. I continue to sink further into darkness and then fall on my back through a net of hanging reeds. My fingers shiver at an oddly pleasant touch. It's like a puddle of glitter, and in my mind, it glistens violet and indigo and shimmers silver, and triangles tingle. Warm and safe, it sucks in my hand and then all of me.

Somehow, I'm deep in the oasis, and before I have time to process what's happened, I run to a tree and hide behind it. I'm near enough where I was spat out in case I need to jump through it again; surely, it's a two-way system. Also, Edgar will likely expect me to put as much distance between us as possible, so this might be the only advantage over him I'm going to get, especially if I must kill him.

Soon Edgar appears, sniffing for my scent like a wolf. Tick-tock. It's not long before his neck is in line with my tree, inches from me. Tick-tock. But I won't stab him, because I consider guerrilla warfare to be a grey area in the killing manifesto; because he's unsuspecting, it isn't a fair fight. Tick-tock. And because I'm a coward. Tick-tock.

And I'll never know if he smelled me or heard my heartbeat, but the man with nothing left to live for lunges toward me, going in for one final kill.

And then a pink and silver sword flies though the air and crucifies him on some bark.

The blade cut through some timekeepers; others fall to the ground and their faces smash and hands freeze.

I don't know how long it takes for him to die exactly, because he stole my watch.

And then the she-elf elegantly, proudly, and aggressively walks onto the scene, her eyes fixed on me with an expression that says: *you're next.*

# 5
# FIGHT, FLIGHT OR FRIGHT

She stares me out of it when I recoil (by which I mean "freak out") at the touch of her cold wan skin on mine. Yet she is patient with me, despite the hovering tension her premonition casts over the oasis. She beckons me to the pool and supports my lightweight feet step-by-step. Still, I cannot shake the feeling that she's merely sizing me up until she strikes me dead.

Every hop to the pool is so excruciating, it blinds me. It is only her hands, one in mine, the other around my waist, which prevents me crawling like an animal to the outer pool. Once there, I lower my bare charred legs into the water. It chills my sand-lined scratches and spilt petrol bruises. After about a minute, the pain oozes from my skin in mighty wisps and bubbles away. The foreign objects in my legs disgorge, followed by silkworm scarlet threads. Then tissue forms and skin sheets stretch over my flesh wounds.

My arms next: they are so swollen and damaged I cannot even lift them; all that remains of me above the waist is helpless dead matter. Seeing this, the she-elf tears off my shards of shirt—my broken corpse appearance is so beyond human likeness, I don't even try to shield my nipples from her for decency's sake. I gaze at my filthy brown shirt. The inside is shed in my onion back and snakeskin. Through the employment of my last shred of motivation, I inch over to the shallowest area of the pool and slip down onto mossy boulders. More wisps. More bubbles. Skin stretches from somewhere and wraps around my punctured wrists, ratty chest, acned and slashed shoulders. I cup some water in my hands and delicately rub it over my cheeks and forehead. My face boils like a kettle, and the wisps steam. It scorches me as the blackheads flare from my pores and injuries from my eye. Then comes relief.

I don't dillydally too long, and immediately dry myself with large leaves behind a bush. Then the girl returns with baggy sweats and a sleeveless blue jacket with gold interlace, two sizes too big, pillaged from Lanky's baggage, no doubt.

"Thank you," I say and dress. A condenser, she only nods, and we engage in not even small talk for an hour.

"Princess!" an old chirpy voice calls out. "And my dear lad! How good it is to see you both alive and together." It's the sorcerer, and an occasional grunt and mutter tells me he is not alone. From behind a barricade of trees and hanging leaves, the first thing I see is that the wizard has found his hat. When he comes into view, he breathes with relief at how great I look. I begin to wish I hadn't coated my wounds with the magic water, so he could see just how *great* I really am.

"You're here to kill me," I state, tensing up. That leaves only one more wizard I haven't met.

"If I wanted you dead, I would not have asked my reluctant associate to tend to the abundance of wounds you have no doubt suffered." He's got me there.

It takes the other figure a few moments to catch up. Dolled in wine-red garments, he looks like a tea cosy. Undoubtedly a dwarf, he's the only man I've ever met who is shorter than me. I smile awkwardly at his unfriendly eyes rather than introduce myself. He grunts rudely and turns his face, beadier than the silver crown that sits atop his head. The wizard whispers loudly that the Dwarf King is just angry because he believes I'm destined to kill him.

I stare at the elf and she at me.

"Goodness me, introductions! I go by Mósandrirl, the Elder Wizard." His greeting is abrupt and almost a week too late, but I go along with it. He says he is unconnected, in terms of agenda, to the Triune, the wizards who want to sacrifice me to serve their own ends. That's good news, I suppose. Instead of elaborating, he begins musing to himself. "Of course, I do have many names: Willaiesa to certain rebel factions who hold me in a low esteem somewhere between dislike and indifference; Harlfang to the Men of the West and North-West, but not to the South-West or North for they call me Wizardia Gesu; Chooey to the Werewolves, again uncomplimentary; and Bucket-head to my late brothers (it took me about three hundred years to trade in a metal helmet for a hat, you see). In fact, I have been called so many names over the years that I do not even remember my real one. I suffered a nasty hit to the head some years ago, you see, so everything before the year 507 is sketchy. No matter," he shrugs it off. I think he expects me to smile, laugh, or sympathise, but all I hear are the over-honest ramblings of a drunkard at a party.

"This," he says of the elf, "is the princess of Loux Laxciila. I am taking you to her parents' kingdom for safekeeping." Her name cannot be shared without the King's consent, apparently—Laxciilian politics, and all that jazz.

"Thomas," I say. The wizard smiles as if to say, *I'm pretty sure it isn't*, but he doesn't give me away.

Promptly he serves us lunch (I think he "magicks" it into existence) and promises that he'll answer as many questions as he can on the journey to Loux Laxciila. I cannot wait. The dwarf grumbles that he's not hungry and, axe in hand, gruffly declares he will scout ahead—he is met with no opposition. Once he has departed, the other two talk amiably over fruit, bread, and green vegetables. It's quite a bland selection, but after the week I've had, this is a fiesta. The meal mostly consists of him sharing witty tales; for example, about the time he drank from the River Slythe and grew ten feet taller; how he was accidentally crowned king of an island of little people ("no offence," he winks at his present company); and how, contrary to the history books, the first dragon he ever killed was only a prepubescent, and a Múrayvian dragon at that, so its head stood no taller than his kneecaps. She laughs in a ladylike tone and I smile whenever he looks in my direction. Not to sound ungrateful, but I feel lonelier than I did as Edgar and Skull's prisoner.

When lunch is finished, the wizard whistles a four-note tune and in response the earth quakes beneath the thunderous gallop of two equestrians. Where they come from, it is not even clear if the wizard knows. The three of us wander out of the kingdom of bark, cross the pool, and scamper up the slope and find a horse larger than any I've ever seen and a meaty spectral unicorn with a rainbow horn, innocent in its childlike representation. The wizard climbs onto the horse's back and the elf jumps onto the unicorn's and pats it and whispers greetings and compliments.

Unused to not being the best at everything, I am filled with embarrassment when I cannot board the third steed that had strolled along at a steady pace behind the others. Add to that the fact that I hold animals in less esteem than humans, creatures I already regard as sub-zero standard. The wizard offers me his staff to stand on and helps me up.

We travel a long time in silence through a valley and over desert hills, the likes of which Haggard describes in *King Solomon's Mines.* "Would you like to hear the origins of Angoria, Thomas?" the wizard asks, and since I'm in no position to decline, I smile, "Why not?" At this the elf squints and glares round for miles with distrust, filled with acuity that even lifeless deserts hide the ears of bad company.

The wizard begins: "First came the Seraphs, or the Higher Orders. Heavenly spirits from your world, Thomas, the Earthen Star, they created a rudimentary planet called Angoria, and they loved it as their own. Some of the Seraphs stand as watchmen above the Great Firmament, overlooking the righteous whilst others judge the wicked. Some have taken to writing the great annals of life; happenings, hypotheses, and predictions. Still others govern the day and night as great lights and stars; these ones determined that an Angoric year would have four hundred days. It was the Seraphs who created the wizards a little lower than themselves, a race of nine to shepherd Angoria."

Apparently, the history books here are slightly misconstrued; they claim there were ten wizards, but Gingerbeard suspects that they're counting Liriondias twice… As if that name means anything to me, besides being one of the Triune! This leads onto an itemisation of the wizarding folk.

The Elder Wizard, or narrator of this history lesson, is the oldest. After him came Thom the Blue, Wizard of Water and everything in it. Then there was Scarl the Colourless. The air was his to monitor and cleanse of impurities, natural and supernatural, for the Seraphs envisaged the eventual swarm of spirits of sadness, sickness, and strife. The winged beasts were also entrusted to his care. Next there was the Purple Wizard, Silas. Fixed on my wide-eyed and open-mouthed reaction, the Elder Wizard can tell that

I've heard that name before. A psychic, it was Silas's responsibility to advise the elves later created and Men later to arrive, and all created things, on how to construct the most adorned and wisest of civilisations, and to serve as mediator between the created and the Creators.

"Silas sent mercenaries to kill me."

"Oh, Thomas, if Silas wanted you dead, you would be. No, the Triune wanted you signed, sealed, and delivered to their home address alive. Then they wanted to gut you, so they would be free of their mystical prison, and get up to all kinds of mischief. Your blood is one of the most powerful things in Angoria." Edgar once said that the Triune were spirits and that killing me would help them get their bodies back. I suppose I could share this, but I'd rather find out what my present company knows first.

He continues in the same manner as before, as though I never interrupted: then there was Merrick the Gold; he was granted the power to manipulate the elements. The wizard *hmmm*s to himself as he tries to remember what power belonged to which of his next two brothers: Arl'nok the White and Harl'nok the Black. In the end, he equates stability with Arl'nok and chaos magic with the other. His lips mutter silent things as though he debates whether to tell a story, but in the end, he decides against it.

"And then we come to Liriondas Exeter Liriondias the Silver, or Lear as his name was shortened to over time, my closest friend among them all. Power over metal, he has."

He concludes: "The ninth and youngest was Kohl. My favourite. He died before he had even grown his beard. He wore green robes initially, and then brown when he discovered it was impossible to keep clothes clean when you have power over the soil and the task of making things grow." The beasts of the field and underground were placed under him, and he adored each of them as himself.

I ask what's-his-face what powers he has. I remember logs floating around outside the cave and not much more. He fidgets with a sapphire ring on his right index finger as he responds, "Oh, yes, that information could be helpful. I am the Red Wizard of the Flame."

All things considered, he is perfectly mismatched and peculiar: his threads are red, brown and grey, and he looks like he has forgotten what it is to bathe. These combine to give him a strong vagabond look. As well as these, from his clothes hang several trinkets and keepsakes, such as a feather, a bead chain, a discoloured and half-smelted bronze medallion, and what I sure hope is not a mouse tail. Add to that, he wears a ring on his thumb. I won't enquire, but he must catch me looking because he explains: "The midnight ring, Thomália, belonged to, as its namesake suggests, Brother Thom. The turquoise bead chain was Kohl's. Kalmbyne, it is called in the Common Tongue, originating etymologically from the first flower the Seraphs gave Kohl to plant in this world. Blue like the first forest Kohl ever grew."

"Is each wizard's power connected directly to his"—I'm a little behind on my mysticism, so I add flatly— "object?"

"The essence of the given wizard's spirit is in his *charm*, an item sealed to him by a blood ritual"—he signals to the oddities that hang around his neck— "but the capacity to use that power rests predominantly in the blood of the wizard to whom that power was entrusted." However, he says, if one wizard's charm is lodged in another magic user's staff, then the staff serves as a channel to access that wizard's power, albeit to a lesser extent. This is ridiculous. "Yet in my experience, Thomas, the greatest power a hero can have is knowing when not to use the gifts they have been given." Ah, here now! "For example, I never use mine unless an alternate method will prove futile. The best way to prevent falling into temptation is to avoid temptation."

"Is that why your battle with the trolls drained you so much? Because you're unused to using so much magic?"

"Well, that, and the fact they were trolls," he laughs gently. In fairness, I walked into that one. We ride a couple of kilometres without saying much else over the barren nothingness of mandarin-coloured sand, cattle bones, leafless Camel Thorns, and rocks cracked like skin or scales, probably to avoid my brain frying following information overload. Finally, I say that Edgar called me the Chosen One. The elf and wizard exchange glances.

"Kohl was the first wizard to fall," he responds randomly, "at the hands of Gideon, an imperious reprobate and, having assumed the identity of the Dark Lord seven times, the perennial threat to Angoria. After his most recent reign and consequential plummet from power, Gideon was temporarily slain. Moments later, though, his heart was restarted only so he could be trapped in torturous suspended animation and locked away in a cage. I fear the Triune aim to locate and unlock this entrapment. To what end, I can only surmise, but Gideon's role in this dramatic production is far from over."

Should someone partake in the offences of grave-robbing and reincarnation, I assume I am expected to put Big G back in the ground.

"Do they know where his prison is?"

"Not yet. Its whereabouts is known to only one man living. And if that secret belongs to whom I suspect it does, he is actually more 'imp' than 'man'. He is little more than a devious, grinning backstabber that we need to keep an eye on."

"Rewinding a few conversations: the Triune are imprisoned, too…?"

"The spell that created the Maze backfired to a certain extent and buried them beneath a mystical force in an underground chamber in their dark castle in the Black Sands. It would take one with considerable power and knowledge of the Secret Arts to cast a spell that unlocks that seal, and thankfully, the Triune as-yet have no one matching that description on their payroll."

"Okay, so there are still four wizards"—assuming Thom is dead, too— "against three. Those are good odds." I haven't entirely disregarded the possibility that this guy is the third villain, but I want him to think I'm onside for as long as I can.

"Not quite," the maiden speaks, eyes fixed on the path ahead. "Lord Mósandrirl is the only one left." He says nothing for some time; only bows his head in solemnity.

Finally, he elaborates: "When a wizard dies, his body shrivels away as food for the ground and his soul moves on to its respective Eternity. His essence remains in his charm and his power seeks a source in which to dwell. His spirit, on the other hand, oh, his spirit remains in Angoria. His spirit is his timeline, his fundamental undying personage. It existed before he did, likewise, it transcends his mortal state and coil. A potent force, his spirit ripples throughout Angoric time, and Normalcy's space. That is how you made your way into this world: unwittingly, you gravitated toward the convergence of mystical energies that emanated from a wizard's eternal remnant. Or it sought you out. Both are true, in most cases."

Ri-i-i-i-ight. Well, that didn't just go over my head. Anyway, back to more pressing concerns: "I have to ask, what exactly did Lear, Silas, and... the other one... do?" I remember Lanky telling me they messed up the geography a tad, but that's more of an inconvenience than a crime. Plus, I want to see if Lanky's account marries with the old man's.

Whatever-she-called-him speaks again: "Consumed with fear and repugnance, my brethren became disillusioned with the world as it was. So much carnal lust, urges and surges, suffering, and war... Evil was relentless. Of course, so were we. But there came a day when they collectively wondered, 'Why bother?' Each era, a Dark Lord rose and a Child was plucked from Normalcy, or the Earthen Star"—his names for Earth— "to render the Dark Lord diminished. Again and again, eleven times so far, and once more, according to the prophecy. So much death, so much bloodshed, so little regard for life, but the Tapestry never stopped weaving.

"In the wake of the last Apocalypse of the Dual Cycle—that is, the fray between the Chosen One and the Dark Lord—my brothers cast the curse that created the Maze. Environmental terrorists, they laid siege on the peoples of Angoria to hold back the utter decimation of the planet. It's extreme, but it's worked.

"But it is a false peace. It was not fought for, won fairly, or earned. There was no choice, no love, no negotiation. It was imposed upon a world that did not ask to be enslaved. The Triune turned their back on all that was good, and performed various kinds of magic most unnatural, until finally they forced upon the world the warren. Thom and Scarl fell just before the hedges of the Maze rose, or—more specifically—before a carbon copy was painted over the authentic Angoria, accustomed to the likeness of the Triune." An ardent reader of Baudrillard and Lewis Carroll, I understand most of what he says.

"They have trapped the once-free peoples within blocks, each with its own traps, orc wardens, and sky. And in each sky is a False Eye." Yeah, it's called the sun. "And the sense of being constantly watched, humiliated, of being rendered powerless... It has traumatised the prisoners more than any loss on a battlefield could have done."

It's a panopticon. A prison of observation. Infamous for shattering the minds of internees, it was forbidden as a means of punishment in democratic countries until recently. The President, once a humble resident of the big house on Lincoln Lane, was the first to reintroduce the fad, if my limited knowledge on twenty-first-century politics serves me well. After that, it seemed that every politician woke up one morning and just so happened to forget everything from their criminalisation to human rights to the Geneva Convention. But if you're evil and do not care about such things, then it's genius.

"You three don't look trapped...?"

"The Resistance has inside help."

"How large is the Resistance?"

"Small."

Bringing it back to the Maze: "How could anyone be *that* powerful?"

Days before the Hedges were erected, the Triune and their upper-level demon associates culled ninety percent of Angoria's population. Before their souls had time to get very far, Silas used his mental powers to snare the fatalities' personalities on the astral plane known as Sheol; an alternate post-life dimension that exists in the fabric of the Maze walls. Thus, he used the jam-packed energy supply of each soul as a battery to power the magical prison structure. Given that technically three hundred years have passed, most of the raw pure energy has been used up, hence the movability—and in extreme cases, disintegration—of certain parts of the hyper-reality. Of course, the Triune are rumoured to possess the ability to move segments of the structure in accordance with their plotting, too, as Lanky noted.

"But this is insane. I mean, there's no way this can be real."

Yet rather than hot-headedly asserting his authenticity, he surprises me by smiling gently and saying, "If this is all a dream, you might as well enjoy it. Whatever has gone before, whatever your present reservations or future doubts, own this moment." I'm ashamed to admit I don't know how to do that. I have always been outshone by duchesses who allowed their self-orchestrated dramas, fears, and prejudices to eclipse the stars I could reach for. They spoke death over me and, after a while, though suffocated, I could not exist as an entity separate from their mould. Because who wants to be a hero when you can be a victim? "Allow yourself to be someone daring, heroic, brave, or new; whatever it is that you are looking for. Be the hero."

I begin to daydream of each of these things, and gradually drift off to sleep.

Mayhem! I wake with a start to the panicked drawing of swords and gallop of hooves.

A screech splits the air like nails dragged down a blackboard. A perverse abomination of black skin, silver bones, scraggy legs, and bat wings hurtles over the golden dunes. It looks like an assemblage of multiple animal parts has been thrown in a pot of glue. Too-stretched necks and handicapped horse heads jut out of the fleshy mesh like birds in a nest. Several appendages lash the canvas of blue and send the grotesque ball in a tailspin. Orange flames burst from many mouths and the beasts screech in misery over their torture. Ladies and gentlemen, meet the Warpers: Mark Two. This one I nickname Abomination.

"Go!" the wizard roars.

He reaches over, grabs my Aladdin jacket, and throws me onto the unicorn behind the elf. The startled proud steed neighs with anger and confusion, and initially tries to throw me off. The elf clearly isn't expecting this and jerks into me, giving me a face full of smooth silky hair that smells of strawberries and lemons. Her stupid unicorn stops its sprint entirely and stands on its hind legs and shimmies to shake me off like I'm a tick. But a quiet word from the elf is all it takes for it to come to its senses and bolt.

A horse head catches up with us from the left. Sensing danger, I instinctively throw a jab, only to crack a bone on the leathery furry face of the Dwarf King (when did he get back?).

"The portal through which we journeyed to reach you has been resealed," the elf explains in little more than a whisper.

I didn't even know there were portals in this world—though that would explain how the glittery, tingly sensation caused me to vanish from inside the log and reappear elsewhere when Edgar was chasing me—so I just nod, "Oh," then proceed to be *that character* who turns his head and states the obvious: they're gaining on us.

Whilst steering, the elf tries to help the dwarf from his pony onto the unicorn, but he slaps her hands away, saying he has been touched by no elf since the War of the Ten Cities two thousand years ago. Aggravated, the wizard gallops to his left and tosses him aboard.

The Abomination is almost upon us. How spit and the smell of cattle exude from its gnashing teeth! And pony. I can confirm the Abomination has just eaten the dwarf's pony.

Lastly the wizard jumps onto the unicorn's back and faces the oncoming waves of piranha mouths.

"Forces of nature," he addresses, "twisted and turned by the Dark Arts and engineering of my brothers, you will do us no harm." And he apologises to them. His right thumb and the two fingers nearest it shake like a gun, and then all five springs open and unleash a fiery ball. It spins through the air. One of the Abomination's smaller heads and several limbs explode. The conglomeration squeals and thuds on the dune and washes a wave of sand into our ears and hair.

"Stallions, a village lies two miles ahead. Go there," the wizard commands. "Find the poorest peasants and serve them as best you can. Full speed!" And they're gone.

"Nala! Take flight!" he shouts. Intangible wings of unearthly brightness lift us into the air, and the spinning spectrum of the unicorn's hooves blinds the faces of the beast whose elongated necks and snapping jaws entangle and devour one another's flesh—well, some of them. Several of the creature's hydra heads still pose as great a threat as before.

148

"Ha! I know your name!" I shout to the elf-maiden.

"Nala is the unicorn, ignoramus!"

The wizard throws a few more fireballs and every explosion is signified by a sound like the squawk of a crow that got shot by a pellet gun. Now I may hate animals (especially crows!) but I cannot help but pity the hybrids. After all, it's not their fault they had been tortured, moulded into something hideous, drugged, disassembled, and reassembled in this heinous image.

Then the wizard bellows with almighty thunder: *"Haerodheim anglashima ... An ru'ark callah hepzibah!"* Large jets of light gun down the Abomination. It splits into scraps of animal flesh, innards, bone, tentacles, brains, and flushes of hot swampy slime that ooze poisonous gases. Meaty chunks fall onto the rooves of dome prisons and sizzle into nothingness. My eyes widen in amazement.

Wordless hours pass. Sleep threatens my eyes, but I fight to stay awake. If I drift off, I don't put it past any of these three people (are they even people?) to throw me to my death. Sure, the elf killed Edgar and the mage killed the Abomination, but I remain unconvinced that they are trustworthy. Is it because they are killers? For if that is the reason, then we're peas in a pod. Or is it because I can't shake the feeling that there is something significant they have yet to disclose? Or is it because I know, deep down, that none of this is real, that this is all one great hallucinogenic musing of a social phobic dreamer with a borderline personality disorder?

I mean, how could it exist? There's an azure reef with age-old geological imprints in the middle of a desert. Next to a barren wasteland inhabited mainly by the skeletons of great beasts are kilometres-long green hills dotted with scrawny sheep. A vintage provincial town shares water with the epitome of pollution. Two neighbouring mountains: upon one stands a bronze watchtower like a beacon of strength; the other a smoking volcano. It's crazy! It cannot be—this is an impossible planet!

The dwarf jabs me in the back with the handle of an axe so hard it will leave a bruise. It's not the strike that bugs me, but his insidious phlegmy laugh afterwards. I spin with a scowl and see that behind him the wizard has a look of expectation on his face. I think I was asked a question.

"P-pardon?" I point to my ear and squint and wince and employ a score of tonal voices and take classical acting to new extremes, and pretend the non-existent wind is to blame for my deafness.

If the wizard sees right through me, he has the good graces to pretend otherwise.

"I said, we are nearing the coordinates to the portal that our informant opened when the unicorn and I set out for Troll Cave, and that I am most assured our spy will come through for us again." Good memory, I return, but he does not accept the compliment. "Magical energies leave a unique trace or residue, invisible to the untrained eye. Thankfully, both of mine are most habituated with the supernatural. I see magic in colours, Thomas."

It is near nightfall when we *zip* into a multi-coloured shimmering circular structure that resembles a ship's porthole, and next thing we know, we're in a pitch-black woodland. The dwarf hollers and applauds like an airplane passenger, but the wizard silences him. This is the first time I detect a hint of fear in his voice. Unsurprising, since the only thing safe about this place is that it is so dark no one could see you to kill you.

"We are vulnerable to any number of dangers until we are within the city."

The elf asks why we weren't transported into the city. He hesitates one second too long in answering her which tells me he is stumped. Regardless, he poses the possibility that perhaps this was a precautionary measure taken just in case a minion of the Triune found the portal before we did. It is a good explanation, but his tone betrays him—he doesn't believe a word of it. I hear him draw his sword, and I pull out my knife. We dismount and the unicorn bolts away despite the hushed demands of the elf and is soon totally swallowed by thick shadow.

"Follow my lead," the wizard guides, tall and stern, and lights a tongue of fire with his thumb. "Pray do not think me impudent to lead the tour of your own grounds, sweet Lady, but when it comes to wandering these parts, I am the more experienced."

Wait. This is her kingdom? She replies with airy distance: "I have no qualms with your leadership, Mósandrirl, and I thank you for your consideration."

We walk as long as three hours with rigid consciousness not to stray from the tiny mud path. Beasts behind the bushes purr and growl, but none rear their heads. The dwarf criss-crosses his front with an axe and hammer and occasionally half-pounces at the rustles and snarls. Ultimately, the cantankerous pug never steers too far from the elf, but I think it is so he can throw her in front of him if faced with too great a threat.

Finally, a raspy voice slights us from a few metres ahead. I don't know what it says, but it sure is impolite. The wizard casts a light in the direction of the words and a long snow-haired sneer steps into view. His ears are pointy; his skin looks hard as leather. He wears skin-tight green material and a cloak. And his sharp eyes cut me. Right hand in the air, for a moment he looks to be making a pledge; that is, until I hear the hidden archers pull their bowstrings in unison. He glares at me murderously as the dwarf so often does, and my family before him.

By the wizard's flame, the male elf's eyes turn to the princess. And his arched eyebrows contract above a smile of joy.

"Sister," he says with relief, or another word like it, and runs to embrace her. I wrinkle my nose at the inappropriate level of enthusiasm with which he hangs to her. Then he chants something worriedly in their native tongue and shakes her so violently her cloak falls off. She seems lost for words but gradually pieces something together in the quiet tone of a guilty child. I think she says "Gau'blí'na" which I suppose means goblins, which is odd since I haven't seen her fight any. The wizard remains silent and lets them talk it out, though he listens intently to every word.

When she has finished speaking, the male elf dismisses whatever she has said and points to something behind him that the wizard's light does not illuminate. The wizard tires quickly of the elf's rudeness and barks at him in Elvish. The dwarf, who has been edging for a fight since we met, takes advantage of the angry atmosphere and begins shouting all sorts of nasty things at the fox-eyed elf, and accompanies these with hostile hand gestures. The wizard's voice booms and all quake:

"Alk'erion! Enough of this madness! You will deny no member of this party passage!"

Alk'erion's eyes and razor teeth flash at me, and I think I'm the source of all this contention. What? Has he never seen a fifteen-year-old who has gone almost a week without shaving before? Sue me. The pointy-jawed prince shouts something, then grabs his sister's arm, and with superhuman speed drags her through an invisible gate behind him.

And a mighty orchestra of arrows cut through the air.

I shut my eyes… I keep them closed… And nothing happens.

I chance peeping through them, and gradually they widen.

The wizard has dropped his centre of gravity and stabbed the ground with his staff, and forceful ripples are sent through the air. The archers are flung into the forest floor and their missiles laid waste.

"You must excuse his behaviour, Chosen One. The King is particularly hard on him, so he takes out his frustration on everyone else. Everyone but *her*—usually. Come along, you two!" He walks in the direction where the other two had vanished.

The Dwarf King begins to secrete so much negativity I nearly slip on it, and eventually, the wizard spins on his feet and smacks him across the back of the head with his hand. I'm guessing he's the only person in this world who could do that and not get hacked at the knees in retaliation.

"I do not need an Elven book of tricks to unlock a secret door *I made*, Master Dwarf." He proves this when he opens it ten seconds later.

That's when the prince, who has somehow gotten his hands on a crossbow, shoots me with an arrow in the chest. Time loses all meaning for me, and next thing I (think I) know he's trying to drown me in a bath full of minty slush.

Get in line, young panther, get in line.

# 6

# PRIDE AND PREJUDICE; OR FIRST IMPRESSIONS

I wake and smell life, not death.

There is a youthful energy about the place, like the very air contains de-aging properties. For example, according to my reflection in the glass wall that overlooks the half-bustling, half-sleeping city, my facial hair is gone. Oh, I could fist-pump.

Under the blackness of night, I see a great house of wealth and a city of carnivalesque reproductions, but no culture. I think I'm losing my mind. Maybe I'm just lucid dreaming. I go back to bed and decide to dream of Roop, my one and only constant. But sleep does not come—it seldom did before I came here—so I settle for replaying The Incident in my mind. Again. And again. And again.

My right hand runs over my naked chest—there's not even a scar. No sign of my beatings by the traders. No hint I was ever shot with that arrow. I'm not too sure what happened after that. I have flashes of minty green slush. It stung but was curative. I remember almost drowning as Alk'erion submerged me, and beyond, the wizard's voice resounding and beating him away, reaching out his mighty right hand, and pulling me up to safety.

And now I'm here, somehow.

I turn my head and see the first flickers of morning ascend on the horizon like they used to in the White Room. And I drop into dead slumber at the sight of it.

Judging by how restless I feel, I must not have slept long.

Suddenly there's a gentle knock on the door. I sit up, wipe some sleep from the corner of my eye, and climb out of the sandwich of comfy blankets. My baby blue nightshirt—I'm not even going to ask where this came from—drops to the woolly navy floor. I'm not sure what or who to expect, so I prepare myself for three combat scenarios. "Enter."

The smell of strawberries and lemons blows into the room before her cold suspicious crystal blue eyes do. For a princess, she is dressed a lot like Cinderella—pre-magical intervention. Beneath her exquisitely patterned headscarf, a stray golden streak of hair curls around the back of her right ear; other than that, she might as well be hairless. Add to that, she might as well have no breasts beneath that dirty brown Amish gown for all the femininity it suggests. She doesn't walk with the elegance and grace I expect of a royal. In fact, she squints so agonisingly with each step that I assume the slippers she wears are too small. I'm tempted to tell her this might result in in-grown toenails (something I know more about than I would like) but something stops me—fear of her wrath, probably.

She places virtually all blue clothes (which can hardly be coincidental) on the locker beside my bed. I thank her. She nods. I feel I should say something more, but I have no idea where to begin: *What was it like to kill a man? Things were a bit hit-and-miss there for a while with that Abomination, huh? So, your brother is… interesting.*

"Would you prefer to breakfast here or in the dining-hall?" she asks with a tight-lipped robotic smile that freaks me out. (She doesn't speak

English, I think. A memory springs to mind of the Wizard putting me to bed and telling me that my brain would automatically translate most polite, contemporary languages, and, before I could tell him I was uncomfortable with it, he cast a spell that enabled me to comprehend the world's leading languages, too).

"Here, please." I hate social interaction.

"Very well, Master Thomas." I half expect the psycho to draw forth a dagger from her parachute brown skirt.

"It's Benjamin. Joshua. Benjamin-Joshua. Benjamin will do, though. Thomas is... Just Benjamin. No 'Master'." I'm not sure why I trust her with my real name, because I certainly don't trust her. It just feels like time, I suppose, to break free of the illusion that this is all make-believe. Messed-up, definitely, but imaginary... I think it would be stubborn and naïve of me to say that.

"Very good, Master Benjamin."

"Princess?" I don't know whether to snort or curtsy.

"Yourself, Master Benjamin?"

"I-I-I j-just wanted to thank you for, you know, not telling anyone what you saw in your... pr-premonition at t-the cave."

"Who is to say I kept that little nugget to myself?" She arches a wicked smile designed to intimidate.

I just shrug, "I'm still alive."

"For now."

Her shiny eyes darken with ire and her neatly trimmed eyebrows crease like snakes. She looks like an ugly, angry man. "But when you show your true colours, I will be there, rejoicing that a dirty, scheming, peculiar malformation like you has been exposed and neutralised."

"You know nothing," I spit. "The context. My reasons. If that is even accurate or interpretive."

"Master Benjamin," she struts over awkwardly in her too-small shoes, voice thick and cunning, "I value the insight, rank, and experience of Mósandrirl more than any other in all the land, but he is wrong about you. I *despise* you. For what you have done to our people. For what you have yet to do. So, enjoy the upkeep of this broken-shy-teenager charade for as long as Justice allows, but rest assured: your villainy will be held in Loux Laxciila at the appointed time."

*What the frack is this broad's problem?*

"My absolute and utter dearest one, sincerest apologies to criticise, but you don't know me well enough to hate me." I've always admired my ability to speak without a stutter whenever I reach boiling-kettle mode on the anger spectrum.

"I know you are a killer and a threat to this shining civilisation I have built, and that situates you on a par with the Triune."

This riles me up more than I should allow it to, and though I don't want to resort to vengeance, I turn the tables on her. "Takes one to know one. Or does Edgar not count?"

"Begging your pardon, who?" Her tone is one of superiority like she genuinely has no recollection of her aggressive role in recent affairs. She cranes her neck and points her nose to the ceiling like I'm no more than dirt. Well, I never could stomach the pride of lesser sinners.

"The man you slew and nailed to a tree. His name was Edgar. He had a wife and three children, all of them illegitimate, so I won't be sending them any condolences cards. He had a thing for watches. He stole mine. Too bad he didn't *watch* out for you."

I smirk callously as her arrogant horsehead comes crashing down; her eyes lose their money and her lips their self-confidence. And it is as though a completely different person stands before me; the immensity of the change is surreal. What remains is no more than a battered teenage girl.

And I feel ashamed. I want to apologise, but I'm so unused to admitting I'm wrong that I don't know what to say. How about: *Look, I know you only did it to protect me?* Or *Listen, that was bad form. I swear, I'm normally not like this?*

Only I am. Every day. I just don't say it.

"Perhaps I should have allowed the merchant to carve you up and trophy your head on a pike!"

Well, that escalated quickly. I thought she was here to get me breakfast. Our hearts pound towards each other, and suddenly both of our fists are clenched. I feel my chest rise and fall as adrenaline pumps in overload. Her neck vibrates and sizzles with animosity. Before something happens that I'll regret, through gritted teeth, I demand she leaves.

She whips away.

"You cannot die soon enough for my liking!" the man-faced maiden says.

"Keep my secret and when the Apocalypse starts, I might just spare you!"

"I am afraid you will not live that long."

I take this opportunity to throw the first words she ever spoke to me back in her face: "Do not fear, just trust!"

She slams the door shut behind her.

In view of this unfortunate encounter, my deduction skills conclude that I am going without breakfast today.


It's like trying to fix a Rubrics cube, but I eventually turn the shower on, though I have no idea how to adjust the settings. Stone cold. Shampoo in my eyes. Hideous. Turning it off is near-impossible, as well, so I just close over the bathroom door and hope the problem goes away.

I bury my fingers in the comfy fabric of the clothes your one left me. There's a recurring design on them imprinted in silver glittery shards: a rhombus with an inner eye; left and right of it stretch elongated figure threes with a dot inside each curve. I assume that it is a family crest or national emblem. I gently trace my fingers along the design on the chest of the hooded baggy shirt, but it's so sharp it nips my distal phalanx. In my mind's ear, I hear Blondie cackle. She's also left me navy long johns to wear as trousers—just as well, given the oven heat. I check them for explosives, but technology isn't that advanced here yet. Next, I throw on a scarlet scarf that strangely leaves me feeling cooler. Finally, I pull on a pair of thin thigh-high boots that make me two inches taller. I size myself up in the mirror and feel like an absolute fool.

But contrary to her wretched attitude, the princess has left me a treasure more magnificent than any of these: a thin small silver headband that somehow weighs at least one talent of gold. Incisions of swirls and lozenges speak meanings I cannot articulate and in the centre is a circle like torchlight or an eye. Four wings in flight, two on each side, it looks as though it might lift off and sail on the wings of the wind at any moment. The feathers are pearls, rubies and jasper, onyx stones and inlaid stones, red stones and those of antimony, and alabaster and (my personal favourite) lapis lazuli. Sapphire stones that change colour depending on how the sunrays hit accent the crown on its left and right.

It probably belongs to the princess and she's already reported it stolen. Ah well, I don't care enough about her to give thought to her intentions. Yet I cannot tear my eyes from the crown. Just holding it makes me feel powerful... and chosen. I sit on a small plush chair before the locker mirror by the bed and place the precious artefact on my head. It isn't a perfect fit, and I feel embarrassed, stupid and vain. But I imagine myself as a king on a throne, and I force a small smile.

Then I hear the door creak open menacingly, and heavy feet scamper into the room. Whoever it is must move with lightning-quick movements for Mirror Me sees nothing. I don't have to turn around before the corner of my eye catches enough snowy hair to camouflage a full-grown wolf. My eyes widen with horror. My shoulders leap and my heart hurtles so forcefully it threatens to smash the mirror.

In a second, he is behind me and his anime spiked fringe pierces my scalp and causes my neck hairs to stand and shiver. He slams the side of my head into the dresser and I go momentarily deaf in one ear. He sniffs me, his nose red and blistered, like he's suffering from frostbite or an allergic reaction to the sun. He reeks of a desert smell and burning, and he sets my empty stomach turning and twisting.

"G' morneen, prett-ee face," his fox eyes mock.

"It was!"

He rasps, "It is Benjy, yes?"

He fumbles and rolls his tongue a lot between syllables. And I'm pretty sure he just yipped at me. I'm reminded of a dog the One-Armed Man treated himself to years ago and named Benjy, which I tried not to take personally. I basically relocated to Roop's at the time; not because I fear dogs, but because I dislike animals marginally below humans. I must have annoyed Samson Junior though, because within a week the mutt was buried and Roop had packed my Return Home bag.

"Close enough."

His smile is terrifying and savage, his mouth a cave. "Now where did you get... these clothes, Benjy? Did you-u-u still th-them... thief? *Grrrrr.*"

I assume he meant "steal", but he doesn't look like the sort who appreciates correction. I stutter like a buffering music video, but "The Princess" is the only audible phrase that comes out.

"She sh-sh-shhhould not have"—he struggles to pronounce the next word— "*done* that, Benjy."

His teeth tear the scarf off my neck. His warm doggish breath chills my Adam's apple. I shudder as his frequent spits acid-attack my flesh. He tells me the helmet (I think he means "crown") is the only thing keeping him from ripping my heart out. In the space of sixty seconds, he has just reminded me why I don't have guy friends.

"It be...lon...ged to the fffounder *growl* of Loux Laxciila." Bless his heart, but I could not care less. "You will be punis-s-s-shed faw your cwimes again' my people, Mex Confetricus." I have no idea what that made-up word means, but I bet it's dangerous. Though it's hard to consider him a serious threat when he speaks so babyishly. I mean, come on, Alk'erion: *"Cwimes!"* Seriously? On second thought:

He wrenches my chin between overworked hardened hands, chickenpoxed with cuts and blisters. What I initially mistake for finger hair are splinters—so what, is this guy the feline from the fable "The Lion and the Thorn"? He sinks his bladed talons into my cheeks and I feel slugs of blood bubble and spurt. Then he slams my head into a wardrobe. Bone versus wood. Wood wins!

And with a doggy tongue he licks clean my blood.

"Now I can find you anywhere."

Is he an elf or a vampire?!

Reflected on the wardrobe door, I see the crown emit a glow. A wisp of smoke stirs. And a spark spits at Alk'erion's bench-strong fingers. He leaps back and covers his hands in his sleeves, unsuccessfully hiding the fact that that hurts. A lot. Enough to send him packing anyway.

His beastly eyes fix on me as he scampers to the door.

"I kno-o-o-ow what you-u-u a-a-are. I smell it off you. And I will always find you. ... *Murderer...*" And from outside the door he calls back, "Stay away from my sister!"

At the click of the shut door, I pause, paralysed, for a long moment, then draw so strong a breath of relief that I almost pass out. Years' worth of unshed tears boil volcanically. My heart pounds and jams so forcefully I think I'm having a heart attack. To stop from crying, I bite down on my earthquaking bottom lip so tightly the skin shreds. I claw the locker to hold onto my sanity.

ABC 6-5-1-18 9-20-19-5-12-6.

God wonderfully and fearfully fashioned me, adopted me as His own, then stashed me away in the darkness of His jewellery-box of saved collectables, and forgot me. But somehow, I died—and now I am in Hell.

"I'm sorry. God, I'm so sorry. Please forgive me. I'm so sorry. Don't leave me here. Please! I'M SORRY!"

The wizard calls in on me after a while and catches me in a particularly prom-queenish moment, admiring my crown—the only thing that kept me alive from that perverse twat. He presses me for details regarding my new injuries, but I hold my tongue.

In fact, the only thing I ask is if someone who tastes your blood truly can track your scent anywhere.

"No one in this kingdom has that power," he says.

I take so great a sigh of relief that I almost pass out.

After an intense interview, the wizard throws me an instant-healing ointment and gives me an "I'm here for you"-style pep talk, then tells me I'll find my journal in the top drawer of the locker. Before I can ask, he assures me no one has read it.

"I also found a marked leaf on your person that I included inside the cover page," he adds.

I have no idea what he is on about, until I turn to that page. It is Lanky Legs' message. I never properly examined it before now, but I'll come back to it. I don't want to read his last words with someone else standing a metre away. So near the end, writing this was the most intimate moment of his life—other than Edgar cutting him down, of course.

The wizard offers to give me an orientation of Loux Laxciila, but I politely decline. I would rather explore on my lonesome for a bit, get lost once or twice, and kill time. He understands perfectly and departs—after I get him to show me how to operate the shower, that is. I give him time to descend the twelve staircases that lead to my apartment before I head out.

Underneath tent material held up by wooden posts, peasants sell anything from live snails that squirt neon slime and wooden toy ducks that quack, to spell books that haw like donkeys. All these are stamped with a seal identical to the emblem on my shirt. Aromas of fresh bread, cooked fish, and overly perfumed flowers, lotions and potions intoxicate every aisle in the marketplace.

And as for the people! The honest boast their wealth and parade their good fortunes while the cheeky swamp their heads in scarves and try to appear poor and swindle sympathy and merchandises, but their rags fail to hide their bulging pearl earrings and well-fed bellies. It's not exactly how I pictured elves behaving.

Laxciila has a provincial but random feel to it, as though the culture is but a background to a drama that features players from a multitude of narratives. One elf looks like Hercules (lion cloak and everything) while another looks like an Austen heroine. Another is dressed as a wardrobe; next to him a feather-duster; and prancing before them is a half-naked circus artist dressed as a beaded necklace. She is dressed modestly compared to some who walk around stark naked, bodies so heavily tattooed they look like animate superhero costumes. *Keep your eyes up, Benjamin.* That said, I feel more comfortable in the nudes' general vicinity than around the freaks dressed as the pets they take for a walk down the gold cobbled lane: sabretooths, bears, pterodactyls, and Cerberuses.

The jester look is also popular this year: as far as the eye can see dance white jesters, pink jesters, dice jesters, and hellfire jesters. One family of a dozen blond ducklings masquerade as sea life, while behind merry-make masked goons, finger-puppeteers and acrobats fresh out of the tavern and twice as mouldy. Confetti rains from the sky, flags sail through the streets on the wind, and banners clunk and clatter down every alley in harmony with the tapping feet of their holders. Music booms and beats and bashes from every corner and crevice of Carnivalesque Civilisation. All around me is noise, noise, noise.

There is nothing remotely bucolic or pastoral in the crass hustle-and-bustle materialism that surrounds me, or in the way the elves shove me as they forge after the smell of pastries or bagels like lions who haven't eaten in weeks. "Excuse *you*," I snipe at one of them, only to pretend I said nothing when he (possibly she) turns around.

The constructionism is just as motley: the buildings, statues, pillars, and pylons look splendid and selfish, and above all uncultured, just created for the sake of spending money. And this is not just my recession-mentality speaking: it's about justice. There's a world out there imprisoned, hungry, and overrun with beasts; meanwhile, instead of organising themselves into a powerful resistance force, these elves live the high life and employ all their time and talents into stupidity.

In fact, the only signifier of any political awareness is the propagandist graffiti of a snake-eyed sneer on just about every wall. His is a countenance that boasts self-importance and omniscience, and decrees judgement on viewers so naïve they are not marvelled by his proud pronounced exterior. Passers-by nod to him, women kiss their fingertips and wave, and parents tell vivid hand-gesture-filled narratives to their younglings.

Claustrophobia threatens to sandwich and squash me between a tattoo parlour and a bakery, so I run as fast as I can until I am good and lost, alone, and at peace.

After skulking along for a little while past hooded monks playing sortilege and bakers oozing of vanilla essence, I join a crowd of flamboyant spectators, each elf as dimorphic as bustards to the one next to him. I'm just about small enough to slip past the hooting mouths, ecstatic eyes, and bizarre costumes, and under the long legs. I slip my way to the front row of a party watching a spectacular parade of colour, riches, and idiocy.

It's impossible not to notice the obnoxious princess under the shadow of a boxed roof on a wooden stage, nose curled up at the repulsive Motley Cow ground-level maggots. She's a fine one to judge anyone else; she has changed clothes again, too. She's been so tightly knitted into a gown like fresh grass that, I suspect, it will tear and cause her grave embarrassment should she sit on her plush, plumb throne. Arms folded, I shoot her the deathly Benjamin stare.

My eyes descend to the peasants. The elves parade in multi-coloured onesies with jester hats, and leashed before them are white-moustached tigers that seem to have stepped in clawed metal traps without noticing. Paint makes their eyes look larger and beadier at the same time, and I'm guessing their noses aren't that pointy, but are instead rubber add-ons (the elves, that is, not the tigers). Some juggle a dozen sticks of fire; others perform choreographed sword routines; one of the wealthiest non-Royal marchers is dressed in at least five layers of thick clothing and has resorted to pegging money at the audience just to get rid of it. Scrap that. He's changed his mind and is demanding it back. Behind, around, and before him, there's more squander, more self-centredness, more carnivalesque everything.

All goes silent though when a woman with skin white as snow, hair black as night, and a head the size of a pip appears disguised as a giant apple, and the crowds bow in adoration. A he-elf next to me even foams at the mouth. When salivary bubbles drip onto my cloak, I step away and look up to the platform. Blondie's irritated disposition is golden, and she is determined to look anywhere but at the double-bent clowns and the apple. Arrogant, much?

The pip-faced wench in the apple garb turns her head to me as she slowly passes. I realise I'm the only person in the whole square standing, other than Maiden No-Name. Eyes fixed on Pip, I give a slight bow, and wear a hostile countenance; not because I have reason to dislike the bold Frau, but to hide the fact that inside I'm dying of embarrassment. Though usually adept at discernment, I struggle at reading whether she is sad or just bored out of her wits having walked at a snail's pace in an apple suit for ages. Her face has a bit of a Mona Lisa thing going on, you see.

After about five minutes of this drag drab stroll, restlessness begins to stir amongst the audience. They get fidgety and disconcerted. There's a universal sigh of relief when she finally bites the bullet and vanishes from view, and the music and rollick resume almost instantly. After them herd trains of gold, ornaments and treasure, stilts performers and exotic birds, dancers and animals, banners and elephants, fizgig flamingo women, giant floats of islands that look like tigers, a heavily maned lion with a palace on his back, and a multi-headed elephant carrying a kingdom with legions of parrots on its tusks.

Leading the entourage is a freakish tall man in a top hat whose long legs arch, bend and stretch like a frog's. Only one ear sits to the side of his snow-white head—and a large and round ear at that, so he's clearly not an elf. In the place of brows, rainbows ring his circle eyes; one iris is a coin, the other a finger. A bulging wart blisters his nose, and this an odd ice-cream cone sculpture that someone stood on. He has no cheeks, just a flat stretched sheet that unites his temple to his jaw and inclines and ascends as he sings of how Loux Laxciila is the greatest kingdom among all nations in the world; welcoming to all; home! What a load of bunkum.

Loux Laxciila!
City of light!
Citadel of culture!
Perpetually bright!

Loux Laxciila!
Under pearl moon and silver sky!
Your golden streets mirror the sun!
And your populace bequeaths joy and integrity!

Loux Laxciila!
Because of whom our freedom is nigh!
Merrily flower follows flower
After the feet of your Most Royal Highness!

His spell has the crowd riveted. Hundreds rave. Some of them vibrate so enthusiastically, it's worrying. The most extreme foam at the mouth; they are so overly saturated with compliments they physically can't hold it in.

But back to the performer: an excellent entertainer and the idol of thousands, still he has known pain. His finned hands are nothing more than heavily bandaged stumps from which emerge three elongated fingers shaped like dolphin heads.

Now he dances like a jazzman; his demon tail serves as a third arm that lifts, throws, catches, and lowers his top hat from which rabbits and pygmy dragons spring. He pulls a diamond-studded cane out from somewhere and blasts wealth, servants, and circuses. Nowhere yet have I seen such vivid, unrestrained demonstrations of magic, such that it makes his skin glow blue, brown, and green. His manic, screechy laugh earns him the name "the Grin".

I search for the princess's face again, but she is invisible behind a pin-thin, six feet tall, robed figure with dark hair. When she finally comes into view, she appears to be seeking me out too for our eyes meet instantly. Hers widen with annoyance. The tall figure whips behind a veil and is gone.

I decide to make myself scarce too, but when I turn around, I see that a young weeping child has dropped his national flag but is too afraid of the multitudes of phony costumed feet to go retrieve it. He looks just like I did at that age, the resemblance is uncanny: huge brown eyes; a mushroom haircut yellow as sunshine; a tan tint to his skin. I pick the flag up for him and smile, "There you go, buddy." Eyes delighted, he reaches out for it, only for his mother or child-minder to slap my hand, and usher him away and snap traduce. She eyes me evilly and wearily, and he with sadness and then fear.

Embarrassed and fed up, I emigrate to a quiet bench in a peaceful park amenity where I sit and relax my mind—that is until two candlestick elves with curvirostral faces appear and debate with unsubtle whispers whether it is safe to sit beside me. Their deliberations are ridiculous, since they so clearly had already decided they would before oh-so-conveniently stumbling across me, but Duchesses starved for drama must get their kicks somewhere.

Their thin angular bodies lower on the bench either side of me, but their spider legs invade my personal space. Their words and what's left of their spindly scrawny body matter pushes me further into loneliness, but I appreciate that they are currently the only ones in all the kingdom interested in sharing breathing space with me, even if that space is filled with their own scandalous stories and dramatic extended pauses.

I put off giving them a proper once-over since I hate looking strangers in the eye, but after a while, I conclude there's no harm in it: one has a starfish haircut of black, white, and silver, with a noticeable bald patch above his forehead; the other a horse face and a Santa's elf hat, only it's about as large as a baby whale. Starfish smells expensive, whereas Whale smells like one of those mad yokes who washes his face in sheep placenta. Incessantly, he flips and catches a gold coin with the propagandist image of Snake Eyes on one face and the Laxciila crest on the other.

They agree that the princess is behaving more strangely than usual. Less quirky and bookish, but more conceited. Hardly ever acknowledges anyone now. She's one step away from regressing into the female Alk'erion, adds Whale. Starfish throws him a perplexed look that says, "Too far, too far, no one is that bad", and then Whale realises the ridiculousness of what he has just said, and they howl with laughter. Next, Starfish hoots like an owl that Loux Laxciila is expecting an influx of foreigners. Just when I think this is a conversation I could join, they go and make it magic-based. Whale, in his gentle unbroken mousey voice, explains that the Chosen One's arrival in Angoria has already begun to upset the Triune's magic and maze. I'm getting a Narnia vibe from them, that my very presence is enough to melt centuries-old icecaps. But before I can learn more about this, Whale tries to begin a discussion on how it is the Elder Wizard's fault that Silas became evil (he was too hard on him, apparently). Meanwhile, Starfish talks over him about how much he wants the refugees quarantined in case the Triune have pumped their veins with toxin poisonous to elves.

After a painful hour of coin flipping and racist miscegenation-centred discourse, they wonder aloud if the Dark One will attend supper tonight at ten o'clock sharp at a very specific courtyard for which they give equally specific directions.

I reach out and grab the coin mid-descent, play the Vanishing Coin trick, and satisfy their semi-invitation:

"I'll be there. And I'll bring my most powerful wand. Perhaps this time I'll make an elf disappear."

Offended, I get up and leave without another word, and throw the coin back at Whale from over my shoulder.

I couldn't describe the route I took thereafter if I had a map, but for about four hours, I see no one, I hear little, and I feel more tranquil than I have felt since the Forest of Melancholia. Then I see something that stops me in my tracks and arouses an anxious but inquisitive excitement.

A wide stone staircase of pallid yellow looms over me like an elevator to Heaven. To the right, stands a lifelike sculpture of a crow and to the left a peacock. Its shoulders are decorated with designs like those I saw on the fountain in Melancholia. The rhombus and its threes recur frequently. As to what these represent, I have several ideas: the first language of Angoria; its history; age-old laws; incantations; the nation's motto; a microscopic illustration of Loux Laxciila's topography. And whether out of boyish curiosity, or the wizard's words about making the most of all this if it really is just a dream, I climb.

I ascend the first of three separate flights of staircases. Someone who hasn't gotten their first *Dan* belt might have given up halfway through the first, but not me. This flight leads to a wide flat surface. If the aura of demise wasn't enough proof that this had been the site of executions, then the bloodstains are a dead giveaway. I tiptoe across the least brown dry splodges. The second flight leads to nothing out of the ordinary. But on the third platform, there is a throne and a view of the entire kingdom, built on an island with four slopes and quartered. Kilometre after kilometre stretch and dot palace after palace, crystal castles, statues of chimeras and hydra, temples, art galleries, museums, great lakes, pyramids, festivals, globe structures, twelve spires, gargoyles, cultish monuments of Leader Snake Eyes, mountains, courtyards, apartments, forests, and magnificent gardens of bloom. Like a living clock face, each quarter seems to be experiencing a different season of the calendar year. Terrified that the slightest breeze on my neck will tickle me over to diminishment, I walk to the brink and peer over. As I wonder why these things never have railings, an unexpected intrusion very nearly keels me over.

"Destroyer, I would bid thou welcome had thou indeed been invited." My shoulders leap with fright at his inhospitable rattle. "Careful now, Mex Confetricus. You are very near the edge." His words are very precise and regal. I turn and... my lower jaw drops.

Her blonde hair is partly braided; the rest falls straight and curls naturally at the bottom. Her skin looks like it's been doused in softener every day since her birth. And her pink tulip dress shows off her curves remarkably. Long sleeves, white and silky on the inside, flow down to meet the stone ground. A beautiful headpiece with a small purple crystal sprinkles down her forehead and works its way over her head in a complex attractive design. But it is her eyes that captivate and disgust me, made exaggeratedly large and hollow by a looming blackness like thick mascara or shadow. Princess No-Name. But that was definitely a man's voice...

"You changed again," I say dumbly, then ask, "Did you know the fox was going to attack me?" I think my insinuation makes it very clear who I am talking about. She only smirks evilly. I repeat my question.

"Who do you think gave him word of your thievery? My only qualm is that he spent too much time doing... whatever he was doing to you... and did not tear out your spleen there and then."

"He is very protective of you." I'm not one hundred percent sure what I'm implying by this, but she can discern that in her free time.

"Alk'erion is a blasted idiot with no friends and no life. He would do better to stay out of the sun and the pathway of everyone else."

"If my existence offends you so much, why hand me a weapon?" I meant to ask, *"Why not kill me right now? There are no witnesses"*, but I don't want to coax her into a sin, the effects of which she may not be able to reverse.

"The Diadem of Loux Laxciila is not just a weapon," she begins, before mouthing off some cryptic crap about how it's the heart and soul of the island, and then delving into mystic-historical rhetoric. It takes her longer than it should to realise I have stopped listening. "The Diadem is neither modest nor common enough to be worn by one like you. Do take it off."

Helmet, diadem, crown—whatever it is—so long as it breathes dragon fire on my enemies like it did to Alk'erion, I am not surrendering this to anyone.

"No."

"I am not asking," she snarls darkly, and her eyes, though still lifeless, seep venom. "You are not a man, but a ball." Ugh, I hate the word 'man'. "A fistful of dark primitive energy made manifest in the wriggling, writhing bodice of a worm with shadowy, fiery destruction on his mind."

I want to make an excuse for her like I did many years for Paige. But I can't. Beauty does not justify shallow rationalisms. And so, we glare at one another in a battle of wills, never backing down, never forfeiting our convictions.

The drawn-out silence ends only when a severely out-of-breath Elven soldier runs up the staircase. He bows to her and collapses prostrate—more out of exhaustion than respect. He lies there like a drowned fish for a while, catches his breath, then pompously bellows:

"O Lady of Light! O Mistress of the Moon!" Veins popping, she grows increasingly irritated with every syllable. "Sister of the Stars! Bedazzlement of Bright Daytime! Nurse and Cure to the Nocturnal Curtain! O Pious Princess A—" He snaps his mouth shut before he acknowledges her by name in front of me. Just as well. I felt a wave of demonic tiredness coming on, and one more alliteration may have sent me over the edge.

The shadow on her face lifts slightly, then faster. Gradually, the blueness returns. She blinks a lot and pretends she is disoriented, but I stare her out of it. What is she playing at?

"Joxer, good sir. Huge fan," he addresses. A guy could get used to that kind of greeting, though it was probably to Blondie's disgust… I like this kid. Joxer tells me in fragmented English that the Elder Wizard has been called away on very important business; that one of his friends is being hunted by an old enemy. Joxer leans in closer and accounts an iffy but vivid description of an erect white-skinned cretin with blond hair and an affinity for wearing red; "the oldest orc in Angoria," he says.

"Thanks for telling me. Um, how did you know where to find me?"

He is stumped. I give him a minute. "Good lord, I believe you… have… what your people call a… lisp." That is code for, "*Oh, I wasn't expecting to be asked that*". Basically, I am being watched.

"It is not a lisp, only a strong S." I smile him away politely. Wordlessly and mechanically, the princess follows him down the steps. I leave enough distance between us before I begin the journey back to my room… on which I get lost twice.

So here is what I know:

One, the wizard has abandoned me in a kingdom where I am considered the villain; two, the company he keeps are hazardous to my health: the dwarf hated me too much to acknowledge me; the she-elf hates everyone; and the gatekeeper prince shot me; and three, the wizard told me I would be safe here. He lied. Everything he told me about the nine or ten or however many wizards there are could also be a lie.

Come to think of it, he only named for me two members of the Triune. He may well be the third. Conclusion: with nowhere to run and no one to turn to, it is dog eat dog; kill or be killed. And though after The Incident I swore never to harm another living soul, I must accept the very real possibility that I may soon be forced to live up to my reputation and destroy them all.

# 7

# THE TRIUMVIRATE

I scour my room for bugs or spy cams, and though I come up empty, the feeling that I'm being watched is so potent that I leave again after half an hour. As soon as I throw open the door, I am pummelled by the collage of instruments and celebratory sounds of dancing feet from every street and rooftop for kilometres. And things must move at an accelerated pace here, because everywhere, masks. Funny and colourful. Mocking and small. Elegant and cunning. Mysterious and evil. Sophisticated and purple and spy-like. Black and wicked and full of malicious intent. Undoubtedly horrific in the dark.

"He may have corrupted the air!" sellers yell from stalls, hula-hoops around them held up by jockstraps and shredded dungarees. "Do not breathe the same air as him! Keep your faces covered!"

So either Wizard Mo-thingamajiggy-thingamabob failed his assignment and his enemy has swept into the safest place on earth, or they're talking about me. Good. Let them keep their distance. They should be afraid of the Big Bad Wolf. And if I am the hero, then pity for them, I don't think they're good people whose lives should be prioritised.

Though twenty minutes early for supper, my bench buddies are nowhere in sight, and all the food is gone. I go to bed starving, but sleep does not come. I have no idea how many hours pass before I give up trying to sleep and am up at the glass wall again.

A huge bonfire blazes in Parade Central, ringed by hooligan elves. I swear, some of these twits must never sleep. But then again, if you're immortal, you might as well stay awake and enjoy it. Above glows a red C-shaped moon, a few hashtag stars, and blood-tinged clouds huddled like armour-bearers against a deep black sky.

And my mind travels beyond the briskly discarded masks, riotous orgies in the apartment complex to my left, and the horseshoe streets to the prisoners in the Maze: trapped under artificial skies like great cornea, forever-seeing, forever inducing fear and mocking. A constant reminder that any of them could be snuffed out as easily as one of these stars. I don't know much about what it means to be the Chosen One, but I do know that the Triune's tyranny can no longer be allowed to continue; that someone has to stop them and set the captives free. And, half-crazed by hunger, half by enervation, I'm just about cracked enough to believe I can do it.

Suddenly, I hear a mighty clang of gates, then a great white light beams. What follows is a thunderous surge of hooves across the stone- and gold-cobbled square. A huge frantic horse rushes onto the square outside my window. Atop it, sits a barely conscious faun, easily distinguished by his bristly goat legs, frothing at the mouth. It feels like I'm down there in seconds.

"Are you alright?" I shout, before realising how redundant the question was. Not that he snaps back any rude quip or retort. All he does is gurgle swampy blood while clutching onto the manic horse's neck with one arm and holding in his spaghetti intestines with the other one. Normally I would pray right about now and vanish before anything happens, but tonight, I am the first response. The biggest challenge is how to calm down the horse so I can treat the patient without getting a hoof to the shin or my ear bitten off.

"Sir, what's your name? How can I help?" And how did a faun of all people make it through the gates of Loux Laxciila? He only mutters broken words and fades in and out of consciousness. It doesn't take me long to diagnose him with syncope.

"*Ost'eolago!*" Instantly, the horse is at perfect peace and lowers so that the faun can be treated. Near lifeless now, he collapses into my arms. I turn and see the princess behind me. I half-expect her to accuse me of butchering the goat-man, even though she probably did it herself, or coerced loose cannon Alk'erion into doing it to frame me.

"What happened?" I shout like a surgeon bursting into a trauma centre before she can cast any aspersions.

"A wraith," she replies. "A spirit that has not moved on to the next life, and in overstaying his welcome, has turned nasty."

"Hear that, sir? You must be pretty brave to have survived that encounter."

"Hardly," the princess spits. "No one survives an encounter with a wraith, lest they are a level five magical being, and even then, the odds are slim. He was sent to us as a message, a portent of worse things to come. Give me your shirt," the mood-killer demands. I'm stooped. "He has lost too much blood. He needs a tourniquet." Every word is spoken with such insistence that I cannot but comply. No sooner have I pulled it off than she snatches it and ties it around his gashed chest wounds. I normally hate to be seen shirtless, but his life is on the line—this is absolutely an appropriate time to compromise on my insecurities. It strikes me that this is twice now that she's seen me half-naked.

As I curl beneath the fey faun's free arm and wrap mine around his hairy back, my fingers brush off the soft liquefaction of the elf's blonde hair. She whispers either Old Elvish or Old Faunish encouragements to him, and I see her forehead and brow gleam with concern and sweat. And we're off, perfectly in step with one another.

"How did he make it through the Maze?" I ask.

She replies mechanically, "The Resistance have made a way." *Ah, yes—the portals!* "And this faun will not be the last to benefit from the philanthropic efforts of the Great One."

"I'm not sure everyone in this kingdom would approve of you calling me 'the Great One'."

"I was referring to my Papa, the Elder Elf."

We halt at the foot of a small wide staircase where three armed knights and six medics sprout from all directions and relieve us of our duties. This must be the Healing Home where I was immersed in the minty slush until my wounds healed; the old man mentioned it before I turned down his offer of a guided tour. It is not long before my toes have been unapologetically stood on one time too many, and I realise my assistance is no longer required. I stand back until the faun has been lifted onto a leather stretcher and brought into the ward, then I vanish back to my room, though, of course, my head is much too busy to let me rest.

Bright and early the next morning, there's a knock on my door. I officially have misgivings of anyone who wants to speak to me here, so I survey the room for potential weapons and prepare battle scenarios in my head. When I'm confident I'll win no matter the attack, I call out, "Who is it?"

It is the Elder Wizard.

"In you come, good sir," I smile, though he should not mistake my pleasantries for trust. He slowly opens the door and hands me fresh blue clothes. From his gaping sleeve, he slips me a box of chocolates which he says he'd swiped from the kitchen when no one was looking.

Caramel, strawberry, honey, mint, cream, truffle, praline, and ice-cream flavours. Delicious.

"You know, Thomas, I heard about the dark hours' occurrence. How do you feel?"

"Life as the Chosen One," I shrug, as though I tend to hacked-at fauns daily, and it's no big deal. "And how is your friend?"

"Alive."

"Good. Is he here?"

"Oh, no. He and the Elder Elf do not see eye to eye. The last time they crossed paths, Lord Mehkabikil threw him into an eternally collapsing star."

"How did he get himself out of that mess?"

"The old-fashioned way: irrespective of how often you fail, try, try again. Get dressed and walk with me for a spell," he says and steps outside.

I look back at the chocolates but, unaccustomed to eating the labours of an occultist's thievery, peg them in the bin.

About ten minutes later, we exit the apartment and walk streets I have not yet ventured on our way to the dining-hall for breakfast. The wizard recommends that I keep an eye out for landmarks—which I've already accepted I'm not going to remember—so I'll know my way around. Little does he realise that travel is up there with my fellow T-word pet peeves—transport and technology—and that geography has never taken up residence in either my long- or short-term memory. Plus, it is a little hard to concentrate on structures when hundreds of Laxciilians queue to get their portrait drawn atop the faun's horse on the blood-soaked flagstones.

When we arrive at breakfast, the hall is already mostly full despite it being half-six in the morning. The room is a long corridor that easily seats two thousand diners at several long mahogany tables. The meal consists of breads and pastries, vegetarian soups, fruit and pumpkins, barrels of oats and nuts, and a cup of tea that is grand but not as good as what you get at home.

Conversation is stunted. I'm not used to being around others as I eat, and I am certainly unaccustomed to people taking an interest in my life. I find that I don't mind so much talking about hobbies, school, and the occasional aspiration, but when it comes to family, I bring the interrogation to a very definite close.

Suddenly, I become all too aware of the hundreds of eyes on me around the room, none more malevolent than the prince's, elevated above us plebeians on a stage at the Royal table. His ceaseless glare strikes me as one a hunter might wear if he so desired the head of an eagle for a trophy. I decide to subtly pat my crown just to spit in his face, but when all my fingers tap is hair, I realise I've left the diadem in my room. The wolf laughs with mockery, and I instinctively withdraw my gaze from him. In fact, if the wizard wasn't here, Alk'erion would probably have killed me already. The wizard notices this.

"Did the impetuous prince behave himself when I was away?"

I mumble, "Mostly," and then nearly choke on gloopy oat cereal.

"That is not nearly good enough. How dare one begrudge and grieve the Chosen One!" Before I can say anything to dissuade him, he storms over to the stage and throws a tirade of quiet harsh words at the prince.

Sharkey, for "Starfish" is no longer appropriate given his new hairdo, pops out of nowhere, and unsurprisingly Whale isn't far behind, both eager for an exclusive on last night's events.

"Oh, marvellous Dark... I, we, we mean, Chosen One, is it absolutely true? That a faun came barging through the gates and died in your arms?"

"He didn't die. To the best of my knowledge."

"But a mortally wounded faun *did* arrive, yes?"

"Very injured, yes."

"Typical! Did I not tell you the foreigners would come and ruin everything?"

"Technically, you told Whale." I then remember Whale isn't his actual name, and then cough awkwardly. Not that either of them appears to hear me. Sharkey continues, "Use up our much-needed resources? Disrupt our perfect peace? Smear the cobbles with a ghastly substance? Typical foreigner! He will be after our jobs next, just you wait and see!"

"What 'jobs'?" snorts Whale.

"Don't be ridiculous. A man... faun... almost died!" I interject.

"Temper, temper, O Child of Time and Darkness. I am merely acknowledging a categorical fact: no Laxciilian would have the gall to break into someone else's kingdom just so they could commit murder and make a scene. Especially when they were not even invited."

"He didn't kill any—!" I snap, before realising he's talking about me.

Smoke practically trails out my nostrils. I don't know why this gets to me so much: because I heard similar rubbish back on Earth, maybe. Because denying refugees solidarity because you consider yourself racially superior is just wrong. Because the social mores he associates Laxciilians with are blatantly misguided, from what I've seen. Because I too am a *foreigner* here who has been vilified, ostracised, and shot since passing through the gate of an apparent haven.

"*Is mise Beircheart! Tá mé cúig bliana déag d'aois. Ithe mé sceallóga prátaí agus sicín don dinnéar. Cáca milis. Milseáin. Cathair. Fuinneog. Dún an doras!*" Convinced that I'm putting a hex on them, they scurry away like the rats they are.

I don't wait for Mósandrirl (at least, I think that's how the dining-hall cleaner pronounced his name) to finish his renunciation of Alk'erion before I slip out of the dining-hall, slink back to my room, and dig out my crown from underneath the clothes I wore yesterday. I feel like a fool for wearing it, but I also feel safe, so it's worth it. A weight off my shoulders, I set out to return to the hall, but Mósandrirl meets me halfway.

"Confound you, boy! I thought those rodent twits had done something to you!" So rather than assume I went to the bathroom, his instinctive surmise was my abduction. That's rich coming from the guy who pronounced this the safest place in Angoria. Yet another discrepancy in the old man's tales. Just more proof that he cannot be trusted. "I was all but ready to track my biggest suspects down and anthropomorphise them into toads, buzzards, and gnats until they revealed your whereabouts!"

After a twenty-minute walk, we arrive at a limestone temple of white triangles, sturdy piers, dozens of flying buttresses and pinnacles, countless triforium, convoluted native designs, eerie verticality, idealised monuments of elves, arches, dragonesque and mermen gargoyles, and dark stained-glass windows. Its scale and magnificence blow me away. It is easily the size of a national museum, but the wizard tells me that there are eleven such museums circled around the kingdom like a clock, and that some of the few Laxciilians that have a labour ethic are currently building a twelfth. However, Mehkabikil, the Elder Elf, has assured them that this is a futile project that will never reach completion since I will have destroyed them all and sunk the island by then.

Mósandrirl chuckles in disbelief like it is all some great joke. Little does he realise, sinking this trove of covetous backstabbers before they bury me seems like a sound idea right about now. I don't stand much of a shot winning over the lost sheep if the shepherd thinks I'm a bad egg. I ask him to elaborate.

"Zseson Mehkabikil, Lord of Loux Laxciila, is our cockroach in the Triune's circle."

"Don't you mean 'triangle'?"

"Oh, they have a small number of confidantes. They're sociopathic, not sociophobes. It was he who arranged for the portals to be opened for the unicorn to travel through. However, lest my wayward brothers suspect he had a hand in assisting you, favouring honour over hush money, Mehkabikil has instead skilfully decided to turn the nation of Loux Laxciila against you. This will ensure the Triune's continued trust. But be warned: Mehkabikil makes for quite the convincing actor. Expect for things to get somewhat intense, but fear not: the elves are on the strictest orders not to kill you." My mind flashes to my last two physical assaults. Alk'erion could have fooled me. I'm not sure he got the memo.

"The Triune consider Mehkabikil trustworthy even though he's keeping me from them…?"

"The Triune does not yet know you are here. They will grow suspicious if Mehkabikil fails to locate you after too much time has passed, but for now, your whereabouts are secret. The ally I aided yesterday is running around masquerading as you. But we need more than delay tactics and tricks: we need an army, so the Elder Elf, with nothing less than floruit dexterity, has systematically begun to release captives of the Prison Blocks and ensure their safe passage through the Maze and lead them here." We must simultaneously conjure the blooded faun in our mind's eye, respectively, because he quickly says, "Relatively safe. Gradually, we will gather a force sufficient enough for you to lead into battle against the anarchists and reclaim this land for those in bondage."

"Okay." Because what else is there to say? That I won't be killing anyone. That I don't feel safe either side of Laxciila's gates. That that sounds like a bland potholed plan for a group of fairy tale misfits who have had three hundred years to think up a better one.

Inside the museum, it is the strong waft of old age that hits me first, then the spectacle. Rich red banners fall from the ceiling with gold threaded *ONE*s on them, indicating this is the first museum. Its artefacts and data cover the time span of Year 0 to 68. The wizard explains that the First Age began with the arrival of the Seraphs and the creation of the wizard race and ended after the First Great War of 64 to 68. After that, each age of Angoria began when one Great War ended.

A few metres inside the door stands a map of the island which highlights the whereabouts of the other museums, and the corresponding time frames they document:

The second: 69-124;

The third: 125-648;

The fourth: 648-853;

The fifth: 854-1003;

The sixth: 1003-2005;

The seventh: 2005-3147;

The eighth: 3147-3256;

The ninth: 3256-4856;

The tenth: 4857-5123;

The eleventh: 5123-6778; and:

The twelfth: 6778-∞.

"What year is it?"

"6779-plus three hundred—so-called for it has been three hundred years since the Triune created the Maze."

Scarcely have I torn my eyes away from the map on the billboard that my head begins to spin and my heart beats forcibly in my chest. It's breath-taking! Towering shelves divide the sturdy wooden floor into six or seven aisles. Weapons! Ancient swords, ornately carved staffs, bronze shields, catapults. Precious stones that light with fire on the inside. Giant caskets house fallen elves; their faces illustrated on parchment atop the coffins. The remains of a ginormous dragon or water creature hang overhead; were it to fall, it would take the floor with it. Murdered bodies recovered from bogs. Sun stones and idols almost Aztec in design recovered from some of the first kingdoms. The first poems and books. Even the first trees, uprooted from some grand excavation, look fantastic, and I couldn't care less about botany.

"So... what do you think?"

This world... it genuinely believes it exists.

"My suspicions that all this is a dream have officially waned." It's just so authentic. The wizard smiles proudly at his world and tells me that Angoria translates in the language of the Higher Orders as "Second Chance". A place that offers new life. A second birth. A do-over.

After a few moments of silence, since this masterpiece of historical accumulation deserves one, he gives me a brief lecture on the First Age. In the Year 0, the Higher Orders came from my universe, where they'd been known as angels, cherubim, seraphim, and the host. Angorians usually just collectively call them all "Seraphs", "Higher Orders", or "Those Above." By Year 1, they had invented the planetary sphere as well as a rudimentary Angoria, ten plains or continents and water. In Angoria's second year, the

Nine Wizards arrived, and they tended to the earth and its needs and spoke life to trees and other previously inanimate natural phenomena. A year later, the Seraphs plucked from my world birds of the air, beasts of the land, and monsters of the sea. In the fifteenth year, the Higher Orders created the elves, first one female and then a male. By Year 25, the Higher Orders had experimented with creating yetis, centaurs, the Minotaur race, and just about every other crossbreed fairy tale or legendary creature I've ever heard of.

He checks that I'm not overwhelmed, because he's just gotten to the part that concerns me. *Bring it!*

He leads me to a wooden square plank. I follow his lead and step on. He says, "Fourth floor, please" and we're whisked away a great height. There's no rope to hold onto, and I feel so physically sick I cannot look over the enchanted elevator. I hop off it first chance I get on a floor that is entirely dedicated to the aforementioned Gideon and the Void. I make an enquiry regarding the latter.

"A vacuous poison that masquerades as true power. The Void is Darkness itself. Evil incarnate. The very personage of corruption and wickedness. I believe you are familiar with it in your world."

Painstakingly. As we near it, a horrific hologram appears in the middle of four diamonds. Its eyes are fire. Its inconstant body—shapeless, black, horrid and evil—made of tendrils with serpent heads. Its skeleton is made of teeth. A mysterious and fearful purple, red and black aura circles before it like a shield, portal, or spirit. Above the image floats a square screen that answers any questions that have sprung to mind in the last ten seconds:

NAME: The Void.

ALIASES: Adam; Final Ode; Hades; Malice; Saturn; The Blackness; The Calamity; The Darkness; The End; The Essence of Evil; The Furnace; The Horror; The Nefarious; The Master of The Underworld; The Negative; The Origin; The Personification; The Power; and The Source of Evil Incarnate.

LAND OF ORIGIN: Earth, Solar System, Milky Way, Universe the First.

KNOWN POWERS: Energy Balls; Hypnosis; Immortality; Immunity; Mind Manipulation; Optic Fire Bolts; Parasitic Host Possession of a Willing Victim; and Fear.

KNOWN HOSTS: Gideon; Leviathan; Warlord Kahn; the Imp; and Caligula.

"In the First War, Gideon suffused his soul with the Blackness, amassed an army of tens of thousands, and led an assault on Angoria that decimated its numbers by a quarter."

I walk ahead and look around without trying to seem desperately curious, which I am. Dozens of statues depict a beautiful tall man with fierce eyes, tight features, the clothes he wore, the equipment he used, and a warrior's visage. On his belt are elongated figure threes with a dot inside each curve.

"Gideon was a Laxciilian. What a betrayal."

"You are sleeping in his room."

Why am I not surprised?

Though this happened thousands of years ago, it pours like salt on an open wound for Mósandrirl. "One must pity a cretin who could stoop so low as to murder to his own community."

"Indeed, you do."

"We still cannot pinpoint the moment when evil slinked into our world and tempted him. There are those who speculate that it was intrinsic within him, but I do not believe that evil is born."

"I do."

"Even in a perfect world?" He seems genuinely baffled.

"Perhaps not."

"Oh, had you only known him before he gave way to wickedness… So remarkably handsome. Unsurpassed in playing the harp and the flute. His voice was full of power and majesty, yet in temperament he was delicate as a rose. His eyes like blue crystals. His perfection and integrity boundless." I must say, if this is the Dark Lord he's describing, I feel inadequate as the Chosen One. "Whatever methods the Void hired to lull him from The Way must have been grievously deceptive." He's awfully sympathetic to one who has committed such evil; I'm a little envious.

Then he describes how the Void used Gideon to entice fleets of elves with hisses and black magic, and thereafter tortured and warped them, so that they became goblins. Those he killed, experimented on, and resurrected became orcs. And Higher Orders—the Fallen, he calls them— who did the nasty with human women bore giants; those who popped human virgins' cherries bore trolls.

It follows that Gideon became a personal favourite of the Void, and the perennial threat to the Free Peoples of Angoria, regularly returning deadlier than before and claiming more and more lives. But since killing him had always proven a temporary solution at best, after his most recent defeat, he was brought back by a grudge-holder and then trapped in a tomb in which he hibernates in suspended animation. Daggered. Frozen. Crusted. Drowning in molten lava. Buried deep beneath the earth in a chamber sealed with hundreds of enchantments, none of them benign.

"Whoever did that was just asking for trouble," I say glibly, at which point the wizard's eyes blaze and his mouth becomes a sword, either at the memory of Gideon's offences or current punishment.

"If 'whoever did that' is who I suspect, we are working on him very carefully so as to extract the location of the grave, but he is… difficult."

He then estimates that the Triune aim to find and release Gideon from his dungeon first, so that he emerges as the Twelfth Dark Lord; there being no candidate with more credentials.

That doesn't sit right with me. "But wasn't the panopticon prison world designed to deter the End? Bringing Gideon back just accelerates the countdown to the Apocalypse."

"Our intelligence briefings typically present contradictory evidence."

"And if the Triune lets him out, won't he just usurp them? Nihilists are not known for power-sharing."

"Maybe they tire of running the world," he says with some severity, "and are now ready to overturn it to fire, despair and shadow."

Inner's blood boils with fury. "Excuse me? Three masterminds are struck with a case of lethargy, so they decide it is perfectly fine to end all that is?! Are you for serious?"

"The world is full of rumours," Mósandrirl shrugs, "but void of authentic witnesses, and truth is on the way out."

"So why am I here? Really? Edgar said I was the Chosen One. Well, he said it in Creole English, but, you know, whatever… Have I been predestined to rid this world of the fearsome foursome: the Triune and Gid?"

"I prefer to use the word 'foretold'."

That is a little disquieting. One word specifies definitiveness, the other conjecture. It is just that little bit too neutral or non-committal for my liking.

"So, I'm not guaranteed to win? The future is not written in stone?" I can't help shake the feeling that he knows I'm about to die.

"Chosen One, Thomas, what you have to realise is time has never been as destabilised as this. We all exist in a pocket universe outside of our conventional understanding of reality. In each Block or Zone in the Maze, the poor beggars have been living the same day on a loop for three centuries with little variation—the primary one being that if you die, you're dead. And this catastrophe is not helped by the fact that the prophetic Seraphs have not spoken in three centuries. Many wonder if they are even still there, and if they are, if they can even predict the end result—this truly is the most unfixed era in the history of Angoria." And before I can beg him to say it, to speak clearly and not in science-fictive ramblings, he confesses, "Success is not an assurance."

"Do you believe that I will win?"

The look he gives me is a killer:

"I do hope so," a.k.a. he's already penning my epitaph.

"Why me?" I ask weakly like a child, my eyes pitiable as a puppy's. "Why was this task ordained for me?"

"I cannot endorse the case that it profits a man to ask such questions. Human brains operate linearly in narratives; that is no fault of yours, merely a symptom of your design. You have no concept of eternity, not really. You cannot fathom the whens, the whats, the whys, and how it all knits together as part of the Grand Design, when the loose threads, blurred colours, and snips so potently wrestle for your attention. Mortality casts a veil over your vision so that you see but the back of an elaborate wall-hanging, but—"

"The Tapestry never stops weaving," I finish, and his jaw drops and his eyebrows leap with curiosity.

"I believe it will if you fail." Mósandrirl opens his mouth to speak again, but instead, someone else's dark royal voice eerily snakes from a chamber corner dimly lit by torches. This person must speak in an old tongue because my brain does not translate its words despite Mósandrirl's automatic translation spell. Every syllable this new figure speaks hangs in the air with the force of a punch behind it.

Gradually, with the shifting of the flames, an erect figure taller than the wizard slithers into view with small, powerful steps. He wears an elaborate crown of thin metal, styled like a cluster of thorny branches, fitted with precious jewels. When he steps beneath the light of an iron black chandelier like one found in a medieval dungeon, the longevity of his head but fist-smallness of his face becomes apparent. His presence is suffocating, his snarl fearsome, and his reptilian eyes are so arch-window-thin that a knight could shoot arrows from them with no fear of himself getting shot. This is the sneer from the propaganda paintings—the one I'd called Snake Eyes.

The wizard's cloak brushes closely over my shoulder like he's a mother bird taking me under his wing for protection. I stare into the elf's eyes and see that they're not eyes at all! They're daggers! And double-agent or no, there's no feigning the repulse his pupils vomit over me. To this cretin, I genuinely am the Dark Lord. That much is certain.

It's not just Alk'erion who hates me. They all do. I'm not safe in Laxciila. The wizard has lied to me again!

I shrug free of his protective gesture. "My Lord Mehkabikil, Elder Elf, and Angoria's wisest counsellor," the wizard bows his head. The corner of my eye even spies the crook of his staff lower at the elf in a subtle threat just in case he tries anything. Well, I don't bow to the Most High at church, so I have no intention of bowing to an enemy. I maintain my straight-spine posture much to the monarch's unconcealed but well-managed offence.

The two ancients stand still and silent for a while and stare each other out of it. The concentration is so forceful, it practically has physical properties as their great minds shape the very atmosphere around us. It could just be my science-fiction leanings, but I'm convinced they're engaging in a telepathic conversation of which I am the topic. After a few minutes, the elf's head tilts at me. His pupils enlarge, fury quivers in his lips, and his closed face fumes at the wizard. What is his problem? I wouldn't put it past him to strike me, so I run a finger along my hairline and curl a lock behind my ear, but really, it's to feel for the Diadem. Yep. Still there.

After an uncomfortably long time on the side-lines of the intense cerebral debate, the wizard ushers me away and promises to continue this discussion tomorrow. He digs deep into his pocket and hands me a great leaf on which is an itemisation of books he recommends I read in the library over the coming weeks. "As the Chosen One, you have a great deal of natural ability and supernatural power, but you still need the knowledge and skills to best and most wisely hone them, Thomas."

"Benjamin. Thomas is my middle-name. My name is Benjamin." Mósandrirl nods with a small smile. Because I want to look around further, and because I want to avoid the seasick feeling of taking the escalating plank, I choose the downward staircase in the chamber that the Elf must have taken. I make a note to return here as soon as possible to do some destiny-historical digging, preferably alone.

My eyes stray from right to left, up and down at miniature models of gargantuan vicious beasts, talismans of gold, unimaginable treasures, coloured glass sculptures within which are living flames, and crawling mummy hands.

Yet I soon wish I'd kept my eyes to the floor. On the far wall is a vast canvas painting, mosaic style but in explicitly dark colours: an artistic representation of the premonition Princess Blondie had outside Troll Cave—an idealised, owl-eyed me running a blade through a crowned midget with stubby legs. I am killing the Dwarf King.

It's still wet. She must have been up all night painting it. And there's no way Mehkabikil didn't see it on his way in.

It's got nothing to do with the First Age, so the wizard must have told the princess he'd be taking me here today, prompting her to place it on this floor to psyche me out. It's working.

I physically can't breathe. My lungs burn. Every cell of my body dirties as they did after The Incident. It feels like the walls are closing in and that everyone has seen this painting and is now looking at me, judging me, and aiming a missile at my back. Sight and sense seem to evade me more and more with each passing second. I scamper drunkenly for the door. I'm seconds from passing out when I finally reach the front door and burst outside.

I immediately drop to my knees and feel the red hotness in my chest fill with air and relief. The sensation of my insides tightening and smouldering relaxes and evaporates. My vision remains blurry for a short while, and I cough up phlegm. Seriously misjudging our distance, I throw my head back against the stone wall—hard.

"Ow…"

As my vision returns to focus, the first thing I see in the street outside the museum is a trauma scene. Two dozen Elven guards face down on the ground, littered with either raisins or mouse droppings, dead.

"They are not dead, silly," a peculiar voice remarks from behind the museum corner to my left. "They are just frozen. Paralysed. It's not permanent. But it gives them a little taste of what the rest of Angoria have suffered the last three centuries." The voice cackles horribly at his warped sense of justice. "It is curious, is it not, what the Royal Guard were doing here?" Pressed against the wall pretending to smoke a long and stylised glass pipe is the Grin. A bow tie nooses his hairy green neck. His filthy shirt oozes a musty smell beneath his brown suit with sleeves and legs too short for his limbs. Tardy footwear warms his feet like gloves, but tennis balls pop out the shoes' heels and bony talons from their toes. He plays with a deck of cards. His analytic eyes are looking for one in particular. "Is it because the King is here? Or because you are?"

He has changed his tune. During the parades it seemed no elf could commit a sin in his sight. A closer examination shows me that he has only a bottom lip. An extremely thin lip. Like Luke's. I count ten yellow unevenly divided teeth above it.

"You really should not make personal remarks, Triumvir," he says with a mixture of boredom and comedy. "Do spare a thought to my poor sensitive feelings."

"Are you…?"

"Telepathic? No. But people always comment on the lip, verbally or otherwise." He smiles hungrily, but it's frightening since he only has a bottom lip. I want to grab a marker and draw an upper one. "Tell me, lad, do you feel a ghostly chill next to you as you roly-poly around Gideon's bedsheets?" He makes a swirly motion with his right arm every time he opens his mouth, as though winding a Jack-in-the-Box crank. His left arm hangs by his side deadened.

"No." I get the funny feeling Mósandrirl and I had an eavesdropper in there. Surely the Resistance wouldn't make my accommodation public knowledge… unless they hope someone burns it to the ground while I sleep.

He steps closer, and I see now that his pipe is actually a Dutch tear. Beautiful. I've never seen one in person.

"Interesting." He must not be all together in the head, because he jumps forward, swirls his hand to a melody only he hears, then laughs like a mad scientist, exclaims, "Bazinga!" and I wait for his rainbow eyes' hoops to fall off like candy canes when you shake a Christmas tree. He flings all his cards in the air, but they come back to him and shuffle themselves.

"They have no reason to fear me. I'll stop the Triune from getting to Gideon and I'll stop the Triune."

"I wouldn't be so sure," he says knowingly. Mocking pity mounts in his eyes at my naïveté, and oh, it rubs me up the wrong way. I don't take too kindly to being treated as a joke, especially by a man who is one.

He has himself in fits of laughter again for some reason and when he finally calms down and regains some level of composure, he asks me what I am going to do about the other one.

"I don't follow."

His eyes suddenly bulge, peering into my soul. I'm repulsed, but do not for a second take my eyes off his. "You *do* know that you will have to kill him, right? Now forgive my being forward," he says, and sizes me up cruelly, "but I feel unled to believe you are prepared for that."

"I am stronger than I look. I am pretty sure I can take care of the buried-alive sleeping Laxciilian."

"I am not talking about Gideon," he hisses with anger. His face scrunches like runny icing on a gingerbread man. "I said 'the Other'. The Third Triumvir…"

"A government consisting of three members?"

He face-palms. "You incompetent! The Triumvirate! The Chosen One, the Dark Lord, and the Deceiver! The Deceiver, sometimes called 'the Pretender', is *the other* Earthen Child! He masquerades as the Saviour until the appointed time when he must do battle with the true Deliverer. One will live, one will fall, and one will die. But regardless, in the end, the only victor is Darkness." I am flabbergasted. His next words cut deep:

"Oh, Thomas, did you really think you were *that* special, coming here all on your lonesome?" That hurts. "What else has the wizard neglected to tell you?"

The Grin feeds into my doubt of Big Moe, but I don't trust that this slimy green hairball is entirely upright either, so I choose to play it safe.

"We were interrupted." I nod to the King's men on the ground.

"Ah, by Lord Mecky." He's as unconvinced as I am that the wizard would have shared everything concerning my destiny, but thankfully he drops it. "Oh yes, he has it out for you and his hesitations are well-deserved."

I give him a quizzical stare so lengthily he asks me my age.

"Fifteen," I say slowly.

"Forget I said anything. I'd hate to be erased for having disrupted the timeline," he says, pointing upward to the sky, before grinning and shouting "Bazinga" again.

"His hatred isn't just an act to curry favour with the Triune. It's real and very tangible. Why does he hate me?"

"Nah-ah-ah-ha-ha-ha-ha-ha! Spoilers, dearie!" He vanishes in a puff of smoke—the word POOF literally appears—then reappears again, double-bent, and gasping for breath, like he's just run a great distance. He has a grand variety of top hats piled on his head, and he holds a rod with a bedsheet of clothes or something hanging from the other end. His deck hovers in the air and continues to shuffle itself. He telekinetically draws a card from the deck: a Lady. Hearts, I think.

"Going somewhere nice?" I ask, and then flash my eyes to the conked-out elves.

"Exile. I've betrayed you all and my double-crossing has been made known to Lord Mecky. They're discussing it right now. These days not even his oldest friend can calm his temper—I'll be beheaded for sure!" He cackles and honks like a goose. "I expect we'll meet again, Triumvir, sooner or later. But I had better get the heck out of dodge for now! Zellazellazellazella-ding-dong-bang-bang!" He literally splits his sides with glee.

"What did you do, if it's not too nosey of me to ask?"

"Nose, nose, nose! No one knows, knows, knows! Right under the Elder Wizard's nose, but he didn't have the wit to see—and he doesn't deserve to now! Dong-dong-dong-zellazellazella!" He stretches out his big hairy green feet and turns the head of all the elves that face us to the opposite side of the street. "So on the day of your arrival, signalled most unsubtly, might I add, by flashes of light and a rampage of thunder, I made my way across the Black Sands and revealed Gideon's burial place to Lear the Silver!"

He teleports about thirty times in a twenty-metre radius in the space of ten seconds. He's very brazen for someone who has just admitted to putting steps in place to plague the world with its nemesis. Well, at least I know the Triune are now infinitely stronger.

"Why would you do that?"

"Not 'would', Tomasheen, 'did'. Keep up!"

"Why *did* you do that?"

"This world has gone on long enough."

"That's the Triune's reason, too, according to Mósandrirl."

"He's wrong. Mósandrirl is too simple and one-dimensional a goodie to comprehend the complexity of the Triune's politics and plans, both individually and corporately."

"Help me comprehend you," I say.

"I am almost as old as the wizards. I was born something like a tadpole and crawled out of my mother's slime in a prison tower"—at this, he uses his right index finger to swab my jaw and then he sucks on the saliva he's extracted— "during the reign of an Earthen Starian Lincoln Lanian. The things I've seen, felt, done... Angoria has long since passed its expiry date... as has a certain creature whose whereabouts only the Triune could tell me."

"What kind of creature?"

"The only kind that causes a man to annihilate all that is: a woman."

"I see... She cuckolded you, huh?"

"Nothing as serious as that, Triumvir! I'm too petty to rely on such a quality reason to scour the world for vengeance. Oh, and one more thing! I am also going to free the Triune from their prison."

"Why would... *will* you do that?"

"Because I will demand that they consult the Fear—the eye in the sky—to tell me where the witch is! Then I will kill her! Then you will kill them, and then the Other will kill you, and then the Dark Lord will kill him, and then I will scorch the earth!" His white face grins at me evilly in the shadow of his top hat. Its wide-brimmed lip sticks out at me like an arrogant tongue. "THE WORLD IS GOING TO BURN! AND I WILL BE RESPONSIBLE! HA-HA-HA!"

He's mad! Insensible. Presumptuous. Nihilistic. And mad!

"I'm telling the wizard." Ugh. What am I? Five years old?

"I expect no less. Now then, payment. My information does not come free."

"You admit to involvement in a global felony and now you expect an award?"

"WHAT?" The glass tail in his mouth, he grips my right hand and pulls me in close. He sincerely believes he has done us all a favour. "I have foreseen, Triumvir Tomasheen, that your paths will cross with the witch from my past. When the time comes, disarm her and scream, 'Come hither, Mister Imp!' after which I will appear, and you will hand her over to me. Or I will end you. Nod if you understand."

And before I decide whether to nod or spit in his face, he is gone. There isn't even the stench of smoke. No poof. Not even a wisp.

And all that remains of him, all the evidence that this bizarre meeting ever happened, lies plainly in the palm of my hand: the Dutch tear and a card. I hold it up.

It has a single image, and it's too specific to be a coincidence: a Grim Reaper.

Just like the statue in Roop's back garden that, until The Incident, had meant nothing to me. The all-seeing monument. The sculpture under which all my secrets are buried.

So basically, I serve up this infamous witch to the Grin on a silver platter, or he'll unearth Roop's corpse, bury me beneath a Grim Reaper of my own, then all Angoria.

# INTERLUDE
# AURORA

"Uhhnnn…"

The seeds or pellets that knocked out the gold-plated guards whisk away in a gentle breeze, and the guards groan awake. Chances are the Royal elves will find some way to blame me if I'm caught at the scene of the crime, and forge more ammunition against me, so I should probably skedaddle. In fact, I agree impassionedly with the Grin's resolution that the best means of survival is to get off this island—all four-hundred-thousand kilometres of it. This morning, I took with me my pen and journal so I could write notes on my Chosen One-centric findings; I don't need anything else.

It's decided then: I dart from the museum. There are probably several gates into the city, but it makes sense to race to the one I am most familiar with: the one I came through. I may not have the most pleasant memories of it—getting shot by Monsieur Wolfe was a low point in my messianic career—but it's all I've got.

Surely the forest beyond it leads to a ferry. Or a raft. Or sea turtles. Or Daedalus' wings. Or anything that can help me escape the island, because I don't trust a single person here. The Triune's courtesy to keep Laxciila from harm has perverted itself into suspicion and apathy of anyone who: one, has a moral backbone; or two, does not celebrate their way of life; and I cannot operate in such an environment as this. Seriously, how could they stand by for three hundred years and do nothing?! What is wrong with these people?

I know I've arrived at the gate when I come to an expansive shining structure, not dissimilar to the gate into the Dendropark near Al-Farabi. The plains at the feet of the gate combine to form a marvellous stage for two ornately crafted golden Elven kings and a faceless forgotten queen. Two stand back, equal in height, large though miniature in comparison to the middle figure, the lord who now reigns. The gate itself is unimpressive, made from brittle dark metal smothered in leaves and weeds.

I look around for the Grin, but he's nowhere in sight. If he came to this gate, he probably teleported here ages ago, a lot less sweaty and dry-mouthed than I am now. Dozens of elves lounge around on the grass or merrily feast and dance or waste away on entertainment. In stark contrast, refugees in filthy mismatched clothes who couldn't have arrived too long ago stand around awkwardly, starved, and ignored, as others waddle through the gate in dribs and drabs. Their eyes are hollow with dismay and grief, but there is an undeniable attempt on their part to lean on expectancy and hope. I doubt it will last long. It didn't for me.

I squeeze through the crowds to get to the gate, touching as few of them as I can. The nearer I draw to it, the more I notice that the gate emits a dim hazy glow and hums like an elevator or a fridge. A veiled figure in a magenta dress and vivid pink pogo boots appears before me. I don't need the veil to be lifted, which it is, to know whose face lurks behind it. Madame Snarl.

For a fleeting moment, I convince myself that if she tries to stop me leaving, she won't try a second time. But only for a moment. Deep down I know that I could never hurt her: firstly, because she's a girl; secondly, I'm not that kind of guy; thirdly, at the end of the day, she's nothing more than a product of her environment—a lost and confused carbon copy fashioned by her culture, peers, hopelessness, and greed—and lastly, having seen her in action against Edgar and witnessed just how fast these elves can move, she'd probably break every bone in my body before I could get within an inch of her.

I determine to show a brave face when I raise my eyes, half expecting to see a sword slash my head clean off my neck. Instead, I see a beautiful countenance, and a young lady graciously poised.

"With the exception of a few licensed and heavily monitored sellers and a tiny number of historically impactful persons, we have a prohibition on magic usage in this kingdom, as per the instructions of the Triune. Yet I traced a magical signal from the First Museum to this gate. Why was that, I wonder?"

I shrug. "Because you like to play sheriff and cuff scarecrows with hairy feet and ice-cream cone noses?"

She compares me to that description, clearly not catching my drift, and then stares at my feet. At first, I think she's using x-ray vision to count the hairs on them, but when I look down, they're tapping like crazy, eager to get a move on. Her eyes shift to the gate. A little smile forms.

"I do hope you are not thinking of leaving us so soon, O Master Benjamin. Surely you will stay for tea?"

"'Thinking?' No. 'Decided'? You bet."

"Oh, very well then. I am sure this kingdom was a little stranger than what you are used to. How unfortunate it was not a fit."

"It was too similar, actually."

"How unexpected." I feign the widest smile I can. "Would you like some food for the road? Some weaponry, maybe? A bucket? I am leading these nature folk, our new dear guests, to the dining-hall to raid the pantry. You are more than welcome to join us," she says, and links arms.

She's choking me with her lemon and strawberry perfume or conditioner. I never understand people like her. They have nothing to say to you all the time you spend together, then when it is time to depart, they pretend you are intimates. Two-faced wench.

"I really shouldn't. In fact, I suspect I've already outstayed my welcome."

"That is not untrue," she sighs. "Though I will let you in on a little secret: we had such plans to more purposely accommodate you."

"Yeah. In the dungeons," I joke. Her eyelids flutter in agreement and she nods. "Well, now you can offer the room of Gideon, who I imagine is a consanguineous relative of yours, to someone with a destiny less cyclical and dark."

"Will you be joining us again?"

"Hopefully not."

"I should hope that is a promise."

"Milady," I bow, not bothering to hide the detestation in my eyes.

"Before you go, be a darling and return the Diadem of Salvation, forged in the fires of Maldr in anticipation of the day my King would march into Loux Laxciila, City of Light, and depose the vile impetuous Ratsach, which he did."

It could come in handy, but technically, it is theirs. I have just reached up to remove it when, next second, I'm chilled to the bone. The air turns to fog, ice cold, and blocks out the sun. All the grass, fruit, plants, and trees turn white as sleet, wither and die. My breath circles like steam against a windowpane, beating helplessly but trapped. Everyone's does. And everyone wears the same ghastly expression—even her. Reality screams. Hurricane winds rush and howl. Evil sets in.

The princess, who is apparently suddenly aware of what is coming, is about to shout, but nothing comes out. She freezes like an ice sculpture. I tear the diadem from my head and slam it down upon hers like a crown of thorns. Then I push her away from whatever is on its way. But, bewildered by her fear, she jumps in front of me. And then I see it, this wicked thing, reminiscent of Botticelli's Zephyrus.

Keen, cruel eyes that drink heavy gulps of light which it drowns in black salivary darkness. A tornado for legs that spits the occasional icicle. A start-stop upper-body. Lifeless colourless hair flows from his meaty head. His arrival is marked by the accompaniment of lightning which also crackles from his fingers. He is death in flesh and burial robes. And I have seen him before… The night I first arrived in the Maze… This is the same ghostly creature I saw stalking the woods. I'm certain of it!

With bolts, the assassin slashes an assortment of refugees and Laxciilians to bloody heaps of unfed skin and brittle bones. Palms blister and smoke. Eyes flicker and melt. Metal wagons scorch scarlet and brand naked legs. The revolting smell of cooking flesh sours my nostrils. Against my better judgement, I reach out to push the princess, then get the unfortunate sensation of a monster eating my hand. With a streak of light, the princess's body is flung like a ragdoll, buried within a cloud of broken stone and thick brown dust.

The spectre's aerokinesis stops and he walks on human legs. Start-stop, start-stop, until he's mere metres from me. The demon then sizes me up for slaughter.

I shout at the nearby Laxciilians, "Cast a spell to trap it, or something!"

They're frozen with fear and admiration. The few who let on that they heard me hunch.

"I thought this was supposed to be a magical world! Forget rules and regulations! Do the right thing!"

The apparition creaks its neck and gazes at me intently, as if to make sure I'm the one it wants. When satisfied, it extends a hand to me. *Go to Hell.*


"Ancient creature, aged about seven *mile*,
Leave now Loux Laxciila!
You made a mistake if you believed you had won,
You are hereby expelled by the Chosen One."

Nothing. Understandably. That was terrible. "Won" and "one". What was I thinking?


"You use your powers for evil gain.
This shall be repeated never again!
Your threat on my life has been in vain.
I banish you to the astral plane!"

Again nothing. And I really took liberties with the "gain" and "again" half-rhyme. You'd think being the Chosen One would come with perks or superpowers. Ah, crap, this is going to hurt.

And then, I too am blasted into oblivion.

I flinch on my pint-sized stool as she taps the damp cloth on my grazed forehead. Too embarrassed to look directly at her, my eyes fix on the lapping flames in the great black hearth. She gently places her hand on my cheek, slowly, afraid she'll turn to stone, and turns my face to hers. She wrings from the cloth minty healing water in her other hand and wipes away a few loose stones that clog my scars.

In her eyes, there is pity; behind her thinly parted lips, an apology; in her touch, reconciliation. She drops her eyes to the pail and makes an indistinguishable sound. I have zero experience with making the first move, so I don't know what to do or say. She weeps tearlessly, and then looks straight at my face with the countenance of one dying. I want to ask her what's wrong, but I can't quite get the words on my tongue.

"I'm not that ugly, I hope," I joke, but am soon weary that I've just invited abuse.

Her grey lips quiver but... nothing. "Of course not." No "O Master" nonsense this time. "Thirty-seven people died. One refugee survived. You almost didn't."

I think I'm going to be sick or cry. No. Forget that. I feel so sick that I think I'm dying.

"You saved me," she says, tearing up, looking for a logical explanation.

"Thirty-seven. Dead. Just… gone. All they wanted was sanctuary. And I failed them"—the most disparaged F word in my vocabulary, and never one I use in relation to myself. "It was my job to stop it. Destiny assigned me that task, yet I let *it* in."

No wonder they all doubt that I'm the Chosen One. Today I was not a hero. I failed to run away. I failed to save thirty-seven innocents. I failed to keep the princess from getting shot. And after eleven years of martial arts training, I failed to defeat the bad guy. Today was a bad day; so bad, that I'm actually delighted that so little information travels through the corridors of the Maze. Now the families left behind by the refugees can convince themselves that their deceased dear ones are off fighting orcs or plotting the downfall of the mages; not mushed and smoking on a stone bed in a vault somewhere beneath this circus waiting to be identified by some thoughtless, checklist-carrying elf who's probably painting their toenails at the same time.

"Benjamin," she says sternly, directing my face to hers and emphasising every syllable: "The key to the gate had to be inserted in a control room in Central Tower. You do not know where that is. You did not open the gate. I did. I let the immigrants in, and a murderer followed in after them."

I wince at the sharp pain as she washes the pebbles from the slits in my skin. She dampens the cloth again and her lips bubble like a baby's.

"Because of me," she says, "all our safety was jeopardised."

"I failed them," I repeat.

"No. You were excellent. Insane. Ridiculous. Unexpected. Unsuccessful. But excellent. Please, do not allow my failures and fears to eclipse your brilliance."

"They're dead. Everyone's dead."

"It was a lot of death for one day."

Not poignantly, and certainly not gleefully; she just says it. She asks me why I saved her despite having every reason to suspect she meant me harm.

"The same reason you were willing to take the blow for me. It was the right thing to do."

"Before I lost consciousness, I remember... despite your burns, you crawled over and... cradled me..."

"That doesn't happen often. I have a standard 'No-Touching' policy that I take very seriously. In life-or-death situations, I make an exception, clearly."

I don't know why she's doing this. Doesn't she have taxing business to attend to: writing letters, attending parties, or lounging around on plump cushiony couches as someone draws her idealised portrait?

"You can go... if you want to. You have medical elves on Laxciila's payroll who've spent centuries sitting around waiting to treat burns and gashes. If you need to be somewhere else—"

She shakes her head a little and silence ensues for a while. She busies herself with creams, lotions, and potions and rubs them on my face. I feel my wounds healing already. She looks almost perfect herself; like nothing happened at all—on the outside—at least.

Mósandrirl was there when I regained consciousness at the ward. Moments after I faded into blackness, it was he who valiantly chased the Wraith out of the kingdom. Thankfully, he didn't ask what I was doing at the gate, though that may be a conversation we'll have tomorrow. However, what he had to say about the princess was very revealing.

It turns out the Tornado Man wasn't the only foe who has been attacking her lately. When the diadem was placed on her head, her eyes were opened to the realisation that, unbeknownst to her, she shared a psychic link with someone. Thus, she intermittently and *cough, cough* *accidentally* operated as his vessel, which is to say he *cough, cough* *unwittingly* superimposed his hatred of me onto her and *cough, cough* *undeterminably and frequently* channelled it through her. Hence, why she was a witch to me. I don't think she knows that I know, or if she can quite remember who it was. Mósandrirl said that when she tried to remember, she saw only a shadow.

She scrubs my neck with the cloth and wipes off a cake of dust.

"Mósandrirl told me you weren't actually the bitter Madame Snarl I thought you were."

"'Madame Snarl'?"

"Never mind."

She repeats it and smiles. Then I repeat it in a French accent. She giggles.

Then, in a more serious and inquisitive voice, she prompts, "The Elder Wizard told me that once you had awoken, you stood by my bedside until I was clear of Death's jaws."

"That is not entirely true. I stood there until Alk'erion showed up. Then I ran for my life because that Dionysian bacchanalia party-goer scares the living daylights out of me." She laughs, then blushes in embarrassment for having expressed such an emotion. I look at her seriously. "You know, you saved my life, too."

"Hardly. The Wraith is an upper-level assassin. Had he wanted you dead, you would be. My presence and interference merely prevented your flight from this circus, this funereal monument…"

"That crown saved me from your brother."

"*Pardon?*" Her shocked squeal takes me by surprise.

"I thought you knew. I'm sorry. Please, pretend I said no such thing." Her memories of the last while must be scattered.

She sniffles as she tenderly washes my arms. With each wipe, my scratches fade and my skin stitches itself back together: first as threads, then folds of baby flesh. These, she wets with her tears.

"I have made such a ghastly mess of things," she apologises and then itemises them: abandoning her principles and campaigns for a better Angoria; accessing powers she does not possess; inhospitality; murder. "I wish you had known me before all this started. I think you would have liked me very much."

"It wasn't your fault." I can scarcely blame her for being brainwashed. "You weren't in control of your mental faculties." Now roles have reversed and I'm trying to convince her of her innocence.

"I failed everyone."

"That happens sometimes. So how about we forgive ourselves, and henceforth do not so much as acknowledge what any defamatory naysayer slanders?" She nods. "Give us a smile." She lights up the room. "Your hair smells of strawberries and lemons. I noticed when you walked in, this blooming fragrance. It's beautiful." Gosh, I'm giving compliments now: I don't sound like myself at all tonight. I should get blasted with lightning more often.

"I think it encapsulates my personality. Sweet and sour," she smiles, and for the first time in forever, I genuinely laugh. And I get the impression that it's been a while for her too.

I don't even have to look at my arms to know they're healed; I can feel the power of the restoration within my limbs like wellsprings of life and energy. Next, she slowly, gently removes my slippers and rolls up my trouser legs, soaks and squeezes the cloth over the metal pail, and treats my scrapes and the clotted gash on my right foot. And she kisses them once each. And dries them with her hair.

Then she rises, reaches behind her to a dark blue cloak, and draws the diadem.

"The King, indignant that the crown ever found its way into your possession, searched most diligently for it this afternoon. Thankfully the Elder Wizard retrieved and hid it before the King could."

She crowns me and curtsies.

I mumble thanks, but hopefully without appearing ungrateful, advise her to keep it.

"Skylar, my blessings are mine to give to whosoever I choose." She is gracious and sweet, but stubborn. There's no arguing with her.

Confused, I repeat "Skylar".

She explains that in Old Elvish, it means "Chosen". "It is an identity I recommend you become familiar wearing."

"My absolute and utter dearest one, I do hope this does not mean you revoke your earlier adamant conviction that I wish to, what was it, overturn Angoria in fire and shadow? What would your old man say?" Her jaw drops in anger, but before she can argue a case for her then-mental incapacity, I reassure her I was not serious. "You know, if you are going to call me by a nickname, I think it is only fair that I give you one, if I may be so cheeky?"

"How about I hear it first? Names are very important constructs."

"Aurora."

"I hate it."

When she asks how I could bring myself to utter such a disgusting sound, I explain that Aurora is Latin for "the dawn" and is etymologically linked to the Northern Lights. By the time I have delineated what they are, she has been enchanted, beguiled.

"How beautiful and somewhat reminiscent of a spectacle we used to witness here often, before the Triune covered over the sky. Now it happens so seldom I had forgotten the feeling it gave me; that sense of how small and inadequate we really all are, and how microscopically insignificant our problems, if only we look up."

"You got all that from the name 'Aurora'?"

She giggles and wipes away a tiny shiny teardrop from her lashes. "Tell me, sweet Benjamin, do you have such affectionate names for every girl you meet back home?"

"Goodness, no. This is the first proper conversation I've ever had with a girl," I smile, then realise how sad that sounds.

"Do you mean to say that your dark brooding demeanour and mild manners fail to woo any potential female companions?"

"What can I say? Tough crowd. Not that I can say I'm surprised. It was always going to require a very rare young woman to melt my heart of black ice into living streams."

I beam, and she beams humbly. I flash her my sultriest eyes before I remember seducing her is not on my to-do list.

Before the moment becomes too soppy, I feign an exaggerated yawn, and remark that is has gotten very late. I take her by the right hand and kiss it as any gentleman would and thank her for everything she has done.

She smiles coyly, grabs the pail and cloths, floats to the door and stops, then half-turns.

"Good night, Skylar. Good night."

And she's gone. Like she was never here: no bucket, no mess, no scrapes. Nothing but the lingering scent of strawberries and lemons.

# 8

# COVENANT

Day Twenty-Four in Loux Laxciila, and everybody worth mentioning is in the dining-hall eating lunch. The Royals are, as always, skewering me with their twenty-twenty vision and ancient, demonic eyes.

Why Mósandrirl always parks us at the table right before the stage where they dine, knowing full well that the men hate me, I'll never know. Maybe he's hoping Alk'erion will shoot me again. Between a spoonful of potato and parsnip soup and a forkful of watermelon, I randomly wonder for the first time ever if the Queen of Loux Laxciila is alive. I could just ask Mósandrirl, but instead I fantasise, much like *Northanger Abbey*'s Catherine, that the queen has been disposed of within a secret chamber in the walls by the King or Alk'erion, who today is clad in leopard skin and strange *Pinus halepensis* earrings.

"Well, don't you look positively androgynous, your highness?" jeers Inner who measures the size of his hand against Alk'erion's Aleppo pinecones. His shirt's open embarrassingly low, revealing chains of Elven bling that poorly mask what was probably a well-deserved plum bruise. His sharp elbow daggers across his lemon-haired sister's plate. She is baby blue today from her crown to her lips to her shoes. In fact, she's bluer than I am, which I find aggravating. She stares at her food, and occasionally her family, with so bored a look that it's hard to tell if she sees anything. Meanwhile, to her left, her fanged father's especially mobile jaws whisper things in her ear, though she looks so distant and blank, it's hard to tell if she heeds him.

After a while, Aurora looks up at me. (Well, it's about time!). She smiles widely like a gorgeous grinning baby, and then tries to hold it in by biting down on her bottom lip. That just makes her sexier.

Afterwards, absolutely stuffed on breads, potatoes, pastries, eggs, lamb chops, sausages, custard, fruit, and tea, the wizard and I roll off our chairs and waddle down a grassy plain for a leisurely stroll. The sun is low and blinding.

"My regrets for the ungainliness of our discussion yester-noon after the Elder Elf's inadvertent arrival."

Mósandrirl had taken me to the Rink, an interactive training-zone that simulates battle scenarios. Designed with the very best technology that Laxciila had to offer for its soldiers to practise, Mehkabikil handed it over to the Triune days before the Maze-curse was cast as part of their neutrality deal. Now, a captive segment of the Fear simulates the threats for trainees to fight, not that any Laxciilians are interested in that. They just lie on the grass all about it sunbathing around stone peacocks and crows that I think I've seen before; getting drunk on every-flavoured cocktails; and discussing identity politics and their wealth.

That happens a lot—Mehkabikil interrupting us when we're alone together—like he's afraid I might prompt Mósandrirl to deny the Grin's snake-rattle that the King's behaviour extends beyond his double-agent mystique. I confided in the wizard what the Grin had shared about confessing to having gone all-out nihilist and allying with the Triune. He said he'd take care of it and that a host of Laxciilian soldiers had been dispatched to arrest him, but I don't think it's amounted to anything.

And then Mehkabikil came over and for forty-five minutes drably talked about the weather in a tone as dry as the grass, at which point I left.

"That is quite alright," I say to the wizard, and kick a ball of grass that suddenly grows limbs and a face and berates me. "So, are your top-secret sessions beginning today?"

Since the Maze was erected, just about every race, village, and culture has been divided in Domes, Zones, or Blocks with virtually no outside transmission, meaning most towns do not know if the rest of their country exists let alone what's happening elsewhere. Many of the captured Resistance leaders were decapitated within the first twenty-five years or so, and this information was proliferated heavily via the Fear—the eye in the sky—but not so much anymore. Even the Triune seldom make broadcasts.

The prisoners know they are being watched. That is sufficient.

More recently, the Resistance's top moles sent word to the heads of two dozen races to ready themselves to escape their Blocks, and a week later, these moles triggered a ten-second glitch in the Maze. Those who got out got out, and those who weren't slain thereafter have made their way here. However, the Elder Elf hadn't banked on them each taking dozens of refugees with them, which caused some initial consternation. Since then, the Elder Elf has invited the heads of each race to a special series of private conferences here in Laxciila at which my credibility as the Chosen One will be debated. The head of each race will lead a seminar detailing their views and then open the floor to questions that will surely give way to heated, and oftentimes seditious, discussions. The inevitable words of death by some commentators aside, I am glad they will consider the case of my destiny and/or execution so thoroughly.

The wizard replies, "I am ready, but there are fewer representatives of the Assembled than I would have liked. The Witch has not made an appearance, perhaps because she would be burned at the stake on sight. Yet I cannot help but sense, as I always have, that she will be heavily invested in the Last Days of Angoria, and in your future, particularly. The whereabouts of the First Vampire are also unknown, much to the relief of everyone. He has killed so many family members and relatives of those attending the Meeting that he is probably safer in the Maze than Elven Haven. Thirdly, there is a young Elven prince whom Lord Mehkabikil so wanted to acquaint with, though I fear he has fallen prey to the traps of the Maze."

Prince Darkwood, he says, has played a pivotal role in the Resistance's plans over the last eightyish years: raising up new warriors where and when possible; putting double-agents in influential positions; provoking the wardens who have been stationed by the Triune to mutiny in their camps; and feeding them inaccurate information so that they were ensnared by their own masters' traps. It doesn't sound too impressive given that the Resistance have had three hundred years to execute these minor victories, but Mósandrirl is sober-minded enough not to suggest the results were all that illustrious. However, he adds, their disabling of so many traps will make for a clearer path through the labyrinth when it's my turn to venture through it and achieve my destiny. I guess that means he's betting on me passing this trial that I have not been invited to with flying colours.

I don't want to belittle his efforts, so I pose a critique with an alternate slant: "Three hundred years… What were the Triune waiting for?" I know if I ruled the world for three hundred years, I would have done something a little more productive than plant a hedge.

"You," he replies. Did I really expect he'd say anything else?

I am reminded of an earlier conversation with Lanky. He said that the Triune are bodiless and believe my blood can restore them. I throw it out there.

At this, Mósandrirl rolls up his sleeve and exposes a black scar with deep purple threads and pale dead skin that I suspect will and could never heal. "The magic is in the blood," he says, and then explains how three of his brothers bled him and an enchantress mostly dry and created a hybrid mage son, Sharmedes, now one of their greatest captains. "He calls me Nuncle," he shudders and chuckles, though it's not funny. But maybe his is the ideal reaction. That his own flesh and blood, boys he probably raised, could chain him up and gut him—maybe all you can do is laugh.

"And all that aberrant forbidden magic came with a cost," I surmise.

"'Aberrant'?" he repeats. "Sharmedes now has a son about your age with that same femme fatale enchantress from whom he was made!" That is messed up.

"But how does this relate to me?" I hope I don't sound too unsympathetic.

"As the Twelfth Saviour of Angoria, the magic in your blood is potentially the most powerful this world has ever seen."

A ridiculously boisterous howl from across the park causes an earthquake and disrupts our conversation. I cannot but pull a look of disgust when I see the beery chin and foamy beard of the drunken Dwarf King. For goodness sakes, it's only nine o'clock. Another king with three brains chuckles at how oh so very funny Master Norbrik is, and how his good cheer has made this entire gathering of magical folk worthwhile. Is Three-Brains serious? Norbrik the Dwarf Lord is the most pig ignorant person I've ever met. Alk'erion may be a homicidal maniac, but at least he acknowledges my existence. Mósandrirl says he wants a word with the Dwarf.

"I'll go get us some more tea," I say, and nod to the nearby café of rich wood and open expanses, scented with fresh custard-filling pastries and beer. Beverages are free to non-Laxciilians since technically, we're all homeless, penniless refugees. With a skip in my step, I make my way to the mug shelf and take a red one for Mósandrirl and a blue one for myself. A tall angular shadow stretches over me, and everyone within a twenty-metre radius goes silent. Not typically convivial with authority figures, I brew my tea and say nothing. He speaks first.

"Mex Confetricus. Destroyer."

"Good morning. Did you sleep well?"

"When I was asleep. Unlike you, I hear. Your slumber was rudely interrupted by that unmannerly Curupira."

He refers to a sliced-and-diced ginger in a Hawaiian grass skirt who arrived in the little hours last night. Driven mad by fear and a plague of blisters, the little dote had fallen prey to his own illusions and believed that a peccary sat on his chest and noosed a metal collar around his neck. The princess, healers, and I did everything we could, but he didn't make it. "I reserve my judgement for the Wraith, actually. It is he who chases and maims your guests on their travels, after all."

"You do not like me very much."

"Why ever would you say such a thing?"

"You do not look at me when you speak."

"I am on tea duty. It requires a great deal of attention," I wink.

"And when you saw me yesterday, and again this morning, you glared."

"I am a passionate walker. And eater."

"You leave the teabag in?"

"As instructed."

"Not in your own?"

"Never."

"The pot."

"There you go."

"You can take it back now. ... Oh, I should have offered you the handle."

"No worries." I return it, hand scarlet and melting, to its place on the fiery stove. "Thick skin."

"I bet you do. Would you like a dash of crushed foxglove leaves for your tea?" He reaches into his pocket and removes a tiny canister.

"Oh, no, thank you. I'm not very adventurous."

"Sugar and milk," he observes. "How about a *cerbera odollam* flower on top?" He reaches into his pocket and showcases Exhibit B. "It contains sugar."

"I have an inactive diabetes gene, so I'm cutting down on my sugar intake. Enjoy it, though." Both mugs are brewed, milked, and sugared, respectively. Sorted. "While we are having the most intimate of conversations, how do you take yours?"

"Black."

"To each their own."

"Excuse me. I have morons with less lacklustre than you to speak with." And he's gone. A string of steam like a snake tail from his mug trails behind him, and he cocks his head to Mósandrirl and Norbrik in a "Come hither" motion. I half-suspect Mósandrirl to ignore him and come drink his tea, but over the heads of the crowds of elves and Toad-people, his pointy hat bobs down the lane we had come and disappears.

Murmurs turn to chit chat and whispers to laughs, and soon, the café is in full swing again. I decide to chill out here for a bit and then head to the Laxciilian Library. What Lanky wrote on that leaf makes no sense to me, so the library's my best bet to uncover the meaning in peace. I slip my hand into my pocket just to check that it's still there, which it is. I can't really justify not having researched it already. It's just that I've been spending so much time with Aurora lately, and training for the inevitable battle whenever I can.

Slinking and sliding between all manner of creatures—Domovoy, gnomes, native and non-indigenous elves, and mooncalves—and find a seat in the back corner. The half-built, half-discarded shack has a forested feel to it, like it was built around the wilderness of the great outdoors. It's nothing special as far as buildings go, but it is closer in appearance to what I had expected when I heard I was being brought to an Elven kingdom.

"*Jisa... Jisa...*"

I turn to the counter twenty or so metres away to see what made that distinctive sound. Not to be rude like pointing children, but out of genuine fascination for the variety of creatures that have assembled here of late, I scan the room. Some of their leaders aren't bothered to attend the Meeting, shrugging off the urges of armed Laxciilian guards, wanting nothing more than to sit around creaming off the café's freebies or drinking mango juice all day. Maybe it's for the best.

"*Jisa... Jisa...*" I hear it again. This time, it doesn't take long to make out which creature it was. The elf who serves it at the counter calls it Roz. Roz is a Lustin, one Laxciilian loudly whispers to his confused-as-I-am friend. Lustins are fleshy, six feet tall, snouted asexual beasts with black eyes and white dots for pupils. Near extinct. Roz's limbs, though elongated and skeletal are no signifier of its fragility. Apparently, it could take on all thirty occupants here without breaking a sweat—in addition to the three litres of sweat it secretes hourly already. Incredibly ripe, any elf that nears Roz unsubtly moves several tables away. Roz "Jisa"'s a few more times, and morphs into a beetle-eyed breasted humanoid, and sits down with its company outside in the sun, just beyond the canopy roof. In their humanoid form, all the Lustins say is "A'en'lor" but with ease they understand each other's full-blown conversations.

Head held high and back so straight she must suffer serious neck pains, the princess passes the window. A flurry of servants follows her, including a hand maid she calls Ebed, and try to dissuade her from gate duty. She's stubborn though; very obstinate. Styled as an ice queen, she looks ridiculous, because it's roasting. But gosh, she looks amazing, too. A splendid and ornate silver rhombus necklace on which have been carved Elvish inscriptions hangs around her neck. Her hair is mostly straight with an added bounce from curls that usually aren't there. She's been woven into a form-fitting white dress with the faintest touch of pink, and around her shoulders there slithers a boa and woolly snowy coat. Her long eyelashes are jet black and curled, and her eyelids gleam silver. She has just the right touch of make-up and glitter to look dolled to the nines but authentic.

I feel a blush coming on. My palms sweat. My fingers fidget uncontrollably beneath the table. My chest ups and downs. My shaky feet play football matches under the table.

"You've got dreadful taste in women." I turn and see Inner coolly sip a pint of butter beer. It smells great.

"I don't know what you're implying."

"You do realise she's this world's answer to Paige? Sweet but sultry. Innocent but a python. Compassionate but dangerous. Sex on a stick—"

At this point, I shout at him to shut up, which attracts unwanted attention.

"Like, what would you even talk about?" he asks, ignoring me completely. "Her papa's *Bendetta*? Her brother, Madame Foxe? How the smell of her multi-flavoured hair reminds you of a time you once busted your toe, so it looked like a strawberry while trying to kill yourself in a citric bubble bath? Or how you feel redundant when you're trying to help a dying critter and she jumps in and side-lines you? How she looks like a middle-aged man when she glares?"

"There were special circumstances pertaining to that. Shut your mouth concerning matters you know nothing about!" I growl sternly through gritted teeth, and then become aware that elves are staring at me.

"Fetch." He lets out an *ah* and puts down his glass of butter beer.

"As in, you want me to get you another one...?"

"No. My name. I'm trying out Fetch."

"Fetch. I like it. It's a good, strong Irish name. Do you know what it means?"

"Of course. Do you?"

I don't answer. He runs off to wherever he goes, and then the prince's head comes into view. *Oh, sweet Jupiter, the absolute state of him.*

Like the princess, his entire appearance has been altered since I last saw him—which was minutes ago. Alk'erion is a pantomime mongrel, Dame Wolf. I don't know if he's wearing a metallic green yukata or robe, but whatever it is, it has black lace Elvish patterns, and his hair is like a cluster of polar white reeds. His face, dangerous as ever, smokes slightly beneath a vibrant pink umbrella held up by an elfling. A train of tight lips and resentful eyes drone behind him, swords at the hip, though their staunchly loathing countenances suggest they would sooner slit his neck than an assassin's. Surely, Alk'erion's rich enough to buy elves that at least pretend to like him?

They just stand there for a while doing literally nothing other than breathing. After a few anticlimactic minutes, a purple figure comes into view. An obstructed view since I'm wedged at the back of the café behind a pincer-handed man holding a totem pole with a goat head, but enough for me to see he's a notably older man with a long white moustache that curls at the bottom. His purple robes and his white collar suggest he's important. A senator, maybe. The fluency of his unintelligible words puts Alk'erion's rudimentary phraseology to shame. I don't know a word of Elvish, New Elvish or Old, but you can tell when someone's struggling at a language. As prince of the realm, shouldn't this have been his first? Shouldn't he have been taught this since he was two—or whatever the age of speaking development is here?

I down my tea, leap to my feet, and hide behind a thin wooden pillar to take a peep. If anyone sees me watching him, they either hate him more than I do or they want to see how the drama pans out, because they leave me to my spying. Not one of them shuts up, though, so I cannot make out a single word.

The prince claps his hands. His entourage breathe relief and depart. The youngling who carried the umbrella actually tosses it away and runs for the hills. Alk'erion obviously didn't mean for him to go, because he fumbles at the mouth in a great panic to get the elfling's attention. He fails. And Alk'erion must have some serious skin condition because he begins to combust. His is a long painful scream, pitiable and raw. And the café, who must deeply despise him for reasons that are their own, howl with laughter and glee.

"Stop it!" I say weakly. "Stop it, shush! Please, don't sneer. Stop, stop, stop it! He's in pain. Please be quiet. Stop it! Stop it! This is how the Triune treat you. You think they aren't laughing at your pain?" (What pain?). "This isn't right! This isn't fair! Wh-wh-what's the matter with you?!"

I turn to the window just as the senator Alk'erion calls Dol'ver shields his suppurating, scarring, smouldering master with the umbrella. He has suffered a severe case of sunburn, but he'll be fine, thankfully. No one should die of a recklessly abandoned umbrella.

Terrified for their lives following their indecency, and rightly so, everyone in the café suddenly reverts into defensive mode. Some drop to the floor, others cover their face and cower in fear, the Lustins morph. The barman, who had been taking an order near the window, drops his checklist and points to me and dons an aghast accusatory face.

Only I stand perfectly still. And Alk'erion's evil eyes glare at me with an age-old contempt as though I'm the root cause of every offence he's ever suffered. And in those arrow pupils I see reproach, pure plenished delicious hatred, and maybe even a tear.

I tap the diadem on my forehead, mostly for my own reassurance that it's still there. He sprints as fast as he can down the forest track, Dol'ver hot on his tail. Curiosity beckons me to follow; that and some innate need to apologise for bearing witness to his mortification, and to assure him that not everyone considered his comeuppance—discomfiture! —a laughing matter.

Out of sight, their hush-hush undertones lead me to a rusty brown shack in a dismal shingly courtyard, cramped and tomb-like, dissimilar to everything else I've seen in Laxciila. At least the graveyard has flowers. Chains and shackles sprawl out over the stony ground, either bolted into the concrete or the mountain faces either side of the rat-hole hut. Scratched into the stone walls are a series of white carvings that look as bad as a child's drawing, but together they form a coherent narrative. I could be wrong, but I think they're self-portraits.

The first picture shows a happy crowned prince and a witch (if the pointy hat is anything to go by) with a heart between them. The second image shows that same witch, but with an angry countenance this time. After that, there's an image of the prince metamorphosing into a shaggy haired wolf-man. By day, according to the fourth picture, the prince conceals himself under the shade of an umbrella. And then, there's a hideous array of images detailing his experiences of night: more beastly in demeanour and mien, he lives here among the tombs. No one can bind him, not even with chains, though many have tried. He just tore the chains apart like they were made of daisies and broke the irons on his long bony feet. No one was strong enough to subdue him and live to tell the tale. Night after night, he cried among the gravestones and cut himself against them—and ate pigs, people, and birds.

One of the last scratches in the wall shows a princess—identical to that of the prince, only with longer hair—smiling alongside the prince.

There's a heart between them, too. The final picture shows a tall elf with a five-pronged crown, a sceptre or a staff, and two soulless evil snake eyes above a small cunning smirk.

The grating of my ears to the horrid tune of crow caws, clicks, and rattles draws me out of the world of primitive art and back to the reality that I am standing in a graveyard, following in the footsteps of a sociopath. Still shivering at the memory of him almost combusting, I tiptoe to the dusty flaky door half-lying against, half-hanging off its hinges. I wonder for all of two seconds where Alk'erion and Dol'ver have slipped away to; but off to the right I hear them shovelling the rock pile floor and pulling something up from the ground.

I open the door, slowly as I can. It almost falls on top of me. Alk'erion doesn't charge toward me, though, so I must have gotten away with it. A wafting musty odour of sweat and urine immediately hits me. It's putrid! My nose wrinkles. I squint. A dark red four-poster lies in the middle of the floor, covers tattered, pillows stained yellow and brown, and the bed frame deteriorated. One window looks out to the courtyard. Black iron bars cage them shut. Mould slimes up, down, and across the discoloured glass. Its corners are smothered with cobwebs. The only thing remotely flattering about this mangy cesspool of filth is a precious painting of Alk'erion and his sister. He doesn't look half bad when he's scrubbed up and has his evil mouth shut. He even looks pleasant. Or maybe that's just the effect his sister has on him. Or maybe he threatened to eat the artist if the male subject wasn't idealised.

It is inconceivable to think that I'm still in the centre of Angorian civilisation and not a prison. Strip away the pomp, the celeb status, and the music, and this is all the Laxciilians truly are: wild venomous slaves in expensive clothes and soiled bedsheets who are afraid of the light because it exposes them and the dark because it's when their inner animals come out to play. They're no different from the people back on my world, and not one of them has peace, joy, or transcendental freedom. Not really.

Before I break into a soliloquy, Dol'ver's mumbling breaks my concentration. Just in case they decide to make a pit stop, I suppose I should probably conceal myself. I'm about to hide under the bed when the sight of a chamber pot hurtles me into a wardrobe. I slide down a clatter of helmets, axe-heads, and metal bits and bobs so encased with dust mice that I sneeze.

The wardrobe door was already slightly ajar, so I leave it as such for surveillance. I comb my fringe behind my ears to avoid singeing it if I'm forced into battle and my diadem retaliates. I take one last deep breath and cover my mouth before the door cacophonously creaks inward—I have an awful habit of laughing in moments of grave tension.

Alk'erion enters first, turns his back to the bed and leaps onto it. Dol'ver enters and stands in the corner of the room, head bowed the entire time (to cover the fact that his shirt is covering his nose), a large bag strapped around his front. Alk'erion does most of the talking, plotting, and hyena cackling. Dol'ver agrees with everything, but when he offers input, it seems cruel and clever to Alk'erion. They either speak in code or an Old Laxciilian tongue, the likes of which doesn't automatically translate for me.

After several minutes, Dol'ver throws the bag on the ground and removes a bow, a plethora of arrows, and a jar of something black that I go ahead and assume is poison. They repeat the same expressions to each other, drilling their plans into each other's heads.

When they take out a map of the kingdom, I wonder if they're setting up a camp somewhere. When they trace along a specific route, I wonder if they're planning on jumping somebody's carriage and taking their gold, since a Laxciilian can never have too much of that. I know Mehkabikil advised them all to cry poverty so the foreigners wouldn't suspect Laxciila of dodgy dealings or of profiting off the rest of Angoria's misfortunes, though just about all of them ignore it, even Mehkabikil.

Then they mention, to put it mildly, the King's name and pluck a bowstring, firing a pretend arrow. I realise what this is: assassination! Oh, my holy days. And the wolf-man is just about crazy enough to do it, too.

Then they mention someone called Underwood, which, I've learned from my extensive studies at the library, can also be pronounced 'Darkwood'. The wizard said there was a young lord by that name who hadn't made it to Laxciila for the Meeting. So, what am I to take this to mean? Are they going to kill him too, or have they already?

With all the excitement, my legs get giddy and restless. Like I'm sitting in a paddling pool, I try to rearrange my feet and cross my legs. Epic fail. My foot slips and I fall out of the wardrobe, squished by metal clutter. I keep my eyes on the unswept stone I swim on as the wave of black metal tools continues and wait for their boots to bruise me. Oh, better idea! I'll propose a team-up!

Alk'erion grabs me, hoists me to the air, and, not quite knowing what to do with me, flings me to the floor again. And both elves pound my nose and cheekbones. Blood gushes from one ear and I can't open my right eye. Maybe I should block their attacks, but I'm more concerned with protecting my sol plexus and respiratory system than my face. I recall Proverbs 4:23's warning to guard your heart above all else—your face can heal.

Fetch leaps on their shoulders and bites Alk'erion's ear off. He kicks Dol'ver away repeatedly, seeing him as no more than a useless secondary character—a mime, a Prince A echo—whose only purpose is to outnumber me in this confrontation.

Any second now, crown! Please, hurry up!

Right when I need it most, the crown blasts a proportionate scorcher of heat at my attackers. Snakes of red fire at the bed, burst through the glass window, launch Alk'erion onto the wrecked mattress, and lift Dol'ver through the air so forcefully that he crashes right through the door. Flesh burns. Eyes plum all around and sting with smoke. Cheeks puff swollen with fluid, black with ash and hissing wisps. And the battle ends.

I stash my satchel with their dug-up plans and portable weaponry. I will give them back, I convince myself. Someday. Then I arise and go outside and brush the crackling embers off my scarf. My black coattails flutter before me.

"Though I am sure it is no consolation, I am sorry."

Unrepentant with pride, "He broke into our room, first," Fetch sulks pettily. And I walk on with a tight little smile to the backdrop of crackling flames just as the roof caves in on the shabby dank hut the prince called home.

Out of nowhere, all I can think about is the day Lincoln Lane menace, Toni-with-an-I, nephew of Rita (I never did know her surname, come to think of it), supplied Roop with Japanese fireworks. Roop stashed them in The Governor's letterbox, caused considerable damage, and then gave me my first demo of manhood: he took a hike.

I turn, immediately repulsed by Alk'erion's hideous grinning face under the shade of Ogham stone knock-offs and ruins, soaked with sweat, streaks of tears, and foamy pus. The bloody gurgle between his teeth. The choke in his throat. He's manic, incapable of registering his distress. But I am not.

"I sincerely regret that it came to this." I shut my mouth fast before I gag or bawl.

"Careful, B," Fetch interjects. "That almost sounds like a second apology. I would hate for you to make a Guinness World Record you might regret in the morn."

"I only ever wanted to help people."

"You-u-u-u-u-u... on'y... wa-a-ant-t-ted... self-f-f... pwe... sssss... erv-v-v-ve..." He coughs and spews life by the litre.

"If I have affirmed for you the suspicion that I am the Dark Lord, then that was not my intention. Though I judge you not for your conclusions."

"I kill-l-l-l... yuh..." he gurgles from his bloodied splashy mouth. "Yuh end de... Eldah El...uuifff..."

My thoughts turn to how I dealt with Roop.

"I can't allow you to see that first part through, comrade, but as for the second: you will have your revenge. Leave that to me."

# INTERLUDE
# THE MADNESS OF MEHKABIKIL

For the first time in my life, I feel like a man. It's not a word I ever liked—'man': "Hey, man, 'sup?", "Well, what's the *craic*, man?" Oh, it's sent shivers through me over the years. And don't get me started on the word "dude". But 'man' is starting to grow on me.

Anyway, as I leave the Rink, Laxciila's virtual reality battleground, I feel like a man. In my mind's eye, I see the training centre in operation by another of Angoria's most esteemed warriors. I went for a walk last night—the sky was black, illumined only by a crescent moon like the smiling mouth of Wonderland's Cheshire Cat—when suddenly I heard the grunts of the Elder Elf followed by metallic slashes. Hoping to find Alk'erion stabbing him, I had to see what was going on for myself and so diverted from the woodland walkway.

And there was Mehkabikil, gutting orcs, tearing out the hearts of a Minotaur squad, clipping the wings of avian humanoids (the aarakocra, maybe), and beheading wild dogs, uber-grizzly bears, and wolves like it's nothing. And he was marvellous. Powerful. Lean. Valiant. Everything the Laxciilians claim he is, and more. Epitomic of manhood. At least, a picture of dominant manhood.

Then the purple-pink cloud appeared—and showed him me. I still remember his yell, his screech. The thud as he crashed to his knees. How low his jaw dropped and how fast his hands sprang to block his ears as he descended into madness.

From a monarchical point of view, it couldn't have happened at a worse time. Hundreds of nonconformists had just begun to leave the kingdom. The dream of Laxciila as a utopia quickly unravelled as farcical what with the recent "kidnapping" of the princess, the horrific testimonies of the refugees (which apparently the Elder Elf made efforts to silence), and the Wraith's attack. Then there were those who simply object to the new rations policy and prohibition of celebrations while the Assembled's meetings are in progress; only two of Mecky's attempts to disguise just how well his pompous deuce-dressed throng have had it while his guests were starving to death and stricken with malady. Some of the guests were so indignant at their discovery that the Laxciilians spent the last three hundred years getting bloated on drink and custard tarts that they left the city with more enthusiasm than they had when they arrived. Some even cite the Elf's misrepresentation of me, particularly based on their leaders' reports on the Assembled's private meetings, as their foremost reason for leaving this den of beverages, Lucullan splendour, miserliness, and bliss. Even now many drag their belongings behind them on carts. Others do not care for such things. They just want out.

Lest any intruders try to sneak in and kill us all again, the doors are heavily monitored and exodus is permitted for exactly thirty minutes at the eleventh hour of daytime and night. I have decided to put the nation's distraction to good use: it took me a few weeks, blisters, and tumbles that twisted my body in ways God did not intend, but I can now roll and fire a crossbow. Not very well, but it's an improvement from my first attempt. I can also shoot any one of the training zone's projections but my target, which is fine by me since I excel at hand-to-hand combat anyway, so long as I don't freeze.

I'm most familiar with fighting with swords, Sais, bamboo sticks, and staffs, so I train with none of them here. I can't have the Laxciilians knowing all my moves, especially since I might just meet them on the opposite side of a battlefield someday. Instead I try my hand at hammers and axes, as well as a leather wrist-strap that fires stakes and poisonous darts. My least favourite part of the day, hands down, is returning these beauties to the Hive: a shelter a short walk away from the Rink that houses a sampling of all manner of beautiful weapons.

With every passing obstacle in the Rink, I feel a stronger sense of leadership, purpose, and faith that I can achieve my destiny. More than that, there's a willingness to make a difference that had until now undergone privation having spent so long lost in the miry throes of depression and apathy. But I'm back. I'm focused. Headstrong. On a mission. I am a man—I'm sure sweating like one, and I'm beginning to smell like one, an unfortunate side-effect of being a world-saver that I'll rectify in a moment.

Ah, go on sure, one more round.

"Final level: activate."

A purple-pink cloud presents itself to me. It calls itself the Fear. It is a spirit, a dark angel that wants—*demands*, even—our awe, emotions, our very lives. Like a baby, it craves nurture: feeding, cradling, attention, one-on-one time, to be handed around like a Pass-the-Parcel sausage-shaped wrapper, to be changed and refreshed and doted on, until finally it has contaminated all who held it, and left us used, isolated and barren. Fear wants a name.

But in my weakness, I affirm its surrender to the Name Above All Names.

But then it shows me The Incident. Suddenly, out of nowhere, Fetch leans in close and whispers in my ear, "ABC 6-5-1-18 9-20-19-5-12-6." I cancel the session and the simulation ends.

I am a man now and nothing is going to bring me down. I need a shower anyway. I turn toward the Rink's pantheon seating arena, and there sits the snarling Aurora alone with a most caustic expression and spears for eyes. *Now what's her problem?* I expel the thought immediately. She's being played again by an as-yet unknown puppeteer, I'm sure of it. She rises silently and smirks her family's trademark evil look, and leaves.

And I pray to God she did not just see me bash Roop's head in with a stone, stake him in the chest, and bury him beneath the Grim Reaper. It could prove damaging for my reputation.

[Aurora]

I run my hand through my long blonde hair and style it with a large clip with a diamond-encrusted rose. I stare in the mirror—my room has many mirrors—and dozens of big blue eyes smile back. I debate whether to expose my Elven ears or not. I choose not to.

Ebed hustles and bustles around my room, mumbling and bumbling at times to me, mostly to herself, occasionally bumping into her many reflections in all the mirrors, carrying bottles of strawberry and lemon scent, squeezed from the Seven-Fruit Tree in the Garden of Every-Flavoured Trees. As always, she knows virtually everything that takes place on the island: who got caught in the rain; who started a barroom brawl over a peanut with a foreigner; how much fish are selling for at the market; and who is dead now for our murder and mortality rates are on the increase.

Today, she spends most of her time yammering on about an explosion that occurred this morning at an apothecary building in Efac. Apparently forty witnesses can place Benjamin at the scene. I take the liberty of severely doubting those claims though, as little does my starlet nurse realise that that part of town has long since been deserted ever since the main square began selling pints for a pittance. Finally, something she didn't know!

Ebed is just about to leave when she recalls the one thing she is actually obliged to tell me: the King has requested I come into his presence.

"Are you ceremonially clean, Lodes Heddwen?"

"Sugar nurse and my one-time weaner, you know surely that I am."

"And have you ceremonially bathed, Lodes Heddwen?"

"I have, sweet maidservant. You were there."

"Oh, of course, Lodes Heddwen. Forgive my forgetfulness. My remembrance faculties are not what they once were, Lodes Heddwen. The days all blend together, if one knows what I mean."

"They do, I suppose. Ebed, could you be a darling and fetch me my lyre before you retire for the afternoon? I suspect Alk'erion took it and gave it to... herself... that she might find amusement, if such a phenomenon were possible."

"And should she not be wanting to return it, Lodes Heddwen?"

"Then tell her that my purposes far outweigh hers. Not an absolute fool, she should understand the implication and respond accordingly. Thank you, darling." Ebed scuttles from my quarters, then shimmies back thirty minutes later with the lyre. "My word, what happened to your hand? It is positively dreadful looking," I gasp, as blood runs like ribbons onto my floor.

"She put up resistance, Lodes Heddwen. I was not prepared for it. I had to break her nose, I am most afraid."

"Do not be, darling. She surely deserved it. She is a dreadful woman. Anyway, I am sure she has a plastic surgeon stapling on a new nose already. Do put some ice on that."

I dismiss her and give her the afternoon off—after she wipes the floor clean.

I had hoped that through Joxer, one of the only Laxciilians I describe as loyal and trust to carry out a task correctly, I could arrange to meet Benjamin at the café for tea before departing for our true mission. However, no one has seen him for days. I wonder if he joined the increasing number of disillusioned citizens and left on the sly.

No matter. I find Benjamin myself. Jealous stares burn on the faces of all my subjects when they see me holding such an elegant ornately designed lyre, yet when Benjamin sees me, he instantly blossoms and lightly remarks that I look as though I'm wearing a kimono, whatever that is.

"It is an essential robe for women to wear in the presence of my lord whilst in his private chamber, mounted in precious stones: agate, amethyst, beryl, chrysolite, emerald, jacinth, jasper, onyx, ruby, sapphire, topaz, and turquoise," I explain. I should not permit Benjamin access, but after I told him how I would spend my afternoon, he said he was curious to see a more sympathetic side to the Elder Elf. Add to that, should anything go awry, he wanted to be there to help me.

We take our tea with us as we cross the city to his apartment.

"Has word reached your ears of the most recent scandal of which I am at the centre?"

"Surely, Skylar, is has. It begs the question: Did you do it?" I grin.

"Yes," he says seriously, then stands stoic as a soldier.

"Your sense of humour, rarely as it is shown, might amuse me, Skylar, but I would not be in too great a hurry to say that again were I standing in your tenuous position."

"Has Mósandrirl searched the premises for foul play? I heard the prohibition on magic rule had been violated there in Efac, and he sees magical traces in colours. At least, I think he told me that some time ago. Saying it out loud, it just sounds made-up."

"Magic is not forbidden. It has been restricted. Some people have special privileges, limited though they are. And to answer your question, Mósandrirl was called away on business yesterday to help more Toad-people cross the Tanck Sea without getting eaten by the Lizard-Men. You are aware of this. You wrote him a Stay Safe card. It was adorable."

"You saw that, huh?" His face cutely reddens with embarrassment.

"You are ceremonially clean, darling, yes?" I ask him in the doorway of his room.

He thinks about it for a second, then understands what I mean. He laughs awkwardly, as though he has never been asked that before. Then he says he is. Hmm…

"And you have ceremonially bathed?"

He says he showered for an hour and clipped his finger- and toenails. Close enough.

Now I had already sent for manservant Erikk to fetch the required clothing for him. When Erikk arrived, I stood outside what Skylar calls Gideon's Gaff while he dressed. He emerges after a short moment attired in a blue ephod, decorated with gold filigree and four precious stones on each shoulder. A breast piece was also fashioned for the ephod: bright purple in colour, a span as long as it is wide, and folded double. On his feet, golden slippers of great elasticity that curl at the toe; and for his head, a turban decorated with a red-violet stone and a plump peacock feather. We don elbow-long gloves and horrid masks with black eyes and pointy noses, for none may enter the private quarters of the King, skin on display, and live.

Before we enter, I remind Benjamin of the situation:

"The King is a secret emissary. He often seeks counsel with Liriondias of the Triune with the aim of discovering their short-term plans, which the Resistance consequently upset by positioning figures in key locations or stirring dissention. Much of this communication has been achieved through a *Radharc*, activated by the spoken word of the King: '*Treoir a Shocrú*'. One consequence of his bravery and valiant pursuit of good is that the horse-headed spirit Fear has forged its way through the *Radharcs* and now torments him whenever it pleases. This most often happens when his paranoia of you peaks."

"That's awful," he says horrified and saddened. "And Fear does this? The actual manifestation of Fear?"

"You have seen it before. It is the final level of the Rink, the purple mist. The true Fear lies within this room, whilst the Triune have multiplied its essence and littered the Maze with its copies: in the heavens, on the roads, in its people. Now Benjamin, I must be strict, Papa's condition is classified information. Not even the Elder Wizard knows. The Elder Elf does not want him to... He feels ashamed, he says."

"This isn't all some elaborate ploy to get me alone in a dark room and arrest me for that explosion, is it?" he asks with a cheeky grin.

"Well, that would be tacky, and a waste of a perfectly good ephod."

My response is more than adequate to persuade him I can be trusted. He steps in front of me, pushes open the door, and permits me access.

The fireplace blazes but only a dim light emanates across the room. Worms and maggots wrinkle, sliver, and spread on every leaf and plant in every pot, vase or tree that springs up from between the tiles. All the chairs are overturned, the great table is split, and the candle holders are misshapen. The candle wax has been scrunched and stepped on by heavy feet.

Papa is heard long before he is seen. His fret. His peeve. His discontent. Melancholy. Screams. Morbid agony. His cackle. His bones breaking and healing and breaking some more. His song to the anonymous blonde woman on the torn fabric banner overlooking the fireplace:

"Of orcs I have slain not thousands
But tens of thousands,
So too of mammal, sea creature, and man.
I am a guardian of this dusty world.

Honour, pride, and wealth I justly deserve.

A brave and mighty warrior,
Well-spoken, lean, and strong,
After all these millennia,
Still the purest Laxciilian.

So tell me, O Hela,
How he kills my spirit dead;
Sends my courage down to the pit of dread.

O tell me, sweet Hela!
Why I see him in the purple mist,
Sword searing my heart,
Feasting on my flesh and trampling on my bones!

Progeny of perne and gyre!
He is a liar! Forget not pyre! He is the Darkness incarnate!
Driving me to madness! Filling me with hate!
O Hela! Fill me with vengeance divine!
Vanquish this shade with my glory's shine!
Surrender him into palm mine
So that he will die!"

I throw my eyes to Benjamin. His face invisible beneath the mask, I can only judge his sculpture-still physique. He appears unmoved, though doubtless he knows the portents of the lyric are about him.

"What are you thinking?"

"That there's a very fine line between desire and detestation."

Papa hangs in the black corner of the stone ceiling. His skin is ghastly and bruised; his hair white; his eyes hideous, swollen, and black. The Silent Monks try to beckon my Lord to come down, but it will take more than urgent hand gestures and the occasional five-centimetre jump. A shadowy black spirit bounces from wall to wall, gnashing curses and encouraging Papa to take the most non-sanctimonious paths.

As always, when the spirit is upon him, I play the lyre. Then relief comes upon Papa. Typically, as his condition improves, he scales lower down the wall, though today's progress is slow. Atypical too, today, the spirit addresses not only my Lord, but all of us:

"The King I know very well. His servants are no strangers. The Silent Monks I would go as far to say are my friends. Even your name, O Lyre Player, is plain to me." Then it turns to Benjamin. "But who are *you?*"

Its eyes roll back in its head—or rather, they would if it had eyes or a head—and it must cross-examine Skye's profile with what all the other versions of ABC 6-5-1-18 9-20-19-5-12-6 have seen. They are, after all, the same spirit, divided and subdivided and distributed all across the Maze.

The spirit assumes an equine shape and must get its answer, because it says: "Ah, yes! So it is you! I have heard great and dastardly things…"

In a moment of inexplicable recognition, Papa's eyes bulge from their sockets and he leaps from a great height, draws three spears, and tries to pin us to the wall. Benjamin saves me each time. Then Papa charges towards us like a madman, overpowering every Monk in his way. I claw off my mask in the hope he will see sense, or that I may plead for mercy, I know not which. But no words come out, and his pace remains constant.

Then Benjamin picks up a spear, and— "NO!" I scream—wallops Papa across the jaw and he falls to the ground, senseless and out cold.

"Skye! You cannot strike a King in this realm without reaping the death penalty upon your head! The only reason the Monks will not have you quartered or stoned in the streets is because I am accountable for you here today!"

The Monks take Papa in their arms and strap him with metal plates into bed. I resume playing the lyre. And the evil spirit leaves him and returns to its hiding place behind the blonde woman on the fabric banner.

All the while, Benjamin is silent; his expression secret behind the horrible pointy nose, great green cheeks, and black planet eyes, until eventually, without warning or speaking, he leaves.

I turn to the head Silent Monk.

"Ozymandias, will you accept my humblest apologies on the behalf of the Triumvir? He did not know what he was doing, not really. He is a Man—a race of simpletons—and, by and large, ignorant of our ways."

The head monk removes his massive hood only to reveal stitches and scars where there should be eyes. Golly! Did Papa do that, or did he remove them himself? He faces me coldly. He has no respect for my office or crown or position, because he knows he outranks me every time on the basis of what hangs between his legs.

"You have a birthday coming up soon, don't you, princess?" He asks it with a smirk and his tone is one of intimidation and threat.

"We live every day on repeat, darling. I have not had a—"

"I know you count the days, missy. I know how you celebrate it, who you celebrate it with, and your star-counting tradition. Nothing you do is secret to my Order. The same is true for his activities," he says of Skye.

"As I have already told you, I was accountable for whatever he did today—"

"And accounts will soon be settled. Princess," he nods, then shoves me out the door and slams it shut; my Papa crying out madly from the back of the room.

# 9

# SOMETHING WICKED THIS WAY COMES

*"A storm's brewing. …. Yeah, we're on the Lane now. I'll be home in a minute. Ciao."*
*Roop hangs up the phone and insults his mother under his breath. I can tell by his*
*breathy snicker that he expects me to laugh, but that is not happening. He asks if I had*
*fun.*

*"Our walk to the carnival was most enjoyable." Then I smile that smile that*
*signifies restraint. "And the remainder of the evening was peaceful and quiet."*

*"All hail Benjamin-Joshua, Prince of the Land of Passivo Aggressivo!"*
*bellows Inner, who then pulls out a trumpet that wakens every child in a five-block*
*radius.*

*The carnival was hardly a blast; far from it. But Roop already knew that. He*
*knew he invited other kids along who hate me. He knew I had no idea what they were*
*talking about half the time. He revelled silently in his rudeness whenever I made an effort*
*to join in on their conversations, and they'd all pretend not to have heard me. I was*
*literally invited to hold onto their change whenever they went on the fast rides just because*
*they were too thick to wear jackets with zipped pockets, and I was too short to ride the*
*good amusements.*

*But Roop, emotional manipulator that he is, pushes me for an answer. Finally,*
*I give him one in what must be our first honest, raw tête-à-tête.*

*"To tell the truth, I felt lonely. Embarrassed. And used." I don't know what*
*"used" means, but it sounds good.*

*"Well, I had fun," he says cockily, then sticks his arrow-head nose up to high*
*Heaven.*

*"I should hope so, given that your existence was acknowledged. This was*
*supposed to be a Troop night. Thomas and Roop. No one else." That's meant in the*
*most unselfish way possible.*

*"Not Fatty-Mc-Fat-Fat Toni, the Screw-bald brothers and Paige," Inner*
*chimes in. "You're supposed to be my best friend, not theirs!" Inner's close to pushing him*
*off the curb.*

*"I didn't throw away an entire evening just so I could be nudged by your*
*cronies, creamed off as a coat-hanger, and get my face painted by a suicidal clown!" I yell.*

*"No one told you to get your face painted by a clown."*

*"He looked lonely, too. I felt sorry for him."*

*"Well, you shouldn't have. If anything, I feel sorry for you. You look a right*
*state. He did a hack-up job with that red paint."*

*"He didn't paint my face red. It's a rash. I'm allergic to face paint!"*

*"Why would you—?"*

"Because I'd rather get hurt than stand alone and embarrassed. Because I prefer pain to invisibility. I'm telling you, next time we meet up, you'd better talk to me, or—"

"Or what?" He looks at me pitiably. He knows he has all the power in this relationship.

"Or I'll stop talking to you." It falls flat before I've even finished saying it.

"Ooh, great comeback. Good luck with that one." He knows I'm a loner. He knows I need him. That nothing short of an atomic detonation is going to send me running, no matter how awfully he treats me.

"My mom said I deserved a better friend than you."

"Tough words, Mrs. C. But while we're exchanging home stories, my mom told me that you're responsible for the One-Armed Man's accident." (Dang it). "And everyone thinks you're such a nice guy! A goody-goody-two-shoes. It would be an awful shame if people found out what you were really capable of, you dirty little hypocrite." He'd tell people too. I know he would. If he hasn't already. "Tell me, did you cry? Did you apologise? Did you show any remorse?"

"Breathe. Just breathe. Keep breathing. And don't cry," Inner chanted.

"Ooh, Thomas. You've gone quiet on me all of a sudden. I do hope I haven't struck a nerve. Answer me this, sweet Thomas, did the One-Armed Man hate you only after you made pork chops out of him, or was he always repulsed by the sight of your dwarfism and that irritating squirrel squeak you call a voice?"

"Shut up," I mumble. My cheeks swell like balloons, and my right hand forms a fist and vibrates. Inner hooks Roop's snaky smirk and knocks a couple teeth out.

"Careful, angel. Next you'll be swearing."

"Shut your flipping face!"

"Huh?" he taunts, melodramatically taken aback. "A de-handed dad. The assist in a couple criminal offences. And now a loose tongue. Gosh, there's no Benjy left. Wouldn't it be such a shame if Momma Bear caught wind of all her Golden Boy's secrets?" And, irrespective of how vilifying his role in events, he'd disclose every iota of information in a heartbeat. Just out of spite; just for the laughs.

We walk up the road silently, now begrudging the closeness of our homes, and turn to our respective driveways, as thick rain clouds gather on the horizon. And then I have a thought that stops me in my tracks. I turn and call to him with confidence:

"Rupert Lucifer Samson!"

"My middle name is Gabriel, but go on."

"Threaten me again, and I will destroy you."

And there's a look in his eye—for no longer than a second, but it's there—that tells me he knows I'm serious. But the villain shakes it off, hoping I can't make out the sudden fearful gulp in his throat amidst the twilight and gentle thunder.

"With what? A cryptic text message containing a really bad word, signed off with an anonymous blue B?"

I don't reply, firstly, because I'm rubbish at comebacks; and secondly, because he's right. But also, the spoken word, the threats I make—the threat I pose—should be *more powerful than a display of that power. Instead, I flash him a smile and rhyme, "I spy with my little eye something beginning with 'die'", and to say I have never seen a look of terror shiver through him more than in this moment. His fear is so delicious it's kissable.*

*That was the first time I ever saw the childhood sociopath afraid up to that point. Little was I to know he would never look that afraid again until The Incident, the day he died.*

I wake to another mighty clash in a battle that has raged for hours between the Elder Wizard and the Wraith, the same one who blew Aurora and me to Kingdom Come not all that long ago. How I fell asleep during the carnage at all, I have no idea. The flames and the flashes illuminate outside. The weatherman pummels his might against the city's barrier while the wizard does everything in his power to fend him off.

It makes my skirmish with Dol'ver and the prince in the shack look like child's play. I turn and stare as the thick grey clouds slot into one another like jigsaw pieces, blocking out the night's white orb. Pale stars pepper what's left of the sky, but I see few and their twinkling is irregular. They spend more time switched off than doing their job.

In this, the dark night of my soul, I allow Roop to goad me for hours about my crimes, my fears, and my futile future. As I cannot gather the strength to contend, he is bored. When he leaves, it is on his terms—I am not all that entertaining tonight. I just lie here and listen to the eternal cacophonous thunder applaud its primitive friend lightning. The cloudy boulders continue to spit rain like venomous fangs. It never lets up, not once. Darts of water ping off my window. The stars continue to go out.

The Laxciilians had supper early tonight. Forbade to wine and dine until all hours as they usually do, the early birds queued in the courtyard and received doggy bags of snacks and drinks. When the last bag had been distributed, everyone was sent to their houses or rentals and the King announced curfew. All the elves are probably hogged around their windows surveying the elemental warfare and making in-house bets.

I, on the other hand, never had much interest in battles. Even in History class, I was more interested in why so-and-so went to war and how so-and-so came to be so-and-so's to begin with, but not in the military side of things.

Tonight, I am protected behind my glass cage, safe and sound, as oblivious as I choose to be. Untouchable. And free to plot.

Alone at the breakfast table, between committing the great offence of gluttony on fruit pyramids, cakes, and wheat meal, I decide to pay the wizard a visit. He defeated the Wraith, but almost perished himself, bless his heart. He's not as fiddle fit as he once was, and that's the truth.

Laxciilian and non-native elves, gnomes, werewolves, Toad-men, oracles, fauns, and Crab-men sit at segregated tables, their curious and cruel eyes locked on me. I don't know what the fauns' qualm is. They wouldn't even know that the lockdown was lifted had I not gone out of my way this morning to tell them; I didn't see any Laxciilians rushing across the meadow to divulge the fact that streets could be walked down and food eaten without the threat of getting shot at.

An hour of this is all I can take before their rudeness becomes too toxic for my heart, and I've just decided to up and leave when suddenly the Elder Elf enters the dining-hall. Everyone stops what they're doing and stands solemnly to attention, more out of fear than respect. I am relieved not to be the sole name on his hit-list today. His snake eyes sink fangs into a few Laxciilians: one dressed in blue and gold; a dark-haired one dressed in red velvet; and a few others I cannot make out over the ridiculously shaped heads of some of these creatures.

His narrow eyes then trace along the empty stage and the tail of his wine-red robe slithers down the aisle and up the steps. Scurrying, the members of the Assembled clear out.

He eyes me and tilts his head like he thinks I have something to say.

"Busy day?" That's the best I've got. I usually pre-plan my conversations, so I'm all out of juice.

"The usual: saving Angoria, one kingdom at a time from her most prominent threats." There's no doubt about it: he means me.

"Do you not think it is a little cheeky to take advantage of the wizard's comatose state by trying to strengthen your grip over the magical community? I mean, he almost died protecting Loux Laxciila."

"You mispronounced 'Loux'. Silent X." I try again. "Silent O, too."

Okay, fair enough. I'll give him that one—I have been here too long to mispronounce the kingdom's name, so I blame it on his intimidating aura. (I'm confident that I usually say it correctly). It's like foreigners being in Ireland for six months and still calling it "Irlanda" and thinking that it's part of the United Kingdom!

A lethargic tone to his voice, notably less sophistication to his dress, and pupils so bloodshot, it is a miracle they are still open wide, the King must have had a restless night. Dare I say he looks indolent? I do hope the whole Lapping up the Life of Luxury-thing hasn't finally gotten to him. Hence, it takes me by surprise when he springs suddenly and slithers down the stage steps and out the front door faster than a hand could catch him.

I make tracks after that, but no sooner have I reached the front door of the Healing House when I say to myself, *Ah, sure, the old man's in a coma. He won't feel upset if he goes without company for a day or two. He'll be grand, so he will.* Instead, this is a morning for study, so I dash to the library and hit a copious number of Anglophonic books hard, as well as books which Mósandrirl's interpretation spell enables me to translate. A defeated undead Wraith is not the same thing as a dead Wraith—or a dead undead Wraith—

251

and I need to know what I'm up against in case he makes his way in here again.

Literature explains that this Wraith is the first of his kind. A mortal man who lived in Laxciila, he is renowned as the First Murdered in Angoria. The first victim of Gideon—formerly his best friend—this mortal man was slain long before there was an Afterlife for fallen heroes and peaceable citizens to enter. No record of his original name exists, and seven commentators across thirteen volumes estimate that he probably does not remember it himself. His most common alias, though, is Malachi Dartport; a name he adopted for a time in honour of the first man he killed.

One text says that the First Murdered gave heroism a try for a couple weeks but, desperately lonely living out his un-life as a silent sightless ghost, he swiftly went mad and put wicked efforts in place to ensure that he wouldn't be "oh so alone" on the Other Side anymore.

My favourite document on the subject is very splashy and jam-packed full of colourful pictures on the Wraith, so he must have got over being "sightless". This document is also the only one that adds, unsurprisingly, that the Wraith has harboured an intense hatred of that same Dark Lord who killed him. In fact, he often publicly endorses other Dark Lord hosts, leads their armies into battle, makes slaves of his enemies and forces them to do hard labour and build sky-high monuments to the despots, exclusively on the basis that they are not Gideon. Why the Triune want to resurrect Gideon then, confuses me. Maybe they think they can control him if they get to him first. He's sure to be a little groggy after being tormented by injurious spells in his suspended animated state for so long.

I read on. The first Wraith has abilities the other wraiths do not, namely limited weather control. Cooler still, he can float on the winds he summons—not to mention that spinning-top, tornado-legs thing. His not so unique talents include: shooting balls of lightning from his hands; literally sucking the life out of someone so that they become wraiths, too; and merging with shadows so that he appears... well, invisible. He is invulnerable to physical and psychic attack, though his form has limited physical properties when he so chooses to carry something, arm himself, or whatnot.

When I ask him about the villain, the librarian (a modern-day Norman Bates, occupying a deserted building everyone else bypasses without a second thought) stutteringly says that the Elder Wizard has killed two wraiths in his several millennia-long career of peace-making. And that's a record. It would help if Norman Bates could tell me how Mósandrirl accomplished these great feats since the wizard is not in a position to brag on himself right now, but that would make life too easy, and we wouldn't want that, now would we?

Not entirely useless, though, Norman Bates does direct me to a mammoth-sized volume, *Judgement and Salvation: A Collection of the Predictions of Minor and Major Prophets—Book III* compiled by K'k'ko Zset. According to one ancient thinker, there is a legend that foretells the casting of an armament forged in black fire, a weapon so great it could finish off the immortal marquis, and all other immortals, too. I am sure that weapon is the one the wizard and the princess retrieved from the cave.

Finding the princess is a top priority then, since the wizard is out of commission. Hopefully she knows where the weapon is. But I make a pit-stop first...

I'm not sure why, specifically—to create added suspense to our impending doom, perhaps. For the thrill of living life on the edge? Unlikely. Maybe I just want to humanise the poor devil and hope to God I find a reason not to kill him. But irrespective of the beautiful day that has blossomed despite the turbulence of the night, still I shiver outside what was, epochs ago, the Wraith's house.

The building reminds me of Glenveagh Castle, only its slabs are silver and shiny. Though nowhere near as elaborate as virtually every other edifice on the island, for the first time yet, I feel a sense of home or belonging, like a piece of Ireland just popped up and said, "Here I am! Proud to be Irish! Hugs all round!" with a possible hashtag somewhere in there.

The near-silent swish of a green coat behind a wall up ahead breaks my trance. Pity for the sneaker that I specialise in silences and the unsaid. I turn, planning to run like there's no tomorrow and get, make, or imitate myself a weapon.

But before I can move, I hear a screechy whirl against a thunderous hurricane wind and lightning clatter. The Wraith has entered the city and leaves devastation in his wake.

Now I've never had a vision before—besides that shared premonition experience with the shrew—but that is the only word I can use to describe what I see next...

[Elsewhere, in the dungeon of the Triune's castle in the Black Sands, a prisoner of Lear's was dreaming of the very same thing Benjamin was seeing in a vision. This dreamer was of the Race of Men and had come from the Earthen Star on the same night as Benjamin. This is what they saw...]

*The Wraith, like Botticelli's Zephyrus, had pale skin and wide deep eyes that drank heavy gulps of light, and consequently drowned it in black salivary darkness. His features were white, their outline blue. As he moved, his body, head, and arms were visible, but his lower half twizzled like a tornado and spat electric sparks.*

*When he arrived in front of the palace, he came to a stop. No longer moving at such an excessive pace, he moved like a damaged H.B.: forwards, backwards, left, right. Really very jagged, he was caught between movements and moments just as he was caught between this world and the next.*

*He saw an elf, dressed in blue and gold, and yawned, "Treason." Before the elf could draw his sword, a fatal ball of lightning was thrown. The elf's skeleton lit up like an X-ray. Sooty grey smoke sizzled off his corpse and cloak as he dropped to the ground.*

*There cried a little child nearby. Whether this was the progeny of the fallen, a child abandoned in the hustle and the fear, or just a random child on their way to their friend's house, was unclear.*

*The Wraith came nearer.*

*The flowing tears, choked sobs, and stringy snot sniffles stopped.*

*The child slowly raised his head and stared into the contemptible creature's hollow sagged face, looking for life, or meaning, or... someone. He gave the murderer a hug, looking for some kind of solace or support and blew his nose on the ghost's robes. After a few seconds of this, the boy stepped back and blankly observed the Wraith's face.*

*The vile man offered the child a single gift: a ball of white-hot electricity.*

*The child gazed, tempted, but declined; then stopped crying.*

*The Wraith snuffed the gift, then simply went away.*

*Outside the Department of Justice, a block away from the Court Room, he moaned, "This one caused political upset" and tossed a magnesium-white sphere with blue barbed-wire sparks. Another Laxciilian dropped dead. By the Western Pond where blissfully unaware elves boat-rid, picnicked, and sported, a third victim, a purported thief, died. This one had a wife and young family. His wife bypassed his scraggy dark hair and melted skin and went straight for his red robes, golden rings, and silver teeth. The robes and rings she put on and the silver teeth she put in. Then she walked away.*

*The Wraith's long stringy hair webbed across his face and—bored out of his wits—he forced a laugh. Passers-by from far-off places chucked apples at him. The clever Laxciilians fled for their lives. Some Elven guards fired arrows, none of which made an impact. Shattered arrow heads strewed the golden streets and bloodied the bold bare feet of unsuspecting people like glass shards.*

*The Wraith stood unchallenged and considered all the carnage he had made. And he saw that it was good. And at the sound of a storm, he tornadoed from the scene and flashed like a star, then sought out the last two names on his list.*

*A girl that both boys care for deeply!*

*And the boy who was standing outside the Wraith's house at that very moment...*

I have an outbreak of goosebumps like acne. My hairs chill and stand. The whizzing sound of a tornado stops. I know the ghoul is behind me.

Fetch asks, "Did the oracles send you here to kill me? I never trusted those scraggy-haired geezers. It was the blue tattoos that turned me off them initially. Not to mention the way the five of them have only one sense each. Freaks."

"Hello!" I greet. "Are you here to kill me?" The Wraith says nothing. His silence makes my skin crawl like a slimy worm down an oozy hole. "'I will tread on the cobra and the lion; I will crush the fierce young lion and trample on the dragon'."

He looks at me coldly. "Dark One…"

"You."

"Kneel…"

"Poor sap," Fetch says. "Benjamin Thomas kneels to no one."

"I will bow to my opponent as a common courtesy, but I will not kneel."

The Wraith shoots a small bolt at my chest. I fall to one knee. "Kneel…"

"I won't fight you." I tear off my crown and throw it in the air before it roars angry red flames. "You were a man once, weren't you? Just a normal man who lived a normal life and did normal things with normal people." The Wraith spins like a drill and at the slightest touch I'm lifted maybe four metres into the air. I crash-land on the hard grass, but without delay get up again. "You had a conscience. Codes by which you lived. Friends you did life with. A family who adored the ground you walked on. Hobbies you enjoyed. A favourite brand of toilet paper you always bought even though it was more expensive. Until one night, you were murdered. It wasn't your fault. You were just a normal man living your normal life going for a normal walk to your normal home via the normal route, and for the first time in your normal life, something unpredictable happened. And suddenly, you were no longer a man."

"No'me," he says.

I continue, "And the ones who should have foreseen it, or should have had a solution, were blindsided. Caught unawares. Left stunned. And, poor soul, you had nowhere to go. And *this*"—I gesture to him from top to bottom— "became your new normal: the paranormal, the unnatural."

He mutters, "Nmorrrrrr…"

"Their solution came too late; their solution being me. They drafted me in of their own volition to put to justice the Dark One who treated you so unfairly and, should the need arise, to vanquish you. I mean, that is sick. You epitomise the Maze. You are a man out of time, utterly displaced, a victim of the moral degeneracy of your world, just like every citizen of Angoria trapped in those Blocks and Domes. You are a microcosmic manifestation of my macrocosmic destiny. Gosh, I came to save these people, and they hate me—I think the only person I should be saving in this kingdom is you! We've both been played for fools. Just as the Higher Orders assigned me to kill folks like you and planted me here amongst haters, so too the Triune sent you to finish me off, so they can resurrect your murderer."

This is clearly news to him. Well, I'll speak for as long as he'll listen: "They've pit us against one another like this face-off is incumbent. But it isn't. And if it starts, it won't stop. It never stops. Not when the deed is done. Not when you close your eyes. Not when you sleep. Not when you think you've just about forgotten it. Not even the next time your life is on the line—the next *incident*—and you trick yourself into thinking you can justify killing all over again. So, let's stop. Let's stop the violence, the dying, the hurt, the pain, the killing, the cycle. They say that "the Tapestry never stops weaving", but it does, *if* we take a step back from the loom."

At this point, the Wraith roars, "NO MORE!!!"

Since I'm now confident that I know the answer, I ask, "Have they told you they're trying to bring him back? That they're looking for his tomb? Gideon's?"

He replies, "Do *not* say his name…!"

"I'll take that as a no," Fetch surmises. The Wraith's eyes widen like a skeleton's and his robes flutter. He's going for the kill.

Just then, a hooded stranger in a green coat jumps between us and faces the Wraith. (I'd almost forgotten about him). His arms stretch out like a cross. "We finally meet, beast. Tell me, how did we spend so long pillaging this earth without running into each other?"

"Green Coat is all confidence," Fetch narrates. "I don't like it."

"Wh-who are you?" I ask.

The Wraith answers, "I am the First... the Last... and... the Power..." I don't have the heart to tell him that I wasn't asking him, so I just smile politely. Suddenly, the Wraith waves farewell to the tornado legs and his robed lower half appears. He's here to stay. His long white hair stretches in all directions, drawn like magnets to the wind. Some locks slide across his face, at times covering one of his eyes. Forks of blue lightning surround him protectively. His big lips pull his jaws into a tight smile, as though held in place with clothes pegs. "Die now..." he says in a droning voice before hurling forks of blue lightning at us. Much to my surprise, however, nothing happens. Upon closer examination, I conclude that Green Coat's long glistening outstretched blade must have absorbed or deterred the attack.

"Impossible!" shouts the undead thing.

"Oh, very possible," says the newcomer. "This blade was formed by a shard of the Nagari Prism."

"Fair enough," says Fetch, before thinking it over. "It wouldn't also, by any chance, have been forged in black fire?" Fetch walks on and surveys Green Coat's face and then mine. "There's a strange similarity between you two, aside from your total lack of long legs and his lack of blue clothes."

I don't have time to verify this before the cavalry arrives. They silently climb onto the roof of the Wraith's one-time home and surround the perimeter. Arrays of expert and lazily planned arrows fire at the ghoul. He must be able to sense them, because he turns his head full circle and creates a light purple electromagnetic force field which sends the arrows bouncing in all directions. A few splints nearly stab my booted feet. The Wraith turns his attentions to the archers on the ground, claps his hands, and sends a ripple effect through the air that pushes them over. He throws them a few magnesium-coloured lightning balls for good measure. The obvious fate befalls them.

The apparition throws more bolts in Green Coat's direction, though much too high to do him any damage. Then it hits me—he's aiming for the building behind Green Coat. I jump in front of Green Coat and push him out of the way of mass chunks of the Glenveagh-lookalike debris. We're both flour-sack-thick in dust and sport scratches, but neither of us is fatally injured.

Our enemy tornadoes over to me and chokes me with an outstretched hand. No elves come to my rescue, either because they fear for their lives or because they think he will do a better job offing me than they ever could. Rather than focus on the pain, I just imagine my oesophagus bruising in purple and brown patches. Pain can be oh, so beautiful if we just focus on its colours.

Before I pass out for the hundredth time this adventure, Green Coat stabs the creature in the hind leg with a wide dagger, and in the back with the sword.

Wheezing and near-voiceless though I am after that choke, I shout, "Stop! You're killing him!" Green glares, aghast. "What? I feel bad for murderers. Now, back off!" He doesn't. "No more death! Please! Enough!

This violence will not stand. Do you hear me?!" I demand, though I still haven't recovered my breath.

Soon the scene is cluttered with swords, arrows, lightning, and rubble. Any Laxciilians who get involved get killed. Fetch gets involved, too; he's biting arms, tripping people up, wrapping his legs around people's necks and somersaulting them to the ground, and tearing people in half. I knew he was unhinged, but I didn't realise he was capable of such savagery.

Eventually, Green gets arrogant and makes a thrust for the ghoul that could only ever have had one result—the spectre buries his phantasmal arm in Green's body and grabs his heart.

Suddenly Fetch stands still and gets a distant look in his eye. He speaks like he's reading from a movie script: "Black Cloak who killed the goblins that had earlier trapped Benjamin appears. Black Cloak's face is concealed beneath a horrid evil mask. From head to toe, Black Cloak is garbed in the most primordial blackness, darkness from the Deep. Some consider Black Cloak to be black like the night, but that is unkind to Night for it offers the promise of beauty: the moon, the stars, the dawn, a new beginning. This shifty phantom offers only hopelessness and despair. Black Cloak lavishly bathes the Wraith in fire like lava and leaps to the right and disappears. The Wraith's scorched skin looks like a hive of the most hideous spider bites: raw; a mixing bowl of red and brown and bone, all tinted with that haunting blue. His lips melt into a paste, sealed. Green Cloak is not entirely sure what he saw, only that his heart is in exactly the right place now."

I don't have a bull's notion what was meant by any of that, only that that is a very accurate description of the current state of the Wraith and Green.

Next the princess enters the scene from the right, followed at a short distance by the Elder Elf. Her eyes are clear; she's in her right mind, then. "Oh, my! What disaster has befallen Malachi Dartport's house? It is ruined! Whatever happened here?" She freezes when she sees the historical site littered with corpses, and hears the heavy gasps, in between the screechy whistles of the resilient Wraith.

"Oh, the Dark One is here. Well, that explains it," says the King.

Aurora hops the wall and circumspectly tiptoes across the grass. "Golly, Malachi, you have returned home," she says to the spirit.

The Elder Elf sets his sights on Green. "What in the name of Hela are you doing here?"

Green replies mock-politely, "My liege, what in the name of Hela took you so long to get here?"

"I do not answer dogs."

"Perhaps Mósandrirl did not tell you, I have been called in to fight the Darkness in a more... official role. Less vigilante vagabond-style."

"How are you still alive?"

"Oh, it takes more than casting me into an eternally collapsing star to keep me away from the Shining City. You have redecorated. I do not like it. How is your wife?" Green makes an obscene licking gesture. Mehkabikil flutters his eyes in disgust.

"Still off the market."

"From which you paid a handful of copper coins, right? Or did you purchase her with blackmail? I forget..."

I take advantage of their distracted state to speak to the tortured and suffering Wraith: "Malachi, keep your eyes on me. Focus. Relax. Breathe."

"How did you get in here?" Mehkabikil asks very loudly. "I will not ask again."

"Your daughter let me in. Yet another woman in your life who prefers my rugged good looks and way of doing things to yours, I suppose."

Green nods to the embarrassed princess. Head bowed, she awaits a strict and painful punishment. Not waiting around for the Elder Elf to give her one, I tightly grip her arm and throw her behind me. Arms outstretched like I've been crucified, I shield her from any potential outburst from the King, but my eyes remain glued on the Wraith. I try to remain calm to reassure him that he's safe now.

The she-elf hits me a couple of times for defending her against an attack that never came—and against her will—before walking over to the villain-turned-victim. "Control your breathing, sweetheart. Steady your pulse. You are home. Nothing bad will happen to you here. You are safe now."

I chime in, "Come on, Malachi. Stand down. It's over. Show the Triune that they do not own you; that you are no pawn in their sick, twisted game—a game they must surely know they have already lost."

Mehkabikil rolls his eyes at me—well, I'm not looking in his direction, but I assume he does. "Look at the trouble you have caused, worm. You knew that I was chairing the meeting of the Assembled to decide your fate, and you took advantage of not only my absence, but that of the highly esteemed Elder Wizard. I am one with Loux Laxciila…" He carries on with this twaddle in the most excessive, hyperbolic language I've heard for a while. "When I felt the earth move and the air change, I had hoped most sincerely that you were not at the epicentre of it. But alas, you are, again! Mex Confetricus!" He very unsubtly eyes the Wraith at this point, egging him on so that he grows increasingly unnerved and agitated.

"Enough of this drivel," Fetch says. He makes a gun gesture with his hand and blows the monarch's brains out, not that it accomplishes much.

"You don't believe that—" I begin.

"Silence! Though it must come as a startle, there are some concerns so close to my heart that they dwarf your proclivity for feigned gullibility and your incessant need for attention. You are the Dark Lord! You will always be the Dark Lord! You are as cursed as a hanged man on a tree and as pollutant as vermin to everything you put your hand to, and on the day of your reckoning, swine, only microbes will gather to mourn you!"

The Wraith has heard all he needs to hear—or rather, all Mehkabikil wants him to hear. I plead, "No, no, no. Don't listen to him."

The defeated foe rises to his feet once more and roars, "Deceiver! Manipulator! Mex Confetricus!" and unleashes his full fury on as many of us as he can, and the losses outweigh the survivors.

# 10
# HAPPY BIRTHDAY

Another fabulous midmorning in Loux Laxciila. How grotesque.

Having used up all my breakfast calories during a three-hour training session at the Rink and studying up on toadflax, jacklebeet, and ogres with Aurora at the library, I treat myself to a detox from world-saving prep and social interaction. But my plans for some alone time on a park bench are swiftly disrupted by the kingdom's two greatest gossips, Starfish and Whale. How they tracked me to this amenity, I have no idea, but at this point, I wouldn't be surprised to discover they are in the King's employ, hired to spy on me whenever they are not getting their hair done.

The grittier tougher-looking Starfish's hair has been shaved and snipped back to seven spikes, the likes of which a rock band disciple might sport. Three are orange, three are purple, and the one in the centre is black. To cover the bald spot that makes his forehead gigantic, he wears a hairband with a fake unicorn horn. Basically, he looks like an octopus punk-rocker. The only thing he's missing is "McLeather" stitched into his jacket. Whale, on the other hand, looks like he's been thrown into a washing-machine with a Joker card and Spidey's arch-enemy, the Green Goblin. His nightdress and nightcap are purple, his clown shows are yellow and curly at the toe, and his cheeks have been painted green and dotted red.

They usually slander anybody who is anyone, including me, and try fiercely though unsuccessfully to eke a reaction, but today, they remain perfectly silent. As bad as nasty blether is for my heart, I trust their silence less. Suddenly, there is a murmur from nearby. Rosencrantz and Guildenstern (actually, those are better names for them) spring into sentry formation like they belong to a meerkat clan and suppress wicked knowing smiles.

"What is it?" I ask, interested more in satisfying my curiosity than mollifying their lust for drama.

"The Hooded Scribes," they chime in their shortest-ever sentence. I don't get it. I shake my head. "The Silent Monks of the Elvish Law." At the risk of stating the obvious: they don't sound silent. "They are passing judgement." They bare their teeth and gnash and grin.

I leap forward and sprint to what began as a feint chant but is now a death sentence; and though they do not follow me, the gossips' cackles louden the further I run, not quieten. And then I arrive at what must be the busiest road in the kingdom.

*"The criminal has aligned with the Adam-Son,*
*Eons ago predicted the Dark One.*
*She put our Master in grave danger*
*By leading the Dark One to his chamber!"*

Dozens of goony costumes howl, fist-pump, and cheer with ugly toothy faces, toadying the Pharisaic judge, jury, and executioners; all men of strong build and medium height garbed in black cloaks that bear the propagandist symbol of the Elven King—his Snake Eyes. The Monks stand around in a semi-circle about six metres from a beautiful and ragged figure; teary-eyed but resilient; regal but undone; powerful but like a carnivorous animal caught in a snapping metal trap seeped of its strength, now the prey. And for the first time yet, she smells less like strawberries and lemons, but prevalently of fear.

*"The criminal has turned on Loux Laxciila!*
*The Council of Monks agree: We cannot redeem her!"*

Gosh, just when I thought the verses couldn't get any worse. Go back to not speaking, Monkey Boys.

I push my way to the front of the queue of savagery-seeking spectators, and her eyes catch mine. "It is true, Skye. I have brought shame to my people. I will pay the price," she weeps. I ignore her.

"'Council', you say?" I call out, my impassioned run now diluted to a confident walk. "You look more like a Cult of Mebakakeel to me." I realise I said his name wrong, so before anyone notices, I smugly add, "Or whatever his name is." Fetch pinches someone's fez and pops it on his head, and suggests I whip someone's bowtie, but I put him on mute.

*"You dare insult the Master!*
*You must indeed be dull!*
*The Fates depurate you, be it ever so severely.*
*Monks! Stone the elf-wretch! Shatter her skull!"*

She drops her head to the beady desert dust and covers her face. And I bend down in front of her and draw a square around us.

*"By the Supreme Silent Monk of the Pyramid Temple Paragon,*
*The wench has been found guilty!*
*Her contact with your innate uncleanliness has rendered her*
*Corrupted! An infidel! Filthy!*
*Dark One, your days are numbered, but our war is not with you.*
*Now remove yourself from the line of fire.*
*The Order of Ozymandias said: MOVE!"*

Within each side of the square, I write a *Tau* with my finger, then I straighten up. "I don't know much about your rules, but honestly, I like rules. Rules make the world go round. Eternal contract before emotional contact. Power before people. Framework before friends. Imperatives before interests. Relationships before rules, that's where it all gets messy. So, okay, if she's legally yours, go on. Have your way with her. Throw and stone and shatter and batter and kill. Do what you need to do. On one condition. Just one. One teeny-tiny-itsy-bitsy-little-condition."

*"You delay the inevitable.*
*We grow tiresome—"*

"And I am tingling at the thought of how you were going to make that rhyme, but last time I checked, I WAS TALKING! (Where was I?) ... Ah, yes. *Just one.* One hoop to jump through. One stipulation. Can you do that? One!" I am on my feet and I am riled up and bouncing! And I take their silence for a "Proceed". *"Think about who it is you're dealing with.* You say I'm the Mex Confetricus, the Twelfth Dark Lord, the Destroyer, the Harbinger of Darkness. That I am the boogieman who haunts your nightmares; the shadow that trails your footsteps late at night, stalking you, but invisible when you turn around; the monster who hides under your children's beds; that face you see in the mirror one second that isn't there the next. That I am in and of myself death; a mystical sphere of malefic energy, the spawn of conflicting buffeting pernes and gyres. That I will reduce your world to ash and make history end... That's it. My one and only requirement is that you just think about that. Now, if any of you is without fear of my wrath, let him be the first to throw a stone at her."

At this, I stoop down and fix my eyes on her. I hear the motley crowd's feet shuffle away first, then the Monks, until only the criminal remains, wet eyes cemented shut, kneeling in a pit of dust dry as a sack of bones. I smile, rise, and lift her up.

"Where did everybody go?"

She's lost for words.

"You saved me from the trolls, Edgar, and Alk'erion, the Wraith, and when I manoeuvred you out of the way of oncoming spears, it was your instrumental talent that chased the spirit away. That's a lot of debt to repay," I wink and walk away.

[Aurora]

In my room hang many mirrors. Big mirrors, small mirrors, circular mirrors; mirrors with diamond frames, gold frames, strawberry and lemon frames, and cockle shell frames; and mirrors whose glass was borne of Laxciilian stone peacocks that show what is and what was and what was perceived, but not true. And though the object of their desire is the same, each shows me something very different.

I have much of everything unimportant but am forbidden to give them away. They are not mine to be generous with, says Mama, who rarely rears her head except for birthdays and occasional public parades and functions. My reflection examines the unhappy wench. Her hair is jet black, short on top, with two solar rings above each ear. Double-bent, her neck is invisible behind her pink collar. Her dress is red like blood. And her nose is still ballooned and horrid after Ebed broke it to snatch from her claws the lyre.

Sour and nerve-stricken as I remember, Mama combs my hair and adds the strawberry and lemon scents. I sit before my favourite mirror; tonight, its glass tells a story about two unhappy she-elves, dead inside, looking right at one another but not really seeing anything of worth.

Just then, Nurse Ebed walks in, sees Mama has assumed her hair-brushing role, apologises, and leaves.

"Do I look absolutely beautiful?"

"Very lovely, Mama."

"Your waist looks willowy, your skin lithe, your lips like rose petals."

"I am getting more sunlight, Madam."

Papa's face enters the room, and the existing awkwardness flees, only to be replaced by a newer and more toxic one. He is a great deal taller than Mama. Mama skulks out the door like Ebed did. How difficult it must be to be wed to a man one despises with every fibre of one's being. I fear that is what love is: a fleeting delusion or primal need for progeny-production mistaken as a need for eternal togetherness. My books imply otherwise, and I do want to believe them, but their message of hope has not been endorsed by my reality.

In one hand, Papa holds a staff with a disturbing golden disc fashioned like an all-seeing eye. I vaguely remember him telling me years ago that during one of their conference calls, Liriondias had said he'd arrange to have the Triune's most elite squad of servants—the Triune-in-Flesh—go to what had been Silas's tower in the East, grab his talisman, and bring it here to amplify Mehkabikil's telepathic powers lest he have need of them.

In the other, he holds a most magnificent necklace. He nods at my reflection. I brush my extremely high pony-tail—held up by a net of white diamonds and blue cords Ebed has blessed me with—in front of my shoulder and tilt my neck. He locks the silver choker in place. It pinches my skin, but I give no response to the pain. A wide gold chain dangles from the choker in the shape of a V, and on a rhombus of blue lapis lazuli, boasts a sapphire ruby. He tightens the choker as much as he can.

"After what happened the other morning with the Wraith, I was not sure if I would have the opportunity to give you this."

"When did you find the time to buy me such a gift?"

"I did not buy it for you. It belonged to my former consort, the one whose fangs begot the dog."

"Papa, please do not speak about Baba Alk'erion so."

"I will stop presently. Anything for my little girl on her big day."

"When did you retrieve it, Papa?"

"I had Joxer the servant retrieve it from her pile of ashes in the Royal Tombs Chamber and dust it thirty days ago. She was wearing it when she died."

"So you still miss her terribly?"

"I have only ever loved you."

"Not even Mama?"

"Do not make me laugh," he says dryly, and I crack a small smile.

I run my right index finger along the choker. "How personal…"

Neither of us mentions how he approved and signed off Ozymandias's warrant for my arrest and execution only a couple of hours ago—but we both know that we both know—and that is sufficient for the both of us.

He breaks the silence: "And how do you feel about the boy?"

"Like I might one day grow to love him. We have had such a splendid time since I washed his feet and nursed his wounds."

"Put all nonsensical thoughts of that brat out of your mind. You are going to meet a suitor tonight. I pray it goes more swimmingly than the last few attempts."

"Another one, Papa? How desperately you try to get rid of me!"

At this, he almost shoves his rod in my face.

"Do you know why I have dragged out the exploits of the Resistance for so long? It is because, out there in the Maze, the prisoners do little other than work and weep and wither away into shallow graves. The wardens get the first fruits of their labour, and we get everything else. You see, far from being free, the Laxciilians are as much a part of the Maze as all the others; they just do not know it. More disgusting than informants, our elves unwittingly cream off the rest of the prison planet, only instead of being rendered into submission by work and the sword, they are made docile and compliant by bread they have not baked and circuses in which they do not perform. But your... distraction... might just have the power, one way or another, to topple everything that has made us who we are: the ruling-class, the elite, the materialistic superpower that everybody wants to live in.

"But what will happen if the Maze comes down? The money will run dry. The flow of food will stop. No more wild beasts will be sent to fight in our underground arena. You will have to get a job—and being a brainwashed cleaner for a couple of weeks for failing to assassinate a political rival will not cut it. Our elves will have to learn trades, artisanship, and actual life skills. It would be chaos! They would not cope.

"That is why you will give your heart to your date tonight—we need another stream of prosperity before we get swallowed up in bankruptcy and, should Fortune forsake us and history brand us as co-conspirators with the Triune—we get economically decimated paying out reparations. Now I believe it is within your womanly, athletic abilities to tie him down, but you have proved to be disappointing of late—and time is not a luxury I can afford. Hence, embarrass me again, and I will take it that you are lost, in which case you are a liability.

"First, this pretty face of yours must first unlearn libellous secrets it knows. Secondly, bind him to you maritally, or go mad and kill yourself."

"Papa," I say, in complete agreement, "That would be the only way!"

"Do not remember any of this conversation."

"Thank you for the gift, Papa."

Then he leaves.

When it is almost four p.m., two buffoons with a penchant for fish and mammal hairstyles, Makkan and Ogun, arrive at my door to fetch me for lunch. Never once taking their eyes off me for fear I might make a run for it, they lead me to the private dining-room and stand to the side of the door in statue-formation like toy soldiers when I enter. Previously my childhood allies, they have recently become most yoked to the ideals of the King.

"Enjoy, Lady of Loux Laxciila," they nod in unison.

"That is the Queen's name," I reply, bored, and remarkably irked by their presence, "and I do not think the most patient elf could enjoy this charade, no matter how starved of food or company."

"Lady Louxandria," they mutter in allusion to the chain of seven stars under which I was born, the brightest of which is the silver Gwawrddydd. Then they walk away.

A staple tradition at my birthday dinner, Papa toasts to the first time he placed me in the arms of the sulking she-elf across from him. Nanny, who insisted on tending to us during mealtime to mark the occasion, interjects that an Earthling named Amanda delivered me. Neither of my parents are impressed by this exclamation, so I expect her head will, as Papa sometimes colloquially orders, *get the chop* for her brazenness on the morn of the morrow.

Pity. I have always approved of Nanny.

I look to Mama. Her skull-white skin, black-dotted cheeks, and heavily coloured lashes stare down the table at me with disinterest as Papa resumes his tale where he left off. Most curiously, he delivers a very different narrative than the one he shared this time last year. He has been doing that a lot recently, even going so far as to tell our people and guests that he was the first of our kind and the only ruler Loux Laxciila has ever had. Knowing full-well that I am deluding myself, I lay it down to stress. Benjamin's response to Papa's nonsense is typically more monosyllabic with an angered resounding "Bull," whatever that means.

Papa and Mama are soon preoccupied with a discussion about how my birth led to a dispute of international proportions with Gideon, and that he sent ships to our shores, killed an annually-increasingly-exaggerated number of our kin, and so on and so forth. All the while, my arm bruises and my skin crawls as Alk'erion tries tirelessly to get my attention through words, nudges, sniffs, food-throwing, and snarls, but after what Benjamin implied of his cold cruel antics, I cannot look at him.

I sigh. "Sweet guests, I suffer the most terrible headache ever to plague a she-elf and I feel faint! Permission, my Lord, to lie down? It could prove beneficial."

"Dismissed," he hisses and then goes back to fighting with Mama and making the occasional slur at Baba.

In fact, having excused myself, I lead Nanny to a well-supplied underground safe room where, hopefully, no one will think to look for her. Am I overreacting? Quite possibly. But Papa has killed women for less offences than correcting him, so one cannot be too careful.

Then I stand in the courtyard, chilled to the bone but perfectly content. The sky has gotten darker hours earlier than usual—it's still early evening—but no matter: I count a star in the faux-sky for each of my genuine (and otherwise) birthdays.

After I have counted one hundred and twenty-four stars, plus three hundred, I take a stroll to the art room I had Ebed prepare for Benjamin.

Many haughty women blindly pass me by, necks outstretched and noses uplifted, tripping along with mincing steps to the jingle of ankle ornaments. And something churns within me, a repulse for their finery: the bangles, headbands, crescent necklaces, earrings, bracelets, veils, headdresses, masks, ankle chains, sashes, boas, perfume bottles, charms, signet rings, toe rings, nose rings, fine robes, capes, cloaks, purses, linen garments, tiaras, shawls, Laxciilian rods, combs, and mirrors. For a brief but fundamental moment all I can think about are the bald, sored, branded heads the refugees see in their mirrors. (In my room hang many mirrors).

What sorcery prohibited me from seeing the vulgarity of this excess before now? No. Such questions may lead to the revelation of answers I prefer not knowing.

I am still quite a way off when I see a crack of light through the art room door. I walk faster now until I break into a gentle run, then slip through the old tattered door to a studio alight with flaming candles where Skye is engrossed in his projects. Drawings and paintings hang from wires that stretch this way and that. His stories are organised by chapters and sit on a corner table waiting to be edited. Funny, freakish, and wonderful false-faces stare at me from all around the room. This boy is a wizard of the most magical kind—the imagination.

I sneak up behind him, slide my arms under his elbows and wrap them around his stiffening chest, and rest my head on the back of his neck. He jumps, as always, not out of fright, but because he hates to be touched, especially when he does not see it coming. But deep down—far beneath his quiet, contemplative, hard, cold exterior—I know he likes it really; to feel something other than hatred. "Strawberries and lemons," he breathes in and exhales deeply.

"Not the three words every girl wants to hear," I tease.

"You're absolutely right," he returns. "Happy birthday, Aurora."

A brief examination of his canvas is sufficient for a poignant appreciation to quicken within me and stir a peculiar recognition, a reification with the two-dimensional beauty. With little deviation, she is baby blue from her petite crown to her small lips to her fairy shoes. She is bluer than Skye which, were I a betting elf, I would expect aggravates him somewhat. I find the idea of the Maker yearning, fawning even like a panting puppy, for the things of Creation fascinating. Silver circlets and green gems illuminate her smooth golden hair as a bold pink skirt tears through the centre of the canvas and ripples from her waist to her feet. Pencilled lightly, though entirely colourless, girdles of forest plants net around her shoulders and breasts, and on one breast, a glittering teardrop fallen from the adequately contented though distant windows to her soul. In every meaning of the word, she is unfinished.

Most curious of all, for Skye entitles all his work, pinned above the image is a blank card.

"What is her name?" I ask. He is torn between two: "Unfinished" or "Undone".

"She is charming."

"She certainly is."

"Careful, dear. Next to fear, pride is the greatest stumbling block for the righteous."

"I wasn't complimenting myself." He blushes with embarrassment and hides his face.

"Mmm, who knew you were a fully-fledged member of the scented candles parade? Is that honey I smell?"

"As spending money, Mósandrirl gives me five thousand of those peacock-backed coins a week, and honey flavour was the cheapest at the market. There are one hundred and twenty-four large blue candles because that is my favourite colour, and three hundred midget pink candles because that is your favourite colour. That is a pain in the neck number of candles to maintain, because the flames won't stop going out and the wax won't stop melting." He carries on with his project, as though this all means nothing. And although he's trying to show that he cares, it probably does mean nothing to him.

"Thank you."

It really is the most perfect sight I have ever witnessed. Skye does not look too shabby either, not that I have ever noticed such things. The heat of creativity exudes from his shirtless body. He has become more muscular and "done something with his hair" (I believe that is the expression that he uses). He has transformed so much from the scared boy with the bloody chin and the staring problem I met the day Surtskvasír and I retrieved Skylar from the troll nest.

From the loneliness of creativity, I hear his heart. It calls to me. I am intrigued. And from the depths of my heart, I answer.

After applying a few more brushstrokes, he turns to face me, and splodges blue paint on the tip of my nose. Like he is being tickled, he recoils and descends into hysterics for he believes himself hilarious, though when he calms down, he is speechless, but it is not awkward. His toes curl and rub against each other and he puts his hands against my shoulders, leans in, and, terrified, kisses my forehead.

Then he slides free of my arms, tip-toes to a small three-legged table, and wheels over an upside-down pineapple cake, a four-layered trifle, some cutlery and cups, and a pot of tea. Next, he carries over a tray of lemon for me, and milk and sugar for himself.

"Ta-daaa!"

And he tells me that I may claim any piece of artwork I so desire as a gift.

"Aurora Undone", of course.

"Happy birthday!"

[A few hours later, Aurora returns to her room. She has just had dinner with a suitor of her Papa's choice. She is overcome with sadness but is not sure why. As observed by the Enenra]

Through the window, I see her maid is early. Good! Punctuality impresses me. She is a snoopy little thing, though. Does her mistress know she eats the biscuits from her bedside jar? Tsk, tsk, naughty, naughty.

The door swings open. "Good evening, Lodes Heddwen," the startled bumbler greets, over-enthusiastically, pretending she was smoothing her hand over the unwrinkled bedsheets. (Over the biscuit crumbs she dropped, maybe, but that would be the height of it).

"Ebed, darling." She shuts the door behind her; probably the most laborious task she has completed all week, other than the time she stood silently and stoically, stiff as a matchstick, handing out baked goods to the mentally challenged internationals.

"How was your dinner, Lodes Heddwen?"

"The same as always, unfortunately. Ogling eyes for starters, talk of post-Maze empiricism for dinner, recommendations on how our guests could revolutionise Loux Laxciila for dessert, and lascivious suggestions that warrant tongue-maiming over tea."

"I am sorry I brought it up, Lodes Heddwen. It is just that the idea of a wedding at such a time as this—in our current crisis, resounds of such hope, does it not? What greater way to defeat the Triune than to show them that they cannot steal our joy and happiness? Still, I did not mean to upset you."

"Not at all, Ebed. You are a dear to have asked."

"And was this one grabby, too, Lodes Heddwen? Young elves have gone quite the way of dwarves of late!"

"Alas, he was. I had to break a few of his fingers, and you will have to sew this skirt. I tore it with a knife so I could kick him in the nose. My aim was off, though. I got him in the teeth, instead."

"Never fear, Lodes Heddwen. There is someone out there for everyone, even in our current crisis. Just be patient."

"I do not believe that for a second, actually," she says sadly.

"Is it the child of the Earthen Star?" the nosey servant asks. Were I her employer, I would have her tongue removed and eaten for interfering in the affairs of her superiors in such a manner. "Do you love him?"

"I do not know how I feel, only what I think I feel."

"There is chemistry, Lodes Heddwen. I do not, by any means, profess to know the boy, but I have seen the chemistry between you two during my subtle chaperoning."

"But I do not believe he is capable of love. Passion, yes, and great bravery and righteousness. But even when he is present, he seems a thousand kingdoms away. The mission is of the utmost importance to him, and thereafter, I think he has settled on retiring in a coffin six feet underground."

"He is a brooder. Darkness is where he feels safe and so it is where he dwells. But a love like the one you can offer him can thrust him into the light."

"It is not just him. To be perfectly honest, for the longest time, I did not really predict marriage in my future. I thought it remarkably selfish to seek out bliss when the world outside this sham is suffering, and I thought it cruel to bring an elfling into this moral sewer."

Ebed turns to face the princess's romantic novel collection but says naught.

"Yet still you entertain all these accomplished and handsome Elven suitors, Lodes Heddwen?" Ebed winks cheekily and snickers to herself.

"Seven suitors in a lifetime as long as mine hardly signifies loose mores, Ebed." She's both shocked and excited by the boldness of this conversation.

"I mean no offence, Lodes Heddwen. Only that it is a shame that you are forced to spend—not that I insult his ever-gracious Kingship (he has been very kind)—idle time socialising with princes of disinterest when your time could be better spent bathing, washing floors, or organising charities no one will donate to. Alternatively, Lodes Heddwen, you could take up assassination again, or are your murderous days over now that your brainwashing has been exposed?"

The sweet fragile doll smiles too widely at this. "All great suggestions, Ebed, but when Papa—excuse me, *his Lordship*—goes to such lengths to grant these suitors safe passage through the warren, one must be hospitable and make their great escape worthwhile. And it is only an occasional and minor impediment on my time. Anyway, I learn much about their experiences out there in the Maze and I leave well-fed, two very important preoccupations of mine. Overall, I think the entire experience is very good for their self-esteem."

The Lady bursts into silent tears and sobs. Ebed pretends her heart is breaking at the sight of her mistress, but really her eyes are on the biscuit jar.

"My stern rejections of these suitors have sparked political conflict between the leading Elven families, so the King has made a decision on my behalf. Oh, Ebed, he has done something awful! Logical, wise and dreadful!"

Ebed is silent. She would be on the edge of her seat were she not standing up.

"But it is late. That is news for another time. Ebed, darling, I feel peckish. I do not suppose there is any dessert left in the servants' hall?"

"Tart it is, Lodes Heddwen." She smiles, apparently forgetting her mistress' distress, draws a wand, concealed within her apron, and gives it a flick. A large bowl of steaming apple and berry tart foamed with ice-cream appears on the bedside drawer. At first, she is grateful, but then immediately guilt sets in of her high position and comforts, and she orders the luxury to be distributed to a quiet child among the refugees.

"As you say, Lodes Heddwen. Very good, Lodes Heddwen." She flicks her wand again, and presumably, the bowl goes where the Lady has instructed. (Like Hell a Laxciilian would associate with any one of those flea-ridden migrants!). "Now then, the green silk nightdress, Lodes Heddwen, or perhaps the indigo?"

"I simply cannot wear green again after that hideous ordeal with the trolls and that slave-trader. It took me forever to wash their guts out of my hair and their scent off my skin. Whenever I wear green, someone tries to kill me."

"Very good, Lodes Heddwen." She misunderstands this as the Lady requesting the green dress, but the puzzled gawp in the mirror corrects her. To cover her tracks, she smooths out the green nightdress on the bed, then delicately lifts the other one to dress the mannequin. She unbuttons the Lady's form-fitting gown, and she in turn conducts herself rigorously to the removal of her sleeves and tiara.

"Would you like a new hairstyle in the morn, Lodes Heddwen?"

"Oh, please, if you can spare the time." She begins to remove the Lady's hairpins, diamonds, and ribbons. "The day, like immortality, is long."

"Three hundred years long," chimes Ebed, throwing her head back for extra effect and voice projection.

"One must find some recreational way to pass the time whilst waiting for death." The Lady's dead reflection in the mirror betrays her as a wishful truant, one who would do anything to leave this accursed place.

*Soon enough, Lady Louxandria… Soon enough.*

"I shall make myself scarce then, Lodes Heddwen. Good night, Lodes Heddwen."

"Ebed, you have been a delight. Truly, you are most appreciated. And it strikes me as odd that I have never told you how much you mean to me. Here," she dashes to the side of her bed and takes the biscuit jar. "I know how much they agree with you"; the coy way of calling someone a thief but assuring them they are not getting the sack. "Take this and keep it. Fill it for yourself daily. Enjoy. No, no, no. Consider it a gift for all your years of service." It is with great suspicion that Ebed accepts it as a token of gratitude and favour, but the rumbles of her tummy quieten her conscience.

"Lodes Heddwen, is everything alright?"

"Of course, you worrisome woman," she lies, tears bubbling as she reaches breaking point. "Now, off to bed with you. I have imposed on your time long enough. Good night, Ebed! Good night. GOOD NIGHT!" Ebed bows out, confused and very afraid, and departs, either to the servants' sleeping quarters or to the kitchen so she can devour that biscuit jar and tart.

And as for me, I perch in the shadows as I have always done, waiting… until the time is right to make my move…

Goodnight, Lady Heddwen. I will see you soon.

Written in 6779+300, Era of the Maze, Age the Twelfth. INTENDED TO BE THE FINAL WORDS OF THE PRINCESS OF LOUX LAXCIILA:

*Is this home?*
*Among ghosts who say they are my family?*
*Where my heart is*
*Broken*
*Frozen*
*Cold?*
*Where I cannot speak*
*Cannot breathe and*
*Am just a deadened doll?*
*Where my life is meaningless;*
*Future—*

*I have none but empty days.*
*Thorns, they shoot up and crush me.*
*Thrones block out the sun.*
*Agency,*
*Freedom,*
*I have none.*

*From over the walls, he calls me.*
*The promise to set me free;*
*The only one who understands me is the one I cannot trust.*

*A forest that erases memories*
*A papa with whom I have none*
*A mama obsessed with apathy*
*A baba who cannot show love.*
*Is this home?*
*This is home.*
*Is this home?*

*My heart:*
*Broken*
*Frozen*
*Gone.*

Beneath the milky moon and misty twilight clouds, the kingdom's Ophelia ungratefully drinks in the supernatural freshness of the Loux Laxciilian air. Her dress is so chalky, transparent even, that I almost don't see her, and her golden locks are darkened by the shadows of the skeletal-fingered branches above. Yet her wooden face glows eerily; its features etched with a knife and inked black. There is a haziness in her eyes and desperation. Before I can form her name on my lips, she turns to a wood near the castle and runs. I follow.

And it is like I have entered a different country: ancient, magical, pure, and untampered by time and the Triune; the real Loux Laxciila, preserved only by its own isolation and neglect. The sky is coal black. No stars peek-a-boo here. The air's cold as ice cubes and everything about the atmosphere warns that this place is restricted. There laps a small brook of flowing ice, out of which fish too large for the brook bob. No birds sing and no leaves rustle. Elongated, multi-legged crawlers scoot around the big mossy boughs.

Only one log's out of place that I can see, and even then, I only notice it when she leaps over it. This log is nature's traffic-light ordering trespassers to halt. Adrenaline lifts me over the barked barricade and I land with a potentially bone-breaking thud, but I run ever on and will do so until I catch her.

She's fast, but I'm hot on her trail—though, let's be honest, she could outrun me if she really wanted to. (I have seen elves use super-speed). She is lost and heartbroken and doing the only thing she knows how to do, but I have no doubt she wants to be saved.

She freezes when she arrives at the bottom of the Wíshagor Pool. I should have suspected this was where she was heading, since I've seen her reading up on it lately in the library. Moss-topped rocks coin atop one another and stick-thin slanted trees sprout from in-between them. Streams of white, mystic blue, and grey drop enchantingly in mists down the small waterfall and settle in a small pool with a brown base. But we're not here to marvel at the beauty.

"Aurora," I say. I don't follow it up with a question. I just say her name… the name I have given her and pray that it is enough.

She turns and responds hollowly— "To forget"—and looks back at the pool.

I admit, the Styx water is a temptation, but I can't possibly tell her this. Instead, I plan to say that life is a journey made up of good and unfortunate moments. Experiences that thrill and disappoint, but we must embrace them all as part of our landscape. All these things and more shape us, but we must not confuse this with letting them define us. And she plans to compromise herself to her core. This is her chance to be strong, to emancipate herself from the wickedness of tyrannical predators. This is her chance to be a hero, and even if she doesn't feel like one right now, someday she will. Someday she will save someone who feels like this, because her life will be a testimony that living on in the face of adversity, exploitation, and manipulation is possible. Because it plays by its own rules and has no qualms with causing casualties, darkness always appears dominant, but evil knows that its days are numbered. And in the end, all that is left are truth, light, and goodness. Life will out.

"Aurora, don't do it."

She stands over the waters, deciding. All that's left is something broken: a bird with no wings; a star that exhibits neither warmth nor glow; a machine that has fallen on the kitchen tiles and smashed into pieces. And honestly, who am I to tell her not to wash the pain away and emerge as someone new, past-less and free? There are much more dangerous things to do with water.

Her eyes close and her head disappears.

No. This is not the way.

I run towards her and grip her around the waist. Her fingers clutch more firmly to the rocks that mark the pool's base. Her adamant form is glued to it. I'm reluctant to tug too tightly at first but resolve that I have to employ more strength than I've ever intended to use against a girl. Eventually she lets go and falls back on top of me, wrapped in my arms.

Face soaked, hair strewn across her forehead, neck and shoulders, her red face flares at me and her tears stream fast. And I'm glad. I'm glad she remembers the sting, the disappointment, how impossibly awful she feels right now. Because whoever did this has already taken her time, her innocence, and has taken hold of her very mind and body. They will not take her memories as well, no matter how painful.

And this will all hurt tomorrow, and the day after that, and the week after that, but there will come a day when she will rise and stand strong. And it will all have been worth it.

Murmurs from the trees assert continuously that someone called "I" saw an infamous "him" chase "her" and deduce that they must have gone "this way" because it is the only road. I'd know that voice anywhere: it's the Elder Elf. He really will stop at nothing until I'm decapitated. Poor sod. One would think an immortal of all people could find something better to live for.

A blast of fire obliterates the barrier log, and Mósandrirl (who must be fresh out of bed) and the Elven guard charge onto the scene. Mehkabikil sits regally in a special armchair, a beige masterpiece of upholstery; upheld by bronze poles carried by goon-masked, draped servants. He must have been having some personal time for he is barefoot, robed to the knee in paper-thin green-black material, his long lean thighs and arms on display. He's got a glass of red wine one hand, a horrid staff in the other.

Alk'erion is here too for some reason; I hear his raspy ineloquent twang pick fights with whoever's nearest him before I see his bandaged hands and his brown-dyed locks. He has incredible restorative powers for a burns victim; I didn't think the Elder Elf would waste the minty slush on him. Alk'erion's nose and mouth wrinkle to an ugly sneer when he steps into my line of vision. After I've quickly shot him the Benjamin stare, I fix my gaze back on Aurora.

She is my priority now.

As his servants lower him to the same level as the rest of us insects, the Elder Elf predictably yells that I'm trying to drown his daughter. The Elder Wizard gives him a suspect look for his presumptions and fair dues to him, demands that Mehkabikil quit this preposterousness. His Lordship's angry eyes tell all that he is not accustomed to being contradicted by those he does not have the power to execute. And the princess glares Polonius down.

Yet ever the figure of composure, the King walks nearer, despite her spitting venomously at him to stay away. Starfish-turned-Octopus and Whale, or should that be Rosencrantz and Guildenstern, are also here for some reason—probably to see if I was sacrificing the princess on a slab to the Void. Rumours spread fast here at the best of times, but especially when there's been a blow-up or Royal Family drama. All eyes are on the Elder Elf as he walks toward her. But I cut in.

"Wine and no sandals? Tell me, what are we celebrating?"

"The life and times of Ozymandias, Silent Monks Chieftain. He will be missed." He raises his glass. It takes me a second to realise he's killed him.

"Why?" Behind me gasps Aurora, between pants and chokes.

"He had a job to do. He failed to meet our standards."

*To kill your daughter*, you mean.

Maybe it's wrong, what happened to Ozzy, but I don't feel sorry.

"How could you be so cruel?"

"You see, Dark One, in my jurisdiction everyone has their part to play. The Royals. The wise. The dogs." At this Alk'erion scratches behind his ears with some tree bark and bites the head off a bird. "The fools. When every player owns their zone, we experience more peace than Angoria has ever known. But should a misguided visionary tug at the fabric of Laxciilian society, he would send ripple effects throughout the entire strata and tear it. And like all wounds, these tears are best healed with a scab: unpretty but necessary. Leave law, counsel, and tradition as they are, Triumvir."

*Subject to your every whim and moving goalpost?*

"Need I ask what category I fall into, your highness?"

"Well, that is simple. None of the above. You are the enemy."

"I just wanted to build bridges—"

"Bridges get walked over, Dark One, and all extend exceedingly short to cover the chasm that separates both of us."

"What did I ever do to cause you to hate me so much?"

Aurora coughs up more water. I inch a little to the right to entirely shield her from his view.

"Oh, I never trusted you," says the King. Mósandrirl's pupils whizz to the corners of his eye sockets and look at him with doubt. Alk'erion's eyes do the same. This must be the first time those two have ever agreed on something.

"Tell me one thing I have done to deserve such suspicion."

"You arrived on the same night as the Chosen One—"

"I am the Chosen One."

"Very well then. I will play along: you arrived at Troll Cave in a flash of lightning on the same night the Dark One was prophesied to make an appearance. At the faintest touch of your skin, my daughter had a vision of you slaughtering a pint-sized ally in cold blood. Upon re-finding you, her first act was the murder of a mortal, something she awakes screaming about in the night. You stole the Diadem of my people and arrogantly trumpet it around my city on your head like you are a demigod. You have incurred the wrath of my pet and injured him." I think he means Alk'erion. The King cruelly cackles a little at this point, impressed by his own metaphor. "You were seen conspiring with the Imp moments before his getaway, and minutes later, you attempted to flock outside my borders just as an assassin passed through an impenetrable force field and cut down dozens. Not to mention, you have been seen skulking around dark chambers virtually every night since you arrived."

"Skulking!"

"Do not think the missing vials and jars of toadflax, pig's feet, oleander, nightshade, nux oil, mustard seed, mandrake, jacklebeet, henbane, comfrey root, cardamom, blood meal, and beetle toe have gone unnoticed! I can only imagine what Dark Arts you are dabbling in up there in Gideon's bedchamber. You are ridiculously fortunate that the Elder Wizard cast such potent protection spells over your room" –huh? When?—or you would have been kidnapped in the dead of night by now, allocated an underground cell, and had your fingernails removed."

I am speechless, but before I can think of anything to say, he shoves me to the ground and steps forward, avoiding the Diadem's flames. He and his staff lower.

"Enough of this," he says of Aurora's crying.

"Perhaps over-exposure has immunised me," she spits more angrily than I ever remember seeing her.

"Then I will increase the dosage until it has an effect," he hisses too quietly for anyone other than us to hear.

And Aurora stops. Stops sobbing. Stops coughing up water. Stops breathing almost.

And every Laxciilian in the audience pities the poor green girl, who must have been overly excited about her birthday.

But not me. Oh no. I smile. Because I had a view no one shared: *the King* has been brainwashing his daughter! And I've just realised how he's been doing it. *Over my dead body*, I promise—which, come to think of it, he wouldn't have a problem with.

I let out a roar and leap towards the Elder Elf. He's too stunned to move. And with a months' worth of pent-up aggression, I thump his ugly face with my right hand, and with my left, grab from him the staff. I dash to the stone base of the Wíshagor Pool and smash the rod against it. Harrowed voices, commands and incantations shoot forth, as well as jets of milky white cloud and thick black soot that bears a striking resemblance to Silas's face.

The rod's token, a small-eyed golden disc, sprints for safe keeping, but I stab it with the spike at the bottom of the staff. There's a long-winded scream to the accompaniment of an extravagant burst of indigo and violet streams that escape to the heavens and vanish. I hardly have time to contemplate what happened when the King pounces at me like the snake he is, muttering curses in his ancient tongue. And I wallop his head with the staff and he drops mid-air.

Usually I am all for submission to elders but, excuse the phraseology, screw this Elven villain's sovereignty crap!

# 11

# THE LAIR OF THE ELDER ELF

I spend most of the night on a bed in the medical ward of the Healing House as Elven healers ooze any possible infection from my bloodstream (at least I think that's why they wrapped me in tourniquets doused in boiling water). The healing process is agonising, to say the least, yet I refuse to demonstrate pain in front of the elves, so instead of squirming, I dig my nails into the blanket or into my hands. At one point, I pierce the fabric and undo my fresh stitches, and before I know it, my palm's pumping blood.

Kindly elves plaster layers of skin grafts over my raw wounds before shuffling out the door like mice before anyone sees. Once they're gone, I'm alone in a large dark room that brims with pillars, paintings, and fine architecture, though lacks in all things medical. It would make life easier for everyone if they just threw me in the minty tub. Apparently striking the King and knuckling his jaw disqualifies one from having a cosy sludge bath.

I still can't believe his clowns juggernauted into me like that and poked me with whatever drugged-up needles they carry around. Junkies! More to the point, I can't believe they didn't strike me dead or imprison me as soon as I walloped the King across the head (for a second time!). Of course, Mósandrirl would never let those eejits do anything too serious to me, and surely even the dim-witted elves have the smarts to know that it can't be that easy to put a Triumvir down.

That doesn't mean they didn't come at me in full force, for all the good it did them. The nurse kept talking about lightning-speed ninja moves I seemingly pulled and how my hands made electric and fiery sparks. She said, according to the grapevine, I laid twenty guards on their back when they came at me. That sounds like something I'm capable of, but everything after smacking Mecky is a blur, to be honest. (That'll be the drugs, whose influence is thankfully waning now).

Before scuttling out, the nurses added that Mósandrirl had gone to find out how Aurora was doing, but that he he'd return if he could. Last the nurses heard, she was off to visit a head doctor. For her sake, I hope he's neither a hypnotherapist nor working from a corner office paid for by the Elder Elf, or their sessions could undo all the progress she has made recently.

I lift my legs out of the bed; they carry the weight of a sack of potatoes. The stone floor chills the bones in my feet and my toes leap. I press them to the floor again. It's so cold that I'd rather just stay in the toasty bed, but I have a job to do, and time is of the utmost importance.

Aurora once told me she remembered being psychically led to a hidden chamber in the walls of the west wing of the palace. It was there that the King carried out his brainwashing machinations—I'm sure of it! True to what Mecky said back at the Pool, I have been skulking about late at night for a couple of reasons. Searching for that was one of them—but to no avail. If there is anything there that could help me expose him for the fraud he is, then I must find it now because this evening I gave him the one thing he has been searching for since I arrived: just cause to have me killed.

As I stumble for the door, it feels like a needle perforates my right heel, a cluster of dirty amethyst rock. Wincing, I take deep breaths and drag my deadened left foot behind me. The healers told me it would be at least a day before a semblance of strength returns to my body, and that is with all their remedies. But I cannot wait twenty-four hours. Having Mòsandrirl on my side or not, let's be realistic: I could be dead by then!

I open and close the door gently, not wanting to rouse any unwanted attention. I'm a little surprised no one's standing guard over me tonight—maybe the King is hoping someone will sneak in and kill me as I sleep.

The pain in my heel is so blinding that I practically crawl like a wicked thing from the Healing House to my art gallery. I must say, I'm blown away by the vast number of canes, staffs, and sticks that meet me just inside the door. The implication is clear: the King's critics applaud my brave outburst of justice—Laxciila isn't as unitarily-minded as I'd thought. I pick up a cane which looks particularly interesting and decide to lean on it for the rest of the night. Also, I tear off the white tissue-thin hospital apron which, if the breeze is anything to go by, has only covered my front this entire time, and dress in my Laxciilian attire, an assemblage of random fabrics and a blue drooping shirt.

Getting inside the palace will require a bit of imagination, but thankfully making my face is easy: a touch of lipstick, a gold coin large as an apple over one eye, and I top up my cheeks and forehead with paints wherever the mood takes me. Granted, it's not my tidiest work ever, but it'll do. Then I hobble out the door and pass one of Laxciila's hundreds of crow statues—I've never noticed one there before. I make good time in arriving at the walkway up to Laxciila's heart of darkness. Ironic, given that it's got more effervescence and fireworks than Disneyland.

Several Laxciilians shoot me dirty looks as I walk by. I wonder if my stubble's back. Nope, still gone. I run my fingers along the sides of my face: I don't feel like blood's caked to my skin. I feel no visible bandages. My ears aren't still bleeding. That's it! My ears! Round, not pointy. I bounce my fingers off them to prove it, not that doing so makes any sense. From down the slope, I watch maybe twenty elves walk past, all with their tipped ears on display like having them out and proud is a badge of honour.

Thankfully, I see Whale, who perhaps today should be called Sharkey, walking with a woman I can only assume is his wife.

"Sharkey," I call out from behind the shrubbery separating the slope from the path. He doesn't turn around. I've really got to start learning people's names. Lost for options, I do the only thing I am guaranteed will work. I jump him from behind and shove him down a hill off the beaten track.

"Don't scream," I threaten in what in my head was a more masculine voice. He lives for drama, I can tell, so he pretends to flounder with fear, but remains silent.

"Banditry, banditry," accuses his woman as she tiptoes down the hill after us in heels, much too quiet for even elf ears to hear.

Sharkey begs me not to kill him, so I say, "I won't if you do as I ask... *demand*!" I'm unused to playing bad cop except in my daydreams.

He says he'll give me anything.

I politely ask for his clip-on wig—he gives me his bangles, wristbands, and rings, too. Having been instructed by him on how best to wear it, I remedy the obviousness of my human ears with a long bushy wig made from real hair. Ideally this would go above the diadem, but the Elder Elf's medical staff appear to have pinched that back, the critters.

Sharkey then begs me not to tie him up—to a tree of his choice—with a belt he hands me, his wife still chanting, ever so softly, "Banditry, banditry." Well, because he was such a good sport, I decide I will for the *craic*, and when his wife sulks with envy, I tie her up, too.

"I'll give these back," I promise, and then return to my assignment. I get much more approving looks now; one elf congratulates me on not being ashamed of my wealth just because the poverty-stricken foreigners are here. I dig my clenched fists deep in my pocket and smile widely because it is all I can do to stop myself punching the dogmatist in the teeth.

At the foot of the staircase, I look up at the groups of threes and fours casually conversing and drinking on the flight. One dopey-grinned waiter walks over to me and mutters something.

"*Tá brón orm, a chara, ach ní thuigim thú,*" I say, hoping my grammar is on point. I can't be certain, but after he's done nodding, I think he tells a group of three punk-rock she-elves that I've just uttered a credible solution to reversing the Triune's hyper-reality spell. O-o-okay. Fair enough.

I flash a few smiles at friendly nudges, laugh at jokes that aren't being told to me, and walk like a crab whose shell is falling off to avoid suffocating "stranger danger" hugs. The gossips have found a new meeting place at the top of the staircase where they describe something with such detail it actually looks interesting to a pair of useless guards. Octopus-turned-Starfish-again keeps shimmering his fingers in umbrella motions, while Sharkey-turned-Whale styles his hand like a snake mouth (or like the tip of his hat) and makes spinning-top motions. They both breathe "Whoosh, whoosh" and eye each other to reinforce each other's "Whoosh." I turn my face away from them, because they will undoubtedly identify me.

Hold! The phone!

If that's Sharkey, then who—?

Sugar.


A hand webbed to the stone walls, I hobble along on my cane for hours feeling for something suspicious. My misgivings send me upstairs, downstairs, through kitchens, passed conspiracy theorist drunkards planning bombastic attacks against the Triune by candlelight, and past wooden doors too stiff, stony, and forgotten to open. The entire time, my legs take turns pulsating and painful spasms rail down my arms. I'm out of my depth. I'm out of my mind. I can't believe I seriously thought this would work.

And what is it with these blasted statues of peacocks and crows I see everywhere?! It's like they're following...

Oh, no. My subterfuge fooled no one.

Elongated by the flickering medieval torch on the wall, Laxciilians' shadows appear hauntingly down a corridor to the left of a door. Their mad hats look like devil horns and pikes. My heart screams and thumps, but I haven't wasted all this time creepy-crawling like a guilty thing in the shadows to fail to achieve my mission now at the hands of these fools. I press forward. Afflicted, but not crushed. Confused, yes, but not giving way to despair. Hounded, but not altogether cast off. And then, the incredible happens:

A super-sublimely-perfectly-timed plot twist that confirms Hamlet's exclamation that something beyond ourselves determines our steps! Around the corner, I hear the pushing of stone, so of course, I treat myself to a snoop, just in time to see the wall slot back in place like a jigsaw piece. And who should I see slotting the wall back in place like a jigsaw piece but a tall man with kingly tails slithering behind him, and something like red varnish on his talons. Got him!

When I'm sure he's out of hearing distance, my fingers clawing the jutted-out masonry, I drag myself along the wall to where the bouldering noise came from. The soldiers' clangs, chinks and thuds draw nearer. My heel still squeals with pain while my other foot lugs like a sack, but excitement at the possibility of having at last found evidence that he is involved in something shady gives me all the adrenaline I need to carry on. I scale my hands along the wall, feeling for some secret passage or big red button or something.

Behind my back, I hear a slight thump. I swivel but my unsteady feet trip me up and I land on the ground in push-ups position, my nose mere inches above the cold hard floor, and perfectly in line with a stone crow's beak.

I hate birds. Satan-spawn they are; up there with cats on my Most Hated list, just half-a-notch below elves, dwarves, and people, at least for today. And the bird sculpture sings a wicked tune in a raspy voice:

> *"The Dark One skulks, sneaks, slinks, and squeals,*
> *Mehkabikil's secrets soon revealed."*

That's it. No more Laxciilian rhymes. I grab it by the neck, chuck it out the window, and turn back to the wall. Like a frog or scaly creature, I scamper up the stonework, peering ever so closely, until I make out a line so vague it's practically invisible—but it's definitely a door. If one was not looking for it, even an immortal elf could go a lifetime never noticing it was there (speaking of which, those soldiers are almost here!).

Quietly, to avoid detection, I push it in. Nothing happens. I lean back and force my body weight against it. What body weight? I am fifty-two kilogrammes of pounded meat. I take a deep breath, resume a proper stance regardless of the pain in my feet, and throw my shoulders and elbow grease into it. Next thing I know, the door is open, I tumble in, the door shuts, and I miss the first step of a steep staircase. My knees bruise against the marble floor at the bottom, and my bones roar at my stupidity. The floor is so cold my palms sting.

I scramble to my feet and make good use of my cane, deciding I might as well walk while I can, before I'm hanged, chained, or quartered on a table after tomorrow's verdict at the Meeting. To be honest, I almost anticipate Mósandrirl to have a getaway carriage for me prepped by then.

The small room is alight with rows of back-to-back shelves of crystal balls, the insides of which glow with milky white smoke and thin silver wisps. As well as these, a few stone bowls are squeezed into the corners. Gulps of cloudy water swim in them. Dozens of black glass mirrors squish the room's dimensions and give an air of claustrophobia.

I don't believe it. I did it. His every fear, thought, and scheme—mine to browse. I am inside the Elder Elf's brain. And since this place is so safe-guardedly hidden, in here are the monarch's most deeply held secrets.

"Greetings," says a woman's voice from somewhere. I jump as if struck by lightning. But scarcely have I forged an excuse as to how I wound up here when she begins to make remarks that are clearly not directed at me. Most likely, they are aimed at Mecky. As I slowly turn, I behold a seductive face in one of the larger mirrors—an attractive woman in her mid-thirties, maybe. Maybe this mirror functions as a recorder and sensor, replaying whenever someone comes within range. Her hair is combed, long, pearl white. She has piercing fox eyes that warn you are being watched, and the same angular face, razor-sharp teeth, and sunken cheeks as Alk'erion. She's identical to the embroidered woman I saw in Mehkabikil's private quarters. I wonder who she was and what happened to her.

I continue along the thin aisle of walking space and when nothing out of the ordinary happens, I tap one of the crystal balls. Before me appears a meeting around a black marble table in a dark room that could only have happened on Earth: presidents are there, world leaders, famous artists, influential television personalities, popish figures. There weren't enough chairs for all of them, so dozens stand along the wall. Behind their heads hangs a sign, 'The Infinity Association'. The lot of them look so powerful, solemn and menacing, they must be plotting to become the new un-copyrighted Masters of the Universe.

They speak about some oncoming climactic world event, and the many communal benefits that trauma brings, and the financial riches available to those who calculatedly prepare for and respond to it. (So, this is where Mehkabikil got the idea…). Whether they are orchestrating or merely predicting this trauma, I cannot tell. They never specify its nature, but it sounds like a purge, an onslaught, a decimation. For the first time since I left my world, I get an innate impression in my heart to go back. But what good could I possibly do on Earth? Not to mention this could be an illusion in a glass, or the Laxciilian version of fictive television.

Some commentators around the table argue that blame for the incident should be placed on aliens, karma, or a satellite missile, but the leader of the shindig resolves that he will accept responsibility. I press my face close against the glass to make out the head of the Association and give it a twist. Slick black hair, a beak nose, and handsome eyes that draw you into a chamber with no inside latch to allow you to get out. My one-time neighbour and local governor, now better known as the President.

And who is that in the background? The One-Armed Man and his wanton mate, the Duchess! Wow, the Elf must be desperate to get to know me better if he thinks Old Man Gerard, guru of all things plastic is worth keeping tabs on, though how he found out about him, I have no idea. I never once mentioned my sham-of-a-family by name with Aurora.

The video runs its course. I tap the crystal next to it, and a holographic projection exposes more revelations of Earth. Oh, I remember this one. It is the last thing I saw before I left Earth and got spat out just beyond Troll Cave.

I had been twitchy all day and was just about to make myself a cup of tea when the Powers That Be Satellite Station switched on our H.B. and aired an automated live recording to which they felt we all needed to be privy. Come to think of it, I hadn't listened to an episode of the national news since they incorporated a soundtrack into their more dramatic and distressing narratives.

The machine projected a still hologram of the President of America's face. Hair like night, one eye covered, an attractive beak nose, and a look of confidence and intent, his appearance has changed a lot since our time on Lincoln Lane. But ideologically, he's as big an antichrist as ever. Last I heard, the President was all for the increased legitimisation of martial law in the streets and violence towards inmates in prisons; locking up Conservatives who outed themselves online by expressing views he didn't like for a set time for behavioural *modernification*; pro-extreme nationalism; the legalisation of sexual relations between humans and animals and adults and children, because bestiality and paedophilia are both innate, unchanging sexualities; and he's never not been itching for a nuclear war. And people all around the world lapped it up as Gospel truth.

Soon before I came here, he even said that he was whipping up legislation to remove problematic words like "she", "woman", "human", "mankind", and "lady" from dictionaries, literature and the spoken word, because they all have "he", "lad" or "man" in them. To commit these oh-so terrible crimes would result in being punished with a hefty fine, and for repeated offenders, even a short prison sentence where convicts would be educated on the impact such triggering aggressive language as this could have on the female population. (Ah, he also wants to blot out "female"). Furthermore, he announced that he would soon be signing legislation criminalising the name "Jesus" in daily discourse. Heck, he's already criminalised churches refusing to officiate the weddings of alternate-lifestyle couples, owners to their dogs, and bereaving species-kind (again, there's no such thing as 'man-' or 'humankind' to this guy!) to their betrothed's corpses.

Beneath this stock image swept links to bulletins of his most recent speeches detailing his support for a European army; a return of all Europeans to the Eurozone; worldwide registration and tracking so technically no one ever goes missing again; censorship of internet and televised ads deemed an annoyance by eighty percent of website users; sex with everyone from children to beasts to stone-crafted false gods; worldwide abortion on demand, and a Dionysian Day, a legalised free for all: free carnal trysts, free punches, free tequila.

And no one in the world saw anything wrong with these but me. No, they were all mesmerised by the heartstring-pulling magician. But I never trusted him. And I eagerly await the moment when he slips up.

I remember the One-Armed Man appearing from within a newsroom, giving so convoluted an introduction to the President he undoubtedly got a salary bump. On the wide screen behind him was his wife, transformed from only a few days before. For one, her stretched face was less tight and sagged a little on the forehead. Oh boy, someone's gotten the axe for that blemish. Her blonde hair still had dark roots, but was reddish, ending in sword-sharp blades, almost as pointy as the cutlery that hung from her ears. Her eyes were not as thin and slanted as that morning on *C&C* but were emerald and piercing. A crocodile tear glistened in the corner of her eye. I shudder at the recollection.

And that is where the crystal ball resumes:

Thousands of well-dressed students my age and slightly older gather outside their school in the wake of its darkest day. Tears. Howls. Injuries. Heartbreak. Courage. All of them carry lit candles, flowers, teddies, or some other memorabilia or consumerist offering. The shooter, the presenters say, was a student. Ally says it's the worst thing in the world losing a child and I feel her eyes burn my wicked hands through the hologram.

The President walks along a huge stage. The cameraman does not give a close-up of the speech-deliverer which I'm sure all the family of the deceased will appreciate when watching this back; he's just one of thousands of species-beings in mourning following a senseless tragedy. It's hard to hate him when he's so, so good at what he does.

And the next part is a classic—it's what I would have done: the President tells all present to join hands as he recites a Tennyson poem from memory, and the power of the last few lines has never been so potent:

> *"'Though much is taken, much abides; and though*
> *We are not now that strength which in old days*
> *Moved earth and heaven; that which we are, we are,*
> *One equal temper of heroic hearts,*
> *Made weak by time and fate, but strong in will*
> *To strive, to seek, to find, and not to yield.'"*

Emotions explode and the most hardened of hearts at the vigil become the most expressive. It's the most powerful thing I've ever seen, him getting them all under his spell. Oh great, he's even crying now—just as the camera gives him a close-up.

I vaguely remember him being clean-shaven and stern-faced beneath a head of pearly white hair. Now, he has been cast by a new actor: his gelled hair is deep black, styled well, and spikes forwards in talons that cover an eye. His skin looks baby smooth and he frequently wets his lips with his tongue. I see why he's widely regarded as the object of perfection; he looks even younger than his equally ageless partner, who is probably off hitting a mall right now if her Marie Antoinette ways are anything to go by—minus the bad publicity.

But though I sympathise with the attraction, when I look into his eyes, I see devils, claws, and naked bodies baking in flames. And in his dragon mouth, I see a delicious appetite for the boys, girls, parents, and staff that stretch their hands out to him as though he's *Der Führer* and hang on every word he says. I see a man who knows he has just gotten everything he wants.

Instantly becoming the official King of the Blogosphere, all the criers whip out their phones and ping crying emojis, hearts, single eyes, thumbs ups, and smileys into the air. What must Mecky have thought watching this bunkum?

Yet something irks me now, as it did then. The timeline doesn't add up. Wasn't he already halfway across the Atlantic by that stage, en-route somewhere for something or other?

Then, gunshots!

And a blood-haired man with skeletally pale skin worms through a clear path made for him by the pagan mass, and he puts a bullet in the President's head. The Duchess points to him and shouts all the right exclamations and gives the assassin the nickname 'the Ginge'. Funnily, the police don't spring to action with any great haste.

"The President is dead," she cries. "The President is dead!"

Meanwhile, I see that the rest of the world spiral into a panic all its own. Screams pierced eardrums. Mobs break out. The until-now useless security open fire on the crowd. Paramedics arrive almost too quickly on the scene to confirm his death and beat each other with their kits in the hope of being the one to make the televised diagnosis. Don't ask me where the Ginge went; he's invisible amidst the vigil mourners' stampede. I want to reach into the glass and save them all, but, useless Chosen One that I am, I can't.

But that's not all. This madness is all seconded by the universal-scale applause that erupts when the fatal bullet is spat out of the eye the dead politician had had on display... and his fingers twitch. He rises to his feet.

"Stretch out your hands to me," he chants, red-black blood streaming out of his hollow socket. "Let me feel your energy. Praise to the one who has restored me. I was dead, and now I live. That's right. That's right. Let me share with you my power. Just stretch out your hands."

And Lord, bless us and save us, they do it.

The generation who denied miracles, healings, the forgiveness of sins, visions, Christ... the generation who tore down churches, statues, traditions, institutions, and biological truths; they hang on every word he says.

The sight of it makes me sick, hundreds or thousands of people reaching out their hands to him in worship. And I pity my lost world more than ever before.

My fingernail scarcely makes contact with the next glass orb in succession. At this point, I hope nothing shows up. But many things do. I see crashed planes in oceans. I see houses on fire. Someone's left the cooker on. Mothers scream outside crèches. They demand to know where their children are. Masked students with clubs smash their virtually abandoned primary schools. A frightened guardian scavenges the yard, calling out for the name of her charge, but there are no children there. The military patrol neighbourhoods. Cars burn in cul-de-sacs. Lewd behaviour increases, just in case there's no tomorrow. Mosques, banks, and chapels flood with all kinds of guests, desperate for answers to the big questions, and money. Behind tall metal bars, politicians bleed, their heads gashed with bricks, as vulture plebeians scream with mockery and fear-induced malice. The media state that thousands of people have vanished, most of whom are reported to have been disturbers of the peace. I don't see how they can make that assertion since phone lines are down, and the internet is frozen globally. A newly converted couple carry a poster: JESUS CAME & WE WERENT REDDY (I shudder at the lack of punctuation and spelling errors). Others lead marches demanding that we make friendly with the aliens—perhaps we can work something out; a joint-government maybe. Thousands roar "THE APOCALYPSE IS HERE!" and it certainly looks like it is.

And the revenue of all those who were at the board meeting in the first glass escalates off the roof. The whole world goes to Hell and still the background schemers care solely about self and money. I am beyond disgusted. But, perturbing as all these images are, for some reason none affect me as much as this one:

A groom traipses from the backseat of his black limo, smoke puffing from places it shouldn't be. It looks like a jeep reversed into them, but I don't see the chauffeur. The groom runs and pauses and slogs and collapses and crawls to the windscreen. Half his bride has catapulted through the glass. The sight of the groom's face melting into pasty plastic... his mouth widening in such disbelief he wants to cough his heart out... There are no words.

"Olivia? Liv? Liv, honey? Baby, are you alright? Liv? Liv!"

I begin to tear up. I don't know why it's getting to me. Deep breath. Enough of this.

I cross to the other side of the room and shove an ugly pallid cot out of the way. Inscribed on it is "Artaxerzes", which I assume is another name for Alk'erion. A wooden rattle rolls off it and hits the floor. If I get down on my hunkers to pick it up, I may not get up again, so I sweep it under a shelf with my cane.

Then I get this notion to dip my head in a pool of living water in a bowl. (Dangerous things, notions are). Regardless, my face does not wet, no more than on a misty day. As the waves lap over my head, I feel my mind expand. My eyes roll back like Match Three Chilli Peppers casino slots, and I fold in on myself, only to be carried through the air to a couple of mountains that fuse at a point like separate roots that form a single tree. Tall barks give off a bluish haze. Haunting, thick fog gushes down in cylindrical hills. A mountain of cloud races like horses down a mountain of trees.

My astral self lowers down into a marshy land, and I see a younger but just as frightening version of Mecky.

I have no clue what he's up to at first, but it soon becomes apparent. Furrowed brow, nasty snout, incantations, and cultish seasoning: he's cursing sixteen dead men. Something tells me I can't be seen here, yet I feel exposed until I crouch hidden behind a bush anyway. In Snake Eyes' wide hand is a blood-stained dagger. Splotches of the killings or sacrifices are all over the place. It was a messy affair. I'm grateful that, as a projection, I can't smell the blood.

The marsh pools are divided by a thin web of grassy walkways. The lone victor drags the corpses in pairs and throws two into each pool. No, not corpses, not dead. Undead.

These watery pits are the men's everlasting graves, according to the lone monologist. He believed they deserved to suffer like this for abandoning the Allies and joining Dark Lord Argosy Kahn in the Third Duel War between the Chosen One and the Dark Lord.

I observe him closely, and shudder with detestation at his malevolent and giddy smile. He incants a curse in what I assume is Old

Elvish (since the interpretation spell cast over me can't translate it) over the pool, and suddenly, one by one, the pairs begin speaking glibly to their respective partners, perfectly at ease with the whole undead-thing. I don't think they hear the bellowing chatty voices of those in other graves or realise that they themselves are dead. Seasons change. Years roll by. The conversations never end. The entire time, the men are free from sore throats, unfamiliar with tiredness, oblivious to the peculiarity of their behaviour, until one fateful day, a young man stumbles upon them and, well-intentioned, offers help to a pair in one grave. And the moment of realisation dawns on both men in the pit. Suddenly lost in their own anguish, neither of them ever considering consoling their partner, they scream forever.

And I imagine Mecky laughing hysterically like a fox drunk on rabbit blood. I do not want to see or hear any more. My head backlashes out of the bowl.

Another glass ball, another vision.

This one disinterests me most. Mecky tells some spiky-haired Laxciilian decorated in rings of body art to deliver two letters: one is for an Elven prince named Paris who never showed up for the Assembled's Meetings, the other is for Dwarf Mountain. The rest of the scene sees Mecky bully his postman into taking a route he doesn't want to travel. In the end, the delivery guy abjectly refuses to go anywhere, no matter how many maps Mecky promises to give him or portals Mecky promises he'll get opened.

I notice Mósandrirl standing in the doorway; I don't even think either of them are aware he's in such close vicinity. The Wizard is as useless there as he is now when it comes to the Elf. I mean, he's clearly not oblivious to the tactics Mecky employs to get what he wants; yet he abandons everyone to humiliation or manipulation at his friend's hands. But who knows? If I had friends, I might do the very same. But I doubt it.

Then it hits me: I've seen this delivery man's face before. He was one of the Wraith's victims the second time he entered the city! Maybe the Wraith's attack was Mecky's way of culling the herd of independent thinkers.

A muffled, dying-animal noise from somewhere causes me to take a cautious step back, but I must trigger another mirror, because a series of towers appear in one. The startle was all it took for me to accept that I'm pushing my luck. I've been here too long. It's time for me and my invalid feet to get the heck out of dodge, or to find something very incriminating—pronto!

Okay, one more—make it two.

The penultimate seeing-stone shows this:

The King is in here. He takes off his robe (yuck, this better not be a nudist feature) and reveals not scales as I had expected, but hideous scarring. It must be incurable given he has wonder-working medicine here yet still bears the marks. Then he covers his wounds with a thin black leather jacket with wide shoulders, and casts a spell with silver dust, potion vials, and smoke. Suddenly, he spins like a bottle-top—whirlwind fast—and looks to be in an ecstatic trance, hands raised as though in worship. Mystical energies swirl around him like snakes. Fitting.

And through the mist, a voice says, "Open your mind to me... Let us read each other's secrets... Open your heart to me... Let me know your truth..." And an intangible, three-dimensional projection appears that he addresses as Lear. I can tell they speak in a language I don't understand because their mouth-to-voice ratio is off, but thankfully this re-enactment has subtitles.

Lear stands next to a blazing fire—an eternal fire, he boasts (Well, *excuse me*)—and says (more to himself than to Mecky) that he does not remember what heat feels like. Oh, the arrogance of the damned. The heights (or should that be depths?) of their folly never ceases to amaze me. Did he really expect that all his wickedness came without a price?

"The Meetings are going as predicted," the snake hisses, disinterested as I am in Lear's self-pity— "Soon, the Assembled shall declare war on the Twelfth."

"And our races shall finally be avenged—and our world made safe for future generations—when the blood of the Dark One washes over the plains of Angoria… assuming, of course, that what you say is true."

"Is that why you sent the Wraith? To verify that the boy was here?"

"You are infamously slippery. I had to ensure that I had not fallen prey to any of your wiles."

"Tell me, Ambassador, should I expect you and your cohorts to show your faces prior to the Ritual?"

"How remarkably forward of you, Elvenson. You usually conduct your two-timing with more indirectness and flair."

"Once the boy's fate has officially been decided by the Assembled, the Council have demanded that I make a public announcement explaining how the ghoul got in. It causes quite a stir when the princess, a Triumvir, and nameless faceless aliens are massacred on one's front lawn. Getting a 'yes' or 'no' from you will be the simplest task this week. And if you were to come here and kill the Assembled mid-meeting, you would make my life simpler still."

"Pleasant as that would be for you, I am in no position to promise I will be going anywhere anytime soon."

"The Imp still has not arrived to free you?! He is probably following some imaginary lead to his Witch. Be patient with him, though. He typically delivers on his assignments eventually."

"True, but even then, you will not see me in person. It has been decided that, short of a severe disturbance, the Triune shall remain out of view until the Ritual. We are not yet ready to face the Dark One. We need more power and the Void still refuses to give it to three dullards who got themselves trapped under a mystical barrier for three centuries. Be a dote and hold onto him a little while longer."

"He cannot stay here! He will be the death of me!"

Trash talk ensues.

"Do not trifle with me, little King. I *own* you!"

The Elf must be embarrassed since he has no slit-throat comeback—a testament to how fragile their relationship is and how accurate Lear's words are. So he does what any wise person in that situation would do: he feigns coolness and changes the conversation.

"Do you have the prisoner?"

Six orcs enter Lear's presence and drag a roped, chained, and daggered being they call the First Vampire. Big Mo had mentioned the First Vampire was *in absentia* from the Meeting. Well, this explains it.

Giant-sized. Blue skin. A hulking brute with tranquilised beady eyes like pebbles, red like blood. Ears pointier than his teeth are sharp. Black, totem-type markings on his head at which I shudder, for tattoos make me very uncomfortable. He wears floppy bearskin over his shoulders and a stringy brown headpiece that ends with two tusks coated in gold. His bone and skull necklace clicks, cracks, and shatters—like his pride, as he's kept subdued by hideous inferiors and their electric cattle prods.

"That is not the prisoner I was referring to," drones the Elder Elf, bored. Lear ignores him.

The orcs lash the drugged vampire with whips and scar him with scythes. Lear smiles crookedly, and claps. A couple of orcs disappear off the radar, presumably to broadcast someone else's misery.

"You're so powerful but can't leave the barrier... They're so weak, but can enter and leave at will... Fate can be so cruel."

"Three hundred years I have been plotting the events of your life, Di'en, King of Vampires, through the medium of the Maze."

A growl for a response, taken to mean, "I do not answer to that name".

"Of course. *Lord of the Vampires*," the mock-gentleman corrects himself.

He purrs, more satisfied.

Lear boasts that he was responsible for the deaths of the six vampire clans; he had their Domes lifted and exposed them to the harshness of the real-life sun, causing them to explode. Then, by showing heavily edited footage in the skies, he framed certain blocked-off villages in the West full of Soucouyants and Haltijas, for if anyone was going to shatter the Maze before the Chosen One had a chance, it'd have been them.

Having fallen prey to Lear's deception, Di'en was released to ravage the Soucouyants and Haltijas in vengeance. His bloodlust satisfied, he returned to his own prison to find his family had been turned to dust-piles.

And the time the werewolves and giants killed his family, leading him to adopt a new son, so to speak—that was also Lear.

His every step... and every wrong done to him... it had all been preordained. How cavalier of Lear to admit to it with a grin! But Di'en is utterly desensitised to it; he's so sold out for evil now that it doesn't even register with him what a victim he is!

His only response is to hiss, "I will be used in no sacrifice, Mage," alluding to a pre-holographic conversation.

"How incredibly presumptuous of you."

"Will his death profit our purpose?" Mehkabikil enquires, in an unexcited voice.

"And spoil the fun? Why no, little King, that could set centuries-laid plans irreversibly backward. You keep your eyes on your objective, and I'll focus solely on mine."

"Do not be spikey. I merely thought useless bloodshed was beneath you. Ye wine-taster-type villains are usually classier."

Shuffles and curses sound from beyond the camera lens.

"Bring him in," Lear demands, and orcs carry in a boy vampire no older than ten in human years.

"Da! Please!" the child screams, white-blue in colour, coated in black tattoos. Brown bruises print his half-naked body. Yet no orc is strong enough to inflict the injuries I see. They think they're strong with their chains, but they don't even trust their legs to hold them up. In fact, the only one there that I can see in any way capable of inflicting such a wound on him is Di'en.

And whatever shred of pity I felt for the First Vampire is gone.

"Take him. Use me. Whatever you need, I will do. Just let me live forever."

That's it?! His only response?! That's barbaric!

"Very well." To the orcs: "Bring this one to the dungeons. Lock him up next to the Chosen One."

Oh, my holy days!

"How incredibly illuminating. That is all for now," the Elf nods. "Return to your machinations. I have a... *little kingdom...* to run." The Mage severs the connection.

What the Hell did I just witness? Is there dissension in the Triune's ranks? I mean, Silas was convinced I was the Chosen One, and he wouldn't have given the Elder Elf his staff if they were ideologically opposed, surely. And whose side is the Elder Elf on? Will that little Vampire be alright? What do the Triune have planned for the First? What will Lear do to the boy he thinks is me? And why is he alive? Why not use his blood to corporealise already? What is he being kept for?

Right. Okay. I need a moment to catch my breath, to think all this through.

Scarcely have I thought that for a second when, like a junkie, I tap another glass.

I see myself. I've grown. Go me! I have dyed my hair and grown it long and bushy. Either that or I'm wearing a blond wig. Potential Me is dressed in ceremonial blue clothes, identical to those Gideon is most frequently depicted as wearing in paintings. Alk'erion sulks in the corner of an elaborately decorated balcony. *Now, now, don't be sour!*

This is my big day. Potential Me turns at the sound of trumpets and Aurora walks down an aisle, beautiful as always, flowers in her hair, radiant as the spectrum. Jonathan Harker-Grey is there for some reason and nudges me.

"Wow… Congrats dude, she really is something." (Well, this is a pile of drivel. I would never tolerate anyone calling me "dude". Ugh).

"Yeah, she is." Potential Me beams with an open-mouthed smile that reveals perfect white teeth shinier than Jon's self-proclaimed medical condition.

About a year passes in an instant, because the couple now have a child. Golden-brown skin, owl eyes, sandy hair. Gosh, my palms are sweating. That's my son. He's actually mine. And he is awesome! I'm falling for my own little family. Mine! The dark, lonely, cobwebbed assemblage of brokenness and despair; the glass half-empty… has a family. And they're all mine.

Stop it, stop it, stop it!

I need to cop myself on. I've read enough comic books now to know that these futures are alternate, not definite. Don't expect good things. Hope is the greatest weapon at the enemy's disposal, for unfulfilled expectations are to the heart like an anti-flu injection that reduces the patient to writhing, vomiting, and bed sweat. A little more relaxed, I go on watching.

As this is Mecky's lair, I feel no sense of shock whatsoever when Potential Me transforms into the Dark Lord, murders his bitter Black Queen, and raises their heir to be so tyrannical, he offs Potential Me in his sleep. (The things I have to put up with… Stress of life!).

I hate waste and vandalism, but I don't mind *accidentally* knocking this crystal ball off the shelf and crunching it into smithereens with my one good leg.

That's when I hear a whimper. My head instinctively darts to the staircase even though I know the sound came from elsewhere. Slowly, my eyes survey the room. I croak a hello, but I'm not even sure I heard it. After a forced little cough, I repeat it louder.

Someone mopes like a child. There! Behind the mirror that showed me the towers. I stumble on over and lift the frame off the wall. And I gag.

A starved crippled form is tied to something like a banjaxed spindle-wheel with thorn vines. Clumps of hair are missing from his head; it must have been plucked by the handfuls. His throat bubbles with blood. Slices of his ears look like the hacks people get between their undried toes. As he gargles, I see that his orange teeth are misplaced and coated in silver slime, the roots of several eerily visible. And he mouths, *"Help me…"*

How could anyone do this? There really are no words to facilitate such cruelty. Deep down, I thank God that there are hot hobs in Hades for the wicked. It really is what they deserve.

When the shock has begun to wane, if even it can, my nose is first to enliven, and all it does is wrinkle at the smell of filth and churn my innards to sickness. At first, I wrestle with the question: why would the Elf do this? What was the point? What is his endgame? And then it hits me. It's Dol'ver! Alk'erion's accomplice. The one I abandoned to the flames.

"Hang on. I can go get some help. Just…"

His head shifts to one side, and he dies with a repulsive, crooked smile. He held on for who knows how long just to be found. Just so he wouldn't diminish into oblivion without the knowledge that someone realised he was missing. And then he saw it was me—the reason he was arrested in the first place—and rather than listen to my pitiable attempt at a Hold-On-Choose-Life speech, let go.

Well, if ever I'm feeling my list of incentives to rid Angoria of evil is running short, I appreciate the King going to the effort to lengthen my list. Congratulations, your Excellency, you have just made it onto the Chosen One's hit list—I don't care what the Wizard thinks of you.

The Mirrored Lady speaks again, and I know that Snake Eyes is there. I turn and fume at his stuck-up snout and lemon-sucking lips through which he somehow hisses something in Old Elvish at me. He has a poppy bruise from where his head hit a rock after his tumble this evening.

And for the first time, I'm not afraid of him.

"Well, if it isn't the ubiquitous Destroyer," he greets. "Although I had the courtesy not to throw you out on your ear the second I first laid eyes on you, I was unaware this gave you the impression you had free access to roam every square inch of my house."

"I was just exploring."

"Let us use what little time we have left most economically and refrain from lying to each other."

"Agreed. Let us be epitomic of integrity and truth." "Epitomic". I'm pretty sure I pronounced it incorrectly.

"What are you doing here?" He looks like I'm giving him a migraine. Oh, bless.

"Curiosity. Now I know it's killed a cat or two in its time, but I'm pretty Zen about that. Felines, really not my thing. Listen, do you have a pan and brush by any chance? I had a little accident. Your ornament..." I nod to the crystallite debris and dust.

"What have you done?"

"It was the one about your grandson," I smirk. His eyes widen in horror at the idea of us being family! "It made for an unusual pre-bed screening, but if home videos pass for quality entertainment around here, then who am I to criticise?"

"Who, indeed?"

I look up at the blonde woman in the mirror as her greeting draws to a close.

"She is beautiful. Was she very dear to you?" Of course, she was. I know this for sure, even without the stray, subtle quiver in his eyes. He has her immortalised in a downstairs compartment in a room that shouldn't exist.

"Was she Alk'erion's twin? Alk'eria?" He throws his eyes in disapproval at my impertinence. *That'll be a no.* "How did you know her? Like, was she a maid here in Laxciila? A friend? A... sweetheart? *All three?*" His silence is all the answer I need. "I cannot help but notice what sharp teeth she has. Alk'erion, too. This, as well as his... summertime skin condition... one draws all sorts of conclusions..." Ooh, I struck a nerve. His veins pop. "Can elves and vampires reproduce? I only ask because, in earthen fiction, vampires can't. Not naturally, anyway. Or were they bitten as adults? Or was she bitten, and then converted him? Where is she now?"

"She died. At the hands of one who would like nothing more than to see your charred bones in a glass case in Museum the Twelfth."

"So you killed her?"

"She, like you, posed too great a threat to be left alive. As such, I feel obliged to urge you to cut off ties with Loux Laxciila and flee into the dark of the night to pursue your true destiny, effective immediately—and to leave my home alone!"

"Well, that would be rude. The final meeting is tomorrow, and I'm sure the guests who have been thus far detained by your Abaddon sermons have expectantly waited some time to get a close-up of me, socio-prophetic celebrity that I am."

"Goodnight."

"Goodnight." And no one would ever guess that my feet are in bits the way I strut on over to the staircase, leaning on my cane as little as possible. "Oh, good sir," I begin.

"Hmm?" He doesn't look at me.

"There's a little something-something behind that mirror over there. You might consider swabbing it down with a dishcloth; maybe tackle it with a mop. Goodnight."

# 12

# MAUSOLEUM

It is custom here to mourn for at least a week before burying the dead and hosting any funeral processions, according to the books I've read in the library. I'm not sure why the first round of victims was simply shut away in a vault underground then. Maybe Mecky was waiting until Aurora and I'd joined them, hoping we'd be offed in the second confrontation with the Wraith.

Despite what I saw in his lair—that clip when he asked Lear if he'd only sent the Wraith to see if I was here—I still think Mecky knew more than he let on. I remember him skipping breakfast and coming into the dining-hall late that morning and staring at certain individuals. I'm almost certain that everyone who got the stink-eye that morning ended up dead by day's end, besides Aurora and me. Being a Triumvir, I have a little more invulnerability than your average Joe, and I pushed her low to the ground, and Green Cloak covered us with his magical sword. I have no idea where he ran off to after the smoke cleared. Maybe he chased after the Wraith, who got away again.

A few Laxciilians were paid to mark their respects and bury the victims, but I couldn't stomach the false wails, profiteers selling their overpriced bouquets, and tearful readings, so I skipped the funeral. Sure enough, King Mecky had the gumption to paint my absence as evidence of a stricken conscience, since even I knew (deep down in the bottomless pit of my black soul) that it should have been me who died, not anyone else. So passionate was he at this point that he even shed a tear. The sight of that alone makes me regret not going.

Still, I attend the funeral meal. I'll do anything for a good dinner.

All around the hall, refugees—usually so subtle—make no secret of their distrust of me. (The ones who supported me by showering my studio with canes either aren't among them or have intimidatingly recoiled into a posture of silence). They glare, whisper, and throw the food at me that their over-starved bodies can't digest. One re-enacts with breadsticks my assault on the King. Downing tea by the gallon, I sit alone since everyone I like is either on bed rest following their last venture out of doors or is busy at the eleventh hour trying to clean up after my most recent antics—proof that going outside reaps only heartache and stress, and that everyone should just stay indoors and drink tea and watch H.B. shows.

Mecky must appear in the doorway for my shirt feels one hundred and twenty eyes lighter, and everyone automatically ceases what they were doing and stands. Immediately, a flock of non-Laxciilian elves and oracles, as well as oddballs from a variety of other races, lockstep to the exit. Today, the Assembled reach their final conclusions about me and then bestow their biases upon my shoulders in the Enchanted Inner Court. Fun times ahead, so.

I am such a slow eater that by the time I have finished, all the other breakfasters have long gone. The Elven maids, unaccustomed to the vibrant material excesses of the other Laxciilians, usher in. Cloths and aprons everywhere, they sweep and clean, and though they fiercely protest it is contrary to their ways, I stay behind and assist.

Every effort I make is denigrated as the meddling of one who thinks they are helping but is in fact merely adding to the burden; but I persist until eventually, one of them hands me a brown sack of leftover food. I'm glad I am a martial artist, or the weight of it would take me to the ground and slop all over tiles we've just mopped. The elf who involves me is frail, bony, an avid squinter, and older than any elf I've seen. Her ears are covered by a white headdress. Before I can ask if she is human, she bows her head and hurries off penguin-style. The head maid, denoted only by wearing colours that aren't sickly, scorches her with raging eyes hot as dragon breath. I wear a questioning look for a while, and I'm finally directed with a nod through the kitchen and out to the dump.

As I near it, the heat gives rise to a mighty mixture of smells, a great deal more pleasant than the sight: piles of squishy pressed fruit, squeezed but uneaten. Shining sprinkles of metal: coins, swords, wires, tools, jewellery, teeth. And such wonderful garments: dresses, cloaks, gloves, shirts—worn once; others brand new but immediately discarded, by the look of them. From a barrel, milk flows like frothy foamy mountain streams. It cannot have been abandoned here any longer than two minutes ago. Brown bananas, thrice the size of those bought in Ireland, flow down them as though canoes on a river bend.

Loux Laxciila: the safest country in Angoria. The only free country. The only one not confined to a life of recession and turbulence, captivity and need, rationing and little. And they waste it—gloriously.

But light shines brightest in the darkness, and from over the dump hill, a purple heart-shaped jewel blinks. I gaze a few seconds before I realise it is a ring. (One man's trash is another man's treasure, as they say). I trudge through enough food to feed a town of several thousand, enough fabric to clothe them for a generation, and enough precious metal to pay off the Witherspoon mortgage. The haggardness of my movements because of my limp must make me look like a desperate scavenger, especially when I occasionally trip and surf; but I eventually make it to my destination.

A nasty rumour circulates back in Ireland that I have sticky fingers, because after a dinner party, I once "stole" (purportedly) kilos of sugar and dozens of pies from the banquet hall and a basket of apples from the reception area of a swanky Dublin hotel. But I will go to my grave swearing they were all included in the price. I scan the area to make sure I'm being stalked by neither elf nor bird, so I don't have a repeat experience with a six feet tall body-builder security guard in the doorway of said hotel.

"Oh, I'm a student. I live below the poverty line," I explained to deaf ears.

"Ah khom frum Nahgeria. Luh m' tell you abou' livin' bene' de povartee lahn!" snapped the S.S. Commander.

What followed was a lengthy lesson on global differences, economic challenges, and a sob story about how her husband was cheating on her back home, under the presumption that she was oblivious. Cry me a frickin' river.

I take the ring in my hand. On either side of the jewel are curves like the golden hand of Midas. From the tips of these droop wings. The ring is further decorated with silver seashell ornaments and hearts, lozenges, spirals, and diamonds. It is beautiful. I decide to give it to Aurora as a "Get Well Soon" gesture and slip it in my pocket.

I make my way back over and down the hill and peer into the supposed slops bag I was handed. Hell, no! Tossing this away would be a sin. There are fresh foods in here unsullied in every way, meanwhile, the world beyond Laxciila's border is starving! I hoist it back to the kitchen and am not ashamed to tell the questioning stares that I am not dumping that sack—a reservation not shared by the head maid who pours it all over the floor, squishes it with her foot, and screams for Mrs. Unseen Ears to clean it up.

Then the head maid cackles at me silently with a venomous expression that goads me to hit her twice as hard as I smacked the Elder Elf. And I think: had I built the Maze, I would have filled it with people like her. And that is the politest thought I have of her for the rest of the day.

Fists clenched, I turn and walk away in a huff; her cackles and barrage of insults still taunting me all the while.

Having looked for her in every room in the hospital, I venture to the library, but she's not there either. Then the café—still nothing. The last place I think to search is the Laxciilian Garden, for she told me once that she enjoys reading among the flowers, though my sheer indifference to all things botanical means I've never been there. If she's not there, I'll assume she's doing royal duties like being pampered, receiving guests with unpronounceable names, or rigging community competitions so that she'll win.

By the time I find the Garden, four hours after my rummage through the dump, I am hungry and fed-up. But there is a certain sustenance or refreshing quality about the area. The first thing I notice is how deathly quiet it is. But that isn't a bad thing. It's the sort of quietude deep people adore.

Surely, I spy my beverage buddy quickly enough, but she does not meet my eye. She is far too indulged scribbling in her little red diary. Therefore, I do the rational thing, and instead of walking up to her and saying hello, I hide and plan conversations we could have, and plot how I could manipulate or dictate these conversations whatever her responses.

Lest she turn and see me staring at her, I play naïve and pretend that I'm fascinated by an average hedgerow and follow its leaves into solitude down one of the many paths divided like a maze (which is in poor taste, if you ask me). Each path is strewn with flowers: roses, lilies, tulips, others I cannot identify. And all around the lawn stand to attention, military-style, stone pentagons and marvellous engravings of wood elves, celestial beings, deer, birds, griffins, manticore, roses, smiling youth hanging out under a tree bough, and dancing nymphs and dryads donned in delicate blossoming garlands.

Granted, the latter ones are a little risqué, but all in all, this truly is an undeniably beautiful garden: three large pools reflect an army of wine-red flowers and mustard shrubberies. Behind these is a fabulous and unguarded entrance either to the palace or somewhere else of great import. Palm trees tilt; their umbrella leaves offer shade. Meadow flowers, yellow like the sun, blue like bluebells, and red like flames beautify the labyrinthine walkways. Crocus blossoms among wide dark red leaves. Scarlet triangles peek like napkins in a gentleman's suit pocket out of cup-shaped flowers. There's a patch of every shade of pink I've ever seen and more. Plants perform, bow, and stand for applause. In one box of grass, a patch of thin bluish-white trees tangle and knot, arms fanned like a Y, topped with leaves like frizzy eighty's style hair. On a small hill, bushes trimmed with precision depict Elven war heroes and beasties. The equilibrium of the grass suggests that this sacred ground is not casually trodden on.

Despite having only complained about this country since my arrival, I feel quite at home here in this forgotten Eden. In fact, though I have always considered the Romantic poets a tad over the top, I too now hear that call to embrace the sensuous. To experience the feel of something good. I slip my right foot out of my beige slipper and dip my big toe onto the lawn. My toe perspires and the flat of my foot sticks to the warm grass like it has just been coated with paint, wet with the beads of nature's dewy sweat. The sunny Laxciilian air breathes through my curls of leg hair and lightly brushes my arms, and I want nothing more than to tear my clothes off and write a poem about bushes.

I pull away from the yearning and return my foot to my slipper. As I turn to leave, my eyes catch sight of an open book made of stone that must weigh hundreds of kilos. Dozens of names—none of which I recognise—are carved into it, and next to this, their date of birth. The year of their death is the same: "the Maze". Some of the carvings are still smothered in dust and must only have been inscribed today.

Newly awakened and eyes open wider than before, I take another survey of the trimmed hedge figures, and realise I recognise more of them than I would like from my last two face-offs against the Wraith. And unlike me, they didn't make it. Suddenly, I realise what this is: a graveyard.

All at once, the dozens or hundreds or thousands or millions of people I will kill or who will die in my name flash in my mind. Heck, it has already begun. All this time, Mósandrirl has been telling me that I'm the Chosen One who will restore peace to Angoria whilst the Elder Elf has been prophesying my future as Mex Confetricus. Little did either of them tell me, it is inconsequential which hat I wear—Saviour or Dark Lord; there is no difference. Fatalities will be excessive either way, and the violence and carnage only stops when I have destroyed one side or the other.

I wonder if any of them will be buried in such a beautiful graveyard.

No sooner have my thoughts rowed down such morbid canals than I feel Aurora's eyes on me.

I've come to always feel her when she's around, like the air her body mass takes up is pushed through the wind and crashes into me like a pleasant storm.

I mean no disrespect to the dearly departed, but I instantly lose all interest in them. None of them mean anything when compared to her. I shut my eyes and sniff the potent aroma of strawberries and lemons. She slinks into me from behind. Her arms slide beneath mine and wrap around my front. Her head rests on my nape. Her silk skirt brushes against my bare lower legs, sending shockwaves down to my feet and up to my calves. Always tense, I eventually exhale and relax, and we stay like this for what feels like forever. It's so peaceful here in our private place among the dead that, at some point, I may even drift off to sleep while standing for when I finally gather the courage to turn, she's gone.

And an Elven guard stands there instead. He tells me it's time, that the Magical Community requests my presence. As if I have a choice. This is no request. This is a command. To stand before the most powerful personalities in Angoria after the Triune as they seal my fate. And powerless to do anything on the contrary, I follow him.

He leads me down streets of gapes and wide eyes; this is the first hint of recognition any of the plebeians have given that they are even aware of the meetings. Most of them scowl and spite as I pass; some brave or melodramatic enough stand proudly, nod to me, and fall prostrate. Acknowledging none of them, I keep my eyes fixed on my chaperone almost the entire time. At the end of our walk, I follow him down silver stone steps that lead to a pastoral garden, nowhere near as beautiful as the graveyard, and twice as grey.

I count four dozen archers planted in the bushes, obvious as cenotaphs, arrows' teeth moistened to lick me should I get up to any funny business. *Dear Lord, let me be brave. Help me be brave. Make me be brave.*

Eventually, we make it through the armed Elven barricade and before a shimmering wall. Mustering all the courage available to me, I step through the force field, and if I wasn't a born and bred brooder, I'd laugh at the ticklish sensation. Unsurprisingly, the first person who jumps out at me is Mecky. I see him pick up and relocate facedown an ancient stele, then he turns his wicked horse head to me and hisses at me with those cruel eyes.

His messenger, my warden, leads me to a stone chair in the centre of a ring of magical creatures, then bows out and departs. Engraved on the seat are ten suns, which according to the books I've read, represent the leading powers of pre-Maze Angoria. Also, there's a fiery head, and beneath it a flame. It must be the symbol of the less than peaceful Chosen One, because it's the one of three that gives me the fewest chills. One is undoubtedly the Dark Lord, a wraithlike shadow king with a five-spiked crown, the middle one being twice as wide and thrice as high as the others. Its symbol is a twisted beanstalk of thorns, suggesting: he's a giant? Or his growth in power and influence? Or how he will choke the life out of the ten kingdoms? The final image is an eye wearing a two-pronged crown. A wing stems from behind each horn, an angel's and a demon's. Beneath is an unhelpful and equally ambiguous miniscule depiction of wings. This represents the third Triumvir, the Other, or the Pretender.

Afraid of giving the visage of nervousness, lest I wring my hands, I shove them deep in my pockets, yet there is nothing I can do to stop sweat seeping from the creases on my forehead and down my back. I try to look calm, but it's hard when the committee are a fireball's throw away from me. Speaking to me interrogatingly. Accusing me with hand gestures of things I'm not even going to speculate. Condemning me without trial with their eyes: some beady and dark, others large and bright, and some hungry and green. All the while, Mecky smiles at me with snake eyes and a snake mouth, certain that his problems are almost over. Little does he realise, I have yet to unleash a snippet of my holy vengeance upon him. He hands a bowled chalice of something red to the centaur next to him. It smells sickly and familiar, but I cannot put my finger on it. The centaur is the only one drinking anything, so the volume of each glug is amplified tenfold, the equivalent of the one earthling eating crunchy sweets at the theatre, or whose phone goes off at a funeral.

The Elder Wizard's here, too. He looks like he's been put through the ringer—which he has—but it means a lot to me that he's made the effort to support me through this.

I walk over to him and, in a whisper, protest, "You shouldn't be here. You have saved me enough as it is. All Angoria is indebted to you. And your part in all this is not finished. You are not finished. But you will be if you don't slow down and rest. Go back to the House of Healing. Rest easy. Sleep. Gather your strength. This"—I indicate to the ring of clowns— "is not worth setting you back or digging yourself an early grave."

Hands clasped, index fingers together, he says nothing for a moment, then: "You would prefer to do this alone, because that is what you are used to, and that is what you fear you will always be. But I say: 'No longer'." And just when I think he's about to break into a memorable, poignant, powerful speech that moves people so deeply that they later post a status about it, he nods to my chair, and averts his gaze.

As I return to the centre of the ring, I drink in the twisted sight of democratisation in the world of fantasy; their preconceptions on display; their judging attitudes; their spite. I see why the Triune tried so hard to keep them apart. Collectively, these heroes are one acidic unit.

I eye the freak show before and around me. I notice that every one of them passes around and then wears shells on their collars or chins— maybe these are translators. That is how I come to learn that what I had originally mistaken for forest growth are in fact Talking Trees. One sits on a rock, probably desiring the change. Next to the sitter are Gwendaldorfs, wizened male humanoids with living beards, multiple brains, and Asiatic eyes. Then there are the grotesque and evil-eyed Toad-Man and Crab-Man. Graceful elves sit next to these crossbreeds, putting them to shame. Immediately distinguished from Laxciilians, these elves are dignified, pure, honourable beings. No tattoos, no mad hairstyles, no ladies' magazine editor countenances. The males are dressed in thin garments woven from sheep wool, and the females in tissue-paper thin silk material, yet they look less promiscuous than the most fully clothed Laxcillian. Come to think of it, this is one of the only parties in which females are in attendance.

Now that I think of it, none of the leading Laxciilians who left the dining-hall for this earlier are in attendance, though out yonder, to the simultaneous flutter of flapping flowers or butterfly wings, I hear the feint ring of fake news proliferation. They must already be filming the announcement of the verdict against me—that I am the Dark Lord elect.

The foreign elves are sandwiched between the most unattractive beings present, for seated beside them is the head of a werewolf pack. In his human form, he's over six feet tall and his hair spikes dangerously. His eyes are wide and fearful like his claws and large flour sack muscles balloon from his every limb. Next are the Oracles, pupil-less men and women of fair and dark skin, moonlight hair, and knowing countenances. One of the women hashes witchy comments at me in a language I can't understand.

Next up, pixies and fairies look pretty sour. Oh, for goodness sakes, what did I ever do to them? Wait. No. It's not me they're seething at. It's the Elder Elf. Well, that is a relief. It's nice to have more than one ally at my side. Beside these are Lions: bigger than usual; sealed mouths; very fantastical. Next to them are the Eagles, bound in human form in view of the flight ban in Angoria. And then it's the Dwarf King, whose eyes tell me he wants me dead.

"Oh, lighten up," Fetch calls, and plonks down beside what Harper Lee would call the "bantam cock"—"I haven't killed you just yet, tuts," he winks.

Nearly everyone rolls their eyes as the Elder Wizard rises to stand. He begins by very importantly stating the absentees, something they've probably heard at the beginning of every meeting, given the chorus of groans: Paris, the Witch, the Vampire King, and more. Then he introduces me: Benjamin Thomas.

"Hello, everyone," I wave, and the succeeding silence reminds me of a particularly awkward eulogy I once gave at a funeral.

After an intimidating pause of silence, glowers, and pursed lips, Mecky rises. The hush that descends on the dining-hall whenever he enters falls here. He repeats my name. The sound of those five syllables from his sly crooked tongue is so wrong, so unnatural, that I feel unclean. I remember the last time I used pottery: my hands caked with thick grey clay; a webby structure outlined the map of my hand; and when I formed a fist, it cracked and piece by piece crumbled like a smashed mosaic. I feel that happening now. My skin and personage crack, peel, and fall to the grass. Suddenly, I'm shedding skin. In Mecky's perverse mind, I'm the deceiver packaged in camouflage. I'm the snake.

"It is delightful to see you like this, son of man," he hisses, tall and proud as an obelisk.

"It is delightful to be seen."

Mecky slithers around his audience and recites a spiel the Elder Wizard's translation spell has not prepared me for. I don't know why, but I wasn't given any seashell translator. The serpent takes advantage of my confusion and flashes me the occasional toothy smile to which I'm not sure how to reply, just to stir my paranoia. He begins to circle my chair like a mist and I feel his acid spit in my ear. Finally, he stops right behind me.

His breath causes my hair follicles to stand, and goose bumps sprout from my neck to my legs. I rub one leg against the other to burst them, but my jaw quivers and my eyes weaken. I am a temple built on quicksand, disappearing quickly for all to see. Even his hisses muffle. I'm terrified. He places his hands on my shoulders. His thumbs might as well be scales brushing off my neck, because vomit mounts. I'm going to faint, and vomit, and choke to death on my vomit. I'm literally losing consciousness.

"Benjamin," the wizard calls out with a wheeze.

I awaken from near conked-out mode and it is like the world waits for me to say something. Maybe it is. "Pardon?"

"How do you plead?" Mecky asks slowly, with emphasis on every hollow syllable.

"Not guilty," I whisper weakly, my eyes not knowing where to look. I mean, what else was I going to say?

"Repeat!" Crab demands in a Cockney accent to the hooting boisterous laugh of Toad, "so all present may hear you, not just those with incredibly sensitive hearing."

"Not guilty," I repeat louder, after a little cough. The Committee seem to wait for a lengthier response. Too bad they're not entitled to one.

Again, Mecky soliloquises to the crowd for a while, and this time I notice some of them shooting him angry glances. I hope his unwillingness to shut up about me is unwittingly losing his agenda votes. When he finally pauses for a breath, I ask, "What was that you said?"

He turns, appalled and thrilled that I have spoken up. "I am itemising your crimes to the Assembly."

Huh. I thought they were called 'the Assembled'! "What crimes?"

"A false face and schemer, you are a categorical opponent of truth and integrity."

"I never lie, dearie, though you are absolutely right to discount much of what I say."

"Theft of my potion ingredients..."

"That again? You're like a dog with a bone, Mecky. Give it up."

"An affinity for being present whenever and wherever trouble erupts. The assault, in front of many witnesses, of a monarch, no doubt!"

"Let me guess: the greatest affront in that example was that there were spectators?"

"The murder of a well-respected warrior king!"

"Oh, please! You don't even like him! You're only pretending to because, for once, you are ideologically synchronised. Not that that is a valid argument in a court of law, given that the Dark Lord's purportedly intended fatality is... still alive." All eyes shift to the Dwarf King who shuffles uncomfortably in his seat. He looks like he wishes he was dead just so he could be avenged already. "Not to mention that if I'm the Chosen One and you murder me, then you're all as good as dead anyway."

"You are *not* the Chosen One."

"Alright then. Consider the unfortunate paradox that, if I am his intended killer yet punished prior to his demise, then you will have effectively shamed and killed an innocent and brought a curse down on your head. Before having proved your theory and merited a certificate of sanity, you will have been reduced to the same lower rung on the morality ladder as I stand on. Now you don't seriously believe that murder goes unpunished in this world or the next, do you?"

"But if you are the Dark Lord, which I ejaculate you are, but are removed prematurely from the equation, countless innocents shall live."

"Keep your ejaculations far from me. No one will be saved if quantum physics kicks you in the teeth and pulls the strings of the cosmos to correct the intended timeline." I've lost just about all of them. Clearly, I'm the only science-fiction fan here.

"Your meaningless rambling fails to secure you from the outstretched arm of my emergency powers."

Remaining on my seat, I lean in as close to his ear as I can. "Is that how you justified slaughtering Dol'ver?"

"You are crazed."

"Oh, I have not ruled out the very real possibility that I am in need of several rounds of therapy, but rest assured, I remain in the right mind concerning at least one thing—*you*."

330

Unrealistic though it is, in a world created with such order and decorum, that this behaviour should be allowed to continue in a judicial proceeding, I lay it down to the court's unspoken deep longing for drama after weeks of Mecky's convoluted monologues and inflammatory rambling. Or perhaps they want to see how I deal with conflict and libel to test my character.

Whatever their reason, Mecky withdraws, gathers himself, and declares it is time to put my fate to a vote; to denigrate me as no more than a piece of paper that may unapologetically be fed to a shredder. Understandably enough, the Witch's, Vampire's, Paris's, and the other absentees' votes are effectively null and void.

"The motion: this boy is the Twelfth and Final Dark Lord, and as such, this house advocates the employment of emergency powers to initiate any and all preventative measures," Mecky shouts. He gets the ball rolling, "Guilty." And we're off to a bad start.

Despite the improper exaltations of the younger centaur, the vote ultimately comes down to his older, more majestic brother; one vote per race or kingdom (as in the case of the elves). Not guilty.

"Thank you."

The Trees. Guilty. The Hell do they know? They're trees!

The Gwendaldorfs. Not guilty.

"Thank you."

Toady and his partner in crime Crabby are of one mind, and they have made their opinions crystal clear since I first stepped foot in this garden.

The elegant elves take a long time to deliberate, and just as I've lost hope: not guilty.

"Thank you."

Their spokesperson nods slowly, his deep and experienced eyes glued to mine.

Faragmor the Werewolf growls a doggish "Guilty." I actually wouldn't mind being the Dark Lord if it meant having an army of soldiers as scary and ferocious as him at my disposal, but I don't know where his allegiances really lie.

The five Oracles waste no time in reaching their verdict. Guilty.

"Every sacrifice we have ever made… Every friend we have ever lost… Every battle we have ever fought… Every disappointment we have ever shouldered… Every stain we have ever inked perpetually on our hands… It all amounts to nothing if we let the Destroyer go free." *Ah, go get eyes, you blind gits! Then, with a fresh perspective, come back to me and express your renewed point of view.*

The one who actually has eyes glares at me. I stick my tongue out at that mute whose chin quivers like tears are inevitable.

The two ginger pixies, a young male dressed like Peter Pan and an older female dressed in pink, give reassuring smiles, as do the two female fairies, a pink-haired female and a brunette whose face is half burnt off. They verbally attack Mecky and his supporters for a good five minutes before delivering the verdict. I mouth a thank you and give them a rare but much-deserved smile. They beam rainbows in response.

The Lions yawningly drone that they cannot in good faith gobble me up for something I have not done yet, and then go to sleep.

It's a tie! The Eagles discuss the complexities of the time stream and other convoluted rubbish, but circumspectly permit me a "not guilty" status; though they promise to monitor my progress. One in the lead! Yet my flash of optimism dissolves at the sight of the small, tight-featured, gruff Dwarf King. I'm hardly surprised by his vote, though in fairness, he is afraid I'm going to pop an axe in his skull.

The Elder Wizard. Not guilty.

"Thank you."

That's…

OMHD! I can't believe it. Eight votes to seven. They think I'm innocent! Hero-material! No one has ever believed in me! And Mósandrirl aside, I didn't even think anyone here liked me! I'm the Chosen One! Sure, it's because a bunch of oddly dressed Halloween characters and animals say so, but now is not the time to nit-pick. Now is the time to shake my supporters' hands (but not mice-catching paws or killer talons) and to assure the people of the world that I am going to do everything in my power to destroy the Mages, their demons, Gideon and the Void, because in this moment, I believe I can do it. The power of having words of life spoken over you!

I am so relieved that I process too late what I see. The younger centaur, eyes blank like Aurora's were when under Mecky's control, drops his medicinal scarlet mixture to the ground. Indeed, smell must be one's strongest sense, because suddenly it hits me: it's what the traders injected the Warpers with! *Bolta!*

The centaur's grey-black hair, pulled back in a ponytail, pounces in the air as his heavily armoured horse parts rise on their hind legs. His pointy ears peak either side of his angular face, too monstrous to be human. The bow, tall as him and slung over one shoulder, jolts a little. He draws from his sheath a wide long sword that easily weighs seven kilogrammes and strikes his older kingly brother dead. And then he roars "GUILTY!" just before Mecky seals the verdict on a scroll, finalising the Meeting's outcome.

The centaur charges towards me.

I sit frozen on my slab chair, my ready-made gravestone.

This creature is going to kill me, and I don't even know his name.

# 13

# THE BANQUET

So much for innocent until proven guilty.

The gargantuan horseman charges toward me, going for the kill. My feet are too frozen to move. An elf with excellent speed loads his bow and lets the arrow fly straight into the centaur's unprotected hind legs. The centaur plummets behind me with a whinny or a neigh or whatever horses do, and his sword slams against my chair. I have no idea what metal the sword is made from, but my chair shatters, and I'm now rolling in a dusty rock heap.

The Elder Wizard, still too weak to cast any magic and so immobile he depends entirely on his staff for support, rises and staggers over. I know that if the sword descends again, he'll gladly sacrifice himself for me—but I will not let that happen.

"Treason! Take him out!" he demands of the company.

The centaur tears the arrows—for more have been fired at him and taken bites of his hind legs—from his limbs and flings the toothpicks to the ground. They stake the grass like birthday candles on icing. More arrows dig into his thinly exposed flesh. His thick muscles pulsate and enlarge with steroids of hot blood and adrenaline. *Shunk, shunk, shunk.* More arrows jut into his limbs, not that he acknowledges the pain. There's an occasional *ping* whenever he moves unexpectedly and the arrows hit his armour. He smiles like a goblin and raises his bronze-handled sword over his head.

And then, I am shielded by the warm shadow of the wizard as he covers me like a mother bird. I slam my eyelids shut and when I open them, he's gone. Talons scratch. Swords swipe. Feathers scatter all around. Fairy dust shimmers as one fairy drops dead. Cats eat horsemeat. Toad and Crab laugh.

I'm too busy crawling for dear life at the patter of hooves and paws all around me to take in any specifics, other than Mecky, a few metres off to the right. He holds a bronze parchment over a chalice that glitters with tongues of purple, blue and silver flames. In sounds unheard of in the Phonemic Chart, he hisses a suspect enchantment. I repeat myself two or three times before he hears me.

"What is that?"

"The Assembly's verdict," he answers. "This centaur's inflammatory charge against you overwrites his brother's misguided unwavering support. With this act, I seal your fate, Triumvir." Mecky drops the parchment into the chalice, and in response, there bellows a roar of thunder and a burst of sunlight and white smoke. He smiles crookedly and his eyes widen and yellow. He really does make the most of every opportunity.

Just then a spear conveniently rolls over to me. Instinctively I grip it and rise to my feet. But can I use it? If it comes down to it, him or me, could I end him? I mean, it's not hard, the physical process of killing someone. Not really. As Sensei taught me the day we met, your body is foremost a fighting machine, and everything else is a weapon. I think I could, to be honest, do what needs to be done. And why shouldn't I? I'm the Dark Lord now—or as good as.

The centaur kicks and slits the Lions and turns his attentions back to me. I look in his eyes for that intimacy that only killers and the to be killed can muster. But all I see is blankness. He gallops and launches into the air, sword poised for demolition, ignoring the arrows as though they are wind.

It is a long second. Long enough for me to see an opening just under his right armpit. To prepare to slice and dice him. To choose not to take it. The Elder Elf is the real enemy here.

I move out of the way when it's too late for him to do anything about it, and I thrust the blade into the back of one of his front legs. He crashes to the ground. The leg that landed properly becomes unsteady and snaps. The wizard appears and clobbers the centaur's head with his staff, but he pulls something in his shoulder, is quickly overcome with spasms, and passes out, down for the count.

The roar the broken creature unleashes from the dead of his sleep is more beastly than human. It is soon silenced by an elf who effortlessly lifts the Dwarf King's axe, its head twice as wide as my body and half as thick, and mallets the handle into the centaur's temple. His catty purple lips breathe their last and give up his spirit.

And everyone falls silent. A younger brother killed his older brother and king today, and now the usurper too is dead. There will be racial, international, and political consequences. They all know this to be true; that the free Angoria they're fighting for may not be as idyllic and hearty as they once believed. The ever-composed Meckster and I are the only ones who don't look terrified. His excuse: because he's evil. Mine? Maybe because I'm Irish, I don't get this whole monarchy thing. So rather than mourn the hybrid who just tried to kill me, I move on to more utilitarian matters: planting seeds of doubt against the chairperson of this sect: "His breath is revolting. Ugh! The smell of dead people…"

All around me, noses more sensitive than mine sniff about his mouth, and soon feline, wizarding, Elvish, and wolfish eyes turn to the Elder Elf. Ah, there it is… The fear…

*Come on*, I egg. *Expose the King. Don't leave me alone in this. Come on, what kind of heroes are you? Don't leave me hanging!*

Yet like the wizard so often has before, they let me down. I can't imagine why. What hold does he have on them all? Or is this what loyalty looks like up-close? What a hideous quality to have. Either way, I decide it's time to make my exit.

I explain all this to Aurora later over tea; it's easier to get a hold of her now than it was this morning.

"Awful, just awful," she chimes. "More tea?" I never refuse. "Now then, Syke, dear, despite this spot of bother, you must come to the Leaver's Banquet tonight. Tomorrow Papa sends home most of his guests, their purpose having been completed... however unsatisfactorily. They will return to their homesteads and prepare their people for when he calls." I don't follow. "Papa has long believed that the deliverance of Angoria will come in the form of global mutiny and that the time has now come to mobilise, even if his methods were initiated in underhanded vogue... But first, the dismissal of the Assembly calls for a night of boundless festivities. All Angoria rots away in squalor and hopelessness, but the party will go on."

"Do you believe it will come to that?"

"Why, yes. Papa has already purchased new cufflinks."

"No. I mean, all-out war." I had hoped this whole saving-the-world-thing would be a top-secret mission and that the fewest number of people would be in on it, to lower the death toll.

"I do not know what I should think. One believes many things, I suppose, notwithstanding how irreconcilable they prove."

"'Irreconcilable'?"

"The illusion projected by the arrogant, ill-tempered warmongers that peace can come through violence."

"You don't believe that some tumours need to be hacked out with a scalpel?"

"Of course I do. In the correct arena. With a knife, hacksaw, or other apparatus of torture? Never. Do you?"

"I don't know." As a Christian, I know I'm supposed to be pro-life and nay-murder, but killing strikes me as being a grey area. Or maybe that's my sad attempt at trying to justify the outcome of The Incident, when I made that fatal choice; when I knew only one of us was going to make it out alive… when I knew it was either him or me. "Yes."

"I am disappointed in you, Benjamin."

Oh, how that gets to me! And her subtle shift from 'Skye', short for 'Skylar'—which means 'Chosen'—back to 'Benjamin'… I'm this close to reminding her about how she killed Edgar.

Sensing that she's ticked me off, she tries to turn the conversation towards a topic that she hopes I'll find more agreeable: "Let us not pretend that every member of the Resistance has the correct motives. There are those who hope to go to war against the Triune so as to manipulate the crisis to create a military-industrial complex that they can exploit as they set out empire-building in (what the cultural theorists are calling) the New Old Angoria."

I'll be beheaded if I'm caught dissing the Resistance after today's murders, since my being me was the catalyst, so I decide that the Resistance's geo-political militarisation is one rabbit hole I can do without going down. Instead, I ask, "Are you sure it is wise to allow your guests a glimpse of what Laxciila has really been like for the last three hundred years? I have not known your people to be particularly subtle or low-key."

"Over the last couple of months, I have organised a charity for each of our departing guests. I should think the far-reaching consequences of the respective financial gift will distract recipients from the nation's two-facedness for one night."

"Were many Laxciilians willing to sponsor?" She chooses to pretend not to have heard me. It wouldn't surprise me if she was her only trustee. "Not to sound glib, but if the banquet's going ahead, does this mean I'm not being executed?"

"Of course you will be. Just not today."

"Tomorrow, then?"

"Perhaps tonight."

"Sure, we'll see how the banquet goes." And since I'm still marvellously ticked off with her disappointing comment (like, who does she think she is to judge me? She doesn't even know me!), I say bye and leave.


As evening falls, pink candyfloss like thumbprints smudge a blue sky. A purple sheet shimmers in the background. I shower, wash my hair, whip out a comb and go for the Gatsby look. I quickly use the toilet, and wipe with the leaf Lanky gave me. His scribbles are imprinted on my mind now anyway, and I don't want anyone stumbling across it and reading it. That reminds me: I rummage through my drawers and extract a few vials of what look like almond essence and I pop them into my waistcoat pocket. All set to go, I take a quick gander in the mirror, and fix my collar.

An Elven maid came to my door a couple hours back and handed me swanky blue threads: blue and yellow boxers; a silver tie I won't be wearing due to a lack of proficiency in that department; grey socks which, for some reason, I find very funny; trousers similar to those worn on Earth but that retain a unique Elvish flair; and a white long-sleeved shirt with blue buttons. They've given me a gold Aladdinesque waistcoat which I immediately adore, and a velvet blue jacket I could rub for all eternity, it's that soft.

"You have outdone yourselves," I said, only to be told by the only humble she-elf in Laxciila that Aurora had made everything and found a comfortable pair of leather shoes that fit me perfectly in the Lost and Found room. The shoes were obviously left behind by a previous earthling who'd slipped through a portal while shopping—they still have the price tag on them.

An unexpected knock at the door brings me back to the present moment.

"Come in, should your intentions be honest."

"Let me get a look at you," the wizard says paternally as he limps in, leaning more heavily than ever on his staff, before he showers compliments on me no one ever has or is likely to again.

"Wow! Get a load of *you*," I reply, and he does a half-twirl. Gone are the grey threads and Kohl's pointy hat. Instead, he sports a wine-red cone with golden glittery designs and a matching cloak and robe. He has pointy tipped shoes and has dyed his beard and hair orange. It is odd, to put it politely, but it strangely suits him.

For the first time since we met, he doesn't look like he's dying. "My goodness, aren't you the figure of health?" Was one not to already know he has sustained serious damage recently, all suspicion would be eliminated in view of how grand he appears. Looks were never a strong point of mine, but I did my best to conceal my pangs behind top fashion brands, when I could afford them. Suffer in silence, that's what I say.

He looks as though he has something important to say, but he isn't very forthcoming, so I don't push it.

Still facing the mirror, I see my reflected lips ask his withholding face, "What would you do if you only had one more day?"

"You do not only have one more day."

"That isn't what I asked," my subconscious rejoinders.

"Oh," he exclaims off topic, "I have something for you." He pulls out from behind him a long sausage-shaped bag. "It is dark blue," he nods, and I pretend I didn't notice ten seconds ago. I lean over it and peak in. It's deeper on the inside and houses clothes, cloaks, at least three different pairs of footwear, rope, swords, daggers, axes, and archery weapons, and I see that he's gotten the diadem back and put that in, too.

"This is all for me?" He says it is. "You shouldn't have. Thank you. But I-I-I can't accept this. I-It's too much. I can't repay you."

"How about you save us all, irrespective of how little we deserve it?"

"Will I have time to come back here later?" He shakes his head, and before I can ask anything else, he puts one finger to his lip and twirls another one in circles before putting it to his ear.

The implication is clear: despite his protection spells, he still isn't convinced that the Elder Elf hasn't found a way to bug the room.

Instead, he touches my forehead and a poem is transmitted from his fingertip to my thoughts:

> "You will know when and be told where,
> And you'll meet an associate of mine there.
> With him to my base you'll hike
> And there we'll launch our counterstrike."

I step away from the mirror, gather my journal and pens, subtly move the vials from my pocket to between the journal's pages, and carefully lower them into the rucksack. He walks into my en-suite bathroom and comes back with kilos of large leaves that we use for toilet paper in Laxciila and buries them deep within the bag.

He *oh*s again, and draws a perfect red rose from up his sleeve in true magician fashion. He fixes it in my lapel, and takes another rose, white this time, from his pocket, and says, "For whom it concerns." Aurora.

"I am neither affectionate nor sentimental."

"Your feelings are unimportant. People are." He eyes my silver tie on the bedsheets.

"There's a full-moon out there. The tie is to keep Fargamor the Werewolf at bay," I joke. He looks puzzled. "Because it's silver." He only stares blankly. "Never mind. I tried to make with the funny. It flatlined." Then I cough. "Could you—?" He reaches for it and nooses it around my neck with a smile as I stare at him in the mirror.

"And now we dine," he says and steps to one side. He bows and lets me lead the way, then we exit my room. And since I know I won't be here again, I whisper goodbye.

We walk from my quarters to Laxciila Palace, and it is breathtaking. The citadel's very outline is lit up in a mirage of luminous colours, none of which include blue. If intentional, that's downright petty. Its towers are rocket fire and great beacons spit fireworks above the doorway. Circuses and carnivals line the walkway: I'm talking fire-breathers, snake charmers, fools sticking swords down their throats, jugglers, gamers, performance artists, stretchy twisty people—the lot! Exotic dancing waiters serve food and wine on trays balanced on fingertips and toenails. Tamed mythological creatures leap and do tricks and give rides.

The wizard leads me down the corridors to the banquet hall. He speaks mostly about the paintings on the walls but I'm too busy feet-gazing to look at them. I feel my social phobia twitching, so I keep my eyes to the floor, inhale deeply but quietly, and try to prepare myself for the vast crowds and threats that await behind the thirty feet high double-doors at the end of this corridor.

We step inside and the room booms. Scary masks, funny masks, elaborate gowns, floating tresses, fingers locked like those of Botticelli's Three Graces', legs longer than nature intended, heels that can't be walked let alone danced in, mad hairstyles, groomed fur, bronze statues of all races, rainbows bouncing from one wall to another and back again, pyramids of sponge balls with cream, caves of nuts, thrones of rolls, a crystal dragon fountain of booze that smells amazing from fifty feet away, pools of soups, life-sized mythological creatures made of fruit and vegetables. The walls are gold. A splendid chandelier wide as a carriage and shining like Christmas lights hangs low from a rope reinforced with a chain. Hundreds of little candles dance jollily, suspended in air above the rectangular floor.

And every class, race, tribe, and kingdom stand socially segregated like they never left the Maze at all. These slavish peasants don't recognise the freedom they have been extended. And on a semi-circular platform sit the Royals. Not one of them looks at the other.

The wizard nods to the top of the golden staircase and says something about addressing the Queen. Ah! She's Pip! The Apple Costume lady! I'm surprised to discover the Queen's alive, although I think I should have pieced this nugget of information together sooner. Not to mention Green alluded to her outside the Wraith's house when bickering with the ever-hated Mecky. I can be so slow on the uptake!

At a glance, I conclude that I can't see anyone else here on ground level that I could ever hope to like, so I tag along with Mósandrirl. With every step nearer the Royals, my anticipation to see Aurora grows. (I've clearly gotten over the offence I took at her earlier). I have to bite my lips and picture endangered seahorses to avoid exploding with giddiness. Yet the second her form comes into my line of vision, gazing upon her beauty is the scariest thing I can imagine. I mean, what if she doesn't look back? Or worse, what if she does? I play it safe and keep my eyes to the floor.

From the corner of my eye, I can just about make out the wizard's bow to the Queen, but my questionable attempt to copy him—since Benjamin Thomas bows to no one—is so downright poor that even the graceless, etiquette-deprived Alk'erion can't resist making a condescending remark. My dagger eyes knife his Manga ones, and he falls silent, afraid I'll burn his face off again. He's a fine one to be scoffing, mind you; he wasn't even given a throne to sit on, only a cushion on the floor. He even scratches his alive-with-fleas hairy ears with his foot. He has never looked more like a dog.

The wizard extends his hand to the Queen, her white skin lifeless as a mannequin's. Thick with layers of powder and paint, her eyes bat slowly and give off a look of bewilderment and boredom. She wears an elaborate crown of three gold spikes, a metre high each, held in place by a ballooned red hat with black whiskers. Her black hair is designed in spider shapes at the sides and a butterfly shape at the back. The whiskers and hair twist and turn so complexly (carelessly?) that it's hard to distinguish thread from hair. Her sleeves are red cones, widest at the brim where her tiny hands peep. She wears an orangey-red robe under a cloak that looks so heavy that I'm not sure how she made it here without breaking her cocktail stick legs. She holds an egg-holder sized goblet in her hands.

I haven't heard anything that suggests elves can get sick, though this woman is the definition of psychological and physiological affliction.

"We have not danced in many an age, Niccolae Firebird," she says—yet another name for the Elder Wizard. It's weird. I had imagined her to either be dumb or to have a squeaky voice, but it's actually very deep and slow like the flicker of her eyelids.

"As I recall, my dear, you danced whilst I swayed on the spot, most embarrassed," the wizard returns with a grin. "And with regards to age, you are more beautiful now than back then, during the Great War of the Eleventh Age."

"Was it really so short a time ago?" I don't think she cares whether he answers. "How time drips like a tap disconnected from a plumbing source when one is waiting for the many-handed bodice of Death to come and take one away," she says, so jaded I think she'll cry if she keeps up speaking sentences that long. Silence lingers on the platform until finally, with a lethargic huff, she makes an effort. "I do not recall any of us looking particularly fanciful during the Eon of the Flame, Mósandrirl." And that's as long a conversation as can be hoped ever to pass through her lips.

"Too true, my Lady. Though, if I may confess"—he moves in as though telling a cheeky secret— "I do miss Gideon's pet Valtor, Lord of the Flame, in view of what we have had to contend with in more recent days. Good and evil were more finely delineated back in his day."

For a short while afterwards, she looks ghostly, not quite remembering who she is or how she got here or why there's a band of fairy tale characters drinking and eating and looking like ants fifty feet beneath her.

Finally, "Elder"—she drifts into a pause as though trying to remember which one he is— "Wizard, shall we dance, for I very much would like to speak with you?" I stare at his outstretched hand. It's probably ailed with pins and needles by now.

"Of course, my Lady." She takes his hand with great fragility, afraid that her own will fall off, and five identical brunette maidens in simple purple dresses usher out from behind a curtained wall, lifting her dress tails. I take her goblet from her and slip something in it, then put it down at the foot of her throne. And they're off, each of her footsteps mightily precarious.

I wait awkwardly until the current song stops playing. Then I look at the princess. She looks positively radiant tonight. Her hair is golden; silver clips and thin rainbow-shaped bars swirl through, holding it in a large ball shape at the back. Her blue eyes are crystal puddles. Her pink lips are content and glittered. Her proud elf ears are pearled. A gold chain that ends in a metal rhombus with the symbol of the kingdom chokes her neck, but she doesn't appear too uncomfortable. Her dress is jet black and hundreds of tiny blue, silver, and white jewels sparkle from the waist down. Long white silk gloves stretch to meet her short sleeves. I have never seen anyone look so dazzling.

"Tell me, little one, are you a religious boy?" It's the Elder Elf. Aurora cringes out of her skin at the sound of his voice.

"If I were to say no...?"

"Then I would ask by what means, short of miraculous, did you happen across a personalised invitation to this function that I never sent?" He doesn't look at me once, just keeps his snake eyes locked on the masked maggots below.

"Well, I could hardly miss my going away party. You are still planning on executing me tomorrow for as-yet unrealised acts of genocide against the biped peoples of Angoria and their good friends, the Talking Trees, right?"

"I had not forgotten," he smiles widely, face straight toward me this time.

"Good. Just so long as we're on the same page." I walk away from him and get down on one knee before Aurora, and shrug off the yelps, *woo-hoo*s, and claps from the nosy figures below.

"A rose for the Princess Aurora," I say and hand the white budded flower to her. She blushes, thanks me, and then extends her gloved hand. I kiss it. She smiles. I smile. Then we both stop.

"Is this the scene when you both profess your undying love for one another?" drones the King, and Alk'erion rolls around on his mat in hysterics. I glare at Mehkabikil and don't dare look at Aurora.

"I don't know much about liking people. I know even less about the ambiguous temporal emotion you've just mentioned. But one thing I guarantee you: two broken people can offer each other nothing better than contented misery… like you and your wife." I'm going to go out on a limb and assume she hates him as much as everyone else does.

"You are a hormonal child with no life experience who has an attitude problem that is nothing short of serious. What do you possibly know about brokenness?"

"Only what I have seen. I have never once met a person who wasn't broken. Everyone has messed up. Everyone is messed up. Everyone wants—*needs*—something. We're all hiding something or running from someone. We all have unfulfilled desires and dreams, expectations for life that haven't been met."

"And what are you hiding?" I shrug and smirk. "So, you played the troubled teen card, and you got a friend out of it… I suppose it is true what they say about misery loving company. I call such a connection 'sad'."

"Brokenness is not a glue; it is the smithereens of a shattered mirror scattered over a carpeted floor and knotted in the fabric. Brokenness is not a badge of merit. It's a fact of life. Being broken doesn't make you a hero, like I once thought it did. It means you're a victim, a prisoner, a slave." I'm staring at Aurora now. "The reason there are so few heroes is because so few people decide to break out of their broken mould and just be one."

"Is that why you were going to kill us all? You were too lazy to slap a dopey grin on your face and get on with life like the rest of us? Were you going to recite a sob story monologue before you put chains around our necks and whipped our backs?"

"I am done trying to convince you. By the way, your wife seems nice."

"Tell me about *your* family, Dark One. First your parents; what beasts were they: a devil and a witch? Are they still surface-dwellers, or did you destroy them before you came to ravage our world? What were their

347

professions: teachers of Dark Arts, dungeon wardens, tyrannical monarchs? Do they see themselves as more sinned against than sinners, victims of your tirades or cursed for having birthed you?"

I still don't know if he's made a connection between the One-Armed Man and myself, so I play it safe and turn the conversation in his direction.

"Oh, little King, I had thought that someone in your stage of life would regard family-centric chats with better taste and decorum." I look at his wife dancing with another man, his son squatting on a mat while eating spiders that had been snooping around his armpits a minute ago, and Aurora fixating on the far side of the balcony. "I mean, family is clearly a sore topic for you. It must be so upsetting that out of the two children you've reared in the several millennia"—he sniffles, about to cry— "in which you've been alive, the only one you lower yourself to acknowledge cannot so much as look at you."

He rises and shows that "little King" was a poor choice of phrase on my part. It sounded so well when Lear said it. He slithers to the balcony, and at the sound of his rattle, the music and chatter instantly halt.

"Loux Laxciilians and guests... *friends*," greets the serpentine King. "I beg your attention a moment." He delivers what he thinks is a joke, but the delayed reaction demonstrates just how greatly the host's popularity has dwindled in recent weeks. Then he spends a good ten minutes sycophantically flattering his other half in the "We Hate Benjamin Club", the Dwarf King. I don't think anyone but the loner stump listens beyond two minutes, but when Mecky branches out in his compliments, the audience warm to him.

Lastly, he welcomes for one night only the special guest who, though now only dominates a platform, unstopped, will soon dominate the world. At first, I'm puzzled, but then I realise it's me. I drop to the floor, but as I'm on the platform, everyone has already seen me.

"Ladies and gentlemen, I give you... Benjamin Thomas, the Twelfth Dark Lord of Angoria!" And the roars of approval I get sicken me. Fearfully, I lift my eyes above the banister.

Every eye of every carnivalesque false face looks up at me. The Laxciilians, distinguished only by their expensive dress, hoot, howl, wow, and cheer. The werewolf bangs a table, drunk or ecstatic. How do they find this entertaining? Those who voted in opposition of the Elder Elf to their credit remain silent, but I don't appreciate their useless unmasked pitiful stares. I glance back at Aurora because she is the only one in this room who, to whatever capacity, understands me. And she is displeased—angry even. Because this is wrong.

I turn back to the crowd and drop my head. My chest tightens. My fists clench. My top teeth sharpen my bottom row like iron. I need Sensei to tell me how to calm my rage, because Fetch is at present flipping Mecky over the banister.

But fine. If they want something to talk about, or something to write about in the case of the gossips, I'm happy to oblige. Shoulders back and head up high, I pompously scale down the staircase with hollow steps—like a boss. I smirk, knowing and wicked and vengeful, at the Royal, delighted to mess with the minds of the Laxciilians, whose women tug on the arms of their husbands with fake fear as if signalling them to draw swords they do not have. And oh! One of them faints. When my feet touch the dance floor, the Laxciilians part dramatically, delighted to have been so close to danger and having survived to tell their embellished accounts tomorrow. A clear path is made for me to an empty table. I walk slowly, drinking in every moment of my solo in the movie that is life, and I sit, my eyes locked on Mecky like a trigger, with the same smirk. There are three things I don't believe in: the institution of family; compromising standards; and that evil will win at the end of the day—so if he thinks for one second that I'm going to keel over and let *him* take me down, he has another thing coming.

After an uncomfortable interlude filled only with the pound of heartbeats, twiddling thumbs, and quiet aspiration that I'll do something megalomaniacal and dramatic, the instrumentals resume, and a flourish of dresses and robes sweep across the dancefloor with more vigour than before. There's a red false face on a seat at my table with a pointy snout and eyes like the Grin's. I hate to celebrate duplicity, but I pop it on and glare at the immovable Mecky. I think I freak him out, for he shudders and returns to his throne. But then, I ruin the moment by insanely cackling to myself until I can't breathe, so I take it off and inhale the thick and sensuous smell of food that shoots pangs through my stomach.

Delaying the inevitable is tough, but I wait until enough creatures have diverted their attention from me before I make my way to the bounty tables. Politely as I can, I push through crowds of Laxciilians that squeak like stepped-on mice and teeter around on their tip toes, shaking their hands so ridiculously, they spill full glasses of wine all over themselves and then lick it up with their cat tongues. When I finally grace the rows of buffet luxury with my presence, my plate fills up quickly: desserts, apples, grapes, lettuce, a bowl of watery brown soup with flecks of green on the surface, black rice, slices of brown bread, and the few remaining chicken slices. I stab my fork into a big brown-red slice of dragon cutlets as well. Its scales look like pineapple skin, and it smells like beef, only much stronger, and vinegary.

When I return to my table, I find a she-elf with a moustached half-mask making out with a much younger he-elf with tardily shaved legs, so I'm quick to scurry away and relocate. Next to the Dwarf King, inadvertently. Nope. No can do. I move again and find another seat. Someone else is there, but they make no effort to converse which suits me grand. Positively famished, my plate is spick and span after ninety minutes.

The return of the Queen's train draws my eyes back up at the four Royals—and what a big unhappy family they are. They don't hold my focus for long, as just then, I hear someone call my name. Over the booming music and high-pitched chitchats, it takes me a while to realise it's the wizard, but he's such a popular guy that he cannot reach me what with the crowds swarming around him. Eventually, he gives up, but his eyes tell me to climb the staircase again. I shrug and use all my method acting skills to stress that I don't understand the implication. He smiles and makes a dancing gesture, and points to the Royals.

I spend ten minutes telling myself no.

Then I remember what Mósandrirl said a long time ago: *"If this is all a dream, you might as well enjoy it."*

I spend the next fifteen minutes considering it, convincing myself that I will leave my seat, planning what to say, and talking myself out of it again for fear she will reject me or that one of the other three will rip my heart from my chest. I itch and twitch and shift so awkwardly and eagerly that my critics must suspect I have fleas. And it isn't because I want to dance, because I don't. I just don't want to part ways with our last conversation being our last conversation. Let's get this over with. I am on my feet.

"Princess," I curtsy.

"O, Accused Destroyer," she grins.

"You look," and I trail off. Beautiful. Gorgeous. Precious. Goddess-like. "Nice." *Nice? Nice!* What does "nice" even mean!? Sweets are *nice*, but... people! <Insert scream>.

"How charming. The only other compliment I have ever been given is that my dress looked tighter than the one I'd worn the day before."

I don't think that's a compliment, but I'd hate to take it from her, so I offer a small tight smile. I'd rather her family not be here for this part, but I offer my hand to her with a little nod.

"Would you like to dance?"

"I tend not to celebrate the events I throw. I would hate to appear unprofessional."

"You did this?"

"Yes. Every idea was vetoed, of course"—her eyes half-signal the King— "but essentially, I was the planner. Do you approve?"

"Very much. You know, w-w-we c-could j-just sit somewhere, if you like, and talk."

"There is another reason I tend not to dance at these banquets," she says airy-fairy-like, ignoring me.

"Why is that?"

"Because no one ever asks me," she gleams with a cheeky look in her eye.

"Well, as the King informed the populace so definitively, I am here for one night only."

"Well, if forever only lasts tonight, I would be honoured to spend eternity with you."

She takes my hand, the white rose tied by its stalk around her wrist, and we both avoid the other three's gaping mouths and popping eyes.

"I warn you, though, I don't dance."

"Then to what do you invite me, Master Brooder, and oftentimes Master of Smirks?"

"To elope," I laugh.

352

"Follow my lead, my dearest one," she smiles, exposing her sparkling teeth in one of those rare smiles she sometimes makes that promises that things can be better, that life can be more than anything you expected. We take each other's hand, and I put my second one on her hip while she places her free one on my shoulder. When we first start dancing, I feel stupid, but soon I'm so entirely fascinated by how outrageously stunning she is inside and out that nothing else matters. And when we dance underneath the low chandelier, she says it is beautiful.

And I reply, "Yes, you are."

Her face is so close to mine I can feel the heat of her minty breath. She thanks me. I ask what for.

"Saving me from drowning," she replies. Oh, right, yes, that.

"You've saved me a lot of times, too. I had debt to pay. I'm catching up with you," I joke.

She backs away a little and looks serious. "Not just from the pool, Benjamin. My whole life, I have been nothing more to Mama than a doll to occasionally take out and beautify, then lock away in a dark cold toy chest. Papa, I can only assume, had his reasons for what he did to my mind, but I do not understand them, nor will I ever give him the opportunity to explain. And Baba Alk'erion terrifies me. For four hundred and twenty-four years in total, I have feared smiling lest they gave me a reason not to. I feared laughing lest they turn my joy to sorrow. I feared excelling lest they not care, their notice of me eclipsed by their own self-worth and pride. I felt I was drowning. Trapped beneath an effervescent surface and citric bubbles, eyes stinging and lungs short of breath. And then you came. You found me."

"We found each other," I say. "You're okay, though, right?" I ask. But I immediately feel bad for answering the question I've asked her. It seems like something Mehkabikil would do, while hypnotising her. I rephrase the question, and it comes across as concernedly as I'd initially intended.

"I am." We go back to dancing; I let her lead, and she changes the subject, diamond tears glistening in the corner of her eyes. "You are most dashing. The suit looks good on you."

"I have you to thank. You made it?"

"I had some extra time on my hands, though I must confess, the shoes are borrowed from a boy called Harker, who is no longer with us. The blue shirt looks good on you."

"You know, everywhere I go, I buy a blue shirt," I whisper, running my mouth up and down her ear, an inch at most apart, tickling her with each syllable. "Louth, Meath, Dublin, Wicklow, Tipperary, Cork, Clare, Belfast, Leeds, Glasgow, Greenacres, London, Birmingham, Bradford, Frankfurt, Rome, Fuerteventura, Ibiza, Tourmalines…" She says that's a lot of blue shirts. "Ireland's chilly, so I have blue jumpers, too."

"You have seen so many places," she says with a mixture of sadness and awe.

"Darling," I say, wanting to treat her as the posh lady she is, "there are entire worlds out there that I cannot wait to show you," and for the next sixty seconds, I forget that I hate Earth with a passion.

"What is it like?" I see her imagination board an aeroplane before my very eyes, so full of excitement, genuine interest, and above all, hope. And for one night only, I put aside my prejudices against life. And I tell her about my four-tier trifle, comic books, the best novels, the most fascinating natural wonders, shows, fresh spring drizzle that everyone complains about but that keeps the grass green, and just for the heck of it, I try to win her for Christ.

"Life isn't all bad, huh?" At first, I think she says it, but when she nods and agrees, I'm more surprised to discover it came from my lips.

She leans in close, and when I nod that she can, she rests her head on my chest. "Your world sounds amazing. I would like to be part of it someday, even just for an hour... when all this is over."

I close my eyes and picture her as a human, and the painful thing is, it's not that hard to imagine. She's everything I ever wanted in a girlfriend, even if I never really thought I would have one. She's a lady through-and-through, drop-dead gorgeous, has a fantastic dress sense, she's pure, and she challenges me to be better. And somehow, she understands me. I'd given up on the idea that I'd ever meet someone who would.

"Why wait until then? *Carpe diem.*" She doesn't understand. "Would you like to go somewhere private?"

"I beg your pardon?"

"Your room or mine?"

# INTERLUDE
# RISE OF THE ELDER ELF

When Ratsach, the mother of Prim, King the Third of Loux Laxciila, learned that her son was dead, she began to systematically rescind the remaining male members of the royal family. But Prim's sister and counsellor Etsah took Prim's infant son, Qal-Shub, and stole him away from among the rest of the royal orphans, who were about to be killed. Etsah put Qal-Shub and his nurse Theodora in an upper room bedroom closet, and hid him from Ratsach and her soldiers, so the child was not murdered. Hours later, Etsah concealed them within a basket which she lowered from the window, and they fled into the night and the vast marshland wilderness of young Angoria. Etsah fell under the suspicion of Ratsach soon after the body count revealed one child missing and breathed her last.

After a few months, Wizard the First found Qal-Shub and Theodora, and he fed and clothed them. Now the human Theodora was well on in years and died soon after. Wizard the First cast a spell of protection over Qal-Shub, and he remained hidden in Wizard the First's bear cave for fifteen years while Ratsach ruled over Loux Laxciila.

In the sixteenth year of Ratsach's reign, Wizard the First, who had become High Priest of the Higher Orders summoned the commanders, merchants, plebeians and the palace guards to come to the lowest chamber in the Golden Dome Palace of Loux Laxciila. (This occurred in the days before the force field had been erected around the kingdom's borders). He made a solemn pact with them and made them swear an oath of loyalty there in the Golden Dome; then he introduced them to the late King's son.

Wizard the First told them, "This is what you must do. A third of you who are on duty tomorrow must guard the Summer Palace. Another third must stand guard behind the palace guard. The final third must surround the entrances into the kingdom so that the Queen Mother of Prim and her loyal servants do not escape. The other two units who are off duty tomorrow must stand guard for the rightful King at the Dome. Form a bodyguard around the King and keep your weapons in hand. Kill anyone who tries to break through. Stay with the King wherever he goes."

The commanders did everything Wizard the First ordered. The commanders took charge of the men reporting for duty the next day, as well as those who were going off duty. They brought them to Wizard the First, and he supplied them with spears and small shields that were stored in the Dome. The palace guards stationed themselves around the King with their weapons ready. They formed a line from the south side of the Dome around to the north side.

Then Wizard the First brought out Qal-Shub, the King's son, placed the Diadem of the Salvation of Loux Laxciila on his head, and presented him with a scroll of the Fate's Laws for Angoric Monarchs. The Laxciilians anointed him with oil and proclaimed him King, and everyone clapped their hands and shouted, "Long live the King!" And he was named Mehkabikil.

When Ratsach heard the noise made by the palace guards and the people, she hurried to the Dome to discover the source of the commotion. When she arrived, she saw the newly crowned King standing in his place of authority on the uppermost step by an intricately designed pillar, as had become the custom at times of coronation. The commanders, trumpeters, singers and dancers surrounded him, and people from all over the land rejoiced and made music. When Ratsach saw all this, she tore her clothes in despair and shouted, "Treason! Treason!" (It had been the custom of Laxciilian monarchs to wear clothes made of a single fabric to mirror their embodiment and headship of a unified state).

Then Wizard the First ordered the commanders in charge of the troops, "Take her to the soldiers in front of the Dome and kill anyone who tries to rescue her." Aware that it was unlawful to kill anyone within the consecrated grounds of the Dome itself (it was considered holy for life-giving streams flowed through its ground-level Healing House) and suspecting no one present would risk reaping the wrath of the Higher Orders, Ratsach ran to the balcony atop the Dome. There she was seized, defenestrated, and, body broken, led out to the gate where horses enter the palace grounds, and she was killed there.

Now Ratsach had erected a graven image of gold unto Maddira, the Sea Goddess, and established a ritual of female shrine prostitution. Wizard the First called down fire from the sky and reduced the image to a river of molten in which Ratsach was buried and hardened. He then chased the sexually immoral out of the kingdom. And on that day, he became known as The Golden Lake Cave-Dweller, or Mósandrirl: *mó* meaning "gold", *mós* meaning "lake", and *andrirl* meaning "cave-dweller". And his fame spread throughout the land.

And Mehkabikil resented him for this.

# 14

# THE BALCONY SCENE

In fact, we go to neither of our rooms, but somewhere far superior. She leads me to the three-tiered Dome, an ancient pantheon I've only ever seen from a distance. Water comes out from under the threshold of the Dome towards the east (for the dome faces east) and polluted water also trickles from the south side.

We climb the staircase until we reach the balcony on the third floor. The large room behind us tunnels further back and is hoisted by ten massive pillars with the most intricately designed pilasters imaginable. The cupola is as large as the two levels beneath us and looks like it could easily be scaled from here. A plaque on the wall documents how every stone in this building was found in a quarry and rolled along on logs, and how no chisel or hammer was required to alter their shape. Created from pale yellow stone, it is by no means the most appealing building in the kingdom, but its complexity and excellence in craftsmanship mark it as one of the most spectacular. I remark this to Aurora, who is surprisingly quick to shoot it down.

"Its self-assured builders were similarly hubris, but I tell you the truth: by the time all this is over, not a stone of this Dome will remain standing." *Killjoy.* "Before this stone pantheon was erected, there stood one of pure gold, multiple times as expansive and marvellous, or so say all the accounts. Constructed by the first King of Loux Laxciila, it operated as his palace, a shelter for the homeless, and a House of Healing through which a stream flowed that had life-giving properties. The Summer Palace, he built for his wife. The Golden Dome was later razed to the ground by Men who our nation thought were our friends. As Loux Laxciila burned, the stream dried up. What little remains is sour and toxic, but we get by."

"How could humans do that?" I'm not surprised. I just want to sound philosophical.

She smiles wickedly and replies, "A woman. A witch, actually, but as a nation we do not discuss her much."

"This witch wouldn't happen to have had a close relationship with Alk'erion, by any chance?"

"You ask because you know the answer is yes. Who told you? Makkan and Ogun?"

"I don't know who they are."

"Oh, you do," she smiles, "though you have probably given them other names."

"No, no one told me. I saw a crude attempt at petroglyph on a wall near his hut."

She breaks into a grin. "Baba liked her very much. The qualm is that Papa was taken with her, too, at the same time!" She breaks into hysterics and there's no point in trying to get the rest of the story out of her—any attempt to utter another syllable results in melodious, undisciplined heart-song.

And it's just like me, after fifteen minutes of sheer unrepressed joy, to ruin it. "I'm leaving tonight. Mósandrirl has already packed me a bag."

"I know." She looks down at her hands and wrings them.

"Come with me. We could save Angoria together."

She looks at me pitiably. "No, we could not. The Chosen One walks alone. He always has. That is his curse. Saving the world comes at a cost." She makes an L sound, but fumbles, and I'll never know how that sentence was going to begin, for she settles on, "Friendship is his." A funereal silence fills the vacuum between us for several seconds that feel like a dozen minutes. "And shepherding this grotesque and greasily opulent people is mine. It is the responsibility placed on my shoulders by my royal status. Whatever else you were to ask of me, I would do, but I cannot abandon my people, no matter how like a prison this kingdom is."

"I commend that. I really do. But Mehkabikil is a malevolent man. Do not think that you alone, just because you are his offspring, will escape his wrath the second Laxciila's stake in this cruel game with the Triune goes south. He will hang you out to dry as quickly as he dragged Dol'ver into his lair and k—." Her eyes narrow and her cheeks tighten, but before she can make an enquiry, I shrug it off and say, "Nothing. It's late. I'm tired. Just promise me you'll be careful."

"I promise." She either doubts my state of mind or her own words, because I never saw so guilty a face for lying. And there must have been something dodgy in that dragon meat, because suddenly I'm having a drug trip to a world where everything is blue:

*"Finality is an illusion and immortality a curse. In the end, all that remains is Eternity, a long stretch of graveyard made of Time and tombstones. Life is sweet as strawberries, and it does Man's heart good to see the sun. Every day is a gift and should be appreciated so. But remember the days of darkness, for they will be many, and when they come, they render all else meaningless. The Tapestry never stops weaving."*

*"Why am I here?"*

*"I do not know. To right some wrong, perhaps. Or so I can tell you... that no matter what... happened... happens... will happen... there is a chance for... for you to prevail. Or so I can... give you... this gift... this promise. I–"*

"Have we met before?"

"Before...?"

"Before I came here?"

"Skye, are you sure you are quite well? I can take you back to the wizard if need be."

"Please, just answer me. Have we met before?"

"Yes. I found you at the Oasis, and before that, at Troll Cave."

"Before that! There was a forest of something... Depression... Mourning... Melanin..."

"Melancholia?"

"Yes! ... So, it was you...?"

"Aside from what I have already mentioned, I have never left this country, as I have told you before. Come," she says sternly, like a mother to her rambunctious children at the park. "Sit by me." I open my mouth to object, but she insists, quite scarily, "Sit down."

I could push the issue, but I'd be facing a losing battle. "You know, I predict that by the time this big, bad, Hell-hath-no-fury war breaks out, you will be the strongest of us all. You're actually kind of terrifying," I joke and we laugh.

"The prophecy never spoke about anything that could strike terror in the heart of the Chosen One," she gasps and teases.

"One thing does," I confess, and my right index finger and thumb remove a stray eyelash from her cheek that's been annoying me these past few minutes. "Starting something and not seeing it through to completion." I lower my hand and cup it with my left and rub my thumbs.

"Anything else?" she asks with such sincerity that, though I choke, and my tongue is slow to formulate coherent speech, I cannot help but answer. She makes me feel safe, safer than I knew was possible. (I really hope she hasn't secretly been some Delilah espionage trying to find out the Dark One's weaknesses all this time). She's everything I needed and never knew I wanted.

"That the final chapter of my story has already been carved in stone by those who know me the least and whom I fear the most." I never said it out loud before, that I fear them more than Gideon or the Triune or the Void, but it makes sense, I think: my mother's a whore; the two men who should have raised me never taught me how to be a man; and while my older brother lies six feet under, my younger brother walks the road that leads to sociopathy. Home (I feel dirty even thinking the word) has been no more than a soul-killer. What if I've somehow been infected? What if I've been exposed to its carcinogenic fumes so long that it has already rotted my soul and bones, and is now coming for my spirit? It took from me my past and present, and now the parasite craves for a feast on my future. I escaped them by coming here, but with the same breath that Angoria pronounced me the hero, she also denounced me the villain. What if I'm playing a fool's game setting out to save the world, and all the while my enemies here see me for what I really am: sinful flesh spreading my sickly fragrance everywhere I step?

"To whom do you refer? Papa? The Higher Orders?"

"My dearest one, I could never reveal to you my deepest secrets. That would be… nonstrategic."

"You know, Papa is correct about one thing: you do not make it easy for people to trust you."

"Circumstance has already hacked me at the knees. One more betrayal and my head might just be severed from my neck. Trust is a luxury I can't afford."

"Not even in a friend?"

"Trusting in the wrong friend is like investing in the wrong business. You're left bankrupt, lodging nothing more than a bullet in your temple."

"You do not have many friends back in your world, do you?"

"I had one. One real one, not that he met the criteria very frequently. For example, on one until-then pleasant afternoon, he blackmailed me with every secret I ever told him and that he had ever overheard, and he threatened to bring my whole house down." She asks me what I did. "I buried him," I say sternly, and her eyes widen. Her mouth gapes, then narrows with intrigue. Her Elven ears must hear my heartbeat quicken to pounding. I inch closer to her and bring my face close to hers. "You are correct when you say I do not make it easy to be trusted, but do you trust me?"

She tilts her head over her right shoulder, examines me up and down, and after a hesitant pause, says, "With my life."

"That's all I needed to know." To conquer my demons. To put the Wraith to rest. To kick the Triune off their three-seater throne. To drag Gideon back to his tomb should he be resurrected. To vanquish the Void once and for all. "I want to be better, because of you. Because of you, I want to want to be better."

"If it is not too platitudinous to say so, hope is another great incentive," she smiles and nudges my arm gently.

"You are my hope." She backs up in shock, either terrified I'll jump her and lock lips or else stunned, having never had a shred of understanding of the impact she has had on me. She pulls her arms back like she's touched something dirty, and her chest sinks in and pulsates with heavy breaths, but this gradually steadies to the regularity with which her peaceful heart is better accustomed. A single diamond tear glistens in each corner of her crystal blue eyes. Slowly, anxiously, she leans over and gently pecks my cheek. It feels dry and fearful, hasty, and leaves no lasting impression or sense of mutual needfulness, but it was nice. I wouldn't have minded had it been a little closer to my lips.

"Careful, O Most Cold and Uncaring Triumvir: for one so reserved and uncomplimentary, that came close to being mawkishly sentimental."

We nervously laugh it off for the briefest moment, but soon we're initiating conversations about stories long forgotten, the likes of which neither of us have ever shared nor expect to utter again. These are the moments divinely appointed for intimacy and healing that are all too few, and that change everything.

I tell her about the day after I dreamed of a pocket-sized universe that I called Pocket—on the eve of my being sent to the White Room. I told Nuala and Dave what I'd seen. He berated my over-active imagination harshly. She sat there drinking a bottle of pure vodka, pretending not to have heard me. I went into the kitchen, retrieved a metal teapot that Nuala had picked up in a second-hand shop—the cheapskate! It looked like it hadn't been washed in two decades. I scrubbed it spotless with scalding water and washing-up liquid for forty-five minutes, not caring about the reddening or shrivelling of my little fingers. Afterwards, when it was spick-and-span, I took a huge sigh of relief and felt so happy, like everything in life could be good again, if it ever even had been.

I also tell her about the time I, a newbie in Ireland, in a fit of rage, threw an interactive reading book across the room against the radiator, and it broke. (The book, not the radiator). I tell her about how absolutely alarmed I felt knowing about the destructive potential within me.

And I tell her about the time, years later, when I ran away and did not return for three days, only to discover that no one had realised I'd been missing—have they realised yet?

After she has gathered her thoughts, she opens up to me about the time she hid under her blankets during a thunderstorm, only for Mecky to walk into her room and lift her in his arms. How beautifully she reminisces his words of assurance: *"The storms of life come each in their season, and they will forever come, but they do pass—such is their nature."*

And about the time her mother tried to force her to marry a cruel arrogant despot under the aspersion that it was a she-elf's place above all else to be shepherded by a he-elf of substance. Aurora, utterly despising the chauvinistic pig, ran to her garden fountain and wept uncontrollably. There the Elder Elf found her and comforted her, saying that she should only ever marry should she find *the one*; that a marriage of convenience leads only to death and disaster. I can almost hear his snake-rattle when she quotes him: *"Prosperity lasts only a little while—bitterness, offence and disappointment last forever."* She says the roles have changed nowadays and it's him who's pushing suitors in her direction whenever he can, lest the Royal Family lose everything but the clothes on their backs when the world is returned to its rightful inheritors.

I instinctively grasp her hand before I have time to convince myself not to. She looks up at me and our eyes meet, then lock.

"I'm sorry."

I'm not sure what I'm apologising for, but I have nothing else to say. And we stay like this for the longest, quietest, most poignant moment. Running on autopilot, our fingertips touch and tingle and create a warm, fuzzy feeling, then interlock. We smile at the same time and breathe in perfect unison. I bite down on the corner of my lip.

*Zoom!*

"What was that?" I yelp, and spring to my feet, though I put so much pressure on my busted one that I collapse on the balcony rail. Aurora isn't spooked though, so I calm down briskly enough, and following the direction of her gaze, look up. Lights appear in the fresh sky over a still lake streaked with white, yellow, and purple. Dark blues, light blues, aqua, turquoise, green, orangey-red, peach, and finally white rays shoot out like hands to all twelve numbers on a clock. Mountains of golden cloud rise from the water but remain low. And there's a cosmological performance going on that I can describe only as musical notes put to colour. I let out an admiring, "That is really something."

"That happens sometimes, but not as much as before," she notes slowly, yet casually. "Loux Laxciila is the top of the world. It has something to do with the sky taking in all the colours. Sometimes it just… gives them back." Standing now, she whispers the last three words close to my ear and it tickles. I stand straighter, puff my chest out more, lean an inch closer, and breathe more heavily, then slowly pull off her glove. I give her hand a kiss and our fingers truly entwine for the first time, my apprehension of skin contact for the time being suspended.

Her eyes close sensually, lost in the moment, and she lets out a quiet *Mmm*, then stops, and begins an unexpected narrative the gossips fed her once upon a spring:

Princess Lucinda of the faraway woodland realm Delhood once watched these lights with her gentleman friend from the race of Men; the night before she was sold off like cattle to the one she would ultimately marry.

The teenage boy had drifted into her kingdom on a plank following a shipwreck, Aurora was told. The princess of Delhood found and restored him. Amnesiac, having suffered a head trauma in a prior skirmish or in the wreck, when the time came to depart, he confessed he was unaware if he had anywhere to go. Yet all could see he just wanted to be close to her. Luckily, King Alabaster and Queen Gerund had grown fond of the boy— he got their friendless moany daughter out from under their feet for several hours a day, so when he insisted on staying to repay his debt, they accepted. It follows that they raised him alongside the princess in their household, where their intimacy grew.

"Hormones?"

"Her only true love," Aurora retorts with a mixture of compassion and disgust.

"What happened?"

Her parents tolerated their childhood fancies to an extent, permitting knowledge of the flirtation remained within the kingdom's borders. Then one day the King and Queen of Delhood were invited to a great Elven Moon Feast in Loux Laxciila. Though they had permitted the boy's amour in the privacy of their own drawing-room, his lack of subtlety and self-restraint in Loux Laxciila (for he had accompanied the family as a servant) proved too incomprehensible for traditionalists and purists who regarded it too shameful an indecency to be allowed to continue. Humiliated, Delhood's monarchs' affection turned to toxin and, when asked about the princess's personal affairs, played naïve to the fling.

Worse than that, they proceeded to declare psychic warfare on the youth and tried their hardest to isolate him from their daughter. Yet, driven by an insurmountable doggish impulse for connection, nothing quite deterred him from his quest for the princess's hand in marriage: not public defamation, nor spears thrown his way, nor a hand-delivered deer heart in a box.

The young woman's engagement, in which she had no say, was announced on the final night of the feast to the peoples of the seven great Elven kingdoms. And who should ask for her hand but the Laxciilian Lord Syaddon Metakiiria, as they called him in Delhood Elvish. Greedy for the riches a Laxciilian union could offer the Delhood Royals, Syaddon promised that he would open his home to their disgraced daughter and purchase her for the required dowry. His condition? The young man could never return to Loux Laxciila or within a kingdom's radius of Delhood. They agreed.

A few short months later, amid disquiet from his senators and counsellors who feared scandal and a sudden surge of loose morals within their borders, the Laxciilian Lord wed the shamed girl. On the morning of their nuptials, he allegedly said he liked her very much—words she has never reciprocated. And how does this delightful story end? On a less than promising note: that Syaddon Metakiira has psychologically maltreated the poor girl blissfully ever since. I know well this man Syaddon, Aurora tells me, though by another name: King Mehkabikil.

Funnily, I am not surprised. Then Aurora's story about the chauvinistic despot returns to my mind.

"Your mother was sold to the Elder Elf, and she still tried to ship you off to incompatible suitors?"

"Do not look shocked, darling. It fattens your cheeks."

"That poor guy!" My heart pangs at the thought of being separated from the one for whom you were made for all time. I mean, if a couple gets together but one passes their expiry date, that's horrid, but at least they have memories. But for both soulmates to live on—forever apart and unfulfilled, connected only in the un-realisation of what should have been, that sounds unbearable. After all, forever is a very long time. And the Tapestry never stops weaving.

Slowly, she rests her head on my shoulder. Lemons and strawberries perfume from her lush golden tresses. After a few minutes, trying hard not to disrupt the intimacy of the moment, I dig into my backpack and rummage through books, vials, weaponry, and clothes, and pull out the ring. I drop it on her open palm.

"I saw it and thought of you." It's a succinct explanation, but I'd rather not say I whipped it from a dump.

"How ornate." She then sings to it, very hushed, and gives it back.

O-o-okay. "Thank you." I throw it back in my man-bag, more than a little confused.

Not a moment too soon, the sky flashes like a lightsabre duel, and the stellar spectacle demands our attention. As I contemplate the vastness of the faux-sky and the colour-changing lakes and hills beneath and beyond it, I ask if she has ever considered running away. She has, but a stone peacock gave her away.

"I hate those birds," we say together. "Jinx," I wink, not that I hold her to it, since I have no clue what her real name is.

"Imagine flying around up there amongst the stars," I muse.

"I have," she responds, then, quickly realising how ambiguous that sounded, verifies she has *imagined* it. There are nine realms, she adds. In order of their birth: the Earthen Star, Angoria, Scylon, Skyatholon, Jebulus, Agog, Fragmencia, Mliko-Blöd, and Golla. When these orbiting realities align ever so neatly, a shift of cosmological proportions ripples through the interstellar constellation and each realm's respective timeline and, olden sources claim, a major event happens across all realities. "What I would give to fly away from here and visit the stars."

"Collecting blue shirts aside, travelling has never much interested me, but I'm sure it would be fun, with the right companion." I hope that didn't come across as too forward.

"Why Skylar, are you suggesting that the pious Lady Heddwen forsake her national duties as tailor and floor-cleaner, and run away with you? I am positively thrilled with the idea!"

"Oh, just think about it!" I squeal, getting way too excited over something that's not going to happen. "The rogue Princess No-Name and her frightful accomplice, the Twelfth Dark Lord, sailing on the winds of time and space on their pet unicorn, getting up to mischief, ticking people off, drinking tea, and staying up until all hours of the night discussing the people they met that day and disliked. Perfection, that is!" My heart throbs and I know she can hear it. I want this. We both really want this. If one were to seriously ask now, the other would leave all this behind and go, irrespective of the Maze—we'd find a way.

"My unicorn is not a pet."

"But it is magical. It could take us there, right?"

"If we had enough food to make the journey." Our faces come up close. "What are we doing?" to which I state the obvious: talking. "It would never work." She's not talking about us talking, or even travelling, but something much deeper. "Look at my ears!"

"Look at my ears! You're an elf and my ears are bigger than yours, albeit less pointy. I like your ears. They're cool." She asks for confirmation. I give it.

Our breathing slows and steadies and merges. We both subtly suck in our own lips with shyness, and then at the same time beam. My insides turn to jelly. My toes feel toasty in my boots, curl, and tickle. And all I can think about is her, and how I need to be kissing her...

I lean in and then back away a little. What if she's not ready or expecting it?

"Do not fear. Just trust," she smiles.

And then she whispers coyly, "*Amandlia Taliana Alcovana alliavuntae*... Benjamin-Joshua." And before I can ask her what it means, with lightning-quick speed, she whips out a folded-up bow from under her skirt, which had been held in place with a garter. She quickly assembles it and points an arrow at my head.

# 15

# THE MIST-LURKER

Embittered, loathsome cries resound from the near distance. It didn't take them long to catch up with me.

I need to make tracks, not that this is an easy feat: my limp is a hindrance and my coccyx an oozy agonising plum, and I've got a cramp in my side like a piping hot iron bar melting me from the inside out. It's so bad, I'm bent over like a thumb or a hunchback. And as for the hunger pangs! Bottomless pit that I am, I might as well have eaten nothing at the banquet for all the good it's doing me. Still, standing here stewing over the stresses of life and the people that cause them won't accomplish anything.

I need a break but stopping is not an option. Never stop running. Just keep on moving… from the Laxciilians with their tattoos, body art, piercings, neon-coloured spiked hair and pikes… from the ever-rising body count… from Aurora; the compassionate, beautiful and probably dead rose of Laxciila. Just run from now until forever and then do it all over again.

Plastered outstretched on the soil and twigs, I do not think I'm capable of moving anymore. I've easily run for ten hours now. Let them come. If fifty of them come at me, I bet I can take at least half of them to the grave with me in hand-to-hand combat.

Despite last night's fiesta, I'm already empty inside. My tongue feels hollow and sore, as often happens when I exercise beyond what I'm used to. Added to that, I must be seriously dehydrated for my urine is filthy and brown. I haven't seen, heard or stepped in water since my escape. Unused to not washing them immediately after depositing waste, I have the destructive urge to rub the filthy flesh off my hands against some bark until the dirty cells are all tattered and dead. *To peel away this life and emerge as someone new and past-free.*

No. Enough of this nonsense. I am the Chosen One. I *am* the Chosen One. I am the Chosen *One.* No one else can do this. No one in all the world but me. I have no idea where I'm going, but only I can venture through the Maze and find the Triune. I may not be able to free myself from my bonds, but someone greater than I chose me to liberate Angoria from oppression. I may never have dabbled in magical affairs before, but by some sick, ridiculous twist of fate, I have been assigned to obliterate the Triune and the Maze. And though I once swore never to take life, if Gideon awakens, I alone can ensure that his cameo is brief. Because I am the Chosen One. And I don't understand it. And it doesn't make sense. And there are greater candidates. But the task has fallen to me, so no more whining.

I drop my bag, throw it open, and arm every limb and pocket: daggers, stakes, poisons, Aurora's ring. Oh, Aurora's ring. I still remember the feeling of betrayal I felt as her arrow came out of nowhere and pressed lightly against my forehead; Fetch joking dryly in the background, "Gosh, she really mustn't have wanted that kiss. Steady, Tiger." The intensity of that focused look in her eyes like nothing else in all the world existed other than my skull and her missile. And I, no more than a flaccid fish trapped in a net, ready to accept my fate whatever should come. I could never hurt her.

*Well played, Master Elf,* I thought. *Getting your daughter to scam her way into my heart only so she could do that which you were always so reluctant to do with the Elder Wizard around. Funny. I expected there to be a larger audience.*

Then she screamed "DROP!" Slavishly I obliged, more willing to die at her feet than the King's. She let loose her arrow on a ground-level assailant. *Ugh!* She got him good. Then she leapt on top of me as arrows rained from the sky and whispered three words in my ear. However, I could take no notice of them when contrasted with how her arrows emitted a force field from the hailing missiles.

She repeated the three words again, just to make sure I had heard them, but I was more concerned with the enemy's fire. More arrows hailed: sharper, quicker.

She chanted in ancient whispers and the arrows *poof*ed into a gentle rain of red roses.

That was when I knew for definite that she was not trying to kill me.

She was willing to die for me.

"Papa!" she screamed. And sure enough, that familiar hiss to which I have grown unfortunately only too-accustomed spat from the ground, streets away, but advanced briskly. No more arrows descended, probably because if the King killed his daughter in full knowledge that she was on the Dome, it might make for bad press—and Mehkabikil liked to get his fingers dirty only in secret.

Aurora spared no time in hurrying me to the far side of the balcony, and practically threw me over the rail. I narrowly got a good grip on the vines, and after some squirming and shaking, my toes slotted into the wooden ladder of rhombuses. I began to scramble down, but the diamond shapes weren't long in caving in under my weight. Glued to the vine for dear life, I dangled for a few terrifying seconds, my heart sinking more and more with each bead of sweat my pores cried, as I tried in vain to regain my footing. Every happy moment since the banquet quickly erased.

Finally, my feet found the brackets and I put my abseiling skills to good use.

"Aurora!" I shouted, too afraid to stretch my right hand up to her as I clutched to the vine. "Please, I don't want to do this alone! I can't do this alone! You keep me from dying! You keep me from going dark! I need you!"

She looked over the balcony. For a second, I thought she would join me. But she recoiled. Then came back. And it all looked so hopeful. And she had enough time. But I knew she would not come down.

"I cannot—"

The last I saw of her, she was surrounded by Laxciilian soldiers' arms and swords and shields and pikes. And she fought them. Oh, she fought them brilliantly. And had I not snapped the brackets above me, I would have climbed all the way up and helped her. And then she fell silent.

Still clawed to the vine, I tried to shimmy upward, but big bushes that jutted out from the architecture blinded me and pushed me down further. This was helped by the pot of scalding water the soldiers threw on top of me. That hurt. Good thing I buried my head in my arms, covered my hands in my sleeves, held on for dear life, hid under the bushes, and pressed myself as close to the wall as possible because that could have proven immensely injurious. But before I could even open my eyes afterwards, the vine and the frame beneath me snapped, and I dropped twelve metres. The thorns of the wall's roses nipped, dragged along, and sliced open my hands. My coordination was all off, so impaired in fact that the armed Laxciilians on the streets appeared to charge toward me in slow motion. I felt like Alice after the Trial Chapter, playing tag with a bull rush of costumed misfits.

And though everything within me wanted to go back and rescue her, those three words permeated in my brain and forbade me: "The Wraith Gate." She wanted me to flee to the gate where the phantom had tried to kill us. And either fear or self-preservation sent my feet cycling there. I can still taste the salt and urea that flushed across my face, the antediluvian Machiavellian hot on my heels the entire time.

Then I heard it—a triangle-chiming wind breathing through dream catchers; a tingle glitter would make were it made of metal. It was the sound of rebellion. A sound that said, "This is wrong." Even though I knew I shouldn't have, I slowed down and turned. The Laxciilians retrieved their bows messily with untrained hands and collectively came to a halt as dozens of fingers fumbled at bowstrings. A few of them tripped over their flowing cloaks. I guess I benefitted from their having had it so easy for three hundred years.

The shimmer belonged to Lily, a fairy I recognised from the Meeting; fair dues to the little yoke; she'd given me a yes and all. She shot jets of multi-coloured dust in the tyrant's path which caused his feet to freeze in sparkling cement. The pink-haired, squeaky little thing screeched at the injustice of me being labelled a terrorist; the venomous toe-rag's fixing of the vote; his blatant falsified efforts at implicating me in various crimes; and now this, his latest offence: attempting to arrest me in the dark hours without any other council members present except, of course, Little Legs who took up the rear from a long way off, his axe bigger than his *Waagh-waagh*-I'm-destined-to-die-pessimism. *Cop yourself on, you dope. Life is terminal. Get over it.*

"Stop this, Mehkabikil," Lily warned. "You must stop. You *have to* stop. You have made your offence and your fears personal and can no longer see the situation clearly." Though irritatingly squeaky, there was such an authority to her words that I could not but be amazed.

"And you, you vainly optimistic little thing, are too distant. You have no idea what he has done, what he is planning, or what he has yet to do!"

"The boy has been remanded in your custodial prison world long enough. Not to mention that he was found innocent of all charges in your farcical show trial!"

"You are an infant in this world and of a hermetic species who spent the last Dual War cosying up by the fire in your toadstool palace. You have never before seen what a Dark Lord can do. I have witnessed it time and time again. I am trying to save everyone!" Gosh, when I replay it now, he almost sounded sincere.

"Who is going to save everyone from your actions' butterfly effect?" I countered.

"I am a fairy," Lily said, confused, thinking I was talking to her.

I just shrugged and sidestepped: "I'll just be over here."

What happened next was almost too fast for me to register.

Mecky mumbled something and his feet broke free from the magical puddle. It shattered into crystals of pink and purple. His mobsters seemed to rush toward me but must have jogged for they kept their distance. Then his arm pounced like a cobra, grabbed the fairy, threw her to the ground, and squished her with his foot. A small poof. An evaporation.

And then just... gone. Not only an innocent life, but more: a foreign ambassador or monarch! This will undoubtedly have political repercussions!

But more than this, what really got to me was his laugh.

I don't know if I was more regretful or terrified, but my run devolved to a drunken stammer. I must have had the appearance of one just mauled by bears.

The first wave of arrows hailed. Off-target due to lack of practice, but close enough to worry me. Survival instinct took over, leaving little room for shock or paralysis. I sprinted in zig-zags. Right. Left. Right. Left. Drop to push-up formation. Roll. Jump. Tumble. Run in intentionally confusing directions. Run to extremer rights and lefts, the Museum outside of which the Grin blackmailed me shrinking in the background.

"The Wrath Gate" had come into view before I reached the Museum, but only as I neared it did I realise it had been opened. I still cannot tell who lowered the force field: The Elder Wizard; Aurora in the unlikely event she managed to escape from the Dome; someone else in the Assembly who voted in favour of my innocence. And beyond the gate I saw... the Black Forest! Not that I held a grudge or wanted to sound like a Doubting Benjamin Thomas, but I was viscerally reminded that last time I stood in that wood I was shot! *Here's hoping for a more preferable Take Two*, I thought, as I neared the all-too familiar unknown.

From the corner of my eye, I caught the ghost of the demolished architecture that nearly buried Aurora and me alive when the Wraith attacked. My senses whirled so ferociously that I could not think of a single good memory of Loux Laxciila, and I wondered: *why have I not left before now?*

Just then an arrow nipped my left heel, and another shark bit my right shoulder blade. I fumbled forwards and my chin and nose skidded along the dry dust. Hurled to my feet by adrenaline, though, I was up and running again in no time, pebbles dropping off my knees like loosely attached gooseberries. All the while, I heard Mecky's feet behind me. In the time it takes to blink, he should have had his hand shoved through my back, my heart squeezed into oblivion, blood dribbling down my big chin. He clearly has no qualms with killing.

Surprisingly, his feet stopped.

I didn't care much to know why, half-hoping he'd had a burst aneurism. All I had to do was pedal my bike out of that trollop's den. Then came his evil voice. It scathed my eardrums to hear him speak:

"Stop running, Benjamin." My name slithering off his forked tongue... I didn't like it. I wished he'd never say it again. Speaking my name without knowing me; he might as well snoop my social media profile pages years before adding me as a friend. It felt wrong and dirty.

Of course, I ignored his instruction.

But just when I'd been lulled into a false sense of security and begun to think I could make the final hurdle through the gateway: A-ha! Plot twist! Six... twelve... fourteen shapes climbed out from behind bushes metres beyond the gate and blocked my path. Archers! Some were hooded, cloaked, and entirely concealed but for their eyes; these rangers all had longbows. Others, all women, showcased their femininity by wearing form-fitting armour and their hair long. Their bows were in the shape of bats and their limbs were saddled with daggers, chakram, and flutes probably containing poisonous darts. The leader of the party had clearly just left the banquet—he was still wearing his mask (I know it was a male elf for his voice was sullen and low, but husky) and had left his weaponry at home. Still, General No Bow aside, these marksmen looked better experienced than the ones behind me. I knew that if they shot, they wouldn't miss. I turned to Mecky, who only threw his eyes to high Heaven in an "*I told you so*"-sort of way.

Thankfully, a bowstring on a universal scale was strummed and events shifted in my favour: I noticed a shuffling near the tree line behind the gateway. They must have sensed it too what with their supersonic hearing, so it must have been loyalty to the Laxciilian High Command that left them planted at death's door. Then something bit hard on their legs, chewed on them with mighty grumbles, dragged them into the forest, and silenced their screams. More elves swiftly raced along the inside of the gate, unconcerned since they were not the fourteen dead, and aligned to bar me in.

But I, embarrassed to be the only one grieved, decided in that moment that absolutely no one would deny me my freedom. As the dawn sun rose in the lower heavens above the humid air, I stood tall (for a short guy) and stared them down.

"Behold, wenches," roared Fetch, "what real power looks like."

Feet apart, arms down diagonal like a bird about to take flight, my palms faced my opponents, and I imagined jets of fire unleashing and burning them all to ash.

And somehow—I still haven't figured it out—that is pretty similar to what I did. A blinding radiant light blazed forth and the world went white. Squinting was futile. The treachery of the judged was held. The guilty fell to their knees, their jaws to the ground. Tears filled their eyes that they were too afraid to shed lest I treat them as harshly as their rebellion deserved. The masked general fell back, stunned. And to think, all I'd planned to do was pounce at them and go toe-to-toe until I'd broken their line of defence or they'd killed me.

Finally, the white light left the world as softly and unexpectedly as it had entered. Only sounds remained: the clatter of swords and bows as they dropped to the forest bed; a unified breath of bedazzlement by the Laxciilian forces; begrudging gurgles; whatever the creature in the woods was (I know now, of course) dashed into the thick blackness, the forest floor pounding with each step; the gentle wind in the trees.

Then I sprinted toward the Black Forest just as the force field began to shut. I could virtually hear the Elder Wizard's voice in my head urging me to hurry up. However, like Pharaoh, reluctant to allow the Hebrews to escape, the wicked King made one last effort to detain me. Charged with hateful impulse and a hard heart, he moved with the quickness of a train, arm outstretched as though for some grand prize at the end of a race. I leapt for the force field but touched it slightly. It retaliated by mercilessly pushing me to the ground and bruising my coccyx. I turned to find that Mecky was somehow still seconds away, so I channelled my pain and converted it into determination and hurled my body best as I could between the jaws of the force field and onto the moist black bed of soggy leaves and wooden chips on the other side. And then, a *Ba-Joom* noise like cartoonish thunder!

Beneath the thick shade of colossal trees, I saw him crash into the barrier just as it shut. The skinny malink propelled several metres. Amidst all the roly-poly as he hit the ground, his crown fell off and one of its spikes broke; but my insides were too on fire to sneer. In fact, I almost pitied the poor fool. Almost.

He mouthed something to me. Words of hate... Disgust... Accusations... Threats... *Rage? Roar? Roll? Rule? Ruin...? Run!*

What the Hell was he playing at? I didn't wait to find out. Instead, I ran for what could have been time immemorial, until the heavy pound of feet came back—the feet of a beast from ancient times.

If not for its silvery supernatural glow, I wouldn't have been able to make it out. Its body was as long as a car. Two vicious needles many inches long protruded from both corners of its jaws, reminding me of the vampire in Lear's dungeon. It had sharp talons on each paw that looked powerful enough to slice through metal. A metallic smell of blood sprayed from its alligator-wide jaws.

Its leopard-like coat strutted out from the bushes slowly, arrogantly. I half-anticipated for it to burst into song like Scar or Scat Cat. Its claws, stained with blood, made splashes and a mess wherever its feet trod. I'm surprised by how like a bulldog its head was, kept warm tucked inside a tardy short mane. Its catty purrs canoodled the mental image of my carcass. Its yellow eyes narrowed on me. Their black slit grew darker.

"Must we do this now, beastie?" either Fetch or I asked, eyeing it intently, with more confidence than I can usually muster. "Time truly is of the essence, and I should not delay. Not to mention I have just had the most straining dawn."

Appalled by my brazenness to talk to such a beast of art and brilliance as itself, it hissed an ugly smell. And for the first time since my exodus, the hammer of my heart stopped. With subtle swift movements, I whipped open my rucksack and shoved my hand inside and grabbed a short sword. Marriage bed aside, what was God's wedding gift to Adam and Eve again? "Subdue the Earth and everything in it." Well, I always suspected power tasted better than sex. *Don't mind if I do…*

Yet still I was paralysed when it pounced.

Fierce choky growls came from its pierced oesophagus as three arrows jutted into its neck and hit the ground hard. The sabre-tooth curled as though resisting labour.

I looked at the beast, and it at me. It had the cheek to crave and beg for pity. "Apologies, lapdog of the Elder Elf, but I'm not much of an advocate for animal rights, I'm afraid." Almost as though it understood, the beast scrambled to its feet and readied for a second pounce. More arrows. Again, it thumped to the ground, heavier than a dozen sacks of potatoes.

One last time, the sabre struggled to its feet, murder in its eyes, though it stood no chance. This was no longer about hunger, carrying out Mecky's orders, primal instinct, or dominance. This was basic, raw, and uncultured; a refusal to be bested in one's own territory, a concept I appreciate. It showcased spectacular resilience, stammering to its feet, and flashing a mouth full of razors toward my blade.

*Now will I do it pat; now he is leaping. "Pat". What a strange word. Now will I eat it pat; now it is cooked. Now will I wash it pat; now the sink is full. Now will I buy it pat; now it is as cheap as it is going to get on a sale, so it is, and never were truer words spoken, by Bodkin.*

Just then, someone leapt between us. Long coat. A sword that shone even in that cheese-thick blackness. I heard a slicing noise, followed by the sloppy drop of the beast's insides. Polite as ever, I extended a short thanks to the stranger—life and death scenarios are no excuse for a lack of courtesy—and then proceeded to get the heck out of dodge.

We're all better off alone at the end of the day.

Hence, it disconcerted me a little when the dark shape edged towards me, and made a threatening, aggravated "Come hither" motion with their arm. I rejected. And though silent and sightless to my naked eyes, they got mad. My accepting their invite was not a suggestion. Suddenly, floods of Elven soldiers rushed onto the scene, only slightly offstage, and I slipped away before chaos became the buzzword. And I darted into darkness.

I have no idea how many hours I've spent on this one spot when suddenly I hear, from near and far, the sound of concrete blocks moving as though by their own volition until they create an empty space like a keyhole. A dead white light blinds and depresses me; I hide my face from its unnatural arrival. A breath of wind whistles its fingers through my hair. I had almost forgotten what a gentle breeze felt like amidst the thick choking density of this forest. I look up and see that I'm metres from the mouth of the Maze.

Okay, let's do this.

Despite the spasms of pain that shoot up and down my body as a result of my fall from the Dome and my unexpected collision with the force field, I determine to see this adventure through until the very end. Who knows, exacting vengeance on the wicked might even prove therapeutic for all the years the locusts have stolen from me. Though some stray drop of adrenaline urges me to charge toward it precipitously—cautious is my middle name—I grab a handful of dirt and peg it through the opening before risking my own skin, just to make sure I won't get fried with jets of flame or anything. Nope. Grand. As you were...

But once it has lulled me into a false sense of security, white misty jets spray about knee-high onto the path from the walls. They solidify like a rolling boulder that chases adventurers in ancient temples in the movies. Add to this, pudgy gushes of vapour spill over from outside the high walls. I scream soundlessly for a few drawn-out seconds until I realise nothing is happening. Another giant watering can douses me, and though I instinctively shake it off and tiptoe from whatever wisps traipse around me, I'm not even wet let alone injured. It makes no sense: why would the Maze, a machination for evil, have any benign features? I mean, it's hardly all for show. No one, not even sadists as criminally insane as the Triune, goes to this much trouble designing a global dollhouse just to indicate the threat of power... or do they?

Embittered cries resound from the near distance. *Dang it! They're catching up with me again!* I need to make tracks and standing here stewing over the stresses of life and the people that cause them won't accomplish anything. My feet are in bits but stopping is not an option. Just run from now until forever and then do it all over again.

Scarcely have I run ten metres when the Laxciilians appear, about twenty in all.

"Is the princess safe? Is she alright?"

"Her fate, Mex Confetricus, will be as she deserves—the same as yours," the squad's commander-in-chief sneers. She has mad red hair, pink tattoos like scars across her arms and eyes, and yellow false teeth. Her face is divided in two by a wide raw scar that runs down her nose like someone struck her with an axe. "Now come. Kneel before us and die with honour before the Maze kills you." Her uncertain feet step forward, backwards, and then tap, electrified with vibrations. Good. She's afraid. I can use that.

"Why don't you come in here and get me yourself?"

"You suspect I will not take you up on the challenge, but little do you realise, the Maze is our friend." Is she for serious? Is she dim? Missing a screw? Slow? Is she broken? The Maze is keeping the Laxciilians prisoner, too! Even their freedom comes at a cost. Does she genuinely not see that?

"That's impossible. It's inanimate."

"Because of the Triune and their wonders, Angoria for the first time ever has peace. Loux Laxciila is a centre of wealth, commerce, and culture; a producer of fine art and architecture. A land of leisure, freedom, and self-expression, set apart from the woes and strife that defined eleven ages. Loux Laxciila is *the* heart and soul of Angoria."

*Hurry up and shoot me, woman. Anything to drown out the convoluted puffed-up airs and graces of this louse; Mehkabikil's undergarment cheeks personified.* "The favour Laxciila has been shown is a cheap way of distracting spiritually dead potential offenders to ensure that they stay in line and don't give way to rebellion. And while the results may on the surface appear attractive, it is still wrong, and you will be held to account."

"You have no idea. You have no idea what it feels like to see women's breasts ripped off their bodies, men castrated and de-toed, and to hear the anguished screams of babies as they sizzle and burn to ash on the outstretched arms of golden obelisks crafted in the likeness of Dark Lords. You have no idea what it is like to see streams turn to fire and vegetation shrivel to brown crisp before your eyes; to see starved men, renowned for being valiant, tear out their own parched tongues in madness because they could no longer bear the feeling of that organ clinging to the roof of their mouths. To see non-natives that you welcomed as your own into your home cry, 'Tear down their palaces! Tear them down to their very foundations!' and parade around the advancing enemy. To have an infant you birthed snatched from your arms and dashed repeatedly against the rocks. You have no idea how it feels to have everything you own stripped away from you, to be exiled into a land of orcs, and upon deliverance, to find your one-time best friend's family eating dinner in your kitchen. To have your fields ravaged; your farm animals pinched and sent off to feed warriors in trenches; and to go months without any food but dry bread, a handful of nuts, and bitter dirty water."

"Neither do you, because you've put on a blindfold, knowing full-well that all those things are happening."

"Nowhere near to the same extent as before. The Triune's sacrifices merely encourage dissenters to toe the line. But things do not need to worsen, Mex Confetricus. Surrender now. Make this easy for all of us. Break the cycle. Stop the Tapestry from weaving."

"I do sympathise. But this is still wrong. I don't know where I'm going, or what I'm *supposed to do* when I arrive. But I will reverse the magnetic poles if it means reversing what the Triune have done."

"You hate peace that much?"

"Your *Tír na nÓg* comes at a price: your knowledge of the very real suffering out there in the big bad world; your freedom to explore beyond strict borders and reconcile with other forms of life; and lastly, your very soul."

"We have peace," she spits venomously like a cult member whose

387

inane beliefs are being challenged.

"Well, enjoy that illusion while you can, because in the world that actually matters and is swiftly coming, you will not find any."

"We have come too far and lost too much. I will not let you destroy Angoria…"

"LOUX LAXCIILA IS NOT ANGORIA!"

The succubus patrols up and down the mouth of the Maze.

"Women," she barks, even though half her squad are men, "Prepare to fire should anything go awry, but until such time, the Dark Lord is mine!"

She charges straight for me. I do not flinch, not even when the vapour takes care of her. Gruesomely. I shield my skin in my clothes, then stretch out my hand. "Go on, take it. We'll…" I don't know: *outrun it?* Anyway, she doesn't. All she does is glare at me, and growl at me, and disfigure horribly like a shifty melting mask, then burst like a pimple—and all her troops with her. The vapour was their enemy all along, not mine. They neither had time to fire their arrows nor scream. That image is not one I am likely to forget any time soon, though there is a strange solace in that I knew none of them personally.

Fetch sneers at Redd, as I go ahead and call her. "She was killed by the very instrument of torture she sought to save. Fate can be so cruel," and though he's half-glad, I think he pities her, too. I snarl that that isn't funny. "Yes, it is, and you know it. That wagon was going to kill you, and you were going to do naught but stand there and take it. But she put her hope in the wrong rock. Poor sap. She chose the wrong bed buddy, and an even worse enemy." He steps behind me and begins to massage my neck and remarks that I'm tense. "You know she deserved it, right? They all did."

I pull away, shrug him off, and trudge ahead. "That doesn't make it any easier, nor does your celebratory masseur profession."

Still pained, I stumble along the narrow path, occasionally leaning on the rock wall for support, though I try not to do that too often in case it's filled with shot guns, snakes, or slice-and-dice apparatus triggered by handprints. After about twenty minutes, I smell something I'd rather I didn't. Five minutes later, I see carts, bags of hoarded goods and clothes. My bones chill. My hair fuzzes like electrical wires. My arm hairs erect, and I vomit.

This is all that remains of the non-conformist Laxciilians who'd departed over the last few months. Their faces are grey, wrinkled rotten masks of emptiness with black patches. The children's faces are worried, sad, confused; frozen as if in a photograph. Their corpses are piled like a blockage or a clot into a hill of bad odour and dry tongues. It looks like a massacre of clowns with all the odd plump clothes, rainbow hair, and stark white faces (for those who still have skin). Misty fangs sink into their remains and savour the taste. One cloudy pincer even licks its teeth clean.

And then it hits me: the mist preys on elves! It eats them. Leaves them to rot and then eats them some more. And he knew—Mecky! He must have, being in frequent conference with the Triune. Yet he still let them leave, let them die this horrible death, this after-death. I swear I will kill the four of them.

But for now, the only way to do that, God forgive me, is to climb over them.

With the amorality of a rodent whose only purpose is to rummage around in rubbish and destroy the dead, and with closed eyes and one hand over my mouth and nose, I climb. Bodies tumble, limbs roll, my feet stumble, and it's like falling off a skateboard on a mountain of clothes and tufts of straw. At one point, I trip and my eyes spring open inches above the icy face of a baby—eyes black, mouth still open for feeding. In my mind's ear, I hear it suck… suck… suck…

I feel no relief until the vapour encircles all, and there's nothing left but a misted scene and a mysterious dung-pile of eyes, shoes, empty hands, ladybird dresses, and bumblebee shirts. If I throw up once, I throw up seven times.

Out of sheer desperation and need, I savagely claw across the corpses (with so primal an impulse to escape I even scrape their foul flesh and stain my nails with whatever blood remains in their chicken carcasses) and take the first turn off I knowingly come to. It's on my right. As a consequence, I easily walk six hours in the wrong direction. I know this because there are no turns, no traps, and no travellers. The Triune cared so little about that path they gave up on it while it was still in the planning stages. I think its purpose is to drive travellers insane.

> *But before this,*
> *The Triune opened the sky.*
> *The threatening, steamy shroud of the air within*
> *Whirled close to the Maze-tops,*
> *Just for a moment, menacingly, reluctant to leave,*
> *But then*
> *Disappeared.'*

That is how I saw the turn-off.

I tear my tie in two, unevenly, and wrap the strips around my hands. Now with the passing of germs limited, I rummage through the bag. It's got apples, nuts, a few loaves of bread, jars of water, a few daggers, a bow, the short sword I didn't use against the sabre-tooth, about a dozen arrows. There's something at the bottom. At first, I think they're stones or glassy bugs. Then I think they're mouse droppings, and to say my hands spring from the bag to the heavens is an understatement. I've got the vials too.

I tuck in close to the wall too quickly for my coccyx's liking, and for a second, I worry that its bruise will burst like soggy fruit... or like Redd's face. Considering the mist has been dining slowly on all the refugees, it must really have hated her to take the short and sweet blood-on-the-walls approach. Either that, or it never suspected so many Laxciilians would venture out in such a short space of time.

As I play the scene over and over in my head, the heat goes out of the sun and the sky spills into a pink-purple pallet, smeared by a few brushstrokes of black. I chow down a couple of nuts, even though it makes for a measly pittance of an evening meal—and I never particularly liked nuts.

Once finished, I take about three steps before I accept the leg I landed on when I fell off the Dome is as useless as a jar of sand. I must have one hideous blister, because when I put pressure on my foot, it's like I step on a spear. I fall back down and can't get comfortable. Yet somehow, sometime, I eventually drift off. But my sleep is haunted by the glassy purple eyes of the fairy and the screams neither she nor the Laxciilians had time to make. And by the mount of corpses, particularly the baby, and the other dozen babies there probably were that my eyes were too barricaded to see. And lastly Aurora who, by all accounts, may also be dead. I can't figure out which offence is most consistent with Mehkabikil's black soul: to behead one of his children, or to break her and brainwash her to hunt me down and stick my head on a flagpole.

When I wake from my restless shut-eye, the ring, which I'd forgotten I was holding, is imprinted in my now-raw hand. I vaguely remember dropping it back into my bag when she returned it so offhandedly, but I can't remember the exact moment I took it out again. Regardless, its intricate stamp in my palm is so defined that, for a moment, it looks like it'll always be there. I press the ring gently against my lips, and then protect it in my pocket, like in doing so I somehow keep Aurora safe too. Then I wonder whose blood will be on my hands tomorrow. And to think, just last night, my biggest fear was that I might have my first kiss.

# 16
# BATTLE ROYALE

I let out a sultry "Ah" as I burst my blister on the ball of my foot and the juice streams down to my heel. Then it's time to get up and be the Chosen One again. Not having rested at all, I spend a good ten minutes standing on the one spot, zombie-like, yawning and stretching.

First, I backtrack to the Dump, as I call the heap of corpses. There are seven turn-offs available to me, which is more than I remember there being yesterday. With no idea where I'm going, I choose the turn-off that looks most likely to kill me. Signposts such as TRIUNE: THIS WAY would come in handy.

I walk several hours before I come to a halt on the edge of a vast slope. The slope is marked by a white strip that runs horizontally along the ground and up the Maze walls. The starting point of the mist, maybe. And just beyond it, at the foot of the slope, skulks a village that stretches about ten kilometres lengthways, and about half that in width—as if I know what ten kilometres look like!

I step into the village with ease, but when I turn around, the Maze is invisible to me, and the village seems to stretch on forever. One thing is for sure: I'm not leaving the same way I came in.

Sand sprinkles as though from a salt-shaker from the round low sky of the globular prison. Dusty hills house little people I can't make out clearly through irregularly punctured windows. Orange-brown twiggy branches guard the huts, marking each family's territory. A cube bronze building, not particularly large, stands in the middle of the sandy terrain. A rotting wooden oval plank hangs by a single wooden nail long as a branch, an isosceles triangle carved on it. Fragile legged pillars struggle to remain upright, holding nothing but the dusty sky. A couple hundred metres off, there's a single stone wall, golden brown, large chunks eaten off the top. Through gaping holes, I see that it once had three storeys. A mushy stone staircase leans against it, leading nowhere. Next to it stands a rectangular wooden door that looks too sand-jammed to open. Spotted around a giant gaping hole are igloo-shaped houses made of mudbrick. I see a single well. It is small and nearly empty.

Well, never fear: the Chosen One is here.

I hear a sweeping sound behind me from where the village line should be and then I'm clobbered on the back of the head with wood. It's not particularly painful, but I fall melodramatically in such a way that I land on my back in the hope of getting a sense of what I'm up against. If they prove an actual threat, I would rather they think I'm out cold so I have the element of surprise on my side when I strike. I peer through slit eyes at the creature who stands above me.

Scarcely visible sonic waves ripple from the antenna which stands erect atop large square brown eyes, his pupils fixed into the bottom corners. The sleeves of his brown cloak drop into sharp points. His body is a tidy whirl of dots of rock. His hands are humanoid but extended, scabbed, and raw. He has three fingers on each hand that curl around the bat he used to assault me. His black mouth, always closed, looks like someone speaking when their mouth is covered by their granny's tights. He makes swishy sounds, made cacophonous and scratchy perhaps due to a lack of saliva.

It's quickly apparent he knows who I am, or at least hazards a good guess. Soon a group of them are herded around me, and it's like the night with the goblins all over again. Decisions, decisions: to kill me, eat me, detain me, worship me, use me against the Triune, hand me over, cast me out, support me, or whatever. In the end, the first and cheekiest Sandster steps forward, still armed with his plank; his aim: to bludgeon my brains out. *Don't try it.*

His spinning-top lower-body freezes, and legs form. He is just about to foray me when I sweep him to the ground, and he drops the bat behind him. I leap to my feet, stamp on his solar plexus, and back-knuckle his face. He squirms and screams, and his antennae send out waves like an emergency beacon as his right hand tries to get a hold of his weapon. I pin his left hand to the ground with my knee, and my hands arrest his wrist. When he yanks his forearm to claw my eyes out, the bones in his arm shatter.

I'm in as much agony as I was yesterday, but I give no sign of it.

As I rise to my feet, all the other Sandsters who merely hooted and buzzed while this went on scatter like the sand they are and yelp.

"I am the Chosen One," I call out, not that anyone cares. "Contrary to the evidence in front of you, I have come to liberate you from entrapment and destitution." I say no more because no one is listening.

The Sandster I defeated zips up again, plank in hand. I conceal my face. Then there's a *whoosh* of fire, an ear-splitting screech, and he turns to glass, the wood to ash. *Woah…* The flame-thrower cackles slyly like a snobby wine-taster. Having dropped to take cover, I roll onto my front and look up at the wall of the Maze. There's a tallish man with a wine-red ponytail and red streaks on the sides of his lips. His face is cruel and wicked: he has emerald eyes, eyebrows as pointy as his nose, and flat cheeks that push out an angular chin.

This must be Sharmedes. I recognise him from the library books. The wizard that never should have been, born of the Triune's spell and the sacrificial blood of the unwilling Elder Wizard. If I remember correctly, he had a son with the witch everyone in Angoria hates.

A purple cloak wraps around his neck and droops like a tongue. I could be wrong, but I think it's the Elder Wizard's—the one Aurora tried to use in their battle against the trolls. Three plates of yellow armour shield his chest, abdomen, and privates, giving him the appearance of an insect. Tight green material coats his limbs like snakeskin.

"Deliver onto me the Chosen One now!" he squawks. His mouth moves at an alternate speed to his speech; it's like watching a subtitled dentist advertisement: most jarring. Impatient and/or too lazy to come get me himself, he gently encourages the townsfolk by most insensitively firing a tree of blooming orange, yellow, and red at a house that consequently explodes. I am surprised by how numbed I feel to the uncertain, tortured screams that rise from the house and all around Sandster village. Nuala and her beau D.W. always said I was cold.

Not sure how to react to such unadulterated evil or my own indifference, I just stare at Sharmedes. And that's when I see him. Behind Sharmedes's stolen threads is a boy. He is amazed at the carnage—there's even a hint of a smile on his cheeks—yet I can see that he is terrified, too. He looks to be no more than a head taller than me. His hair's dark brown, streaked with golden splints. His fringe is combed upwards which makes his face look longer than it is. His forehead is so large his facial features press down tightly on top of one another, yet he is still handsome. His trousers are sandy brown and a little scorched, revealing skin raw like crinkly cranberries. There's no way he's much older than me. I hope one of these

Sandsters kills him before I have to.

Sharmedes raises his hand. He's about to strike again. Should I pretend to surrender? He looks arrogant, so he'll try to kill me from up-close, right, exercising mastery over his prey just before the kill? Then I'll subtly reach in my bag and stab him in the back. But before I can put my rudimentary plan into action, I hear a whizzing sound. It crackles. Like a tornado in a lightning storm.

*Oh no! Not him!* From across the far plain of this village, I behold the rage of the Wraith, half his face smouldered, melted, and blue; this all combines to make him all the more terrifying.

"Dark Lord," he yawns in his monotonous, hollow voice, and then very dramatically shoots lightning bolts at a number of fences and huts to further signal the obviousness of his arrival.

Hold on: Silas referred to me as the Chosen One, as did Sharmedes. Yet Lear and the Wraith (who, I learned from spying out Mecky's lair, are in cahoots) think I'm the Dark Lord. But Silas, Lear and whoever the third guy is are a team. I struggle to reconcile the discrepancy.

The two manic villains shoot bolts of light and forks of fire at each other for a while, so I take advantage of my being a secondary concern and scurry left, but down the street I see an amassing cloud of swishy, slicing sand. The natives are fighting back. I bow to the preparatory stance of a racer and hobble in the direction of the pillars, circling around the Wraith. The pressure that moving puts on my feet is blinding. My blisters now have blisters. But I make it there unseen. I pant silently, my back tight against a pillar. My coccyx shrills. I'm thirstier than I ever remember.

I wait for the *whoosh*es and voltage and demolition to end. They don't. When I finally peer, I see hovels burning; the Sandsters punish the duelists with a sandstorm. This has no impact on the Wraith's intangible skin, but surely blurs his vision. Slits like gills appear on Sharmedes's hands and face and he glassifies them in retribution.

On one level, I want to get out there and be the hero, but it is also the last thing I want to do. I procrastinate and pretend to myself that I'm strategising how to annihilate them both: the wizard that never should have been born, and the dead man who never should have lived this long—hybrids!

I feel the eyes of another on me. I look to my left, expecting a hammer in the face. Instead, behind another pillar I see the youngest wizard in Angoria. Assuming he's here to grill Barbeque Benjamin nice and crispy, I point and spit, "Don't... you... dare!" I make a chasing motion, like I'm going to thwack him. The entire time, I remain stringently shielded from the others' sight by my pillar. He cowers and looks like he's about to take a hike, but in case he does make a run for it and consequently gets his heart ripped out by the Wraith, I tell him he's grand and to stay put. His spiked head nods slightly and shivers a lot, and I see in his eyes such fear as I have only ever seen in my own. I think I can trust him not to kill me. I think I can trust him not to say a word.

Still, I press my right index finger to my lips. "Shhh..."

Closer to our pillars than the carnage, there's a bustle and a wheeling of a cart. I investigate. Though he clearly doesn't want to risk exposure, in view of his jittery digits and movements, the boy follows suit. Copying me is better than helplessly waiting for death, or so it would seem. Beneath the cart, a family of Sandsters finish burying what I assume is all the food and possessions they have in the world: a few jugs, loaves, and better-looking clothes than I've seen anyone else here wear, which is to say their clothes are coloured something other than brown. They must be the one percent. They hug and pat and kiss and flee. I blink away the jealousy. The boy does the same. His irksome copycat ways are starting to bug me.

Finally, there's a lull in the battle. Now if this were a movie, the lot of them would be huddled together on the opposite side of this pillar when I sneak a peek. Instead, the ever so fleeting calm only serves to hype up the next storm. Caught between worlds and moments, the apparition shakes left and right like a mirage of photographs blowing in the wind. His lips bulge horribly as though surgically enhanced, flattened, then ballooned again. Finally, he stabilises, and from a bluish white belt, he draws forth a long black wand with a knotted design for a handle. He flicks it and it extends, widens, and sharpens to become a sword with a rippling oily flame for a blade. And the sandstorm screeches as he slices off many of its faces into oblivion until not one combatant remains. The dust of the deceased vacuums upward through the dome barrier.

Within a minute, the colourless sky is blotted out by brown smoke and bursts of dust. Few hovels remain, and what is left of them is runny mud and charred twiggy infrastructure. I see no inhabitants. And with gruesome majesty, the Wraith stands alone with an air of coldness, un-surprise and lethargy for a countenance—the Warrior Victorious.

With a single flick, black flames jet from his blade and eradicate the stonework of the cube building like an eraser. The Cube vanishes into thin air, and inside it—or, where it used to be—stands the family who loaded the cart, buried in a palace of jellies, cakes, and wines, all of which they have just now been eating. These one-percenters must be the mayoral family, national traitors, and co-conspirators with the enemy.

Without so much as a cheesy morbid one-liner, the Wraith slaughters all but one of them with a black blast a second later. To the lone survivor, he taunts, "Beg for your life…" As if that will do any good.

Colourfully dressed, and his antennae coated in gold rings, the mayor is an anomaly. More importantly, he is beaten. He knows this, surely. Yet still, he kneels before the Wraith and pleads for his life in a common language: "The Triune promised us peace in this New World. They told us we would be greatly rewarded for our acts of service. That we would be treated as royalty and given one hundred-thousand wives! Please, do not send us to Sheol, the Land of Shadows! They promised us immortality!"

He grovels in at least five other different tongues before the Wraith, having droned, "Consider your masters pleased and their conditions revoked" decapitates him anyway. Well, I saw that coming.

The guy next to me did not if his gasp is anything to go by. As white sweat seeps through his pores and glosses his forehead, the boy's head pivots frantically as he looks for Sharmedes amidst the dust and the grating of billions of tiny stones. Distressed, he rocks on his heels and his toes, fidgets with his blood- and dirt-caked hands, and finally buries them deep in his holed pockets so that his fingers pop out his trousers at the thigh.

I quickly throw my eyes past the pillar. There's no sign of Sharmedes. I hope he's dead. But the boy's genuine trepidation moves me to compassion unlike I knew I had, and I decide to create a diversion so he (my enemy!) can look for him. I just need the right moment. Oh, who am I kidding? This is war. There's never a good time to jump out and hand yourself over to the enemy on a silver platter. Deep breath…

I step out from behind the pillar. No fear on my face, despite all feeling. Hands down, diagonal, palms facing the Wraith. I remove Aurora's ring from my finger and clasp it tight between my right thumb and palm, safe and warm. Like a stress ball, I find it helps to fidget with something at times like these.

"Dig those fish-lips, beastie!"

He turns and smiles crookedly with what's left of his functioning facial nerves. He's a crossover of a clown and minced meat, with the perverse laughter of the criminally insane. Daggers of light fire at me, but I avoid every one of them. Every widow and orphan in Angoria is my charge, and I refuse to allow them to kneel any longer in subordination to madmen like this. He begins to show off with his sword. Sucks for him that I'm unimpressed. He almost seems saddened.

He turns back to me and again senselessly obliterates things in my vicinity. I notice that he's intentionally not hitting me with the flames, so I can only assume this is a retrieve mission, not a murderous one, but I don't trust him not to kill me regardless.

Anyway, more to the point: what am I going to do about him? I'm the guy who is too afraid to touch traffic light buttons in case the previous button-pusher didn't wash their hands after their last visit to the bathroom. I'm hardly qualified to man up and battle this undead ghoul from the netherworld.

To be honest, I should know instinctively how to outmanoeuvre him, but I find now that every sci-fi show or comic I'd stored away in my brain is in a password sensitive vault, and I can't calm down enough to remember said password and open it up.

"My Lord." He bows and it sickens me.

"Servant," I say pompously, head thrown in the air in all directions; anything to buy myself some time. I walk around him in a slow circle.

"You escaped the strictures of Laxciilian life unscathed?"

"I wouldn't say that," I scowl, and walk subtly in the direction of the well. I stop and turn. "Lear spoke so highly of you, assassin. Tell me, then: whatever excuse do you intend to fall back on for failing to kill the Elder Wizard or the Royal Family of Laxciila?"

"My orders from the Great Elven House were to kill only the girl and those the King deemed a threat or disturbance, Master Mex Confetricus."

"Confectionary."

"My Lord?"

Oh, wait, he's right. 'Confectionary' means… something else. "Proceed." I walk on, and he follows in slow uncertain steps, but says no more. "Good servant, who is your master?"

"Lord Lear and the Triumvir to whom he swears allegiance… you, O Great One."

"THEN WHY DID YOU TAKE ORDERS FROM THE ELDER ELF?!" Oh, my holy days! He actually cowers. This is golden!

"He lowered the gates that I might retrieve you from the pit of squander and take you to Triune Tower. I was surprised by your hesitation, my Lord, if you permit me to speak so freely."

"You shot me. Repeatedly."

"For appearance's sake."

"I waited months for you to come and deliver me until finally I lost hope! And in my vulnerable state, that horse-faced moron used his wiles and charms to turn me against you. He is a sneak and a liar, and devilment follows him…"

"I was aware Lord Lear had reservations. How much I now regret having considered them unfounded."

"In my world, we have an expression: 'Expect the unexpected'."

"I have heard the First Sinner say it, speaking of which…"

"I only said all that about Gideon to mess with the others' minds. Lear can be trusted. The same can't be said about the other two. They have constantly railed against me. And mark my words: Mehkabikil works for the enemy!" I can't believe I'm painting him as the good guy in all this. Help!

I walk on some more and get more dramatic with my hand gestures, so he doesn't suspect I'm going to trick him into solidifying, going all electric, and then push him down the well. "That vermin cannot be trusted! I tried to break him, but his loyalty to the Elder Wizard was too strong. For every move Lear orchestrated in Laxciila and beyond, I assure you, the Elf has a countermove."

"What do you propose?"

"For your next assignment, easy: I want you to kill the Elder Elf." And just so it sounds as though I mean it— "Kill them all."

Suddenly, the not-so-dead Sharmedes reappears. Well, if I'm honest with myself, I knew that wasn't over.

"Paladin!"

Who? Me? Oh! I have to say, that is definitely one of the nicer names I've been called since I got here. Okay... *Paladin*... I like it.

"Kill him!" I shout to both of them indirectly, wearing my contrasting titles with pride.

The Wraith must finally cop on that I am not his bedfellow, and his sword blanks the well out of existence in an attempt to oust me. He misses by a hare's breath, or a hair's breadth, or whatever that expression is. Next, the Dark Wizard clicks his fingers and sets the bottom of my trouser legs alight. I flay on the sand like a fish drowning on oxygen to the chorus of his crusty cackle.

I put it out quickly. I'm more humiliated than injured. Within seconds, the Wraith's a spinning drill again. He'll be upon me any moment. I leap to my aching feet, about to beat him across the head with my man-bag.

And then a metal blade is thrown to me, covered in a cloth! My butterfingers fumble and grab it tardily. The cloth falls and reveals a most marvellous sword that almost reaches my height: the blade is wide and silver; noticeably ancient. And its gleam atones for the sun that no longer shines over this pallid and barren dead-land. The rhombus pommel, cross- and rain-guard are flat, strong, and decorated with a vine pattern that continues into the fuller where there are six chicken scratch markings—

"Skylar!" screams the Wraith at me—or the sword?—and then we both turn to where it was thrown from.

A man in his mid-forties to early-fifties throws off a Sandster cloak and leaps between the Wraith and me with feet certain as a cat's. He has a small beard, hard features, and wears only brown but for his signature green coat. At the sight of him, I vaguely recall the Elder Wizard telling me a mentor would be waiting for me in the Black Forest. The one who rescued me from the sabre-tooth… who I proceeded to abandon to the beasts of the woods and the forces of Laxciila. (Whoops).

The Wraith's and Sharmedes's reactions to our new arrival are hilarious. Two baddies against the Chosen One: piece of cake. Then a guy in a green coat shows up with plot-twist timing and plot-convenience swords (for he also holds one) and within seconds, Sharmedes has a concussion and even the Wraith falls victim to fear-induced paralysis— probably because he knows he's about to lose the second half of his face, and not a decade too soon.

And I'm certain I could stab him to death with Skylar before he could blink. Angoria would certainly be better off. It would sure make my life easier knowing that this *thing* was not chasing after me.

But can I see it through? Last time I stabbed a person, the entire trajectory of my life was set off-course. Do I really have it in me to kill again?

Then again, his death could save hundreds of lives—my own included. The Triune's, or Lear's, number one assassin—eliminated. But do I really have room for another ghost in my nightmares? They were pretty overcrowded last night. Not to mention the moral implications of offing someone when he is as good as defenceless.

To kill him except in combat would be undignified. Murder. It's not like he's a chicken. He was a living, breathing being once. Just a normal man who happened to be in the wrong place at an even worse time, murdered by Gideon before the Higher Orders knew how to cope with the whole death thing. Yes, he is responsible for his tyranny, but it's not his fault he was a victim; that the appropriate help resources weren't in place when he needed them.

I choose to let him live, though I don't know if honour or fear is the deciding factor.

Gradually he recovers from his lapse.

Having momentarily neutralised the wizard, Green Coat now sprints toward the Wraith, but the Wraith punches him, and he's hurled dozens of metres away. Sharmedes is up again, and from his hands slithers a fiery snake, but the Wraith easily disposes of it with a flushing whirlpool of wind. Sharmedes's attempt was weak, and I can see he's looking downright weedy. He's over-exerting himself on magic usage, since he's probably unused to confrontation on this scale. Excellent!

The Wraith speeds my way and lifts his sword in the air. The black flame hardens to metal. He's just about to lower it when *Shunk*. An arrow shoots right though his chest. One that burns a yellow and red hole through his skin. A hole that bleeds and foams with eons-old sudsy pus.

I jump backwards, bobbing on my blistered feet. His sword continues driving to the ground and turns the sand it lands on to rock.

"Ouch," he yawns, and twists his head full way. An arrow lodges in his skull. Then another. Dozens more pierce his body. More! He drops to his knees, twists his head back properly, and I see the archers: Laxciilian elves!

Gold helmets shield their crowns, the back of their heads, and cheeks. Gold armour shields their shoulders, chests, and legs from the knees down. Blue dragon skin, thin like a jumpsuit, protects their exposed arms, and chainmail their groins. They wear flowing purple cloaks for show; and a sword, longbow, and a red quiver of arrows for battle. Their aim has improved. Green Coat bows his head to the commander, marked by silver armour, a red cloak, and a crossbow, who nods in return.

Unmerciful screams originate from the entrance to the village as Sharmedes scorches their armour and the Wraith treats them to a dose of lightning bolts, nowhere near as powerful as those he mustered prior to getting shot with the power-dampening arrows. Regardless of their combined efforts, for every elf the villains take down, three are on hand to take their place.

I take advantage of the flood of alpha-male testosterone, and limp back to the pillars. That's when I see, from the farthest reaches of the village, screeching sandstorms swarm together like locusts. (Where have they been hiding for the last ten minutes? The hills? The air? The ground?).

When I'm back at the pillar, I realise the boy is gone. I hear a *zip* beyond a nearby obelisk; but when I inch my eyes in that direction, I catch a glimpse of whirling velvet, and nothing else. What is going on here? This is pure madness!

I hear the incessant whir of arrows cutting through the air and slicing open the Wraith's garment and flesh. Those Laxciilians had the chance to kill me, but they didn't. Are these renegade warriors who have abandoned the Elder Elf, or has everything the Wizard said about Mecky being a spy for the Resistance (albeit one superb at his job) been true?

No, I don't believe that for a second. Fool me once, shame on him; fool me twice, and I won't live long enough for it to happen again. But this commander might be ideologically opposed to Mecky. He hasn't made moves against me, so I won't tar him with the same brush as his boss. And without a shadow of a doubt, I go ahead and decide I already like this commander more than the last one; he's less of an Elder Elf's rear end-lookalike than she was.

But how did they avoid the killer mist? Did they just time it really well? Did their armour protect them? Did the mole open a portal like he did when I first came to the Black Forest outside Laxciila? Does it matter?

A piercing scream that scrapes the air like nails on a blackboard steals my focus. I tilt my head slightly over the pillar and see the point of Green's sword sticking its tongue out the ghoul's mouth, mapping it with black cracks. Arrow shafts pin him everywhere like a severely tortured voodoo doll. Blood oozes and blisters burst as needles fly through the air and take up residence in his ragdoll animated carcass.

And I can't help myself: "Stop! Leave him alone! Please! What is the matter with you? He's a person. A human being! Get away from him!"

Green glares at me for a second. His nasty eyes widen. He takes one step towards me. Then one of the Laxciilians gives a verbal signal, and half of them turn on the others. Brother ploughs down brother. I don't see what happens next because individual sandstorms hail through the streets, converge, and attack all the Laxciilians (whatever the cause for that grievance) and the Wraith. With harsh scratch after harsh scratch, the sand shaves the Laxciilians' armour and skin and eats them to the bone.

A few Elven swordsmen and a few archers succeed in making it across the plains, nothing more than sheer indomitable determination egging them on. Finally, they bombard the pillars. Three, five, soon there are twelve. And it doesn't take a mind reader to know they're coming to kill me. I ready myself with the sword, but while I'd like to think myself capable of self-preservation by any means, I don't know how far I'm willing to go.

*Zip!* I turn, more defensively than aggressively. The boy is back; half the purple cloak is torn and coated over his shoulder like a sash. His hazel eyes and stern expression assure me that the sword will not be needed. That he will repay what he considers a debt, my enabling him to look for Sharmedes. He indicates that I close and cover my eyes. I oblige and shield my vision, but curiosity forces my eyes open again and my hands drop.

And the boy does something that earns him the name Pyro. Murder the colour of sunshine sweeps into his eyes. Hot, focused, adamant. His thick eyebrows lower like the elves' life-expectancy. He mutters silently to himself and jets of fire shoot from his hands. Soon, cooked flesh bubbles in our hiding place, and gold rivers lake down shoulder blades. The cloaks disintegrate, while the dragon skin does not even smoke. And my would-be killers lie dead.

Another *zip!* A purple swivel of light like a washing-machine.

Sharmedes. Only metres away from here. Pyro's eyes tell me we're even, and he runs out to his carnivalesque maker. Yet Pyro does not expose me: not when he's within hugging distance of Sharmedes; not when Sharmedes raises his hand to him; not after Sharmedes beats him with a hand so piping hot it glows—and for what? Did he assume Pyro was a coward *zipping* away like that, or for taking his conked-out posterior off the field, or for killing the Triune's Laxciilian allies? Did Pyro *zip* around the battlefield rescuing Sharmedes every time he fell? Is this punishment for making him out to be a weakling, for keeping him alive?

You piece of work!

Over the crackles of voltage and beating and *uh*s and swirls of sand, I hear the muffles of Green yelling my name. Well, he uses the words "kid", "princess", and a whole host of expletives, but I think they're directed at me. I shrink into a ball and scurry behind whatever debris or burning bush that I think will best shield me from the lot of them at a given moment. At one point, I hear him get jumped, engage in a sword fight, and cut several elves down with no hint of remorse. I fear he might be more evil than the lot of them combined.

Every sound I hear is awful, but not one for naked exhibits of emotion, I hold in every urge to scream as each warrior out there is hacked to pieces. And I wait until the titanic battle between metal, light, fire, and stone has ended before I make my presence known.

The Wraith smoulders on the ground, no more than blistered, melted flesh now. Whatever the arrows were doused in has virtually solidified him in a crusty case. His open mouth is humiliated, either unaware of how this happened, or incapable of comprehending his distress. I'm forced to remind myself that the Wraith is evil, deserving of all this and more, and that I'm not supposed to care.

But I do. I do care. And if that makes me a bad Chosen One, then for the first time in my life, I am okay with not being perfect at everything.

Pyro stands a few metres away from the fallen ghost, his back to the apparition. He seems lost and confused, and intentionally wanders from

Sharmedes's ill-thought-out battle with Green.

When Sharmedes finally accepts that persisting in this duel will only result in his decapitation, he covers his face with his half of the cloak, and—

*zip*—he's gone.

Pyro's eyes hone in on a corpse on the ground, pretending he's unaware that he's just been abandoned. And that's when I see it: the last ounce of strength in the Wraith's spidery fingers crawling along the sword's handle.

And despite a limp and blisters, I charge into Pyro and knock him to the ground to safety. And with my new weapon, I slash the Wraith's wand-sword into fragments. There's a small explosion which adds something special to the visual effect of the scene, and then, just defeat. His final attempt having failed, the Wraith surrenders to the sarcophagus he's become.

"What did you do?" snarls Green behind gritted teeth like a dog.

I'm offended at having been spoken to so rudely, so without looking at him, I pout, "He saved my life." I don't know if sticking my nose in the air is absolutely necessary, but it's done now.

"He is the enemy," he growls, and he must think I'm dressed all ladylike or that I have high notions of myself, because he again calls me princess. "They both are."

"Princesses?"

"The enemy."

"Aren't you?"

"Not yours. Not today."

I want to talk to Pyro, maybe see if he'll ditch Sharmedes and join me. I can't but feel sorry for him standing there, frozen on the hot sand; a statue, forgotten by his own maker. Disregarded like a piece of art.

Then, a *zipping* noise. A purple swirl. An outstretched arm, not even Sharmedes's full body. And Pyro is grabbed into the mixing violet swirl and disappears, a wary and unhappy disposition on his face.

"Da-a-a-a-a-a-a-ark       W-o-o-o-aw-aw-aw-aw-aw-aw-aw-n-n-n-n…"

"Hello," I say dopily and wave.

"N' m'… n' mmmm… n' maw… no more…"

"Are you sorry?" A poor comforter, I don't know what else to say.

"Yuh-sss-sss-sss-sss-sss…" he lies.

"Good. Then I'm sorry it turned out like this. Truly."

"C'm… 'ere… pluh-eassssssssssss… D'arck-k-k-k On-n-n-n-n-n…"

I look around the fallen village. Smoke puffs from the wreckage of hovels. Fires crackle and dance on graves. Monuments are… (what monuments?). Fried flesh, most of it burnt, pollutes my nose, and it is hard to hold down the vomit. No one survived. Quietly, Green demands, "Don't you dare." I ignore him but monitor my closeness to the ghoul. I bend low.

"Let me guess: this is the part when you force those crocodile tears down your cheeks; I take pity on you; you tap my hand; and send an electromagnetic shock through my body that results in a heart attack?" Gosh, I'm good. Look at the horror in his eyes at my accuracy. "Now allow me to tell you how this is going to end: I am going to walk away, and you are going to watch, and forever and for always you will remember this as the day you failed to deliver onto Lear the Chosen One. Not the Dark Lord. The Chosen One. My associate is going to imprison you now and lock you away for all time. This, you will spend alone and in agony until time itself has reached its Best Before date, having reaped exactly what you have sown. And should you perchance find a way out, you will behave as decently as the man you once were, for should I learn that you do not, I will deal with you personally. I will pierce you with many Laxciilian arrow heads, solidify you, and then run this blade through your heart until you burn from the inside out with the heat of a thousand suns. Then I will peel off your flesh and feed it to you. Lastly, when you are beyond the ability to beg for mercy, I will decide against demonstrating it by beheading you and sticking your ugly wicked head in a glass box and propping that box over my fireplace. Then, when I tire of looking at you, I will toss your ugly wicked head into a volcano. Nod if you understand."

He nods, and I turn and walk away before I cry and apologise and do everything in my power to heal him.

And with nothing left to stay for, I hobble to the gate at the back of the village. It appears that anything but a Sandster can easily pass through, because I'm soon back in the Maze. Green exits the village within a minute and follows close behind me all the way. Call me uber-sensitive, but I don't want to look at him ever again.

"What did you do to him?" I call back.

"I kicked him down that big bottomless wormhole," he laughs with, I assume, a shrug. Ferocity fills my very veins—why didn't I think of that? Probably because I'm not as okay with killing people as he is.

"But he can fly...?"

"Not after sustaining all those injuries. Levitation is easy when you are a spirit. It is less simple when you have been solidified and mauled."

Subtly, so he cannot see, I tighten my grip on my sword, and convince myself that should he cross a line, I may suspend my not being okay with cutting humans down.

# INTERLUDE
# DAVE WITHERSPOON

From inside the house that I had not yet grown to call home, only one sound, steady and unchanging in rhythm: *chop, chop, chop!*

She carved bulky potatoes into ever thinner slices, her long sink-white arms rising and falling in machine-like fashion. There was a scary look on her face that I was unused to, a crazed look. She had banished me from the kitchen for two hours to a wasteland so sacred it has not been host to children in years—Outside.

I remember seeing her standing there through the kitchen window after my exile, terrified she might look at me, Medusa-like, with a glare so stony it would inject me with shame. The *chop-chop-chop* of the knife as it sawed through the potatoes and bounced up from the breadboard permeated in my brain until long after she dropped the knife.

Oh, it had been such a beautiful day. The sun's heat was rough for Ireland, but it would be a cultural sin to complain about that, despite my increasingly vampiric antipathy for light. After a couple of excruciatingly boring hours of playing alone with the grass I re-entered the cold new house. Semi-detached, even the house had more companions than I had.

My breathing irritated her now more than my presence had ever upset the One-Armed Man; so, quieter than a spider crawls down a cobweb, I took a single step through the backdoor. My foot caused a splash. Oh, how I've always hated the feeling of soggy socks.

The tap ran like a fountain, and a chill sea lapped across the floor and flowed against the threshold plate. I had never been to the beach before, so I was unprepared for the awkwardness of wading through water as the current cemented my feet to the tiles beneath. I didn't like the sensation. I still don't. I struggled across the riverbed, dragged over and stood on a chair, and turned off the tap. That instant, a small waterfall urinated on my hair. I looked up to see a brown patch smudge expand from one end of the ceiling to the middle. Folds appeared to scratch their way across the once-white ceiling and tear. More clear water leaked downwards and spilt on the table, the oven, and the fridge.

I was only nine years of age. How was I to know that Nuala was in the upstairs bathroom drowning herself?

After pulling the feeble creature from the water, red hair tattooed across her face, I rushed downstairs to the sitting-room and flung open her briefcase. My socks splodged and my runners squelched with each step. She had forewarned me months prior that the emergency number was different here—not that that even mattered, for after I'd run for her phone, I realised that I'd never been told her password to unlock its features.

Instead, I grabbed her laptop, whose password I knew instinctively, having done homework on it before: 4xABC2o25s. The second I was in, I frantically set about searching a list of doctors in Louth. I found one. A head doctor. *That must mean he's pretty good*, I thought. And in a moment that I have regretted since, I pushed the call button.

From the instant he arrived on the scene and carried out his rescue mission, he shaped me in a most detestable image—that of a ghost—until he had utterly turned her against me, and his name became my name. Before long, he'd pulled out the upstairs bath—and about half the floor tiles with it—and, more than once, for days on end, chained to a pipe and starved so much that my chicken carcass ribs could be counted, that small room would become my dungeon. I came to call it The World.

I'll always remember the overpowering pungency of the nacre lemon-scented air-freshener atop the toilet cistern, squatting as though taking a dump. A metre or so above the mother of pearl was a small opaque window that rarely let in much light, but every once in a while—though perhaps only in my imagination—it seemed that light was breaking through.

Sometimes I'd play a game in which I'd try to trick myself into thinking I hadn't been locked in there for any longer than sixty seconds at a time, even if six days of body fat had dropped off me and my raw metal-encased wrists had been pared to the bone. During that time, I'd imagine another version of myself—not one who was the prey, but rather a predator—breaking me out of there, and we'd escape to a far-off place where we could be the heroes rescuing the poor helpless victims trapped in the planet prison. Sometimes changing my perspective was all it took to rewrite time and change my understanding of reality.

But it was always the lemony perfume in its seashell container that brought me back to reality. No matter how intense the illusionary prison world, there would come a point where I'd catch a whiff of its acidic spray and sense would break through… and with it, pain.

We moved into the significantly smaller 87 after the next-door neighbours complained about me screaming at the top of my lungs all night long for help. And there a brother would be spawned from the coital amalgamation of the two beasts… the Mad Woman and D.W.

Sometimes I wish I'd let her commit suicide whilst peeling potatoes. I would have killed two birds with one stone.

# 17
# SCATHACH'S ISLE

I hate him. Passionately. I think he might be this world's version of D.W. Between us, we have found no reason to speak, which suits us both fine.

It's not just that he isn't talkative. I mean, I'm not either. It's the casual unprovoked rudeness that ticks me off. The all-round bad manners: the cutting remarks; the gestural stares; the clips around the ear for not conforming word-for-word to his inaudible grunts and mumbles; the random punches in the gut and machine-gun "WHERE'S YOUR GUARD?!" I hate the mercilessness with which he slaughters all foes that come against us with his own magic hawk-eyed sword like he has a personal problem with the lot of them: Nue, Chimera, Demogorgon, Laxciilians, Amphibians, Mermen, Snake-Men, and a murder of crows. Like, I'm the Chosen One, and I'm pretty much of the opinion, sure, give them the chance to say they're sorry, turn around, and walk back home. Sometimes I try to peacefully negotiate with the fiends; other times I just flex my muscles or clean dirt from my nails and let the band of eejits do their thing as Green Coat massacres them. Once in a while, I'm as vicious as he is, and I see Roop's face transplant over every one of theirs. It always ends the same.

The rare times I do speak— "Morning," "Thanks," "Night"—he snipes, offended at having been spoken to. Plus, he has this look in this eye that seems to question why I state what time of day it is in my greetings and closings, like I'm a puppy looking for a medal. It would probably make more sense if I was to wish him a *good* morning or a *good* night, but I don't lie.

Furthermore, his filthy attire exudes the stench of an entire liquor shelf; he unabashedly swigs alcohol at regular intervals from sun-up until sundown. I remember Booze-hound Witherspoon once slurring during the ads of her favourite soap that historically Irishmen preferred the pub than talking. She'd know. This leads me to ponder if something happened that moulded Green into an unscrupulous unrepentant killer with a penchant for downing drink by the draught. Or if he's Irish. But only for a few seconds. He's not high up enough in my esteem to justify making him out to be a complex character of considerable depth.

After three weeks of wordlessly putting up with his nonsense, I ask him if he has a problem with me. He uses and abuses my invitation to speak freely, and says he overheard my sinister conversation with the Wraith; hence, he got the wrong end of the stick. Eavesdropper! He adds it was my "YOU SHALL NOT PASS" re-enactment (when the Laxciilians tried to kill the ghoul) that solidified his suspicions. However, having surveyed me for weeks from the shadows in Laxciila, he deemed me honourless and says he never trusted me one bit.

"What did you see?" I challenge the barbarian.

"You tiptoeing throughout the kingdom when you thought no one was watching." Funny. The Elder Elf accused me of something similar— "skulking".

"And with whom, may I ask, did you share these mirages?"

"I know what I saw." If he has a confidante, he's not spilling the beans. He's cagey and secretive. I don't like it.

"Where, then, did I tiptoe?"

"You know where."

"Do I?"

"Yes."

"Pray tell, whatever did this figure who so convincingly resembled me take?"

"You know what you took."

The implication, I assume, is that he does not. Good. He knows nothing.

For the next few days, we walk in complete silence in a relatively straight line with little alteration through the spindly alleys that spike left and right. Well, Green walks. I limp, wince, scream, and die, and scram from the cat-sized black rats. Reminder to self: if ever I see giant frogs again, avoid the whiplash of their tongues and poke a sword in their jelly belly. Not that I have my sword anymore. Green considers me too great a liability to the cause to harbour anything so dangerous, so he keeps it wrapped in cloths and tucked away in his armoury bag. Probably so he can gut me with it later.

We have two meals a day: one of bread and milk (which is relatively findable in the Maze if you know where to look, which Green does), the other of nuts, fruit, and water. He shoots and/or stabs a few wild beasts daily. Unfortunately, most of them are Warpers, so they're not safe to eat, and the natural creatures he kills tend to be small pests, so they don't make for hearty meals. The path gets hardly any sunlight so little vegetation grows here (aside from the hedges, though I think that has more to do with supernatural influences than artificial climate patterns) so it would be impossible for packs of animals to survive, if indeed they didn't cross paths with a Warper first.

Every night ends the same: Green tosses a stone at the Maze wall he has chosen for us to recline by, just to make sure that hedgerow isn't sentient and won't eat us if we roll in our sleep and make contact. Sometimes though, the leaves are tricky and play platonic until the little whippersnappers think they can drag us into oblivion. To the sword-friendly yahoo's credit, they haven't been successful yet. It probably would be polite for me to offer to keep watch one of these nights, but I'm not mad on the whole notion of giving up my quality shut-eye time to prolong his lifespan.

Honestly, I cringe so much to hear his voice and detest that I am solely dependent on him that, if not for my handicap and lack of a H.M.D. (Holographic Mapping Device) because Edgar stole my watch, I'd have run away already—I still might.

The ruffian has his practical applications, though: he has an expert understanding of the Maze and memory of its roads, chasms, and shortcuts. No widespread sheet of directions for this guy, oh no— "My memory is the map," he snarled the morning after Battle Royale. (I hope he doesn't know the way so well because he had been hired to take me to the throne room of disgrace at the Triune's feet. That would not be good).

Thus far, he has only led us astray once (yesterday)—into a den of giant insects and spiders. It wasn't pretty. The shortest bug was as high as my kneecaps; the largest was so tall the Maze wall shot up multiple feet higher than usual just to contain it. There were pale grey slugs with red eyes and more legs than a millipede. There were butterflies with black and white variegated patterns on their wings, laser eyes, and massive teeth!

Of course, I got trapped in an arachnid's slimy web, green and beautiful though it was, by which I mean no insensitivity to the pallid human corpse that hung next to me. I called him Joe. Bored out of my wits waiting for Green to save me, I even had time to script a mock role-play with it:


BENJAMIN: Hello, Joe.

JOE: Hello-o-o!

BENJAMIN: How's she hanging?

JOE: Poor choice of words there, boy.

BENJAMIN: Ah, 'twas punny all the same though, Joe.

JOE: True that, my son.


Our scripted conversation ended awkwardly and abruptly when I realised he was still alive. Furthermore, it was at that point that the Queen Spider set all eight of her sights on me. Regrettably, I had little other choice than to throw open my satchel with my only unwebbed limb, retrieve an apple I had had such high hopes for that night (dessert!), and hurled it in one of her eyes.

Blinded, I was released in part by the random rabid dices of her spoked legs and chattering pincers, and in part by Green's slashing flashy blade. And then he, a right show-off, leapt from one of her legs to another, until he was atop her hairy body, and then stabbed her in the back and the head.

"Worry not, Princess. I'll make everything better."

"You are quite the spin doctor."

"Have you learned nothing from me during our time together?"

But instead of complimenting him as his ego begged, I walked right by him and then sourly commented, "I guess I'll have to watch your lessons back on the World Wide Web…" and then killed more monsters than he did.

Afterwards, I dug a shallow grave for Joe, who'd died either from wounds sustained by the insects and arachnids or by Green's carelessness. "He probably escaped his quarantine when the Resistance caused the glitch in the Maze to free the Assembled," Green eulogises briefly in funereal vogue… and it's done. Then we left.

We rise at dawn and swallow a dry nutty breakfast. Shards of brown splinters get caught in our throats, though we both try to hide it. There's no milk flowing here, no chickens pottering around. Not even a turkey, which I'd gladly eat right now, despite my deep-seated conviction that turkey is a mediocre substitute for chicken that leaves a queer aftertaste. Green disappears for a little while and prepares a meal of small fish, but despite the cavernous hunger and my affinity for seafood, I can't eat them. The smell of their faeces and guts which he flung right next to me turns my ever-shrinking stomach.

The day feels drawn-out, uneventful, and over too quickly, all at once.

Ready for a kip, I pull off my leather boots and recoil at the whiff of my feet. It is uncanny how much these bad boys sweat a day, and even more so when I consider I haven't showered since fleeing Laxciila, as any stream we've come to ripples with electricity. For food, Green has to stake the fish with wooden rods. Sweat and grime have become me. Everyone commends the bravery, stamina, and heart of a hero, but no one warns you about the body odour. I check to see if my most recent hive of blisters have burst and rub the balls of my feet. Pink flesh peeps beneath saggy white pouches of dead skin on both.

I look over at Green. He hasn't told me his name yet, which is grand since I'm not his friend and names are personal matters. But not knowing the name of the man who has rescued and guided me this far, however indecently, is ridiculous. I take a deep breath and bite the bullet.

"I don't believe I ever introduced myself. My name is Benjamin." No response. "What is your name?"

<Grunt>

Moving swiftly on...

"How did you meet the Elder Elf?"

"Under unfortunate circumstances."

Sugar! I meant to say "Elder Wizard"! "Where are we going?"

The Elder Wizard's house, I'm told. On one hand, this comes as a surprise since it's easier to picture Mósandrirl as a gypsy magician who goes from place to place looking for adventure, perhaps staying for a cup of tea or some music afterwards. The Great Grey Bard, they would call him in the smaller villages where nothing ever happens.

That said, this doesn't contradict the little rhyme that the wizard downloaded in my head when he visited me in my apartment.

However, how far away it is I'm not told. What we will do exactly when we arrive there, he doesn't say. Why his house of all places, whether for magic books, ingredients, or an army, no explanation is given. Afraid my mentor might over-exert himself after so long a sentence, I close my eyes and fail to convincingly pretend that my bag is a pillow. After at least forty-five minutes of struggling to get comfy, and also because it's chilly, I pull a jacket out of the bag.

*Ding-ding-ding.* Something small bounces along the stony path, then comes to a halt. I search the black ground to see what I unwittingly pulled out along with the jacket: Aurora's ring. I try to shield it from Green's intrusive, glaring eyes, only metres away. Too late: he's seen it.

"Princess," he sneers. I roll onto my other side, the ring embalmed in my right hand, and picture ways to break all the main bones in his body should he come at me with evil intent, which he one day undoubtedly will. With these pleasant thoughts in mind, I drift off to sleep…

Only a few hours could have passed when Green growls at me like we missed the last train ever to Disneyland. My sharp nails fly out of my sweaty boxers and I curl up in pain having shredded my scrotum raw and bloody in my sleep. Add to that, my eyes feel baggy and bloodshot, my hair rife with dandruff, and when I run my hand along my jaw, I'm shocked to find how hairy it's gotten. I can't believe I thought the complaining complainer that is Bilbo Baggins was such a whiny twat all this time. *I take it back, Double B.*

Oh, what I would trade right now for some shaving foam, powder, and a shower. But on the plus side, my legs and feet have given up telling me they're sore, so basic mobility should pose no problem.

Green says there's no time for breakfast this morning which I consider a travesty of inter-dimensional proportions, but I suppose it's the first of many mornings like this to come. He arches his head like a dog sensing a storm, as though he hears something I don't know to listen out for. When I catch his eye, I think he's asking me if I can hear it, too. I don't, but I gasp anyway. Personally, I think he's just joshing me and being melodramatic. If we were under attack, his sword would be drawn and breakfast would be the last thing on his mind, which is saying something because this thug likes his food.

I get up as quickly as I can, wrecked and groggy though I am, but this isn't good enough for him and he starts to hurl accusations, insults, and violation-against-mental-health commentary, so I do the mature thing and give him a reason to be annoyed. (Why does he make it so difficult to be liked?). I put my jacket back in the bag slowly, and up the ante on my usual anal retentiveness. And just so I can really frustrate him, I wear my "Princess" ring with pride on my right index finger and get in my early morning stretches. After one too many foot taps, heavy breaths, and eye-rolls, he finally storms off.

It takes me five minutes too long to remember I don't know my way around, so I speed walk after his pungent gin scent around sharp corners and over a bed of bones. When I catch up with him, he seethes on his knees and tears his hair out with his hands. Odd... though perpetually impolite, he's usually calm in his own way. I look ahead and see nothing but road and a haunting mist. I ask what the problem is.

"PRINCESS!" he roars at the top of his lungs, not caring who or what hears us.

*Hello.*

He roars again: "There is supposed to be a door here!"

"Well, it's not here now." As soon as I say it, I want to take the words back. I assume a defensive position in expectancy for the coming blow, the likes of which Sensei taught me.

"I *can see* that there is no door here, *Princess...*" he bears his yellow teeth at me. I hope my teeth aren't yellow. I mean, I haven't brushed them since I last had a brush and running water, but I haven't been drinking tea by the gallon or eating cake by the plate either. I had fun scraping gunky bland plaque off them yesterday until I remembered I hadn't washed my hands since, funnily enough, the same time as I last had a brush and running water.

"What makes you so sure it's supposed to be here?"

"I have read every one of the Resistance's maps. It is always here."

"But doesn't the Maze hide things and move places around?" Heh-heh-heh. I got him there. "Maybe we took a wrong turn," I suggest so quietly he's not supposed to hear it.

"That is impossible."

"Hardly. It only makes sense that we're a few"—by which I mean 'an infinite number of— "blocks off from where you imagined. We've been chased through fly-infested marshes, shoe-nibbling pebbledash roads, swamps like toilets by orcs, a nest of vampires, and Warper wolves—"

"'Warpers'?"

"Magically-genetically-engineered beasts."

"'Hybrids'?"

"Oh, you use that word here, too, huh? I sort of prefer 'Warpers'… as in, they've been warped. *Warp*ed. Warpers. *War*pers, because they go to *war* for the Triune."

"PRINCESS! Shut up!"

"Right. Sorry. Okay. We're lost. Check."

"No, not *lost*, we cannot be… There should be a door here."

"A door?"

"Well, a wall."

"The opposite of a door?"

"No, it opens."

"The door?"

"The wall."

"The wall opens like a door?"

"That is why it is called a door!"

"Steady on there, Gruffy Mc Gruff-Gruff, you Gruffster. You're the one giving poor illustrations! If you mean 'door', say 'door'. If you mean 'wall', say 'wall'. If you mean a 'wall with an entrance', say 'cave'." I gawk open-mouthed at Fetch for being brave enough to say it as it is. He just shrugs. Then I snicker at the idiot.

"You condescend me?"

"Pardon? N-n-n-no..."

"You ungrateful—!"

He moves in to strike me. I throw my hands to protect my face. And a white and startling blast shoots forth from my hands and exposes inches before us a terrific and terrible wall with four limbs, two heads, cruel cold eyes, and a concealed doorway of stone in his chest. We had already stood on that spot, unfeeling and desensitised to the mighty living boulder who, until the radiant light was upon him, had existed in his own pocket reality, intangible and sightless as the unicorn's wings.

Needless to say, Green's arms freeze mid-air like those of Pyrrhus, and I Priam make good the distance between us.

"How did you do that?" he asks quietly, and I catch the first look of fear in his eyes yet. "Never before has a Chosen One had such power... In fact, in every generation there is only one who does, and that is not you..."

"I'll be damned if I tell you," I glare, and he buys the misconception that I myself know.

With lightning speed, he whips out a knife from his sleeve that I never knew was there and I think he's about to gut me!

Not willing to go down without a fight, I instinctively whip out my stake which I had hidden in the exact same place.

For a long moment, we stare questioningly at each other. I won't strike unless he makes the first move, but I won't retract my weapon until I know he's not foolish enough to take me on. Suddenly his countenance of curiosity becomes a second-long sneer, and then he turns, like this is all a hormone-projected bid for attention and I'm not worth his time. Then he freaks me out so much it sickens me: he slices open his hand, walks over to the door-that-may-be-a-wall and places it inside what looks like a handprint carved into the black stone. Markings invisible to the untrained eye flare like fire, and the Wall, now animated because of his drink, asks how many wish to enter.

"A man and a boy," Green replies, and though I don't typically like the word "man", I feel denigrated having been referred to as a "boy" in that sullen tone he does so well.

"Two," I respond, because his phraseology was more of a dig than an answer.

The Wall says that entrance will cost us both a story, and most of all, a secret.

"No. Folly! Definitely not! Out of the question. We can take another route!" At first, I think I say it—I'm certainly thinking it. But then I replay all the expletives my ears bleeped out and realise it was Green. What does he have to hide... the site he intends to bury me in...?

"The days are dark, Watcher. The days of free passage have long since ended."

"I will give you anything else," Green snarls behind bared teeth.

"I am most disappointed in your cowardice," the Wall says in a low, drumming voice, strongly emphasising his S sounds. "Your reputation for courage seems unfounded." Green's ears redden and peak. "Oh, yes, Master Cillian J. Axebreaker, all of Labyrinthine-Angoria has heard about you... the man who escaped confinement... friend of the rogue wizard...

430

murderer of men, women and children... the great revenger who runs ceaselessly and will never stop until all who have wronged him lie dead at his feet."

Cillian J. Axebreaker... Green has a name.

"Are you going to tell them I am here?" I assume he refers to the Triune.

"Hmmm... To set them on your trail could prove very prosperous for me... To hand you over personally, that much greater..."

"What does money matter to you? You're a brick!" Fetch shouts, and the Wall groans.

"I would not recommend that, Obelisk. The boy has Skylar. He could obliterate you from the inside out." Not knowing what else to do, I offer a small wave to the talking head, and then to the snake-like dumb one, so it won't feel ignored.

"You threaten me?!" the Wall bellows and the stones on the Maze floor bounce and stammer. I hear the brisk thud of many feet behind us. Armed stone soldiers like pharaohs that the Wall identifies as the Miton Ra Remnant form a line and point pikes at us, awaiting the Wall's command. My stake won't do much good against them, so I return it to a strap on my wrist. *Enough of this testosterone debacle. It's time for an intervention.*

"Hello. How are you? I'm the Chosen One. Possibly the Dark Lord. Maybe even the Other. How about this? You are free to rat us out should you choose, but I implore you to listen to our stories and grant us safe passage."

"What kind of negotiation is that?" Green yells at the highest pitch his voice can reach.

"You're arguing with a wall! That is so unbelievably sad that even I am lost for words! And no one is sadder than I am! Now behave. He's... they're... under no obligation to help us, so stop spouting your bad attitude and hollow threats."

"The boy does speak sense," the Wall drones on, still with a stress on his S sounds. I say thanks, but he retorts droningly, "I was not complimenting you. For what does it matter to speak sense should no one understand it to be sensible? Therefore, I applaud myself on recognising the rationality of your words... words... words..." He says nothing more for a minute or two, and I begin to suspect he forgot we're conversing and has fallen asleep, until his eyelids flutter and he beckons "Go on. And Cillian, we will start with you."

Green (as he'll be to me until he gives me permission to call him something else) walks over, walks back, and laughs aloud either at the audacity of the secret that has plagued him his whole life or that he has met his match in a stone obstruction. He casts one final look at the rocky persuasions of the great provocateur Wall, and then whispers in his raspy voice:

"His name was Ki-Twon. Race of Man. My best friend, he approved of my upcoming betrothal to his sister, Aliana Kiira." He pauses, lost in a chasm of memories. Finally, he climbs out of it and continues: "One day, Ki-Twon and I were sword-fighting for fun, as men do. We had stumbled upon the blades in the forest next to the town we lived in. A pair of soldiers had stabbed each other to death. It was very sad"—as his smile so convincingly testifies. Then his face flashes into a stretchy multi-sensory mask and the smile disappears. His eyes apologise, his brows raise in shock, and his mouth struggles to fathom the reality of the unexplainable actions of his hands. "And Ki-Twon, his warm body, it… somehow slid down my blade. It took me so long that it defies reason to realise he was dead."

And if that wasn't uncomfortable enough, he then adds that his immediate response to his sweetheart's scream when she came across the bloody scene was to slit her throat and run from that Zone. How he managed it, he isn't asked, but this all testifies to my long-held belief that desperate people are capable of anything.

The only response he gets is an unsatisfied contemplative hum. And I am sick to the core, not by what I heard, but by the Obelisk's ruthless dismissal of my guardian's pain. Flushed with embarrassment, Green's focused eyes glare at me and say, "You're up." I think what he means is 'Don't mess up', like he thinks he just did.

"Make it a good one, Benjy," Fetch urges, while Roop disparages the very thought of me opening up. Though I hate to admit it, I think he's right. I procrastinate longer and more melodramatically than Green did, and to such an extent that he thinks I'm putting it on for show, or so his jeers suggest. But I'm not. I've kept my secrets concealed all my life and was more than prepared to take them to the grave. And now I'm supposed to casually throw all caution to the wind just because what-should-be an inanimate object tells me to? I'd rather chance taking on his statue army with my oversized pencil.

To say that I am hit with years' worth of shame is an understatement, like I'm airing all my dirty laundry for the world to see. The Wall is a camera and beyond its lens, I feel an unlimited army of judges and scandal columnists.

The soldiers must respond to some psychic command for they take three heavy trudging steps towards us and raise their scythes above their heads and poke us with pikes. Here goes…

I have no idea what will come out of my mouth when suddenly I hear Nat King Cole play the piano and I sing:

*"There was a boy,*
*A very strange enchanted boy.*
*They say he wandered very far, very far*
*Over land and sea.*
*A little shy and sad of eye*
*But very wise was he.*

*And then one day,*
*A magic day he passed my way,*
*And while we spoke of many things—*
*Fools and kings—*
*This he said to me…"*

"Yes?" the Wall presses for an answer.

"A lie. Words, words, words that I have found to be untrue."

And then I begin my narrative: I start with the One-Armed Man's crime, the Duchess's "help", and skewer the timeline a little by detailing what little I remember of Ronan's end. I had forgotten how dear he was to me. My big brother. My idol. My hero. He was supposed to be my champion in the age-old war between youngsters and their parents; to teach me about puberty and maturity; how to burp really loudly and make inappropriate noises with my armpits; how to stand up to enemies; how to be cool; how to drive; and how to be a man. But he died, murdered by his own stupidity. And now that I finally have a reason to remember him, I hate him for it.

And I hate that Nuala (Green eyes me scarily at this point like I cussed) and D.W. have overwritten every good thing I ever taught Luke. Because of their involvement, he's going to end up as broken as I am, just in a different way. Then I introduce Roop to my narrative:

While the Duchess and Nuala were speaking, directly across the street, Roop and I stared at 124 Lincoln Lane. In the world of play, my pseudonym was Thomas. Roop, whose middle- and therefore nickname, not that it stuck, was Gabriel. Ironic, since he was no angel... unless, of course, he was that of death. We had played a game once in which we were characters in a fantasy world and adopted different personas— "You can't let the goblins know your real name, or they'll find out where you live and eat the man of the house and run off with the woman," Roop had explained. It totally made sense at the time, and I revelled at the thought of the One-Armed Man being dragged off into their cave and mauled.

Parched in the air-freshener-free house (the Duchess feared they gave one cancer) and a little claustrophobic by the mixture of incense and scented candles, I was positively on the brink of fainting. Roop said he'd get us some lemonade from the kitchen. He left the television on, both sets of headphones still plugged in, and switched on unneeded lights. He pretended not to hear my criticism about how green he was not being. (Ha, Green!). Upstairs, Mr. Samson showered. He always showered those days, except when doing his physiotherapy or complaining that his dinner was cold, burnt, or on a paper plate— "that's what he gets for smashing Mommy's good plates," cocked the unsympathetic Roop.

In our most homosocial moment to date, Roop had just informed my blissfully ignorant and firmly disbelieving longer-named self of things which could not possibly be true about the combined utilisation of the male and female anatomy. He used the television as a visual aid. I felt dirty, though, and could not entertain the thought of watching another scene.

"When are you getting the holographic projector?" I asked.

"Never. Mom's too cheap. You?"

"Himself said it should be soon."

"You know, you could just call him 'Dad'."

"It doesn't feel right."

He'd paused the disturbing show halfway through and we shared our secret crushes. After fifteen minutes of blushing and shyly saying, "Naw, it doesn't matter, it's silly," and "It'll never happen, we're just nine," I named Paige Shauna Andrews, a pretty girl our age who was moving to Ireland soon. Had I known she'd grow up to be evil, I probably would've recorded the cruel antics she got up to with Roop with a SPYDER-cam for leverage. Roop mentioned half the girls in town, and over half a dozen women. And we simultaneously chimed "Ivy".

"Yeah, she's hot," Roop said, picturing himself a stud, before making coarse comments that I patiently waited out like a storm.

I stood on my tiptoes, head tilted towards the window like a seal balancing a ball on its nose, because I was so short. My eyes locked on a stranger eyeing up a house whose teenagers, I can now safely bet, ended up in this world. A little upset that my friend had forgotten to pour me a glass of lemonade, I decided to say something grownup and unrelated. Quietly and very dramatically, I asked, "Do you think he'll buy *that* house?" and with a terrified tone, "The haunted one?"

Roop stared omnisciently. "It wasn't the house that ate Cassie and Peter, stupid. It was the Lights." They appeared and called them by name.

I usually glance over these more banal details of The Incident, but I realise now that these *lights* are the same ones that encased me when I arrived here. I wasn't worthy enough for them to say my name, mind you, but I suppose the Fates have been infamously silent the past number of centuries, haven't they?

Anyway, Roop continued to boast about everything he knew, and to cap it all off, tried a real-life jump-scare, which was ineffectual. I was much braver back then.

Green grunts with boredom, but the Wall to my eternal appreciation listens with patience and drinks in every mundane iota of information.

Then he left, I say of Roop. When he came back, he was unhappy to see me, but before long, pretended he enjoyed my company: "Beejie-Weejie, do you wan' play out back? I've got a really great game for us to play." Taking me walkies on a leash like a puppy kept him from feeling lonely. Up for some more fun, I let the little manipulator lead the way.

Green asks what the point to all of this is, and I suddenly realise I don't want him to know. Every smile, every touch, every experience is a piece of me. Body, soul, or spirit, we're all just fragments of cells, stories, and choices, and he does not deserve them, so I walk over to his blooded palm print and whisper the closest account to the truth that I can jigsaw together: a fabulous tale of arachnid robots, flowerpot baths, and stakes—minus Roop's indiscretions.

"But why?" the Wall enquires when I recount from fragmented

images the burial.

"He is not here to defend himself. Therefore, I offer no charges against him that he cannot rebuff."

"But I am here, Benjamin," Roop objects beside me, before foaming at the mouth, shaking hysterically, and bleeding hot red bubbles by the bucket-load from his chest, and dying.

"What then?"

"We moved," I say. "Before long, Eden"—I say of Nuala— "tried to drown herself. And then I made the biggest mistake I could have: I saved her. Or rather, I brought into our lives a man that I thought could."

He took her away to the hospital but must not have told anyone she had a son for I was alone for almost a week. All he said to me was, "Get rid of all this water before she gets back" for the house was a swamp. "Your mother deserves to come home to a nice clean house."

How he spun it so that she was not locked away in the psychiatric unit for months, I had always meant to ask, but that would involve words, words, words.

Half-starved and mentally damaged after six days of neglect and eating blue furry bread and dry cereal—for the milk had run out and I had no clue where she kept the money—I remember my socks and spindly little legs standing on the auburn kitchen table. I was hanging our fruit bowl clock back on the wall. Had the hour changed? Had I used it for tracing when drawing a picture? I forget. Anyway, that's what I was doing when Nuala walked in with D.W. for the first time.

I took an immediate dislike to him: the way he touched her, how he disregarded everything I had to say, how he liked his tea lukewarm with the bag still in the mug; the musky scent of his aftershave; how he preferred reading electronically to reading books; how he said paper had no future. Oh, the temptation to tell him to get back in that cigarette-smelling *Lamborghini Murcielago* with its unwashed bumper and banjaxed passenger door and leave right then! Hatred still ripples through me every time I look back at how brazenly he snuck into our lives—under the guise of help, no less—only to swiftly and irreparably secrete his toxin.

But more than anything, I remember how, in that very first moment as I stood on the kitchen table, he looked at me as though I was vermin... a problem that had to be silenced or exterminated; knocked and beaten and coiled in the foetal position under that same table.

The next morning, I found his curly hairy chest and sweaty tank legs in her bed. Strawberry stems sat in one of two creamy glasses; the other glass was smashed. Pasty and ghostlike, she emotionlessly brushed her scarlet hair with the uncompromising pace of a pendulum, her dead sad eyes fixated on the locker mirror.

Not long after this, they sent me away to a facility that rightly suited them both. The White Room... And when I finally returned home, I was but a stranger, an intruder. Some people fear dying alone, invisible—a ghost. Worse still is living as one.

I can't say I've come very far. I'm a stranger in this world too, unknown, my identity constructed by the speculations of people who could not possibly know.

Only Aurora knew me. At least I think she did. But when I extended my hand to her, when I asked her to come with me, even she pulled away. I've had a really hard time of it and become so disillusioned. Blind to hope. Embittered. I've become the One-Armed Man. And by the time this war is over, I will have uncaringly left one cataclysmic body count because of it.

The Wall whimpers, and then a door opens onto grassy hills, a gorgeous sun, and a cloudless sky. And for someone who is not particularly fond of grass, sunlight, or heat, even I must admit that it's the most welcome sight since Melancholia, whatever drug-trip that was.

"I bid thee both entrance! I doubt we shall meet again, Storyteller. Goodbye. And thank you!"

"Thanks for listening." The vagabond leaps through the door and drops to his knees on the glossy plains. His grimy fingers fumble at the first foliage he sees and he eats it. It isn't long before the base-low animal has a green mouth. I enjoy my grub too, but I approach the pastoral scene with a more cautious eye.

He leaps to his feet, sprints drunkenly down the dewy hill tearing off his clothes as he goes, and throws himself into the steady river at the bottom. I'm not entirely sure what to make of his naked body on display. Plus, I feel deeply perturbed to see him this close to happy.

Circumspectly, taking care not to slide and mucky my already icky disgusting trousers, I make my way to the edge of the river. One by one, I take off my shoes and socks, fold my socks neatly and tuck them in my shoes. When I'm certain Green won't interrupt me, I strip bare. The black stitch fabrics feel sewn to my skin as I claw them all off for the first time in ages, and a layer of dead snakeskin comes off with each sweaty soiled layer. I then dip my feet into the freezing water, and gradually immerse my waist and shoulders, and soon my entire being. I curl my toes in the soft mud beneath me and rub my chest lightly and count my ribs. Repulsed, it feels like I'm poking a chicken carcass. And speaking of repulsion, I scrape as much dirt off my body as I can before this Zone's traps have a chance to trigger, flooding the hydrogen atoms with blood or electric knife-fish. This place is too prelapsarian for the Fall not to be just around the corner.

"Laundry!" Green shouts from further down.

But he's right. This is the first bath we've had in about forty days. We jump out of the river at the same time, neither of us looking at anything other than our own possessions, and dunk all our dirty clothes in. Then we lay them on the grass beneath the yellow ball and, metres apart from each other, dry ourselves off by lying under its heat.

Later, when he comes over, I remark, "You're not as green as usual."

A long blue coat rimmed with a white lining with blue patterns has replaced his trademark green one. And his face is almost unrecognisable; the river has washed away about a decade from his face, and he's trimmed his beard, so he looks to be in his mid-thirties. His hair has lost its ratty bristle.

"I am not so *sad* that I wear the same colour every day," he retorts. "Get dressed, Princess!"

As I put on fresh clothes and militarise my gear with small weapons, he explains that though we've been here less than four hours, one hundred days have passed in the Maze.

"We could have lost seventy-two days taking another route," he says, though that would have involved battles against carrion crawlers underground, swashbuckling pirates at sea and in the desert, reptile Hybrids at a circus, the Triune-in-Flesh (loyal subjects of the Triune who serve as special operatives on their behalf. They consist of the infamous assassin, L; a snake-whisperer, the Lady of Baalat; and Adonis, a god trapped in human form who causes all who look upon him to fall head over heels. The most monstrous of all, he eats babies to survive), and gambling.

"That doesn't sound too bad." I don't know if I mean that sarcastically or not.

"I do not like people." He says nothing more and leads me to a forest on the horizon where the gaped toothy jaws of the Maze invite and terrify feet stupid enough to trespass in its corridors.

For the next six weeks, we go into intensive training mode. Green orders me to walk without boots or socks because it will initially-tear-to-bits-but-ultimately-strengthen my feet; he teaches me that Native American "Ear to the ground, hear faraway sounds" trick; and he teaches me to cartwheel, flip, and hunt. We spar for two hours a day, and it doesn't take me long to find my rhythm after he beat me to a pulp the first time:

"Fight me," he spat, "but be controlled."

"I am controlled!" I screamed at his bloody muck of a face.

"No. You are reluctant. And that is what is going to get you killed one day."

It's all hard, but it has its rewards.

Each night, we meditate for an hour and the focus shifts to the spiritual connotations of being Skylar, the Elvish word for the Chosen One, as Green progressively supposes I might be.

GREEN: Feel the pure blue Triumvir energy flow through your innermost being.

ME: All I feel are pins and needles in my right foot. And my ears are itchy.

GREEN: The Chosen One should have a sixth sense warning him that evil is afoot.

ME: I'm broody. I know evil's ubiquitous. I don't need superpowers to tell me that.

GREEN: The Chosen One should see things that were, have been, and can be avoided in his sleeping mind's eye.

ME: [That day] I had a dream last night. I just don't remember what it was.

ME: [The next day] I dreamt of Aurora. I mean, the Princess of Loux Laxciila. We... talked.

ME: [The day after that] I felt Gideon, misshapen and manacled though he was, sink his teeth into me and drink me dry. He clawed his way out of that grave.

ME: [And the next day] I saw Angoria on fire.

ME: [And the day after that] I saw history end. But finality was an illusion. Eternity remained; a long stretch of graveyard made of Time and tombstones.

During one of our meditation sessions, I fell into a trance and there I saw the Void: a charming and well-groomed man dolled up to the nines in a white suit, black shirt, and red tie. There were no introductions, but there was a mutual sense of knowing and being known straight away.

"Why am I only two feet shorter than the ultimate evil?"

From Green and my campfire, he led me out into the wilderness for forty days and nights, and there he tortured me with scorpion stings, snake bites, beatings, and every kind of sickness. In all that time, I ate nothing; and I was only permitted to drink bitter water from the Panopticon's copy of a shallow stream.

"It turned bitter when a god who wasn't wearing his seven-league boots fell from the sky like lightning, crash-landed, and broke his neck. From a fiery mountain, I watched it happen with delight! If you are who they say you are, my apprentice, imagine what we could accomplish together!"

"I will never serve you!"

"So… you believe the prattle of the minority… If you are Skylar, and there is magic in your blood, then say the word and turn these rocks into nutritious refreshments. You must be hungry."

I was. "True strength is shown when it is not used."

"If you are Skylar, and there is magic in your blood, punch a hole in my chest." He stretched his arms out, as though hanging on a cross. "I'm wide open. Give me your best shot."

"You are a spiritual enemy. It won't be physical prowess that casts you out."

Then, leash around my neck, he dragged me to the roof of the Dome of Loux Laxciila where the elves goaded my few remaining supporters and shaved their heads. Then they fornicated in circles around my burning effigy, paintings of me as the Dark Lord, and a vulgar waxwork of Death, War, Famine, Pestilence, Plague, and Conquest weaving in and out of me.

"If you are Skylar, there is magic in your blood, so jump. Believe in yourself and you will soar on sightless wings like a unicorn. Astonish them. Steal their attention from the Elder Elf. Or call down fire from the faux-sky and burn him to ash. Then all will know that you are the Chosen One."

"I think you're mistaking 'Chosen One' for 'murderer'."

"Is there a difference?" he hisses.

"Yes. The Chosen One is a slayer of your offspring, but I don't kill people."

"Oh, Benjy. Cillian can't hear us from up here. You don't need to lie to me."

"You literally only brought Cillian into this for the sake of a pun, didn't you?"

He pushes me off the Dome and I land atop the tallest mountain above the faux-sky where the entirety of the Maze is plain to me. He gestures emphatically and monologues in paragraphs regarding all the earthly kingdoms, elemental powers, and cosmological principalities that are under him.

"You will never save them all—even if you are the Chosen One. I am too vast. I am in all. I am working through all. I am over all. I am... all!

Accept the dark power I now offer you, and all my demons, spirits, and servants in the unseen world will kneel before you."

"Dude"—since when do I use that word? "You seriously need a girlfriend."

"Don't force me to overlook you, Earthen Son. I think we could have a lot of fun together."

"Go kill yourself!"

Now his true form is made clear to me: he has horns made of bone; rock-hard black skin; amber snake eyes with red irises and black slits for pupils; razor-sharp teeth; long nails strong as steel; molten lava veins protruding from his mammoth rocky form; and cloven hooves beneath his ankles of iron mixed with clay. He is Apollyon... Darkness... Sin.

The Void wields a sword called Skylar. I see now that what I'd mistaken for a chicken scratch design on mine actually spells "SKYLAR" in a stylised font. His sword looks like mine, only so much bigger in every way. And I feel a sense of familiarity with it—my sword and his are one and the same, only his is as wide as a slim man, as thick as a door, and as long as the fiend himself. The black sword handle was made from his hooves and its silver blade and decorative handle from his teeth. (I don't see either the handle or the blade being crafted; I just instinctively know this). The weapon was forged in the black flames of a volcano called Paradise.

And then the trance ends, and I'm bowing to Green and he to me, eyes fixed on one another's face, set to spar. (How long was I out? And what did I miss?).

And I lose my mind. The Little Terrier they call me at karate competitions, and I show him why: I back-kick, roundhouse kick, head-block, drop to the ground, sweep, nudge, swipe, punch, jump-kick, axe-kick, and throw spinning-kick after spinning-kick. My mind-body communication and coordination is all off! I think my body's freaking out because my soul has moved back in. And poor Green bears the brunt of that traumatic transference.

But he's not playing second fiddle either. His wet, rotting hair lashes my right eye and it stings. His thumps leave bruises. His swipes cut. His kicks knock me over. My snarling face bloodies, reflected in his owl-eyes as he hammers me.

And somehow, I manage to catch one of his usually lightning-quick kicks, and I spin him into a hedgerow. It swallows him whole, gladly, and then pants for dessert.

# INTERLUDE
# K'K'KO ZSET'S PROPHECY OF THE TRIUMVIRATE

[Stanzas six to nine are common knowledge among anybody who is anybody in Angoria. The rest has been progressively revealed to the eccentric prophet, K'k'ko Zset, by the Higher Order known as the Weaver. It concerns the end of Angoria].

The First Inhabitants are going to lay waste to Angoria and devastate it;
they will cast fear over the land and its song will uphold the Warren:
ABC 6-5-1-18 9-20-19-5-12-6
ABC 6-E-1-18 9-20-19-E-12-6
ABC F-5-A-R 9-T-19-5-12-F
ABC F-5-1-R I-T-S-5-L-6
ABC FEAR ITSELF.

The First Inhabitants will hone the power of the Void;
they will ruin Angoria's face and scatter its peoples—
it will be the same
for magical creatures as for humans,
for kings as for the poor,
for the powerful as for the voiceless,
for seller as for consumer,
for the needy as for the taken care of,
for debtor as for creditor.
Angoria will be completely laid waste and totally plundered.
The Higher Orders have spoken this word.
As it was in the beginning, so shall it always be: world with coming end.
Amen.

The land will dry up and wither,
the people will languish, wither, and burn—twelve times twelve,
the heavens will languish over Angoria and with Angoria
silently for fifteen score uncounted years.

Angoria will be defiled by her First Inhabitants;
they will disobey the laws they agreed to,

448

violate the statutes they created
and break the everlasting covenants that they made.
Therefore, a curse of deadened immortality consumes them
and the Triumvirate raid the earth;
Angoria must bear the First Inhabitants' guilt.
Therefore, Angoria's inhabitants will be scorched, massacred, trodden on,
and eaten,
and very few will be left.
The streams will dry up or turn to poison, and the vine will wither or rot;
merrymaking will cease; groaning will be the people's only song.
Celebrations will be stilled, made silent by the sword,
the noise of the revellers will stop,
there will be next to no music across the world.
Those who drink wine will whine;
those who down bitter draughts will be drafted into bitterness.
Ruined cities will lie desolate;
the entrance to every house will be barred or kicked-in.
Everything will turn to gloom,
and anything that does not will be banished or exterminated.
Angoria will be left in ruins,
Everything it ever was will be battered to pieces.

The captives cry, "I waste away! I dread life more than Death himself! Woe
to me!
The treacherous betray! The strong have lost hope!
Fright and snare and Sheol are all that await the people of Angoria.
Alarm and entrapment and Thrush are all that await the Good Beasts."

Triumvirs! Triumvirs everywhere!
Recycled, undead, redundant, and new!

He comes as a chameleon to the cave of gargantuan beasts,
Child of the contumelious shadow,
Where hidden in plain sight will be the Weapon.
He oozes death and death follows him.
And he shall be called Mex Confetricus.

He wears two faces. Duality is his nature.
For the Twelfth and Final Age, a brand-new creature!
You will not recognise him until the Endgame.
And he shall be called the Pretender.

At the end of days comes riding the Lord of Fire:

449

Passion and violence, peace and ice innate.
From a troll cave to Ancient Stone,
From the earliest of days to the end of all,
Even the Oldest Ones,
Flies the double-headed dragon: the Chosen One.

They come like a storm
And they come riding one.

The pernes and gyres will turn one last time,
and the floodgates of the Higher Orders' kingdom will open one last time,
releasing the Power that creates the Saviour one last time,
and the Void will send forth the Mex Confetricus one last time and the
Pretender.

As they war, the foundations of Angoria will shake.
They will do battle at Right Foot Gallows
where the villain will slay the Dwarf King and
one will die and one will fall.
Angoria will be broken up,
Angoria will be split asunder,
Angoria will be violently shaken.
Angoria will stammer like a drunkard,
Angoria will sway like a hut in a hurricane;
so heavy upon it is the guilt of its witchcraft, rebellion and cyclic Dual Wars
that it falls—never to rise again.

And it pleases the Higher Orders for things to end so:
For finality is inevitable and immortality a curse.
When all this is over, all that will remain is Eternity,
a long stretch of graveyard made of Time and tombstone
until even sunlight gives out.
But remember the days of darkness, for they were many,
but by rendering all else meaningless and void,
the peace of Angoria will have been purchased.
The Tapestry will stop weaving,
When all this is over.

# 18
# ENTER THE JUNGLE

*Night vanishes and a neon bulb dangling from the ceiling of the White Room haunts me.*

*The walls whiten and turn to tiles. The door will not open. The tiny window is all barred up. D.W. smacks me around for a while, calls me crazy, and orders me to stop telling lies. He has the audacity to reprimand me for putting Nuala through all this stress with my tales of Pocket, yet he financially creams off her heartache. Moves out of his dingy flat and into her house. Populates it with all his junk with their smoky and scotch smells. Eats her food. Raises her bills. Consumes every iota of the woman she once was, back when everything was perfect, if it ever even was…*

*I know she's just outside the door, from her chokes, sniffles, and occasional squeals. Probably holding a handkerchief to her eyes. Covering her bitter mouth with her skeletal fingers. She's no more now than a whitewashed tomb, ashen and ornate on the outside, but a dead sack of bones on the inside. A ghost of her former authoritative, warm, ladylike self.*

*And I hate her for it.*

I yawn myself awake, not entirely sure what I just dreamt about for it evades me instantly. And I must be having another very strange dream because a bloody man hangs on a crucifix across from me, stark naked as the day his mother bore him. We're situated on a small plot of grass encircled by a vast, thick noisy jungle filled with dinosaur, bird, and bovine sounds, and there's a random picnic basket beneath him.

"Yes, Princess. We are naked."

Green? It's his voice, but I can't make him out clearly. Everything is blurry. I throw my head around but don't see much of anything, really. Just green shapes that I know are leaves and grass, and brown stalks that I know are trees.

I have a sharp metallic pain in my chest like my insides are on display. The cruel cold air cuts my innards. My teeth chatter uncontrollably. My knees shake. I lower my eyes but am uncertain as to what exactly I see. I'm hanging from two planks in an X-shape too, wrists and ankles bound so tightly that blood can't circulate. My skin looks whiter than usual, deathly so, and I am so very, very weak.

"I stepped through the Hedge to rescue you…"

"You threw me into it."

"I was a little bit all over the place in the sanity department."

"You'd been behaving primal and stoned for a month and a half. Trance?"

"Must've been."

"What is the last thing you remember?"

"I have no idea." I fix my eyes on him and screw my face as though that will somehow squeeze my suppressed memories to the fore. It is him… Green, that is… But his beard and a layer of his cheeks have been yanked out in fistfuls. His legs look like they've been hammered with mallets, and the undeniable mark of the Triune has been etched into his chest. I'm not used to seeing him so vulnerable, like a wounded roadside animal. "I'm freezing," I tell him. My bones shake. My breaths are heavy and far apart. "That's a bad sign, right?"

"That will be the hypothermia. They burned you with candle wax all over, then buried you in a barrel of ice. Let's see… what else? Oh, word on the street is they also tied you to a table, removed your right kidney, took a bite, and slapped it on a tray for experimentation."

"But I like my right kidney more than my left."

"To help alleviate the pain you have (in your more semi-conscious moments) been force-fed herbal-medicinal properties."

"That does sound like me. I do hate medicine. No pain, no gain, says I. Suffer in silence, that's my policy. It builds up the immune system, I find."

"They uprooted much of your leg hair. I assume they have their reasons."

"Well, I won't begrudge them that. I imagine it's an improvement. What else is new?"

"Your hair has been dyed blue."

"Oh, my holy days! You mean my *au naturel* look is gone?"

"I thought you liked blue."

"It's true. I do like blue. How did you know?"

"We have journeyed far together these last few months, and I spied on you long before that. By the way, they considered castration, but one thing at a time."

"They chose best. Surely I'd have to sign for that operation."

"Hair can be removed and grown back," he nods.

"I do hope yours does."

"You noticed?"

My vision restored so progressively I hadn't even realised. "You're bleeding," I gasp. "And your cheek looks like a raw damaged slab of meat on a butcher's table."

"Ugh! Chosen One! That is my face you are dissing. Enough with the metaphors!"

"Simile," I smile instinctively.

"Avoid that word. It's too close to 'simians'. Our savage captors find that offensive."

"Are the Triune here?"

"No, but they are coming."

The Grin finally released them then.

"Who ratted us out first?"

"Obelisk the Wall," he says.

"O mighty rock, thou art naught but rubble before my vengeance! Where is Skylar?"

"With my belongings."

"Where are they?"

"No idea." At this, I start chanting *Skylar... Skylar... Here boy...* in the hope that if I say its name long enough, it'll come flying and cut my bonds. I crane my neck any which way to see if it's working. Sensing my nervous frustration, Green asks, "Are you worried?"

"No."

"Look me in the eye."

"Yes. Are you?"

"Always. Benjamin, you and I *will* get through this. *I* will get you through this." With his ordinary, unimpressive, concerned words, he has chased away the fear.

"Side-note: I don't mean to be crude, but is the whole frontal nudity thing really necessary? I mean, it's a little breezy."

"We're just hanging. No shame," he says proudly, and then chuckles, "Unless you look down"—which I do. I'm not sure exactly what I see... It's brown and red like a box of ketchup and smells putrid, kind of like...

"Why would they do that?!"

"Because the instant you stepped into my kingdom, Shaman K'k'ko Zset sensed a great powah, and the powah comes from the blood, and I have devoted my life to discovering how Triumvah powah works."

I have no idea who I'm talking to when I snap, "You'll know what power is and how it works when I get down from this cross and beat you, you aberration!"

Green's eyes widen in shock, and he quietly but ominously warns me, "Do not look." Well, by law, I am now obliged to. And as the villain's fat head comes into view, Green and I explode in fits of laughter that pierce our guts.

Context: Back when I was in school (oh, no, I'll have to repeat the year, I've missed so many days!), there was a special needs student named Gregory Saint Germaine—with an E at the end of Germaine. I don't remember much about him, only that he had a habit of forgetting to bring his calculator to math class and getting his own way. He had a big head, fingernail-thin lips, and a pencil named Mister Howard Kieron.

The resemblance is striking, minus the mummy bandages; someone has spent way too much time in the jungle. This man is short with a spindly body, comic book eyes, a Cheshire Cat grin, and a massive forehead. He holds a long witchdoctor's stick, probably to keep from keeling over with the size of his overgrown brain. He's ugly, grotesque and adorable, and I just want to take him home and stick him in an airtight glass box. He *he-haw*s, snarls, *hoot-hoot*s, and *Oh Nelly*s at regular intervals.

And just look at how his band of eejits bow to him, wipe his brow with a damp cloth, fan him, and hang on every word he says. More warped monstrosities: one of the dogs is four feet high, white and silver, and shark-toothed. Its finny body moves in fishy, wavy motions. It has three yellow claws on each paw, and when it stands on its hind legs, I see it has an extra foot like the first Warpers I saw. Another one's like a surgically enhanced lion, pumped with a tank of blood and organs. It has a reptile tail ending in a metal triangle. Its head is a bulldog and its legs are thin as a warthog's. Don't ask me how it moves. Another Warper that stands out from the pack is a lanky one, maybe six feet tall. Its legs are so brittle and exaggeratedly long that it looks the weakest; like it's been pulled and stretched beyond all limits on a medieval table until irretrievably broken, then stretched some more for the *craic*.

"Now then, as you're finally both awake and lucid, how about some introductions?" *He-haw!* Snarl. *Hoot-hoot. Oh Nelly.*

"The barbarian is called Conan," I say, and "the princess is called Benjalina", he says.

"Nonsense! And your kind claim to be the civilised folk"—he's a fine one to talk about what constitutes being civilised— "There is always time for names. Be honest."

"Oh, I'll give honesty: you, Gregory Saint Germaine—with an E at the end of Germaine, are about to get an overdue wallop with Mister Howard Kieron unless you let us down and then crawl back into whatever pit you crept out of. And mind your head. We wouldn't want it to get stuck in the wormhole on the way down." The bandaged little fellow looks like I've just electrocuted him. ("The drugs", Green explains, apologising for me, remarking how hard it usually is to get a word out of me).

"Don't apologise for me. I am marvellously distempered, venomously ticked off. I set out to save the world, and what's happened? I've become one of those poorly-written characters who could easily be killed off, but oh no, it's not the finale, so instead I'm tied to intersecting planks where I'm forced to sit through this freakish wannabe Bond villain's master plan speech."

"You know, I hate being called 'Freak'."

Oh, no. Pray, tell I am wrong. Not this. Anything but this. He's giving us his origin story! NO-O-O-O-O-O-O-O-O-O!!!

Daddy issues: check.

Childhood experience of bullying: check.

Struggles with fears of isolation and base-low personage: check.

The big head is a medical condition: check.

Tried to kill himself and gets off on telling and shocking people with this gem: check.

Surviving years' worth of criticism has made him stronger: check.

Genuinely believes having a sob story permits morally blind behaviour: check.

*He-haw!* Snarl. *Hoot-hoot. Oh Nelly.* Every time I come close to nodding off, he raises his pitch and jerks me wide-awake. Green, on the other hand, is out for the count, and nothing short of a blow to the knee with an elephant tusk is going to bring an end to his slumber.

The heavy sleepy feeling comes over me yet again when suddenly Gregory Saint Germaine—with an E at the end of Germaine mentions Laxciila. He leans on Mister Howard Kieron with an ancient look in his eyes like he's an immortal bard with a catalogued library of all transpirations since time immemorial. It turns out he was once a scientist in Laxciila who worked closely alongside Mehkabikil, performing autopsies on all the corpses of fallen Dual Cycle Champions they could get their hands on. Why?

"So we could discover a way to kill *you*," he snarls, and I'm grateful he finally withholds his nonsensical mating calls. "Angoria's hatred of you runs deepah and longah than you could possibly imagine." He takes a step toward me but trips over one of his wedding-dress-train bandages.

"Mehkabikil is *not* Angoria," I spit through gritted teeth.

"Isn't he? … No, perhaps not yet…" he answers his own question, and then I think of how he's tried to marry Aurora off to wealthy princes; has killed ideologically unsynchronized monarchs and politicians; and has effectively made himself the head and face of the Resistance. "But soon…"

"Well, I wouldn't take anything he has to say personally. He has the liver of a pigeon, that one. Talks big and manipulates the masses but keeps to the shadows in a permanent pounce position." Fitting for a snake.

He proceeds with his narrative: "Angoria is always imploding in on itself in grave warfare. And after millennia of trying to find a solution to our "You" problem, I eventually found the solution we had been waiting for! *He-haw!* Snarl. *Hoot-hoot. Oh Nelly.* Through an advanced combination of sorcery and science, I discovered we could create an army of… or from… the most powerful beings, collectively infinitely greater than yourself. Behold, Triumvah, my family!" And from behind trees, atop branches, the depths of the lengthy grass, and the innermost parts of the jungle, the biggest collection of misfits rear their heads. There are humanoid wolves, tyrannosaurus-frogs, and rhinoceros' heads on goat-haired forms, and they're just the animals I can identify.

"Warpers? You created the Hybrids."

"No thanks to my dear friend, Kabikil."

"Mecky," I correct. "Those of us (by which I mean just me) who dislike him ascribe to him a nickname that focuses on the first syllable."

It follows that the Elf one day accused him of crossing a line. Classic. The man who has no qualms with killing his own kind lectures a cross-kind thinker on what is right and natural. That said, I'm unsurprised: it is just up his street to be elitist and supremacist with his notions of what qualifies a pureblood. So, typical Jekyll and Mister Hyde scenario: when Gregory Saint Germaine—with an E at the end of Germaine's main ally withdrew financial support, the poor fool experimented on himself, fell into a deep sleep, and awoke the next morning with a big head.

I snort, and just when I think I've succeeded in holding in all my bottled-up humour, Green snorts, proving he's been awake this entire time, and I explode, and apologise frantically between fits of laughter. "This is not a laughing matter," I say matter-of-factly afterwards, and pull a serious face in the hope that no more giggles will force their way through my tight cheeks. The poor devil is red in the face, bless him. I remind him of where we left off.

Mehkabikil chased him out of Laxciila in front of crowds of hundreds of pointers, mockers, sneers, and howlers. Just because he had a big head. That was when Gregory Saint Germaine—with an E at the end of Germaine sought out the Wizarding Order. Few of them shared his suspicions of me, and fewer still his plea for support to create a hybrid race. In fact, only two of them did, initially: Lear and Silas. Centuries passed, Ages began and ended, and his dream of birthing this band of mutates appeared to dissipate into oblivion.

And then, one unsuspecting day, the not-yet-in-power Triune approached him and offered to back his business proposition, and the rest, as they say, is history. They created Sharmedes, their own hybrid son; the Maze; and Gregory Saint Germaine—with an E at the end of Germaine's mutates.

"And they allotted for me this territory, formerly owned by the Elf, to be the site for my Mutopia."

Wow! Some handsome payment that is. It isn't even real. It's an illusion. An image without substance. A shadow of a long-coveted original.

And then he rants about how his wife left him! Oh, sweet jeepers, kill me now. There is only so much more of this I can take. I interrupt him mid-sentence:

"You waited all that time to realise your dream, only to give sole custody over to the Triune?" Dimwit. I know how long it takes to write a book, and I'm only on the second draft. Like Hell I'd just hand it over to someone else, let alone the three most despicable people I know who actually could seize control of Earth: the President, the One-Armed Man, and the Duchess.

"Hardly," he yells with arrogance. "They are mine alone to control." He taps his overgrown temple and grins.

"You're psychically connected?" Maybe that's a contributing factor to why his head is so big... He has a phone in there for each one of them. But the lines of communication must be open twenty-four-seven. Does he sleep? *Can* he?

"With each and every one of my darlings. They are my children."

*More like your robots.* But this is pleasant news to me. It implies he doesn't know that the Triune have armed their servants with *Bolta* and are pumping it into the veins of whichever Warpers suit their present needs. Hell, they're doing it so subtly he can't even detect it.

"I tell one to go and he goes, to kill and he kills, to bring me an offering of fruit and figs and he does it with haste." He taps his oversized head with Mister Howard Kieron. "We share a hive mind"—he unfolds some of his bandages and exposes his skeletal skinless form— "and more."

"What's the connection between your creation of cronies with your decision to hack into my associate and me?" *Associate.* I feel cold just saying the word. But we're not friends.

"If I can piece together from the varied anatomical structures, bodily fluids, and deposits of animal simpletons a new and spectacular species, how much more can I strip away the mortal flesh of men and uncover the secret to what makes one an atavistic Triumvah?"

"But why hurt *him?* I'm the only... Triumvir... here..." I look to Green and his head is bowed, his ashamed eyes honed-in on his dung basket. "Oh, my holy days..."

Betrayal. That is all I feel.

He is the enemy the Grin warned me about: the one I must eventually kill. The Pretender or the Dark Lord, I know not yet. But one thing I do know: he has been nurturing me in the ways of battle only so that I might die at his hands. Well played, sir. Nicely done. Something always did stir within me that prompted me to obscure the true extent of my power from him. I should have followed my instincts and removed his head from his shoulders back when I first held Skylar as we left Sandster Village.

"He never told you...?" Cheers for stating the obvious, Gregory Saint Germaine—with an E at the end of Germaine. He treats himself to a well-earned *He-haw!* Snarl. *Hoot-hoot. Oh Nelly.* I'll give you that one, buzzard.

"Why am I still alive?" I spit, but the freak thinks I asked him.

"I wish to study each of you in detail, find out how you tick, discover which of you is which, and birth the ultimate beast. Usually the identification process is very easy, but at the End of Days, all descends into chaos, even something as fixed as Good and Evil.

"Cut the cryptic crud. Speak plainly."

He hauntingly sings the verses of Shaman K'k'ko Zset's prophesy that relate to the Triumvirate; not that those verses are scary—they're actually among the least bloody—but his singing voice is just really bad.

The goodly shaman suspects many things, he adds: that perhaps I am the Last Lone Warrior of Light who will descend into Sheol to bring deliverance; or maybe I'm the Harbinger of Darkness; or the Pretender who merely mimics the energies of the perennial nemeses; or mayhap I'm half a bicephalous dragon leading two co-existing lives simultaneously. At this, he looks from me to Green.

"Hence, you would belong in my collection of worshippers and friends"—a group that has multiplied in a ring around us— "as the Ultimate Hybrid!" *He-haw!* Snarl. *Hoot-hoot. Oh Nelly.* "The champion of my army on the day of battle when I exact vengeance on Kabikil!"

Bingo. I've just found a way out of this chamber of funny mirrors.

"I had no idea that was your intention. Sorry, but I beat you to it."

"You're lying."

I explain with a smirk: "In my absence, the Elven kingdom is crumbling. Before I left, I set in motion a scheme to decimate the Family Laxciila from the inside out. Mecky has a flock of spies at his disposal. They sneak about looking for gossip, then buzz off, and whisper in Mecky's ear what they've heard. But it is not birdy-encased eggs that these animate statues lay but Seeing-Stones filled with prophecies, predictions, and memories. Mecky keeps them locked away in a hidden passage in the wall. He is kept well-informed. He knows where the bodies are buried. Figuratively speaking, of course," I laugh quietly. R.I.P. Dol'ver.

"One of these *Radharcs* showcased an intimate conversation between Mecky and Lear and contains undeniable evidence that they're working together." I take a second to scrutinise Gregory Saint Germaine—with an E at the end of Germaine's reaction. Just as I thought. He had no idea. "They're in league with the First Vampire. They want to perform experiments on him; turn him into a Super-Vampire, maybe. Seems to me that Mecky didn't disapprove of your brilliance as much as he pretended. They're making their own Hybrids.

"I dropped that egg into the Queen's goblet when the Elder Wizard led her off to dance on my last night there. She hates Mecky already, because of the circumstances under which they were wed eons ago." Green looks up at me, aghast. "If the melancholic wretch has the faintest hint of decency, this should sever any remaining ties that exist, such as familial loyalty or habitual demonstrations that project a united front. Secondly, I hid a gift in their house pet's scorched abode, hoping he'd prove even more malleable than the Queen: the remains of the disgraced politician, Senator Dol'ver."

"Was it Kabikil?"

"I will not speculate aloud but rest assured: he will answer for his sins in due course. He caught me in his chamber, but not until after I'd pocketed a couple of eggs. He very politely gave me leave to return to bed, but instead I hid behind an arras. Soon, two of his most loyal goons who frequently wear their hair in the shapes of sea-creatures arrived, clothes muddy from time spent in an out-of-bounds forest and one of them with a shovel in hand. Together, the three of them carried in a rug the senator and left the shovel behind. I stepped out from behind the arras, grabbed the shovel, and followed at a safe distance to the plot in which they buried Dol'ver. They departed for a nightcap and a nap, and I dug him up again."

"Why would Kabikil do that?"

"It is no secret that the King and his scion hate each other. Dol'ver was the prince's only friend. I, on one occasion, snuck into Alk'erion's den and overheard an assassination plot between them. Perhaps the Elf pieced together a theory that this was so, or maybe his peacocks shared their suspicions. Whoever massacred poor Dol'ver had probably hoped that eliminating one of the faction's key leaders would hurt Alk'erion and end all rebellious mobilisation.

"Anyway, Alk'erion distrusted me just as much as Mecky did, so before I asked his sister to dance at the banquet, I secretly slipped a memory egg next to his doggy cushion. This egg proves that Mecky had been brainwashing the princess, something her over-protective brother would not be able to tolerate, since he wanted every iota of her for himself. Furthermore, sooner or later, his bloodhound nose will pick up the scent of Dol'ver's remains. These will offshoot his most hideous revenge."

"Illogical! You trust your poor attempts of scheming that much?"

"No. I trust in others' brainlessness and foolery. I also trust the potency of the until-now-stoic-and-useless Queen's superior hatred of her husband to spur her to action. She will tell Alk'erion that Mehkabikil has gone dark and show him the footage of the latter conspiring with Lear, and his alliance with orcs and creatures of the night. Alk'erion will then reveal his Seeing-Stone, and…" I wait to see if he's caught on.

"With the Queen's support, the saucy prince's tempah will again boil to rebellion."

"And destroy them all."

"The balderdash you speak," Fetch retorts, but I do not unfix my gaze from the egghead's gigantic eyes.

"It's all reliant on external forces operating in conjunction with your scheming. There's so much conjecture, but outstandingly possible, if what I know of their temperance is true."

"Fancy cashing in on the Family Laxciila's destruction?"

"What do you propose?"

"As punishment for Mecky selling you out and stealing your idea, I ask that you plant three simple words in the furthest recesses of your *beauties'*"—I nearly choke on the word— "minds. They are: 'The Chosen One'. To clarify, you maintain complete autonomy. Just speak those words from your hive mind to theirs, like a feint whisper, a nearly irrecoverable dream, a song you can't quite remember the lyrics to, or a celebration you don't recall being a part of, despite featuring in half a dozen photos. That's it."

"Why?" I have just about lost him. Suspicion soars with each second.

"It's a surprise."

"Not my preferred sort of prize."

"I bet the Summer Palace in Loux Laxciila constitutes that. You could turn it into a lab. Consider it my way of saying thank you."

"That is not yours to give."

"When all this is over and the biggest players are held to account, you will be amazed by what properties are on the market. And you have my word: the Summer Palace is yours, if you agree to my ambivalent terms. Think of how much stronger your children could be hand-crafted in a bourgeois centre like Laxciila with its limitless resources. They wouldn't be misshapen and incessantly moaning in pain. How do their screams not drive you crazy?"

Gregory Saint Germaine—with an E at the end of Germaine clutches to Mister Howard Kieron more tightly, draws him in close, and tenses his muscles and his grip. This is all he has wanted for centuries: the fall of the Elder Elf; his own return to power; and after all this time, to receive credit for his intellectual brilliance in the genetic crossbreeding of perversions that never should have existed. *It's too good to be true*, he thinks. *What's the catch?* Having finally gotten him where I want him, I reiterate slowly:

"And all you have to do is subliminally plant 'The Chosen One' in each one of their heads."

"Let's say, for the sake of argument, I do as you say, but then retract it without your knowing?" He's goading me. He wants to see that my power exists not in words alone.

"Oh, I'll know. And I will defeat the Triune as planned. And then I'll come back for you. And the whole of Jumpstarted Planet Angoria will not be vast enough to hide you from me. And you will be charged for collaboration with the enemy tyrants of the Free Angoria and publicly hanged atop the palace that could have been yours."

*Shut up, Fetch.* "Then you will die stupid."

"What makes you so sure you will win?"

"You."

He says he needs to think about it, and calls to his side a fuzz-ball of thumbs with a one-eyed antenna, a grizzly beast with beaked hands and feet, a piranha-faced penguin, and a centaur whose human half is more demon than man. They retire to a treehouse (the centaur remains outside but looks in through the window) and they confer over recent developments.

"What are you planning?" Green spits, with more accusation and hostility than I think I deserve.

"Who are *you?*" I fire back.

"Your guide and"—he swallows hard— "friend."

"Less friend and more foe."

"Don't sound so upset, chronic deceiver. Don't pretend Andronicus's words weren't the happiest of your life. You have hated me since we met, and suddenly you felt justified for those feelings. The eternally betrayed lone wolf has yet another enemy on his decapitation list. Personal drama wins again."

"Go die."

"Prin–... Benjamin..."

"You and Mósandrirl have played me for a flute this entire time. You are my enemy!"

"Shut up, child!" his cobra mouth hisses.

They're back: the mummified Gregory Saint Germaine—with an E at the end of Germaine, surrounded by his haggard misfit confidantes.

"We have talked it over." *He-haw!* Snarl. *Hoot-hoot. Oh Nelly.* "And we have decided... to abet you on your perilous, dare I say ridiculous, quest." He puts the fingertips of one hand to his right temple and holds Mister Howard Kieron to his left, closes his eyes with the vigour of a constipated child, and subliminally speaks the three subtle words ('The Chosen One') into the echoing canals of his artifice-nexus.

"Good. Now please bring me our bags. I had better be off. Got people to kill."

"You only brought one bag each."

"He wrapped his sticky fingers in bandages one night, slid his hand in my bag, and stole my magic sword, for fear I'd gut him with it. I want it back."

The ball of pollexes must be the jungle's secretary, because he bouncily rolls away, then back again with our bags. He drops mine carelessly at the final hurdle, then gets one of his appendages caught when he tries to open it. ("He's all thumbs," Gregory Saint Germaine—with an E at the end of Germaine apologises). Next, the short man waves Mister Howard Kieron in the air, and a mystical energy eats my bonds and safely plunks me at the feet of my cruciate. With lightning quick movements, I flip open Green's bag and whip out Skylar, and grab my pail and sprint over to Green's and slop in its hideous contents.

"NO! Blood is life! What have you done?!" The little man freaks out.

"The power is in the blood. I won't have you concocting insidious studies on my physiological make-up or deposits when I'm not around. You can have all the Triumvir blood you like when this is over. But you will ask for it. Consider this a lesson in manners 101."

Gregory Saint Germaine—with an E at the end of Germaine's band of amalgam hooligans yelp and clap their wings and whistle at the prospect of a fight. It's more grotesque than watching the Laxciilian Colosseum spectators, since you at least expect people to speak audibly, and to speak horrible words at that. I wonder, if all animals' mouths were opened, would they all cheer at the panorama of us leaders of the food chain squaring up against one another and getting our eventual comeuppance?

"Now what are you doing?" he barks as I near Green. I know I'll regret this, but I cut his bonds and extra mercifully catch him as he drops from his rood. "This is only because you know the way through the Maze. Otherwise, I'd spear your chiselled abs myself."

Suddenly, the Shaman appears, a feathered wrinkled man who

looks more high than supernaturally-inclined, surrounded by his henchmen of orcs. Unlike the goblins who tied me to the Saint Catherine's wheel, these orcs are large, green, and sluggish, but they have adapted well to the hybrid jungle. One wears a buffalo skin, one an eagle, another an elephant, and one a human. They each hold a staff crowned with the skull of the creature they wear.

I bray like a donkey, then break into a wolf's gnarl, and go "Hoot-hoot" like an owl, in jest of the jungle monologist, then "Oh Nelly! "K'k'ko Zset comes yonder!" I tighten my grasp of Skylar and try to work out a way to kill the two men and four orcs should it come to it. They turn to look at one another and suddenly, it's like I've been transported to a barn in view of the explosive chorus of squawks and contented chicken clucks. And this in-depth conversation lasts so long in this manner that by the time they have finished, I feel embarrassed for not having run away.

Then the Shaman steps back in line with the orcs and all nod their heads reverently to Gregory Saint Germaine—with an E at the end of Germaine, who then arches his head at me.

"He is here. Triune Lord, Supreme Silas."

"Now? B-b-but we're not… I-I-I'm not r-ready. I'm—" No. I have prepared for this. I've trained for this. I was born for this. Like a harvested-organ baby, I was born with a predetermined purpose: to save the world. This is my moment. So shine, Benjamin-Joshua Thomas Coffey-Witherspoon. Shine like a sun, burn brighter and hotter than ever before, and blast every one of them into eternity. "I'm going to need clothes."

"Do not be a fool, boy," grimaces Green. "There is no way you can defeat him yet. You are not strong enough."

"When will I be? Why delay the inevitable? Why not just get it out of the way? Anyway, his body is dead and his charm's been destroyed. He's got no blood so he's got no power. Now is the ideal time to strike." But no sooner have I asked these questions than I second-guess myself: saying that killing someone is easy, taking someone's life is harder, but superseding that is living with yourself afterwards.

Well, if you're me. Silas is unaffected by such internal qualms, as evidenced by how he blows up the orc shamans' heads from behind with a six feet long metal rod that emits blue magical energy and electrical sparks. Their bodies shake for several long uncomfortable seconds and then drop only to be consumed by fire. K'k'ko Zset is next to fall.

"Actually, I wisely retained a single droplet of blood in my spirit form, just in case something like this were to happen. Were you really arrogant enough to think you could sever the bond between me and the amalgams and that I would not notice?"

"*The amalgams and me*," I snarl through gritted teeth.

Gregory Saint Germaine—with an E at the end of Germaine shivers with terror. His icicle feet are frozen on the spot. The way his hair stands erect, added with his giant eyes, gives him the look of a cartoon hedgehog who senses his coming death knell. But I won't let that happen— I need him alive…

Yet Silas is here to bury him. He prolongs the agony by blasting to bits several Warpers first with his wicked instrument. Each death sears Gregory Saint Germaine—with an E at the end of Germaine like a sword, and he collapses and sprawls out on the grass.

"Lower the gates. Lower the force field. Whatever keeps them in here, drop it and send them out. Spread them all across the Maze. Go!" I yell. Green keeps interrupting me, but I just repeat my commands louder. Amidst the chaos, the carnage, and the massacre of his children, Gregory Saint Germaine—with an E at the end of Germaine doesn't know who to listen to—Silas, Green, or me—but I hop down before him and swear I know what I'm doing. "I'll keep them safe," I promise, without any intention of upholding it.

Green pulls me up (I'm surprised by how strong he is, even now, after all he's been through) and chastises me. "You cannot make deals with every enemy we meet. Sooner or later, soldier, you have to accept that this is war. We should kill him now." The exact opposite advice he gave in relation to Silas a minute ago.

"You are right. This is war. But *you* are the soldier. *I* am the Chosen One. That makes *me* the commander. And we are doing this *my* way." I wet my fingers on the blood streaming from my side and scribble on my chest. "What is this?" I demand.

"Blood," he says blandly and shrugs. I glare sternly to show I'm not messing around. "I don't know... a rabbit?" He arches his neck to the battle we should be fighting, but he's not getting past me until I've said my piece.

"Wrong. It is only a *picture* of a rabbit, my favourite animal"—at which point he says he thought I hated animals, which I do— "and operates as a metaphor for our great mission. As the Chosen One, I invite you to colour this rabbit with your talents, your skills, and your tenacity for exacting retribution and judgement where appropriate... But I forbid you to rub out any of the drawing. I'm the general for the side of Good—my plan is the plan. If you have a problem with that, rather than waste time with negotiations you are fated to lose, you might as well turn back now and run back to whatever cave you crept from before you set your sights on me."

"You do not have a plan," he scowls.

"I have had a plan since before I entered Laxciila," I deviously grin.

Again, I tell Gregory Saint Germaine—with an E at the end of Germaine to lower the gate and send the hybrids out; to trust me. He nods and clucks to the birds of the air who tweet his commands. The gate descends and the natural-mythical crossbreeds run amok for the exit in the strangest stampede I could ever have imagined: a manic flurry of winged dinosaurs, hare-footed seals, otters with platypus beaks and orc ears, a unicorn-headed man, and a five-headed dog. Each head once belonged to a different breed.

But they all pale in comparison to Silas. His spirit form has really come on since the Grin released him from his Black Sands prison. He's in H.D. now: full-colour, no fuzzy soundwaves, 3D. He looks like a well-exercised man in his early fifties with an angular face and sharp silver brows, a moustache and beard. As it is with Earth and Jupiter's Great Red Spot, his eyes are so beady they could fit into Gregory Saint Germaine—with an E at the end of Germaine's thrice, at least.

"It's been too long," Green greets, pulling out his hawk-eyed sword.

"Ah, if it isn't the Black Rat, chief of the Angoric vermin... I feel you are owed my sincerest congratulations for your uncompromising persistence in spreading your germs and stink across my perfect world. I had thought the border would succeed in penning you in, but your mousey instinct must not have been able to resist running around a maze…"

A gigantic dragonfly with spider legs whizzes past Silas's ear, but he cuts it down with his sparky metal pole. There's a sizzle and a smell of roasted moth, then an *uhnn* from the mad inventor.

"Don't hurt him," I beg, then ashamed of my compassion add, "What do you think will happen to your Hybrid army if he dies?"

"I will get by," Silas smirks, "Same as I always have: by getting someone else to do my dirty work. In fact, it seems to me that the only one who would be put out by the death of Mad Andronicus and his insolent freak show is your two-man army." Wait, is that why he thinks we're here? To build an army? I can work with that. "If it would make your life simpler, call them back." *How?* "Do not take me for a court jester, Benjamin. I saw you when you crash-landed in the forest just beyond Troll's Cave. I saw you in the desert and again when you fled Loux Laxciila. And I have seen you run from the Elf and your destiny ever since. I know you planted your name in the amalgams' minds so you could control them. Didn't you just say that you were the Chosen One and the jungle rat was a soldier—*your* soldier? That he exists only to serve you and obey your commands? Imagine an entire army of soldiers who love you and fear you. Imagine all that power in the palm of your hand."

"What powers of deduction you have," I say, in the manner Little Red Riding Hood spoke to the Wolf.

"Do not let me stop you. Beckon them to come to your aid. Or to save all the children they will otherwise eat. To slit the throats of the ambassadors that my brothers and I have established in each Block; the ones who are fat on human flesh, rich on their people's labour, and black to the core. Send them to Loux Laxciila to make war with the Elder Elf. Cement your reputation as the Defender of Worlds and Ravager of Evil. Stop wars before they happen. Heal those we have damaged. Restore order where only chaos reigns. Call your army. CALL THEM!"

I must admit, I'm sorely tempted, and he knows it. Just look at that crooked, all-knowing grin. I could silence everyone who doubted me. I could give back to those from whom everything has been stolen. I could make these Warpers, these slaves to lawlessness, slaves to righteousness. I could, with a single thought, save the world. But it's not the way. It's cheap. Nothing would be sacrificed or earned.

"Together?" I whisper to Green, who has been ominously silent. He nods and we charge at him. Gregory Saint Germaine—with an E at the end of Germaine scurries off on all fours. Silas tries to take control of his body, but I stretch out Skylar over the helpless short guy, and it absorbs the attack of the mental ambush. I keep this up until he is out of harm's way, and only the three of us remain.

But even the combined strength of our swordsmanship and stealth aren't enough to scratch Silas or his metal pole. Green goes in for the kill with each strike whereas I think my hits through more cautiously. Completely unfazed by the likelihood of his demise, Silas holds the pole with only one hand, and condescends us by keeping his second arm firmly glued behind his back. For an old man, he is one very athletic samurai.

At one point, I believe Green could have delivered the winning blow had I not been in his way, and this sees him get thrown down a hill and land on a large network of thorns—on his back, thankfully, should he have any desire to propagate or employ his twenty-twenty vision when all this is over.

At another moment in the duel, I almost get my head fried with the astral ninja's pole, only I block his attack with my right forearm and suffer a nasty burn and sprain that won't heal today or tomorrow.

It feels like a long time before the severely punctured Green comes back into play, but I regard that moment with appreciation and relief. And against all the odds, we somehow gain so potent an advantage over Silas that we flash him that final, fatal death look. We lunge. But like Achilles before he struck Priam, our swords freeze in the air mid-strike. Our hands shake but it's like nothing above our heads exists, though it is felt. The armoury within our rucksacks hover, as do random chunks of metal and architecture sprawled across the lawn. *Clink*s and *clank*s and thumping heartbeats become the only sounds. It means only one thing.

*Lear!* From far off, a dark-clad figure soars into view. Wrinkle-free, he too looks decades younger than when I saw him last. He wears a mixture of metal and leather, and comes across as both cultured and dangerous, perhaps even more so than Silas because his cruel demeanour is subtler.

"Brother Triune," Silas greets, more than a little surprised. "I thought you were going to Loux Laxciila."

"I sensed a disturbance in the Maze. I thought it warranted a gander. Ah, what have we here? The whore of 144 and Black-Blood. We meet at last." He approaches me and bows politely. Not wanting to be outdone on the manners spectrum, I curtsy. He kisses my left hand (Skylar is in my right) and sniffs so greatly he gets intoxicated. "All that metal in your blood... lead... mercury... magnesium... Mmm. How do they not drive you crazy?" He foams at the mouth and wipes away his spit with a napkin. Then his ghost, equally as life-like as Silas's, takes large steps back until he's beside his wicked malevolent sibling.

I gloss over Green's less courteous responses and re-join the conversation when he asks, "What happened to you? At what point did Lear, lover of lyrics, fine art, and literature, align with the darkness he swore to forever confront and instead pursue power, dominion, and the annihilation of children? At what point did you become a madman?"

"Oh, I am in my right mind about many things, cabin boy." Strange. I never took Green for a Seven Seas navigator. "In fact, it was my intense awareness of the signs of the times that convinced me the opportune historical moment had arrived for the wizards to rise up and take our rightful place as leaders of you substandard scum, wholeheartedly intent on raping our world with your existence, pollution, and wars. Angoria was perfect before *your* breed came."

Now is my chance to test a theory. I say to Silas, "What say we bow and start this skirmish over: the most powerful of the wizards versus Team Chosen One?" Then I quickly glance from Silas to Lear and back again. And it is glorious. That tiny bit of doubt. The flicker of petty fraternal nastiness in Lear's eye like he has just lost a bet. That is all the ammunition I need to tear them apart.

Lear fires some shrapnel at Green. As a reflex, I throw out my right hand to cover him from any debris, but a perfectly sheen burst of light jets from my hand and penetrates the distance between us. The floating weaponry and the tosser are flown backwards.

Meanwhile, Silas wastes no time in trying to execute Green, but we hold him off. Hawk and Skylar deflect his psionic blasts. Yet despite the severity of the attack, it strikes me as odd that I'm still alive. Killing me must not be their priority; either he or Lear could surely have offed me before now had they really tried.

Lear is soon up again and tells Silas it is a useless endeavour: some things have yet to happen. The Weaver has ordained fixed points in time. Destiny cannot be altered. The Tapestry never stops weaving and, though its warp threads are hidden away at the back of the finished product, its threads must inevitably connect.

"Indeed, they must," remarks Silas, a sly glimmer in his eyes. "And, before he died, K'k'ko Zset—however unwilling a participant he may have been—showed me how. I've seen the endgame. And we're going to dictate it."

He laughs evilly and stretches out his arms. Reality becomes a series of blocks. At this, Lear's eyes bulge and he vibrates with horror as though he's been tasered.

"Brother! What are you doing, man? You will weaken the Collective!"

"Buying us the time we need to get the Stone!"

I sprint in Lear's direction and whisper in his ear.

Then I dash to the rucksacks and grab the strap of one. The building blocks of the Maze whizz past me: forests with orphans who have turned savage without parental guidance; an idyllic scene of hot springs, blue sea and turquoise cliffs; a sword-wielding orc captain poking the ugliest spinster aboard his ship in the back, inching her towards a plank; an ancient ruin surrounded by sand; a long-forgotten temple where sits a statue of an old familiar man; a volcano and the insect creatures and blacksmith who dwell in it.

Silas leaps at me and pounds me into the dirt with his weapon. My limbs pinned to the ground, the scorching energy blasts from the pole begin to undo the threads that hold my one remaining kidney inside and, electric pole in hand, motions to maim.

Just then Gregory Saint Germaine—with an E at the end of Germaine jumps in and strikes him across the temple with an elephant tusk, then places his hand on my shoulder.

I see Green coming up the rear of the jungle of nothingness. It's all disappearing.

A block scoops up Gregory Saint Germaine—with an E at the end of Germaine. As the bag-strap I clutch becomes an extra appendage, the mad doctor's grip on me tightens. We are as one: two figures, the same sculpture. The building block sucks us up in the vogue of a black hole, like a washing-machine spinning us into atoms. We are but insects in a pouter experiment and we vanish from the jungle.

All of a sudden, we appear in the middle of a woodland community who stand wide-eyed and amazed at our unexplained appearance, his big head, and my banjaxed, bruised, naked, animate corpse. I hate to accept clothes from them since they are the very emblem of destitution, but they insistently offer, and I sort of need them. Plus, the shirt is blue, so how could I refuse?

But once dressed and calmed, oh, how I laugh! I must cackle away to myself hysterically for about fifteen minutes before I can even think about calming down, despite the slavedrivers smacking me with sticks, spitting, and making all kinds of threats in their choky dry voices. Heck, they just add to the giggles. The generous beautiful slaves have no idea how to regard me even though Gregory Saint Germaine—with an E at the end of Germaine repeatedly assures them in a hushed voice that I'm the Chosen One and must have a spectacular-amazing-undefeatable plan up my sleeve.

But I laugh not because I am shaken after enduring a traumatic experience, nor because I am mad (at least, I don't think I am); not even because I lost my guide and, with the exception of Skylar, accidentally whipped his belongings instead of mine. No, I explode in a fit of laughter because for the first time I know… I just know… I know *that I know* how this will all play out… exactly how the Tapestry weaves in the end!

I know I'm going to win.

# INTERLUDE
# SONG OF SONGS

Written in 6779+5, Era of the Maze, Age the Twelfth. To THE SWEET

GIRL FROM BLOCK 144:

*Aliana Kiira,*
*Three years dead today—is that right?*
*Not a day goes by that I do not think of*
*Your hair strands, auburn and gold,*
*Your freckles, red and tan, and*
*Your grin, wide and bold.*
*How could I?*
*You have been etched in my brain with a poker*
*And in the hollow cut a tumour has been fitted;*
*A toxic mass that incises my innermost parts.*
*You haunt me night and day.*
*I remember*
*Your kissable mouth,*
*Your keenness for hitting balls with sticks,*
*Your heart open and honest,*
*Your giddy laugh,*
*The way you breathed loudly*
*And tripped a lot;*
*The way your arms embraced all living things,*
*The uncanny way your spirit took captive every grievance,*
*And how your sweet soul was admired by all.*

*Your laugh was my favourite sound in the entire world until*
*My blade leapt,*
*Killing your brother dead, and*
*Afeared, I gutted you next.*
*Your lifeless head drooped flatly on my breast,*
*And your cloudy white eyes rolled like reels in a casino slot machine*
*Until they saw no more.*

*Now you linger as a judging spectre,*
*An indignant voice of condemnation*
*That whispers in the morn*

*And goads in the even*
*And hollers from the deep,*
*Cry'n' out to the deep*
*In my deep,*
*In my deep,*
*In my deep.*

*When will you shut up?*
*When will you have had enough?*
*Go. Get a life.*
*Stop haunting mine.*

Written in 654, Age the Fourth. To THE WITCH OF ANGORIA:

*Dearest A-*
*Your hair is a red rose:*
*Passionate, ablaze.*

*Your head is a snowdrop,*
*Bowed with embarrassment. I know not why.*

*Your Naked Man Eyes reveal your many faces*
*But their alien look indicates your many skeletons.*

*Your Psychotria elata lips*
*Keep the dead's secrets.*

*Your body is a crocus:*
*Dark, lean, desirable.*

*Your soul is a blade of grass,*
*Soaring in the spring wind, and taking me with you,*
*But blown away in the morrow or*
*Tossed in the fire.*

*Please tell me your name.*
*I am in love with you.*

Written in 657, Age the Fourth. To THE WITCH OF ANGORIA:

*Dearest A-*
*Your lips are rich fruity wine for my soul.*
*You leave me*
*High*
*Drunk*
*Thirsty*
*Craving*
*And empty.*

*Your soul is a necklace of lapis lazuli—*
*An endless expanse of*
*Sky*
*Colours*
*Lights*
*Golden gases*
*And neutron stars.*
*When I am not with you,*
*I want to be.*
*You consume me*
*Until there is nothing left*
*But animal craving and*
*Need.*
*I hunger for*
*Your voice*
*Your touch*
*Your name*
*You.*

Written in 660, Age the Fourth. To THE WITCH OF ANGORIA:

*Dearest A-*
*I wake*
*Amidst the fabric of the night*
*And do not despair the dark like I used to.*

*No longer do I interpret the blackness*
*As the hours when*
*Fate allows cruel nightmares*
*To push back the light,*
*To reign,*

*To play the tune of that age-old ode*
*That ends only when*
*I am slain in the hunt*
*And the earth is plunged into shadow*
*And what lies beneath devours all that is*
*And all that is*
*Is dead.*

*No, I care not for these things anymore.*

*You rest on my breast as your*
*Sleeping fingers curl my chest*
*Hair and let out steady breaths.*
*Like the coos of doves you stir*
*Something tranquil in that*
*Hidden place within me.*

*Your body is silky and warm,*
*Your heart soft like cream.*
*Your mouth smells of gold and myrrh more precious than*
*All the riches of the untamed lands*
*I travelled before meeting you.*

*Your fingers in my mouth*
*Smell of the apples and raisins we ate last night,*
*Your hair of coconuts,*
*Your body of the juice of olives in which we bathed.*
*I taste your fruit and it is magical.*
*And your grabby metallic fingernails taste of stolen gold coins.*

*And I—*
*Displaced in space and time, destiny and reason*
*(But with you infinity years young)—*
*Try to build the courage to ask you*
*To marry me,*
*All the while knowing*
*You'll be my doom.*

Written in 661, Age the Fourth. To THE WITCH OF ANGORIA:

*"Come away with me, my love!*

*We need not this stolen wealth!*
*We can leave all this behind!*
*No to destiny!*
*No to purpose!*
*No to the rules that hinder which we had no say in!*
*I can fight for you!*
*Defend you!*
*Die for you!*
*Send floods of blood like living streams charging down the hills for you!*
*Keep you until Angoria itself is rolled up like a garment!*
*I love you,"*
*I cried.*

*But you left.*

*Heartless hag!*
*Shunned, spineless shrew!*
*Cheap, cunning counterfeit!*
*Weakling forged from butter!*
*Most hated in all Angoria!*
*Nameless Witch!*

*And oh, unforgotten grinning Imp,*
*Whene'er we meet next I will cut your throat!*
*I swore I would ne'er kill again,*
*But for your part*
*And your endless, murderous, innocence-spoiling vengeance*
*I will have your head*
*And the earth shall drink to fullness your bubbling blood.*

*The Great Beneath will cry out*
*And be satisfied!*

Written in 243, Age the Third. To THE PRINCESS OF DELHOOD:

*Lucinda,*
*Daughter of the High Elves of the East,*
*Your teeth glow like moons around*
*Your blackberry mouth where come your*
*Nard compliments,*

*Honeycomb promises and*
*Gall vinegar lies.*

*One look of*
*Your hazelnut eyes*
*Which first I saw when I awoke, helpless and bewildered, on the*
*Lapping seashore of Delhood*
*Was all it took for you to steal my heart.*

*When I do not know your whereabouts,*
*I seek you.*
*Though guards scorn,*
*Watchmen suspect,*
*Conservative mystics whisper,*
*The thugs of King Delhood secretly beat and bruise me and leave me*
*Naked and pulped,*
*And village boys and girls of higher standing than I mock,*
*Still I charge after you, a gazelle to the clefts of the rock.*

*I need to know why I cannot fully trust you.*

*Your love is sweet,*
*Exudes peace,*
*And feels mostly safe.*

*But I worry that you are oh so malleable.*

Written in 245, Age the Third. To THE PRINCESS OF DELHOOD:

*In the prison that is Loux Laxcïila,*
*The apparent City of Light,*
*Your parents spoke to one they call*
*The Imp.*

*He said he had a message for them.*

*He rolled out a lengthy sheet of parchment with names of*
*Families*
*Friends*
*Strangers*
*Wanderers*
*And all manner of creatures*

*I've murdered*
*And spoke of crimes for which he holds me accountable:*
*Theft;*
*Running around Angoria under false identities;*
*Unauthorised occupation of property;*
*The aiding and abetting and hiding of a felon, and consequently a*
*Romantic dalliance of the highest offence:*

*That I touched in a future time and place*
*The one he hates the most—and it's left a trace: "My witch…"*

*Lucinda,*
*I fear our time is*
*Up.*

*Run away with me!*

Written in 854, Age the Fifth. To THE WITCH OF ANGORIA:

*Witch,*
*You are back again.*
*Your bodice has changed.*
*Your hair is now bistre,*
*Your skin flecked with crystal,*
*Your ears bear the rings of harlots,*
*Your necklace and jewels add nothing to your appearance. Instead*
*They only reflect the shallow temptress that burns and flexes in your heart.*

*Everything about you has lost its innocence;*
*Not that you were pure before,*
*But back then I saw the broken little girl who just wanted to be loved.*
*Now all I see is the heavily perfumed, greedy, ever-taking, empty, whiny wench.*

*I had forgotten you,*
*But your scent is an itch to my brain*
*That scratches all the etches and hollows and crevices*
*And paints so vivid and splashy a canvas until finally*
*I remember*
*Everything.*

*I preferred you forgotten; loved you more.*

*Yet your mouth smells the same as it did that autumn;*
*Of apples,*
*The fragrance of the grapevine,*
*Strawberries,*
*Myrrh,*
*Treasure.*
*And your eyes have the same old look*
*Of need, desperation, desire, and opportunity.*

*I leave you out in the cold*
*And you mourn for our lost love all night*
*Battering on the lintel,*
*Thumping on the door,*
*Thrusting your hand through the latch-opening,*
*Prohibiting me from sleeping*

*Until at last, I offer you the floor coldly,*
*Appropriate for a female dog.*

Written in 854, Age the Fifth. To THE WITCH OF ANGORIA:

*A-*
*It is early afternoon.*
*I hate that we are here again:*
*A cabin not our own,*
*Your body, cold now, on my left arm,*
*Sinking into whatever warmth I have left;*
*Your fingers finding my chest hair again*
*As you dream of*
*Spells*
*The past*
*Revenge.*

*You could have shattered the door to splinters*
*With the magic your Master taught you.*
*Instead, you knocked,*
*Repeatedly,*
*And begged*
*And pleaded*
*And cried*
*Until you broke the wall I had built,*

*Designed to keep you out*
*Forever.*

*I have loved you quickly*
*And loved you slowly*
*And here we are again.*

*You are naked and at peace, now twirling my belly button hair as you slumber.*
*Whatever would you think if you saw the*
*Inked quill in my hand*
*And the dagger by my side?*

*Would you think it rude, pet, that*
*I play you for the fool for which you play me?*
*I know there is only death in your mouth now*
*And when you show your true face,*
*I will be ready.*

*It does not take me long to learn your body,*
*Or the taste of your choice fruits,*
*Or the various pitches of your new voice.*

*And I know this will not last*
*Despite the years*
*My heart died*
*Searched*
*Craved and*
*Cried out*
*For you*
*Without knowing who you were*
*Or remembering our past life.*

*But now I do.*
*And I remember how greatly I loved you;*
*The lengths I went to protect you;*
*What I was willing to give up for you.*

*I feel it now resurface.*

*So love and be loved and know you are loved*
*Because that will make it all the sweeter*
*For me:*

*When you awake tomorrow, I will be gone.*
*I hope your heart bleeds and*
*You cut it out.*

Written in 2813, Age the Seventh. To THE RINGED WIDOW:

*Allyssa Gorgonette,*
*It took me so long to find you.*
*I have been ahead of time*
*And seen epochs pass,*
*And been forged and re-forged in fires,*
*And seen cities burn,*
*All to do the bidding of the Higher Orders*
*And prepare the way for*
*The Twelfth Age*
*When I rise up and take my place as the last Chosen One.*

*My wife,*
*After years of war*
*Bloodshed*
*Skirmishes on cliffs*
*Horseback riding*
*Sieges*
*Ravishing hunger*
*Wearing the same clothes on my back for months at a time*
*Blackmail*
*Espionage*
*Last second escapes*
*Torture*
*Being hunted*
*And hunting*
*I had given up on love*
*On hope*
*On happiness.*

*And then I found you,*
*Or rather, we found each other, both*
*Fresh from grief*
*And too world-weary to postpone marriage or*
*Wait for the next crisis.*

*And every day I heard death bells toll in the air*
*And saw lilies in your eyes, on your palms, and on your garments*
*And I knew I had to marry you quickly*
*Before you met your inevitable end.*
*I am cursed, you see,*
*And I spread my curse to all I touch.*

*My wife,*
*My blue, beautiful, dead valentine,*
*You have exposed me,*
*Broken me,*
*Made me vulnerable,*
*I hate you for it.*

*But not as much as the one responsible:*
*The Red-Faced Man,*
*Who, through this act,*
*Has drawn me back into the game*
*That will not end until I have killed him*
*And everyone else who stands in my way.*

Written in 505, the Third Age. To NOO ALLA.

*I like to duel;*
*You prefer to talk.*

*I consider clothes optional;*
*You insist they are a necessity.*

*I crave adventure;*
*You seek passion.*

*I seek results;*
*You settle for nothing less than perfection.*

*Adrenaline, adrenaline, adrenaline;*
*Caution, intelligence, propriety.*

*Bodily processes exist for a reason;*
*They ought to be kept private, falling outside the arena of social graces.*

*I battle, I kill, and I save;*
*You sew, stitch me up, and drink tea.*

*I am a hero;*
*You a princess.*

*Your eyelashes long*
*Your face bone*
*Your hair is a stream of fire.*

*Your grin cheeky*
*Your laugh short and to the point.*
*When you purse your lips, I hear fruit burst.*

*Your narratives are intelligent*
*Your speech dignified*
*Your walk upright*
*Your person blameless*
*You are a moral compass.*

*Your expectations are high,*
*You are a challenge to get along with,*
*Yet I find myself burning my songs of hatred for you*
*In the embers over which we fall in love.*

Written in 506, the Third Age. To NOO ALLA.

*I guess it is true what they say about opposites attracting.*

*When you bathe in the falls,*
*I admit, I take a peep.*

*When I hear you laugh,*
*I cannot but do the same.*

*When I anger and want to lash out,*
*A glance from you is all my soul needs to calm.*

*When I attempt a rhetorical flourish,*
*You make me shy.*

*When you say "Joshua" in that disappointed but amused tone,*

*I feel like a naughty schoolboy with a donkey's pulse.*

*When you encourage me,*
*I feel strong and believe I can fly.*

*When I am a hill away from you*
*And you tread carefully,*
*Preserving your shoes,*
*I sprint to you like a gazelle,*
*Lift you,*
*Twirl you,*
*Run my fingers through your hair,*
*And finally, after all this time, find your mouth*
*And kiss*
*Your soul.*

*I will carry you to eternity.*

*For, despite tough beginnings,*
*You make me better,*
*Anna-Marie.*
*You make me whole, my love.*
*You complete me,*
*My love, "Noo Alla" in Elvish,*
*Or as you pronounce it,*
*Nuala.*

He knew my mother. As in, he *knew* my mother intimately.

I feel sick. And used. And the tiniest bit excited, too. Churning in my stomach is an equal measure of shock-induced disbelief mixed with uncompromising faith in the evidence his writings provide. It's like some great cosmic joke whereby every peering faux-star above me is an all-knowing eye and every icy breeze is a sneer that asks, "What took you so long?"

But as I ponder it, the signs were there all along, from the very earliest of days: the One-Armed Man's occasional hints that "Nuala" was an alias. My Mo-Mo wooden toy, identical to Mósandrirl. The painting on my wall back in 124 Lincoln Lane of the knight with the hawk-handled sword. My name. Deep down, I always knew it hadn't been pulled out of thin air, that there was an underlying meaning behind it.

There were isolated instances, too. I remember one rare night when Green—I mean, Joshua—inconvenienced himself to light a fire and I got the distinct impression that he had something to say to me. However, Joshua being Joshua, he just eyed me darkly from across the *whoosh*ing crackle of leaping scarlet and orange tongues. He struck a match, lit up his pipe, and resigned himself to silently sussing out my face, his gaze rife with wordless questions and threats. I remember now how greatly his dilated black pupils terrified me, sightless and sinister under the shadow of his soaked green hood and greasy hair.

He held his incriminating glare so long so that the black cloud of smoke stung my eyes and they watered, and though by the end I merely winced through slits, I never once looked away. Finally, he cleared his throat with a disgusting phlegmy spit, and asked scarily, "How does it feel to be the Chosen One?" He cursed under his breath and wrinkled his nose and lower jaws, as if he had asked the wrong question.

I genuinely had no idea how to answer. What could I say? *Hurtful? Embarrassing? Sacrificial? Pointless? That I'm hated for being me by the people who are supposed to support me most? That there are hooligans I haven't even met that have put threats on my head? That no one appreciates anything I do for them, but unremittingly send in their wolves in sheep's clothing to deter, distract, and distress me? That even if I wipe all the main scum off the face of the earth, there will always be evil? That evil lives not only in murderers and rapists and wizards, but in all people's hearts, so unless my job is to send Angoria spinning into a black hole, my objective will never really be achieved?*

"It's all I've ever wanted. To be the hero. To be special. Set apart. On divine assignment. To be chosen."

"You know, the Elder Wizard has claimed to have found the Chosen One before?"

"Oh?"

"He was wrong then—" He spluttered into a harsh rusty cough, and I'm not sure, but it sounded like he said "too" at the end of that sentence.

"Oh."

He spoke no more on the subject, though he clearly had more to say. I think I know what now. I think the Elder Wizard styled him as Angoria's Twelfth rescuer, only to later reconsider. Only to replace him with me. I suppose that would explain why Joshua always kept me at arm's length or regarded me with a sense of begrudge. Perhaps he thought I had stolen his identity, his calling, his reason for being. Truth be told, were we to exchange places today and I watched Mósandrirl pull another Earthling out of his hat and proclaim him Saviour, I would blow a gasket too, and I don't even know what a "gasket" is.

Silence set in again, and it was in no way comfortable. The crumbling of wood within the lowly growling fire was the only sound other than Joshua's occasional drag of his pipe. At long last, he took an almighty puff of it, lowered it from his mouth, and tilted his head as he let out an unmerciful cacophonous cough and simultaneous hiccup. It sounded painful, like an iron bar scratching the inside of his dry grating throat. Then, the seemingly random, brazen question came: "What is your mother's name?" Looking back, I think this is the question he had wanted to ask me all along.

"Eden."

He swore under his breath and threw his pipe at me, but I elbowed it and sent it nose-diving into the hungry leafy-flicking flames. When I looked up from the ashy debris of his cancer-stick, I saw he was already asleep, or faking it. It was the only night he did not keep watch, or if he did, he didn't want me to know he was still protecting me from harm and keeping me alive.

Did he already suspect who I was? Did he know? This dark, anti-heroic, masterful man with many identities: Green Coat, Cillian, Joshua. I can't believe how close I came to missing it. He only wrote his name once in his five-hundred-paged mammoth of tragic romance stories; an absolute triumph for such a sullen, quiet man. Joshua, Joshua, Joshua. The name doesn't suit him, but I like it. Should I have told him that my full name is Benjamin-Joshua? I would have gotten some reaction!

Now, of course, I understand that some people would regard the act of rummaging through another's unpublished auto-biography intrusive, but I'm a Triumvir and I need to know more about the man I'm trusting with my life. (*Trusted*, I should say. He's gone now). Plus, were anyone to ask, I would make no secret of the fact that I am a proud pooching poocher. I like to pooch, to unravel the delicate nuggets of information people retain about themselves in drawers, presses, crannies, and holes in the wall. People are fascinating creatures when they do not know they are being watched. I wonder if the Triune feel that way as they watch the ants of Angoria submit to their will, rebel in vain, and die.

# 19

# REBELLION

I had thought that prying into his personal writings would alleviate some of the greater ambiguities about his personality and harsh exterior but to be honest I have more questions about the enigmatic man than ever: like, why is his timeline so confused? Is he a time-traveller? Is he a physical manifestation or product of the magical energies that perpetuate the Dual Cycle of the Chosen One and the Dark Lord (now the Triumvir Cycle), a recycled historical personage destined to play a role in every era? Or is he like me, just some nobody thieved from Earth, only to be bounced around Angoria's timeline as per the whimsical Fates' demands? And, however he manages to do it, why didn't he just tell me? Why didn't he let me in, or make more of an effort to bridge the gap between us?

Because as much as I hate to admit it, I cannot do this without him. My rogue's gallery is too expansive—Zj'hakim, Sharmedes, the Elder Elf, the Triune, Gideon, the Void, and who knows what else?

"Oh, Joshua, where are you?"

I stop for a quick bite to eat, slump in a heap on the ground under the shade of some evergreen trees, and rummage through his things. All I find is a measly stale cracker he's held onto for way longer than the packet recommended, and a few drops of water in a rusty tin flask.

I have a very different approach to Joshua's avoidance methods insofar as I venture into Zones as opposed to spending irrecoverable days averting them. Sporting Skylar, Joshua's green coat and always something blue, I boldly brave my way into the cesspools of victimisation, colonial oppression, and subjugation, and demonstrate acts of compassion amongst the lowliest peoples.

The slavers usually leave me to it without kicking up too much of a fuss so long as I don't charge at them threateningly first. Perhaps the Triune have commanded them not to harm me because they still need me alive until, well, they don't. Maybe the wardens just appreciate that I am true to my word when I say I could gut them in a heartbeat but won't so long as they behave. Personally, I rather think the slavers get a wry pleasure from watching me instill hope in these peoples only so they can beat it out of them again when I leave.

I find that it's easier to care for these maligned and vigorously beleaguered peoples than it is to care for Ardonians or Laxciilians, since I know my time here is too short for them to get to know me. Though I hate bodies, I wash them. Though I have no food, I feed them with words of life. Though I have no relational connection with them at all, I listen to their stories. Sometimes I think that's enough for them—just to know that their story has been heard; that they have been given the one thing they have been deprived of for three hundred years—a voice! Just to know that their ghosts will not wander aimlessly and moan with inaudible whispers and groan wordless pangs in the annals of history when all this is over...

When the entrapped peoples I meet have said all they want to, the next question out of their mouths is almost always the same:

"How did you come to be here, strange traveller?"

Then I share my greatest adventures and acts of heroism; never once lying, but perhaps minimising Joshua's overall contribution to the success of a given mission: the time he was stunned by a fearsome cave-dweller that tried to flay him and I crept up and bashed its skull with a rock. It survived, for all of three seconds, until Joshua chopped its head off. And the time we were attacked by fearsome wolves and had to jump off a cliff into a gushing river to avoid being made into brekkie. Little did the doggies know, Joshua had an on-the-road-made bomb strapped to the peak of said cliff whereupon the wolves had congregated to rejoice at our downfall. We went *splash!* They went *ka-boom!* Only one species survived—and it wasn't them. The Battle Royale of Sandster Village is a fan-favourite for its complexity, plus many of them know Sharmedes and the Wraith and are happy to hear that at least one of them got his comeuppance. And the whole time, I never once tell them who I am, but the smiles on their faces when they have the lightbulb moment never gets old: "The Chosen One!" Unfortunately, I don't think I'll be getting that reaction today…

"You are not the Anointed One, the one of whom the prophecies foretold!" an old bald man yells, fist in the air like he just doesn't care. I want to snatch his twiggy walking-stick and lash him with it. "You are but Joshua's shadow, his follower! You are a disciple of the true Chosen One! Go back to your own world, little boy! You have no right to wear his cloak!" He has triangular eyes, a snowy white beard dotted with burnt breadcrumbs, and L-shaped kneecaps.

"It's called a *coat*, Old Man Heckler," I snap back, to the raising of eyebrows and the inching backwards of the crowd. Flip. I'm losing them. Let's save this. "Joshua is great. Really, really great. He is brave, daring, skilled, and acutely demonstrative of that skill, takes no nonsense, or instruction," I laugh, "gives short cut-throat speeches, gets the girl, and rides into the sunset without sparing a thought for who he killed that day…" and for once, I realise I'm not judging him. I'm just stating a reality. "Joshua is the reason I stand before you now. He has saved my life more times than I can count and taught me how to defend myself, which comes in handy in this season of separation. But I assure you that under the Twelfth Cycle, he is but an artifice for what real power looks like. Until now, to be chosen went hand-in-hand with death: spiritual, emotional, physical. I am redefining what it means to be the Chosen One. Mine is a way of peace, not war. If I can stop the deaths of thousands with a word, then I have an obligation to try. If I can see to it that the Maze comes crumbling down and that your sons never once have to strap on a sword, then I alone will stand before these demigods. If I can impact the lowly, the forgotten, the rejected, then let someone else gain favour with the adulating crowds. If I can build something great, then why initiate Mutually Assured Destruction?"

"In order to build something great," Old Man Heckler snarls, "you must first dig deeply. This means tools, graves, and sweat. All you want is an audience of listeners to unctuously boost your self-esteem! To delay the inevitable! You are a fearful tramp, treading slowly as a snail through the Maze while the rest of us pay the price for your cowardice. You are not worthy to come in and out of our prison as you please… You're just lucky."

It is terrifying how quickly he stirs the crowd against me. I suddenly sympathise with how Moses must have felt when the millions of Israelites turned on a dime against him. I try to hush them, but to no avail. I've already lost them. In spite of this, I shout at the top of my voice my plans for the New Angoria, starting with how the Laxciilians will be sent in to relieve poverty and help construct schools, medical centres, food stations, places of employment, and public amenities.

"I think it would be good for them to do some work for a change," I slander, though I immediately regret it. I don't want to open a can of worms I may not be able to squeeze back in. It's best that they know nothing of Laxciila's fortunes for now. "Gradually, democracies will be established, and each Zone will be lifted out of isolation and be represented by a Senate. And I will invest all my energies into demolishing the Void."

I have no idea how he heard me over the boisterous jeers, *boo*s, and tidal wave of insults, but Old Man Heckler asks, "And what about our captors?" The city falls unnaturally silent. It's like someone just pushed the mute button on some interdimensional remote.

"Rest assured, when this Maze comes down—and that day is coming more quickly than the Triune think—the orcs will not long outlive it."

"I am not talking about beasts, *boy*." Oh, the condescension in his voice—I could smack him! "I am talking about your breed." *Triumvirs?* "Humans. Seventy percent of slavedrivers, according to our own punishers, originate from the race of Men. Now answer."

Oh, human race, why do you let me down so? Though the source is a right git I would rather denigrate to nothing more than a dissension-stirrer, I have no doubt that that figure is accurate.

"An Angoric Senate will be elected to sit down and discuss an appropriate punishment and rehabilitation programme," I begin, only to be cut off by an almighty: "ROUNDTABLE TRIUMVIRISM!" *You know of King Arthur?*

"You will sit around a board littered with envelopes, blood-money, and wine, discussing peaceable resolutions, before inevitably choosing to sweep their sins under the carpet and move on!" Probably, yeah. "Where was your peace when they pulled our teeth from our gums? Where were your talks when they poured boiling tar over us? Where were your bribes when they hurled boulders on our babes? Where were your deals when our sons were brainwashed into killing anyone who forsook the Triangle—the mark of the Triune? Or when our daughters were taken and sterilised, or thrice-quartered and distributed in letter-boxes and pies?"

Unwanted, I turn to leave. That's when I hear him yell, every syllable like the snap of crab pincers: "Kill the imposter!" And the volatile crowd charges toward me, toppling over and crushing themselves. Grabby hands and skeletal arms stretch out like I'm offering them a grand.

And the Fear—that great eye in the sky whose slit pupil is very much like the Triune's triangle emblem—smiles.

And then the Zone walls unleash jets that scald them with boiled water and bulldoze them with the filthy brown heads of their dead. My reflexes serve me well for the most part, but even I fall prey to the occasional thump of a scraggy-haired woman in her forties, red tongue sticking out of her gob like a dog's. And as suddenly as they started, the jets stop. Scarcely a handful of seconds later, the Triune-stationed captains move in with their shock-rods, nets, circular iron shields, and rusty blades.

And social revolution breaks out: untrained strays clawing at their nearest neighbour in adrenaline-fueled guerrilla warfare, no one knowing what they're fighting for. My pleading for submission and peace goes completely unnoticed. And then the fake skies open to the tune of helicopter wings as millions of locusts descend and eat everything green. Using Skylar as a flame-thrower, I burn to a crisp as many of the gregarious swarm as I can before I'm forced to take flight. This city is lost, and though I take no pleasure in saying it, they dug their own grave.

Obviously watching the mayhem with delight, the Triune reopen the gate to the city that I came in. Usually, Strays—as the wardens call us labyrinth wanderers—can't leave a Zone, Block, or Dome the same way we entered, but we can leave with ease of access through other doorways. They typically don't remain visible or existent long enough afterwards for the locals to run through, though.

The last distinct sound I make out just before I cross the barrier from death to life is Old Man Heckler jeering at me, mouthing off that I did this. And as coldly as Joshua would ignore the hurting, the broken, the down-and-outers, I keep my back to him and step from the Zone into No-Man's Land. But before this, I matter-of-factly say, "You were right. Peace was never an option."

# 20
# HEADS WILL ROLL

Though I keep my weapons concealed twenty-four-seven, I am geared up to the nines. Yet for all my militaristic preparedness, that revolt just now caught me by surprise. I badly wish I could have a do-over. Speak with more integrity and strength. Maybe trap Old Man Heckler in a bunker before my speech. Fight back something larger than locusts.

It's times like these that I find myself most in need of encouragement or a switchboard to whom I can relay my thoughts. I'm beginning to regret dropping para-scientist Gregory Saint Germaine—with an E at the end of Germaine off at an Olympian mountain topped with sexy dancing oracles whose order has taken a vow of silence, not that I think he minds.

I'm not ten feet from the exit when the gate to the city swings open, and a ragged figure emerges. Wild black hair. A grey full beard. Yellow beady eyes, filled with money and hatred. Clad in leather and lances, silk and swords, ravaged sacks of goods and rings. I never did learn his name, but he's undoubtedly the captain the Triune stationed to oversee the oppression of Block 896, or what I'll now always remember as Rebel City. Regrettably, he is very, very human.

Limbs, limbs, and more limbs rush for the exit, but he pushes against the gate to shut them in until they retire to their misfortune or until their limbs fall off outside in the warren, and the *f-k-k-k-k-k-k-k* of the locusts' wings is silenced.

"Much obliged for the exeunt, Big Bad! I almost thought the

Masters Three were going to leave me to the bugs!" And away he skips and sprints.

And something inside me snaps.

"DEATH!" I yell at the top of my voice until it cracks, and I point Skylar at him. His wild eyes widen and his sacks of stolen goodies plummet on his toes with the uniformity of a woodpecker's pecking. His bottom lip drops to his chin, but nothing comes out. "I will give you a thirty-second head start," I warn, "before I hunt you down and end you. And rest assured, Wildman of Rebel City, the furthest reaches of this one-to-one-scale hyper-reality offer no hideaways or magic wardrobes so bank-vault-safe that they can keep me at bay when I am mad at you." I'm so murderously enraged right now I could cry. And something dark inside me takes over. I really want to hurt him!

He doesn't seem to know what he's supposed to do until I start the countdown. Then all that remains of him is the dust of his feet where he once stood. And then I set off hot on his trail. Will I kill him when I see him? It's unlikely. But I don't see why not, though hopefully the Maze will squash him first. For now, all that matters is the chase.

Through chasms that can be crossed by swinging vines, four seasons of weather, valleys, ravines and old creaky bridges, flowerbeds of eyes and anti-gravity deserts, I chase him for easily thirty to thirty-five kilometres without stopping for a break that lasted any longer than fifteen minutes.

While in a town called Gibeon, I pass a great tower. It's one of the towers I saw in Mecky's lair. An orc large as a troll comes to meet me.

"My Lord," he bows. "Lord Liriondias hadn't told me you were coming. But no matter. Come, my Lord. It is almost dinner time. Would you like a child or a chicken? Or a *chilken*?" He has himself in hysterics with that one. I'm still wearing Joshua's green coat, and strapped over it at my waist, a belt with a sheathed dagger. It drops to the ground with an echoing clang as I step forward.

"Whatever my servant thinks best," I beam, with the fakest smile I have ever artificed. Then I take him by the soaked smelly beard with my left hand as if to kiss him. But caught unawares, he is completely ignorant of the dagger in my right hand, and I plunge it deep into his belly and carve a happy face in his flesh. His intestines spill all over the ground, even on my shoes. I wipe them on his isolated head, his face wearing an altogether confused expression.

Not desiring to collect standees like stamps or contagion followers like the Pied Piper, I drag his sloppy muck of a body and chuck him in a ditch. And then the chase continues until I see the Wildman rush into a city by the name of Breathing Stone. Skylar in hand, I sprint to the outer fortification, still unsure what my actual objective is, but I'm convinced now that more blood will be spilled.

Then a right kibitzer in her fifties calls down from the city wall, "Are you the Chosen One?" I don't count the number of times I say I am before she gets the message. "Listen to what your servant has to say, I beg." *Who's that?* "I am." She looks puzzled, like I'm slow or something. "My name is Aarilyn, Wise Woman of Breathing Stone. You may have seen our signpost out yonder." Her grey hair is pulled back tightly. There's an air of Mósandrirl's calmness about her, though she gives the impression of being sharper and snippier.

"Proceed." Again, I don't count the number of times I say this.

"Long ago, they used to say—"

*Oh, for goodness sakes...* "I'm sorry, but I don't have time for this."

"Long ago—"

"There's a murderer... Well, I don't know if he's a murderer..." Why am I chasing him again? Oh, yeah. "A slavedriver, in your—"

"Chosen One, you are being rude." That shuts me up. I'm not used to being told that. Bloody cheek of her. "Long ago, before the Maze, Angorians used to say that Breathing Stone was the Temple of Resolution. No question was too great for our wise counsel of elders."

"Mm-hmm. That's nice. However—"

"We are the peaceful and faithful in Angoria. We are steadfast, upright, and gentle. Anyone who seeks refuge in our city, should he be found righteous, will always be protected."

"I'm not looking to rent a room—"

"You are trying to destroy one of the only remaining mother cities in Angoria. According to the Elder Wizard and the vagabond warrior whose coat you wear, Breathing Stone is one of the only cities whose leaders did not betray their people for status and riches after the Maze walls went up, or burst with boils and perforated innards because of that integrity. We harbour the escapees from each Zone, replenish them, and then send them on their way to the City of Light. Yet you approach our wall with vehemence in your heart. Why do you want to swallow the true pride of this broken world like that?"

"I don't want to kill you all. I didn't know you existed. And I don't know why you haven't been obliterated, but what you don't understand is that I'm here for—"

"You are a Triumvir. You bring only death in your wake. Or do you not know that the Fear, servant of Lord Silas, lights up the midnight sky with visuals of your charitable expeditions (though that cannot be said of your last one) and that the Triune then burn those villages, towns, and countries to ash?"

What...? All this time I gullibly thought I was helping people, but I just made things worse.

"There is a man in your city. He is guilty of the offence of which you claim your people are innocent. Hand him over."

Aarilyn pauses a moment, deep in consideration. Her thought process is brief. "His head will be thrown to you from the wall." It takes me a few seconds to register what she has said, but when I open my mouth to object, she's gone. I try to barricade my way through the gate, but her men obstruct my entrance and consequent interference in Breathing Stone politics.

She reappears not five minutes later and says, "His name was Druan Duran, and he was guilty of such heinous crimes no lady could dare speak." And sure enough, she hurls a miscellaneous object toward the sun. It blinds my eyes to follow its destination.

Is it a bird? Is it a plane? The entrails and scarlet droplets are all the evidence I need.

"Now be on your way, Triumvir, and leave the captives be before there is no one left to save," she drones, before turning nasty. "And should you survive this, and we meet again, it will be your head that I remove from its sinful flesh." Having said her piece, she then tiptoes down a staircase I cannot see.

I take a moment to spare Druan Duran's trachea a thought, and then step over it proudly. Then I flash a wide smile, certain that the Triune are watching, and tell them, "Lear, Silas, and the other one, you're next."

# 21
# DEAD THINGS

The sun comes up another four times and I'm still wandering over the same mountains. I honestly think the Triune are extending the length of this terrain just to mess with my head. I wouldn't mind, but I'm playing it safer than I used to: when I was first separated from Joshua, I followed the logic that if I was lost, I should employ every effort to get doubly lost and since a minus times a minus is a plus, then I'd find him again. Now I'm sticking to straighter paths and taking less mad detours.

With no drinkable water around, thirst scrapes my dry mouth like sandpaper on a wooden floor. Minute after minute, violent sunrays hammer my head. I urinate only twice the entire day and it's brown like dirty dishwater. My hands are so unwashed they're changing colour too. I keep them wrapped in my sleeves to avoid cross-contamination with everything else I touch.

On my fourteenth day without food, I get delirious and scramble up and down the hills at times like a berserker bipedal mammal, at other times, on all fours like an animal. And starved of all else, I eat the grass.

Then there comes a blessed day when, having unwittingly entered a far-off Block filled with shrubbery, briers, and lava, I pinch a crusty cake of fruity brown bread from a tea-party of grabby miserly mice and honking geese, but every nibble sticks to the roof of my mouth. I've barely supped my first mouthful of tea beneath the table since I fled Laxciila when I'm sniffed out and chased from there by pitchfork-wielding pigs.

With nothing amusing to do and no one to keep watch for me, I walk for twenty-four hours straight, more than once averting scores of goblins, growling trolls, and ravenous crows. I see the Triune are breaking their Flight Restriction policy; some of the only exceptions I can think of are the Abomination and the locusts—not that I care about any of this. All I can think about is how my stomach's so small I'm not hungry, and how I'm so exhausted that falling asleep seems too much hassle. The day is long and hot, the sun's a wasp, and I don't know if I deposit a drop of sweat or if I'm just wearing last week's, or if Time is but a day and I'm walking in circles, "squircles", squares, or triangles.

It takes me longer than it should to realise that the reason I haven't seen any potential food around is because I'm chasing them away with my roaring truck breath. Great. It won't be a group of wizards that kill me, or a corrupt paranoid elf, or being squashed by the Druid's Penis in O'Connell Street; but the altogether unimpressively banal global catastrophe of starvation.

I have no idea why or when, but at one point I perch on a blue-grey rock and make a four-note melody with a cartoon bird and spy a large rabbit wearing Roop's face that hops over when he's sure I won't strike, and gnaws the stake in my jacket pocket like it's a carrot. The white fluffy patch is Roop's bloody wound. His tail's the rock. He chatters that he knew all along Thomas was crazy, and my wide dopey eyes grin, reflected in his massive comforting pupils, but all I hear is "Nibble-nibble-nibble."

Next thing I know, I'm inching out of a bush on the mountain spying on Commander Zj'hakim. The bald head, but for a few stray white strands. The pale brown arms. Reptilian scales encircling his black eyes. The orange tongue that makes me want to throw-up. The gipsy hoops in his ears. The tattoos; an unnecessary and disrespectful perversion to one's skin—orc or not. The bag of multi-coloured flaccid foreskins he munches from with indelible relish.

I think I phase through the bush because I have the odd sensation of walking into a television screen. Yet they don't see me. (Am I even still there…?). Why don't they see me? Why does no one ever see me—except when I don't want to be? In true clandestine fashion, Zj'hakim speaks tactics with his sack-of-scum army of forty or so. I think I shout at them to let them know I'm here, but they pay me no heed. Or do I? Or did I? Or didn't I?

There's a reference made about me and whatever "Althrodùr" is. Or maybe they're talking about Joshua. Or maybe there's another Joshua. I thought I saw Top Hat leaping over the literally rolling hills with the feet of a gazelle and the elegance and grace of a ballerina.

"Do not forget our agreement," he calls back as he dances with glee, singing "I saved the Triune! I saved the Triune! I saved the Triune!" Then he explodes in a flurry of snickers. "Agreement?" What agreement? Oh, no, I've forgotten!

He runs rings around me and skips and grins. Oh, yes, that was his name, wasn't it? The Grin.

Maybe that's what they had on the wagon… Not the Grin or all the Joshuas or the Triune, but the Althrodùr. (What wagon? I was talking about the Grin). Everything is so confusing.

Ah, yes. I said, "I'm sorry, sir"—Have I ever apologised for anything? Hardly. I'm never in the wrong— "but I have no recollection of that which you speak of."

He moved in to harm me, but then stalled. "Rumour in the warren is there are two of you running around." Up to the high heavens went his ice-cream cone nose and then his sprightly, airy-fairy leap over the rainbow-coloured snake-wriggling mount resumed.

There's also an in-depth gnarly, snarly spiel in orc tongue about whatever orcs talk about for fun as they load the Althrodùr or the Joshuas or the something else onto the wagon. (What wagon?). Where am I? When did this happen? The past? The present? In days still to come? When all this is over?

I need water. And sleep. And food. And... just one touch... from...

Suddenly, everything screams at me. Stones split open. Every puff of wind is an eggshell that cracks upon impact with my ears, and the drums, drums, drums, emphasise the sound. The clouds roar like spectators in a football stadium. Orcs cackle cacophonously. The grass hisses. The fattened worms 1.8288 metres beneath my feet laugh. Strapped and statue-still swords alike clang, clang, clang. I sweat pop-pop-pop-popcorn beads and the tears roll from my pores with a sizzle like streaks down a glass bottle. I need the world to shut up. I pull off my coat because everything's too loud, but I soon realise this solves nothing, so I put it on again. And every mirror that hears every sound—where'd they come from?—throws-it-throws-it-throws-it back, from the deep, to my deep, in the deep. Shut up. Shut up. Shut up.

I don't know how I get from pulling their cheeks like a baby's cheeks made of goo or melted plastic or water to a pit of quicksand, or how I get out again. But I do know that, giggle-filled, as my azure blue robe (when did I change into this?) pulls me down, I twiddle my fingers to music that's not playing as my legs sludge deeper into the rank brown silence, as Fetch recites Gertrude's speech to Laertes.

I have no idea how I escape the droopy swamp—it certainly wasn't for the want of trying. No, wait. Now that I say that aloud, I know it wasn't true. Not that I said anything out loud. Did I? (Why am I narrating my every action?). How did I get here, wherever "here" is?

Clawing onto bricks of turf, many of which at first give way and lose their footing and roll into my wet cement grave, I eventually climb up and step onto dry land… I assume. Mightily perplexed, I rub my eyelids and moustache and smear them in gunk and contemplation. But the screaming starts up again as soon as my pinkies unclog my ears: the eggshells, the cackles, the drums, and the soccer match and the Gaelic match and the rugby match of my nervous hyperactive feet under the table, and the match, match, match, fire, fire, fire, liar, liar, liar, *whirr, whirr, whirr* of helicopter wings, and the *shunk* of the stake, and *beeeeeeeeeeeeep* in my ears as I crunch Roop's skull, and the *ugh* as he wallops mine.

The screaming doesn't stop until all the orcs are dead, and I am covered in brown, then black, and smell very badly, and I clutch Zj'hakim's decapitated head by the few strands of hair he has like I'm David and he's Goliath—and I'm living and he's dead.

And I'm dressed in my boots, trousers, shirt, and jacket again and sprinting in what feels like six or seven directions at once in woodland terrain as far from the Cornucopia, Agrabah, and Middle-Earth as possible. My bag bashes my knees and threatens to trip me up with every step.

Finally, I pause. Hold on: am I dreaming of the Hunger Games, Aladdin, and Tolkien's fantasy or am I still in the Maze? Am I having a drug trip or am I just dehydrated? Do I wake or do I sleep? Am I even real anymore? My head...

I've seen green evenings and I've seen volcanic mornings. A morning that was a woman recently passed and an evening came with a firestorm. A black sun shot up, the sky turned pink, the sun to ash and the moon to blood... but when...?!

I'm in the White Room with a bed that's marked "N+J", and then I'm in my bedroom wondering why no one's knocked on the front door to come play with me all summer. I wave doltishly at all manner of strange and evil creatures and then I lie in a random tuft of flowers that are probably poisonous. I bathe in the blood of the monsters I slay, and I wake from a restless doze in a narrow stretch of road as though nothing's happened, only my arms are swinging in vicious warfare, pricked by pins-and-needles. And maybe I never left the bathroom with the lemon-scented seashell air-freshener, and I'm still there counting to sixty. How long do I do this every night, every day, forever, for always? "Eternity is an illusion and immortality a curse", or is it the other way around?

*"Finality is an illusion and immortality a curse. In the end, all that remains is Eternity, a long stretch of graveyard made of Time and tombstones. Life is sweet as strawberries, and it does Man's heart good to see the sun. Every day is a gift and should be appreciated so. But remember the days of darkness, for they will be many, and when they come, they render all else meaningless. The Tapestry never stops weaving."*

It's on this day (which day?) that, after a few hours of wandering, I see something that should not be here, that should not exist in so cruel and empty a world as the Maze: a meadow housing the most picturesque family of deer, more deeply lost in affection for one another than most human clans. The stately stag oversees the fawns play and graze and dance and butt heads and make up and leave, until only the doe remains; her reasons are her own.

I think back to my *Bambi* days on Lincoln Lane. Nuala playing it for me from the moment we'd finished breakfast until she'd completed her chores in the afternoon, and then again after dinner. The One-Armed Man was there too, of course, and pained to hear anything that implied my existence, sullied those moments by wordlessly shaking headphones at me with an enticing smile that I found terrifying.

I remember how peaceful it was to be freed from his detestation after we left, though flash forward to potato peeling, soggy socks, fruit clocks, D.W.'s exposed leg sticking out from under the bedsheets, the combed red hair in the mirror, strawberry stems, and the White Room, and the reality must surely set in: I have never once been free. And from my most formative and vulnerable years, one question has never ceased to wrack my brain: *why me?* What had I done to deserve such hatred at the hands of these men? What was so intrinsically wrong with me that all these predators saw: Toni, Roop, the One-Armed Man, D.W.? And I said no to manhood, to relationships, to family, to happiness, to change, to intimacy, to masculinity, to the being God had made me to be.

Roop assumed I already had: *"God shut you away in a jewellery box to be kept lonely until all this is over and you die."* Whirr... Whirr... Whirr... *"You're done."* Whirr... Whirr... Whirr... *"I know the truth."* Whirr... Whirr... Whirr... *"I'm going to bury you."* Whirr... Whirr... Whirr... *"I want you to die."* ... *"Time is a luxury you are most certainly out of."* Whirr... Whirr... Whirr... Whizz... Whizz...

Oh, look. A deer. A doe. A female deer. (Didn't I already know it was there?). Like in *Bambi*. I enjoyed *Bambi* when I was a child. Nuala once said that during my *Bambi* years, I point-blank refused to walk. At two and a half years old, my only accomplishment was having watched that film a record-breaking number of times on my little swinging chair until one day, the seat broke under my weight. By that evening, I was sprinting like a spitfire and two kilos lighter.

This replays in my head as I slit Bambi's mother's neck, cook, and eat her. My thirst is quenched. Her juices slosh down my chin.

Nature retaliates and hurls upon me a snowstorm. I tear out her guts and organs, get down on all fours and crawl inside. And I take shelter in her warmth.

I rub my hand across my face. The ring brushes harshly across my cracked lips. Beneath my long johns, my Herculean bronze legs are outstretched on a plump velvety couch, a mirroring wine cup in my hand. Ugh, two of my biggest hates: underage drinking and cushions.

I hold up the chalice to my face and admire my blond hair and six-pack, as well as the renewal of my recently deflated muscles. All my poppy scrapes, blistering bubbled burns and crocus bruises have healed and been coated with varnish. I take my right foot in my hand and examine its sole and ball; it's been a long time since I had a couple layers of skin there.

Someone breathes behind me. I turn instantly. There's an Aladdin style of dress hanging from a mannequin. Behind it perfumes her mouth-watering, distinctive scent: strawberries and lemons. Then she steps out from behind it.

"Skye," says the voice of light and I cannot help but smile.

"Aurora?"

"Who else, my dearest one, unless you have found another girl on your travels that I need to contend with?" Ooh, sultry. I like it. It suits her. Oh, how easily I could kiss her.

Her face is a valentine's heart, her eyelashes attractively long, and her baby-pink lips luscious and defined. Far healthier than before, she has vibrant colour in her cheeks now. Her skin is perfect, as is her hair. It's not as plastically straight as before, but rather ripples, and gives her a more goddess-like look. (I hope that isn't blasphemous to say. You're still my Number One, Jesus!). Atop her thick golden fringe sits a red hair band with a figure eight design across her tilted head. Her pointy elf ears have even grown on me; still to this day, I sometimes forget she isn't human. Dark pink flowers form a V-neck and end in two red ribbons on her bright green dress, and its sleeves end at her elbows and droop as usual. And far from being squeezed into a gown that suppresses the existence of her breasts, the twins are pretty voluptuous.

"Stop staring at them."

"I wasn't!" I exclaim defensively, and then burst out laughing. In every way, she looks less like Mecky's toy and more like a girl. She takes quiet, steady breaths.

I sit up slowly in case my over-eagerness shatters the dreamy illusion. Gradually, the surrounding scene come into focus. All about her, enchanted harps play by themselves; the articles of furniture slide gently on the marble-smooth golden tiles; and brightly shining jewels, coins and red diamonds relinquish the need for the dazzling sunlight that beams through the pillared doorway. A little indoor fountain laps soothingly, sightless birds chirp lightly in the crevices of the ancient Grecian architecture, and there's a real sense of *shalom* peace in the safe people-less world beyond the crystal sea outside. And there's a glorious Mount Olympus behind our ancient open-space quarters.

"It's nice here," I admire, pretending this doesn't all pale in comparison to her beauty.

After a long silence, I build up the courage to ask, "Where are we?" Her smile dissipates into utter blankness and her eyes flicker away from me for the first time. OMHD. "Did I die?" She pauses and looks at me gravely. Not with a yes. Nor with a no. Nor even with sympathy. Though her look is not cold, clinical, or confused either. Just grave.

"You are very much alive, young protector. You are just not yourself right now."

"I have been acting a little cray-cray lately, haven't I?"

"Only slightly," she says seriously. "I have been a rather uncomfortable spectator to, dare I risk hyperbolising, contumelious behaviour."

"So, this is a dream?"

"Of course, though whether or not that means this is all one elaborate fabrication crafted by a disturbed traumatised mind is up for discussion."

"But I can see your clothes. And your hands. And your perfectly manicured, blue-polished fingernails. You can't see those in a dream, typically, right?"

She just stares, and I fear I'm losing her. Time to salvage this. And though I hate to touch people, I tap my lap and wink, "Get over here, woman." This is but a dream, so it doesn't really count anyway, right? She laughs, climbs aboard the couch, and sits on my lap, and I breathe in her strawberry and lemon hair, all the sustenance I need in this brief, fabled moment between waking hours. I take note to lock her citric scent in my heart's memory, safe from prying eyes, safe from her family, from the world and its falseness, transience, and hollow promises. Safe from even the better and worse angels of my nature.

My hands travel to her small smooth, overly moisturised feet. I kiss them gently, and massage them with my thumbs, lightly at the top, then gradually apply more pressure as I inch closer to the heel, and I knuckle the arch of her feet. It's so unlike her to murmur or grunt that I let out short breathy giggles each time she does, which is very frequently.

After twenty minutes or so, she lies on the flat of her back, almost dosing. "Back at the Dome, we were jumped. You helped me escape, but… they came for you. What happened?"

"Less than has happened to you. Rest now, sweet Benjamin. Close your eyes." But sleeping is impossible for two reasons: one, if I wake, she will not be there; and two, the immaculate vision becomes a melancholy beauty whose dark inner aches shroud even the gleam of the gold coins, the rainbows bouncing off the tiles, and the summer's day. I beg her to come back to me, but she says she cannot. She polishes the ring I gave her on the Dome with her fingertip, and says, "I dwell here. I took a leaf out of the Wizards' book and attached a segment of my being to the article. I did not want you to be alone. You should not be alone. That has always been the cruelest fate of the Chosen One."

"You poured an ounce of your soul into a cheap circlet of metal?"

"'Cheap'? It looks most expensive."

"It was a steal. Wait. I've shot *whooshy* jets of white light on occasion. Joshua said that's outside the perimeters of my power. Was that you?"

"You channelled the fragment of my person that dwells within the ring, yes. That is all we are in the end: fragments, echoes, memories, shadows, half-stories, ghosts buffeting aimlessly between narratives, unsaid sentences."

"Where is the other half of your *sentence*; the real, physical you?" *Oh, no.* Tears glisten in the corner of both our eyes. I gulp and choke, "Does it hurt?" terrified she might respond honestly.

I had forgotten how strong she was; my bones nearly break when she grabs my ringed finger and kisses it. Though small-lipped, she soaks it like her mouth's wide as a hoover. "It is dark. And cold. And I am so very, very tired. But no, I feel no pain. Not anymore. It has long since fled me and left me alone."

"I'm so sorry. I'm sorry for everything." I think I'm going to be sick.

"Do not be. I was a doll and you breathed life into me. I was a shell and you returned to me my soul. I was Princess Nobody of Nowhere Worth Mentioning. I had nothing to my name and everything concerning me was aimless. And then you came, and you made me feel like a hero. What happened was not your fault. Were I to believe you held yourself responsible, I would feel very sad."

"I turned your family against you. I just couldn't leave well enough alone. I procrastinated and delayed and took offence and became so insular. I fought the Triune only weeks ago and left them alive. I played defence; poor, sad, miserable Thomas, enemy of the Big Bad World, when I could have just gone on the offence and killed them. I'm responsible for all of it." I want to ask her forgiveness, but I wouldn't give it to me, so I won't insult her memory.

"You cannot change what has already been, but you need not be defined by it either. The past is only as strong as your present is powerless. Be the hero I know you to be. Be Skylar. Be the Chosen One."

"I don't think that's possible. My list of enemies is too extensive. I don't know where I am. I can't do what needs to be done." And the harsh truth regarding my destiny solidifies in the core of my being: my preordained path as the Saviour never stood a chance at ending in triumphant celebration.

"This is what you must do: go to the Glitch. When the dogs bark, follow your instincts. When you see and talk blue, there is *barely* any distance between you and the shortcut." I shrug. "The Triune put a curse over the land when they built the Maze. The dew on the grass cries out to them, betraying you, like the blood of a righteous man betrays the identity of his assailant. So long as you remain on Maze ground, the Triune can extend these meadows and hills the length and breadth of Angoria and set you on a course towards everlasting nothingness, not that they would be so merciful. Run to the Glitch."

*Is that a place where people live?* She never says. "But if I enter the Zones, the Fear will see me. It makes people go crazy. And the Triune see everything it sees. And then they kill everyone."

"That has not stopped you before."

"Everyone I've tried to save or inspire has died because of me."

"No. They were murdered because the Triune feared their hope. You are winning. You are more than a conqueror because Good will always triumph over Evil. You are the Triumvir Victorious, and I forbid you to allow anyone to tell you differently. Arise and go now and make finding Joshua your priority. And know that I am with you until the very end of this most tempestuous age."

And then I wake, less-Herculean, bronze, and pampered, to the intoxicating stench of doe guts clogging my nostrils and trachea.

It's hard to explain, but it feels like one thing pulls me into the land of the living while something else drags me into the depths. By the time I open my eyes, I'm not entirely sure which side won the wrestling match, though there is the unfortunate and sickly sensation of strong arms retrieving me from a uterus. No matter. Aside from the terror, the quake, and expectancy of being staked in the heart, I'm quite peaceful.

One of his large strong hands brushes over my mop of hair, and then his spindly fingers run through it like rake teeth. His fingernails scrape away at my dandruff, becoming thickly snowier with their flakes. My scalp is so dead I might as well walk around with a corpse on my head. The scratching is pleasant, like I'm being cleansed by pruning, and my noggin feels more capable of breathing with each erasure of white chunks. He pats my hands slowly with his other palm. My cheek brushes cosily against his denim leg. I'd recognise that texture anywhere.

I inhale the smell of his stolen cigarettes and Copper Paul's *Adidas* aftershave on his wrists. He had thought himself very cool being the first of the under-twelves on the Lane to have the first squiggle of a moustache. I rest across the long legs of his skinny jeans and think about how he seldom wore anything else.

My eyes flicker but, unprepared for the intensity of light all around me, like someone has encased me within a coffin of windowpanes each with a sun behind them, it takes my eyes a while to adjust. But when they do, I see him whip out a handkerchief from the top pocket of his shirt and flick it—he always fancied himself a gentleman, despite all the evidence to the contrary: his filthy tongue, his sordid belching, his lack of manners, dismissal of social mores, his penchant for torturing animals, blackmailing people, and killing whatever had the breath of life in it. I think I allowed him away with it for so long in the hope that friendship evangelism had the power to break his ego, but nothing short of a stick of dynamo was going to blow a hole in that pompous sod's cranium and ease the swelling of his pride.

He tries to look happy to see me, but his overwhelming arrogance pollutes his endeavours. Everything he did from blinking to breathing to handstands to scraping an A in spelling tests was, in his impalpably sound mind, a *tour de force*, a *magnum opus*, a *chef d'oeuvre*, confirmation of his superiority over all his subjects in his monarchical delusion. He taps the handkerchief on his tongue in motherly fashion and dabs away the doe blood that's caked to my face.

His red-brown hair is combed back slickly, and his eyebrows are perfectly plucked. I feel ashamed that the one day I see someone I know, I'm bloodied, scabbed, sweaty, and my hair's a mess. He mocks how rampant and alive my eyebrows look.

"Hideous as a wildfire," he judges. There's a black widow print on his yellow T-shirt.

"It's nice to see you again." I don't mean it right now, but I'm going on faith, hoping to prophesy a change in my reception to him.

"You look ugly, Thomas. A right state. Do me a favour and shave before the finale, you hear? And for the love of all that is holy, would you take a bath? You stink. Really badly. I'm surprised every beast in the Maze hasn't come after you." He thinks it over. "Actually, I'm not surprised. And I mean that in a bad way."

"That is the intention: to smell so expired that they stay at bay. What about you? You're going for the goatie look?" I ask, noticing that while his upper lip squiggle is gone, he has grown a small chestnut on his chin. All he's missing is a sunburn and a couple devil horns, and he'll be all set. "I don't like it."

"Jealous of my good looks?"

"Why are you here?"

He presses down and breathes in my wrists. "You don't smell like almond essence anymore," he says, upset. Oh, gosh. I cringe at the thought that I used to rub my wrists with the golden liquid every morning before school in the hope of attracting the ladies—and by 'lady', I just mean Paige Andrews, not that she was much of a lady, after all.

"Am I in Heaven?"

"If you were, would you be seeing me?" he grins devilishly.

"Point taken."

"Remember that time you told me to repent or I'd go to Hell? What was my response?"

I'd forgotten that. Long before The Incident, I saw the signs he was a sociopath, so I put on my gardening gloves and tried to uproot the seeds in his soul before they germinated and blossomed into full-grown ferocious weeds, but something went wrong. My efforts further hardened his heart and turned him into something lethal.

"You outed me as a hater to the entire school. Turned everyone against me. They ostracised and spat on me. I was seven. I wasn't supposed to know what hatred was. Not yet." Who knows how chronic he is now, aged sixteen?

"I got what was coming to me, didn't I?" It's not a trap. For once, he's sincere.

"Yes," Fetch agrees loudly, as though it's the most stupid, obvious question he's ever heard, but I demand that he stand down and go cool off.

"Don't do that," I say to Roop as he cockily waves Fetch goodbye as though I've chosen the redhead over my stronger inner self. "I'm not a fan of revisionist history at the best of times, let alone with regards to The Incident. We were our worst selves that day, that's all."

He rubs my brow. The stench of his decomposition sails like a mist up my nostrils. It's worse than the doe carcass.

"You don't remember every detail of that afternoon as acutely as you've led yourself to believe. That web is too tangled for even your great mind."

Ignoring him, I continue, "Still, you weren't as bad as I like to remember. Not always, anyway. You could be incredible. There were times you stood up for me in a way no one else ever had. And as for the laughs and stories we shared! And there were days I wished time would just stop so that those rare, precious golden moments would last forever. You were my brother."

"You never spoke this nicely to me when I was alive. But then I die, and it all comes out. Maybe there's something to that, hmmm? An innate companionship with the dead that you simply cannot attain with the living?"

It shouldn't get to me—it really shouldn't—but it does; his condescending tone, as though he knows me, understands me. "Roop…" I begin, though I've prepared nothing to add.

"Yes, Little Thomas?"

"I regret how we parted. And I think this should be the last time we do this. I'm letting you go. I'm moving on. You're nothing more than a shade, an echo, and you're killing me."

He struggles to form words between his eye-widening, snorts, *hawing* mouth gestures, and suspicious eyeing. It's like pulling daisy petals: he will, he won't, yes, no, his mouth is open, then shut again. Will he speak? Will he sneer? He holds a dumb stare for a while, then, here it comes:

"You're not serious? That's it? After all this time, that is all you've come up with?" I remain silent. He realises I am deadly serious, then bursts out laughing and sprays me with saliva. I had forgotten he did that. Well, if I didn't need a shower before, I do now. "Little Thomas," Roop practically whispers and his warm breath brushes softly against my face. "Are you really that naïve? I despise you. And the only reason you are still alive is because I will it so. But as soon as you have fulfilled the purpose for which I need you, I will come after you with the might of a thousand grim reapers and I will drink your boiling blood in a cup. I will take from you your pretty she-elf toy. I will strip from you your Triumvir title. And I will tread, as though on a winepress, your ashes and expose you as the fraud that you are."

He leans down over me and slowly, wetly, Judas-kisses my nose, and I shut my eyes tightly. My head hits the ground hard when he pulls back his legs, gets to his feet and walks away. And when, finally, I'm brave enough to reopen my eyes, I awake cocooned in filth and gunk, but no longer in my doe womb, and he is gone.

# INTERLUDE
# THE LAST PETAL FALLS

[Aurora, months ago...]

Mama, Queen of Loux Laxciila, at the bequest of Mósandrirl, lowered the force field, thus permitting Skye to run freely from his material prison. *Run far and fast, My Chosen, and mayhap, we may meet again when all this is over. Oh, to have seen his face one more time...!*

Papa, Lord of Loux Laxciila and Sovereign of the Nine Elven Kingdoms under the Sun, in his great anger and dominance, deeming me Implicated, Lecher, and Traitor demanded that I be apprehended and incarcerated until after the capture, retrieval, trial, and execution of the purported Dark Lord as decided upon by the Assembled.

His guards—my own subordinates—arrested me atop the Laxciilian Dome and shoved me in a long-thought-forgotten dungeon far beneath the cage-fighting Exceptional Animals, the bank vaults, and the torture chambers. Between his meetings with the Assembled and the Triune, and his ceaseless attempts to defame Skye, I have no idea when Papa found the time to do this, but he hand-painted on the walls all the crimes that I had committed whilst under his compulsion.

These include the dozens of times I hunted down Exceptional Animals from the woods just beyond our barrier and forced them into a gladiatorial arena to fight to the death, although secret bribes that went toward building the Golden Palace usually determined who won the day. The inflammatory paintings on the ceiling judge me for how I personally led a witch hunt against any unregistered magic-practitioners' unlicensed use of the Magical Arts, and moreover, the glee I took in removing their heads as punishment. Other images include how I poisoned any Laxciilian senator who gave the faintest hint of having an independent thought in his head. Senator Dol'ver is included in that one—well, mostly... Papa finished him off. Though my compulsion had been broken, the inherent confusion it wrought was less easily overcome, and truth and fiction were hard to distinguish.

But worst of all were the crimes I committed as High Priestess of the evil Ozymandias' Order of Silent Monks. Splayed out dramatically across the floor—and its paint is still wet—it shows how we built fertility poles and idols of sticks and stones in all the high places. The admittance fee to the sites was one hundred shekels of gold per hour, and for a culture that throws its nose up at silver, there were very few who were unwilling to pay to visit multiple times a day. The gold was fashioned into a sculpture of the Triune-in-Flesh.

Few remain who have actually ever met the Triune—that there are no visual images of them helps boast of their mysteriousness, ambiguity and perhaps even the omnipresence of the threat they pose—but not so for the Triune-in-Flesh. Loyal subjects of the Triune of Warlocks who serve as their tangible witnesses and special operatives, they are L, the Lady of Baalat, and Adonis. L is the King of Sheol and the keeper of dead souls. Contrary to religious fables of everlasting peace, all who died in the creation of the Maze and have died since its erection are his. Sheol bleeds the life out of their souls, metaphysical constructs with energy of cosmic-level proportions, and with them he upholds the Maze.

The seal- and lioness-legged and professional snake-charmer Lady of Baalat is mistress of all worms and reptiles. This is fitting given that she is as slippery as the former and as cold-blooded as the latter.

Last is the hunky womanising sex god Adonis. By far the most wicked, he convinced me, in my compelled state, to demand that the seed of Loux Laxcilla pass through the fire. By this he meant that at harvest time each year, a fire should be lit before the Triad-in-Flesh's golden sculpture and every family had to sacrifice one child. The King of Loux Laxciila was only required to make one sacrifice for all time. To show he was serious about his commitment to Angoria's illegitimate overlords, Papa chose Artaxerzes, the son he shared with his elf-turned-vampire consort; this Baba of mine had been kept hidden away in a dungeon in the walls of the palace for centuries.

Adonis called these killings "a tribute", an honorarium to our superiors for their grace in permitting us to live so freely. Any poor wretches who would not get involved, Adonis told me, were to be stoned with heavy sharp boulders to death. My people lapped up the sacrificial instruction like dogs do water on a scorching day. The Elder of the Wizard Folk Surtskvasír, the First Created Being of Angoria back before the Land was named, did not visit us once in those years. All correspondence was carried out telepathically at great mental strain and never for any longer than two minutes.

Baba Alk'erion later told me that the night Skye came, Angoria shook and the golden sculpture and the high places came crashing down. The Triune-in-Flesh, he added, had just left the kingdom having come to bear witness to the tribute. No one has heard from them since. I hope they are still out there for I very much want to kill them myself.

Papa's behaviour also appalls me. Twenty-one moons fell and rose as I withered away in that stylised dungeon without visitors, food, or water.

Alas snuck in Baba Alk'erion, newly a favourite of Surtskvasír. Having disabled the guards with gentle weapons, Baba, carrying a key, peasant cloak, satchel of food, map, and water crept me through the city. Though I had been raised to believe it was my home, in that moment it felt like the enemy had truly taken over and that the world really was theirs. Baba led me to the stables, like some calculating thief under the cover of a black sky and the eyes of a few white stars. He had prepared my saddle, my sword *Agaela, Silver Dwarven Tooth and Goblin-Cutter*, and my unicorn, Nala. Lastly, he handed me a bag of sugar and carrots for Nala.

Baba told me that Papa had determined to execute me to appease the kingdom's lust for blood, unsatisfied by the timely (or inconvenient, by their standards) exodus of Skye. Hence, Baba was helping me escape and sending me to aid Skye in his quest.

"Come with me," I begged. "All is forgiven. Be a hero!"

"The King can't kk-conttt-in-oo breathin', sisteh. Hisss a plague."

"Which is why you are safer with me!"

"Warrrr isssss com'n, sissstar. I mussss fight."

"You have nothing to gain, Baba. If he dies, no one will accept you as monarch. You know this, yes?"

"H' kil'd Dol'ver... Ffffound 'isss corpse... Need r'venge..."

I stroked his face and smirked, "Bite him."

Surtskvasír sought to manipulate the Elven King's affinity for drunkenness and loose living in the crimson room of fire, dance, and music while Mama, assuming the role of a rogue Queen, lowered the force field once more, permitting my escape. A stirring premonition told me she would never do so again, and I wonder if she too knows her end has come... or *knew* her end *had* come.

Sitting on Nala's back at the barrier, I paused for a moment that I could not really afford to consume redundantly to see if her final redemptive act had quickened some slumbering sympathy for her within my heart. It had not. She was a disgraceful woman, undeserving of the breath in her lungs, though I am glad that her death amounted to a little more than the entirety of her life.

Papa has always been most shrewd and suspecting, and if indeed he sensed too great an eagerness for drink from his eons-old comrade, his eyes would have turned upon all that moved within the radius of his tallest tower and the drums would have sounded and all would have been called upon to answer his bidding.

One last time I asked my brother, Esquire of the Dark Woods to which none have consent to walk, himself included, if he would assist me in this operation, despite the misgivings in my heart and head. Palm to my cheek once I had mounted, he told me he would have gone to the ends of the Great Warren for me, but that his part in this tale was over. A little sad, but mostly proud, I fled.

As Nala rode through the windiest, darkest, most secluded paths in the Black Woods I wondered if I would miss anything affiliated with Loux Laxciila. Nanny and Ebed to an extent maybe, but that was all, besides the greatest treasure within that kingdom— "Aurora Undone". My overall disregard of the place was not meant in a cold, unappreciative way, but the seabed degree to which I esteem sentimentality on the best of days is chronically near-non-existent. Indeed, when Nala finally took flight, once we were beyond the borders of the wood and out of sight of the most skilled Laxciilian's arrow, all I felt was freedom and excitement to see what had become of my dearest one, Skye. I longed to see him step into his destiny and become the man he was born to be.

Oh, to hear his laugh one more time…

Yet weeks passed and I never found him. Orc corpses were the only trail available to me, and even those grew faint with decomposition or consumption in the mouths of the Abominable Hybrid army of the Wizards Three. Regardless, however bleak the nights, dark the whispers of the Trees, or wet my cloak with blood, I have never given up on My Chosen. He saves me and I save him. That is what we do.

Oh, to hear his laugh one more time!

He must have slipped on the ring before falling sleep, because a telepathic link opens between us, marrying our minds. I explain this to him and ask if he finds this too great an invasion of privacy, but though he responds that he oh so desires for this to be real, he tries to convince himself that he only dreams. Grieved in heart, I tell him then to take off the ring. I refuse to be implicated in the mental trickeries and perverse abuses of the Host of the Great House of Angoria, yet a twinkle in his eye tells me he believes what I have said. His lips fumble, and between them peeps his tongue as often happens when he speaks, but he says naught. And he looks hairy, unwashed, undernourished, and beautiful.

"I hate Green," he mopes. He is usually such a broody and mature hero that sometimes I forget he is still a hormonal teenage boy who routinely retaliates to whatever stimulus he encounters.

I laugh. "Give him time. He is a little grim-faced, and a little rough, but you have more in common than you yet realise. I think you will grow to love him like a Papa."

"Good one! He hates me," he states, offended to the core by some unkind remark that Cillian Joshua must have made.

"You have a powerful anointing on your life. It only makes sense that jealous heroes and evil zealous enemies would want to snuff out your light."

"That was unhelpful," he says, wishing I had put my hand on his shoulder, encouraged him to cry about his qualms, and urged him to gossip.

I explain further: "Skye, you suffer the inevitable cost of clarity. Had you been instructed in the ways of your destiny by a dream, a night vision rife with symbolism and multi-layered levels of meaning, your primary task would not have been to save the world, but to interpret the dream. That would have been your cost, your penalty, your payment. Instead, you were told that you were the Chosen One; who your enemies were; and that you are to destroy them, and in doing so, this global prison they have built. Hence, to maintain the balance between Good and Evil, currently skewed though it is, you suffer the cost of abundantly clear revelation."

"So, I'm cursed because Mósandrirl is a loudmouth?"

"No. You are salt in a wound that needs healing. You are light in a crisscrossed snare infested with darkness. You are hope to those who have inwardly died without it. There is a target on your back because you are the sharper arrow."

He pauses, and bows his head with embarrassment, not believing any of it. He is thrown into a fit of blinking, as though attempting to erase the compliment—the truth—from his most wonderful, imaginative, and alluring mind. With tears in his eyes, he blubbers, "I don't want to be salt, light, hope and metal-tipped missiles made of sticks. I always thought I wanted to be the hero. But this is hard. Can't I just go back to the shadows and the quiet?"

"Skye, you were chosen because of your pain. Your whole life you were a victim; that is what you told me. You nearly died in the womb. There was a baby-killing doctor in the hospital where you were born who nearly got his claws on you but for the timely arrival of a nurse. You learned to draw hiding under your bed from D.W., the White Room physician. You were despised at school, at home, in your community, and in another world, all because they could see what you could not... Your destiny. Who better to be a slayer than he who had been slain day after day for years?

"You were chosen for your rage. For every time they tripped you up, stole your schoolbooks, urinated on you, defamed you, struck you and drew blood, and although you had the skill and the speed and the martial arts to terminate them, and chose not to... because to do so would have been wrong.

"You were chosen for your hatred of all living things: ever-watching mockers, liars, and bullies; men who represented all you feared you would become; the woman who gave you life yet took it from you again with her choice of bedfellows; leaders and their blind followers; your church for doing nothing to help you; and yourself for never fighting back or being able to lie in the bath long enough for the pain to end in its entirety.

"You, who had been the most humbled and submissive, the most silent in your grief and distress, the strongest in weakness, and the angriest at human frailty and spiritual scourge, would avenge those who had endured suffering and could not help themselves—whether they deserved rescuing or not. And even though the villains you would face would be nastier and larger and more numerous, and there would be neither thanks nor reward, the prey would become the apex predator. The crocodile, the lion, the killer whale, the wolf, the dinosaur, the man... And the ghost you had always been would become a deadly poltergeist and those unsaid words would become action.

"That is why you were chosen, Skye. That is why you fight. For no cause, no nation and under no banner... But because fighting is the only thing keeping you and the other weaklings from being dead."

Delicately, I place my palm against his cheek, and after a while, he warms it with his own. "I know the last memory you have of me is my refusal to come with you. But I would be amiss were I not to tell you what you meant to me that night and what you still mean now..."

"I'm buried in a hole in the earth, sleeping, and I think a metal shoe just stepped on me," he says abruptly, then his front streams with blood.

"Wake up!" I scream, and as they pass through his mind, a mirage of images flash before me, and I believe that my perfect Elven memory can lead me right to him.

Mornings darken to nights, and nights into months, and still I have not caught a glimpse of him. Yet I always find boulders of corpses before long, reassuring me that my efforts are not in vain.

Atop my steed, I am in an empty circle of curled grass, enclosed by tightly knit trees, beneath a metallic green-silver glow. The barks of the trees make devilish faces at me with each passing shadow, filled with mockery, cunning and ill intent. A great silver tree of many branches—each pointing somewhere different and undoubtedly dangerous—stands before me. It has thrown its arms in confusion, perplexed by which direction it recommends. The top of a little door can be seen in between its sluggish trunks, so cleverly concealed by leaves that it is only by Elven sight that I spy it. Perhaps it is home to a family of Talking Rabbits.

Then, flakes appear in the sky. At first, I think it is ash, falling in clumps, following a battle of fire far beyond my hearing, travelling in gusts of wind. But this is not ash. It is cold, so very cold, and at the touch my hand stings wet and red. I think this is snow. I look up and see the most stunning flurry of nature I have ever had the pleasure of witnessing. Eaves of white fall, unique as Men and Elves. I open my mouth to swallow, then tumble painfully to the ground as Nala is shot dead with several arrows.

I leap to my feet as my steed crashes to the ground in an unmerciful heap, undignified in view of the valiant life she lived. In too quick a movement for my attackers to see, I arm myself with *Agaela*.

"Who dares ambush the Lady of Loux Laxciila?" I do hope that does not sound too much like something Mama would say.

It is only when they creep into the hazy green light that I see or hear them. One looks like a man stripped of melatonin and elongated; he rides what could be a boar were it not so coated in steel and digging the ground beneath him with dog paws. Another larger figure sits upon a large four-legged steed with the face of a great piranha. Seven heavily armed hunters, male and female, glare on foot close to wide-barked trees, but remain silent. Like Edgar, these are surely mercenaries who have been offered passage home, or the pleasure of tactility and wealth. A goblin captain almost the size of a Man with a magnificently defensive mask stands strong, blades projecting from his boots and wrists. Behind and around him jeer, hop, and cackle other fawning green-skins. It is like they have never seen a woman before.

But most fearsome of all is a tall figure with a coal face, small ruby eyes with black pupils that chill colder than the snow, a black coat and long silver hair. I believe he belongs to a race that before tonight I had only read about, that of the Almost Men.

"How did you sneak up on my Elven ears?" I order. My enemies shuffle about and encircle me.

The shadowy figure rips a shield from a goblin's arm, unrepentantly tearing off the simian's limb in the process and throws it before me. The heavy snow corrupts with black blood. I drop my eyes for but a second and see all that I need to: a peacock. The symbol of immortality and of my elves: Laxciilians.

This was Papa's doing. "Mehkabikil gave me away."

"Yes," he grins lowly, baring fierce spotless teeth; his eyes burning brighter and crueler than before. "He cast a simple but effective silence charm on the shield, preventing anyone from hearing whoever was behind it... until we wanted to be heard." Then he races toward me.

And my last thought is of Skye, and oh, how I wish I could have heard his laugh one last time...

# 22
# ORC-GORGER

I breathe in the fresh frosty air of the mountain range sandwiched between four walls of hedge, static electricity, wood, and stone, respectively. More clear-minded having seen her, I'm taking Aurora's advice to cop myself on and get off the uninhabited rolling hills and get back in the game, but the trek was a lot easier when I was delirious.

It's been dark all day. When morning light finally breaks through, it is accompanied by a thick wave of moisture that closes in with unnatural haste. The gas fires stalagmites of ice. One only flecks my nose, but it feels like a knife has punctured the flesh. More ice shards pierce my hands. Red patches like polka dots splotch and bleed heavily. The ice pierces my legs with a thousand needles too; I haven't felt cold so nastily since my baptism on Bettystown beach. I throw on my hood and my exhausted legs gallop; somehow putting a vital fifteen seconds or so between us, then stop to slip my boots on my bare feet. I can't risk the loss of toes or my feet getting struck and having to experience the hellish feeling of hacks in a world without *Talcum* powder. Deep down, I never once believe that outrunning the daggering hail is possible.

My solution? To go all-out *The Princess Bride*-mode and hurl myself down the face of the mountain. Every bone in my body aches by the time I tumble to the bottom, but it does the job. One of those things that only works in a fabled reality, I suppose.

Within an hour, the clouds stop squeezing stalagmites overhead. It ceases instantly and gives way to a harmless curtain of drizzle that floods my barren mouth with some much-needed $H_2O$. (For a moment, I was afraid my tongue was going to cement to my palate). I also fill Joshua's canister. In my valley, puddles waterlog stretches of the overgrown mucky hills.

The irregular rocks that weren't drowned in the rain form a kind of stepping stone bridge. I trod the newly formed path pretty well (until I slip) and there must be shrunken icy missiles swimming in the pond because my left hand sizzles when it goes under. Thank God for reflexes, because another second down under could have done irreparable damage. My filthy trousers bloat, heavy with drink which scalds my legs, and pile on ten pounds. I slip them off, carry them by the bone-dry waist, and let them go cardboard-crisp under the sudden blast of arid heat as all colour erases from above.

The sky hasn't been white three hours when it purples, thickens and runs like steaming melted tar, and what is sure to be an extended nightfall fast approaches. But why the sudden need for darkness in this barren landscape? What are the Triune planning that requires all eyes to be blinded? To what does the darkness give speed? It is not long before I get my answer.

From not too far off, I hear toothy punitive grimaces, and smell something foul and expired. It's like rotten eggs, sour milk, and sewage all rolled into one, with a generous sprinkling of post-mortem blood for good measure. The growls soon give way to unintelligible bickering, the likes of which one might expect to hear in a pub full of dumb brawling drunkards. In the background, there's a *chuck-a-chuck-a-chuck* machine-gunning clatter of weaponry.

Keeping as close to ground-level as I can, I scale up the next hill face and down the far side to get a better look and hide behind a large rock.

The rickety roll of the wooden wheels gets notably louder every second and is made all the more harrowing by the silence on the mountains. Two giant headless men, whose faces are worn on their chests, grab my attention first, understandably. They move unsteadily, like the swampy ground sucks their boulder feet down with each step. They look strong but vulnerable. Small simians scream at them venomously.

"*'Acapella'?*"

"*Akephaloi*, Fetch."

"How do you know what they're called?"

"I wrote about them in my book, briefly."

From beyond the corner of the foot of the grey drab mount, I note a mixture of neighing and whimpers. Soon, two reined creatures like ponies in ram coats appear. Lambs worked before their slaughter, they suffer severe blows by their miniature cretin master. One of the Warpers is missing a hoof, so I have no idea how it still walks. Maybe because it knows better than to stop. The basher turns just as his allies come into view: an armada of goblins and orcs!

Both species belong to the *Orcana* family, according to *The Commonest Daemons and Warlocks and How to Vanquish Them*, a book I read in the Laxcillian Library. Both goblins and orcs once belonged to clean or respectable races. Those that sought immortality through Dark Magic became the mindless goblins. They know only to act on instinct, and their instinct is evil! They have an innate drive towards subservience; they need to obey a greater evil or they simply die.

I think back to their smoking corpses on the day they tied me to the Saint Catherine's Wheel and wonder, were they taken by surprise when they were murdered, or did they beg to be cooked when they knew it was the flame-thrower's will?

On the other hand, the orcs, again according to the literature I read in Laxciila's chronicles, came from beneath; turned and twisted by the Void after death. In addition to greater height and upper-level body strength than goblins, they also lust. The methods employed in both species' creation predates Gregory Saint Germaine—with an E at the end of Germaine's pseudoscience, so they aren't to be confused with the Hybrids.

Mósandrirl once told me that when the Triune gave Angoria the head's up that they would unleash the curse that created the Maze, hundreds of thousands of woebegone hopeless miscreants from the world of Men slaughtered themselves with the promise of being reanimated as wealthy orcs. (Though if I was as rich as they purportedly are, I think I could afford a bath). People never do fail to repulse me. According to recent statistics, an estimated seventy million orcs prowl the side streets of the Maze and champion the Triune's power in the Blocks. (How Joshua ensured we avoided nearly all of them is beyond me). Added to that, the wizard also told me that millions of those poor devils were too weak or deeply buried to claw their way out of their graves, so they died of suffocation immediately after being transformed. Breathing dirt is awful tough on the lungs, after all. Serves them right. If they haven't already, I hope they rot!

I wish the same for this filthy crowd. One of the orcs, who looks a little worse for wear, yells at the top of his croaky, cacophonous voice: "Hurry it up, you sacks of scum! We have far to travel and less time to get there than I would like! Hurry, yon filthy mongrels! Smutty curs! Grubby, pinching army of tin! Crusty, slimy gorillas! The Wizards Three anointed that on this day the sun be hidden and darkness fall over all the Maze! Make haste with the blackness afforded to you! Hurry it up, foul greasy rodents! Keep it moving! Even the Lifeless Mountains have eyes! No time for slacking! Misbegotten eaters of rats and cockroaches!"

Funny little thing, their Bat-gwai leader is. It has been awhile, but I'd recognise him anywhere. Zj'hakim! I'm surprised he's alive. I could have sworn I killed him back when I was mad... only a handful of days ago. He's a resilient little fellow.

Some of the goblins push the wooden cart, which is missing a wheel, along the bumpy path. Most surround it casually and leave the work to the Warpers, still getting heavily lashed by the goblin that, I now see, has buck teeth and tusks. His hair is pulled back so tightly I'm reminded of Nuala. A strong gush of wind threatens to expose the apparatus on the cart, but the single-minded slaves of the Triune forbid this from happening. Whatever is on the cart is well-covered by a filthy once-cream sheet and will remain so until the Triune are present to witness the unravelling. Or until I burn it to ash.

Peeping behind the rock, I observe that their snot-coloured noses vary from slits to pointy as the Grinch's. Suddenly, I beware their potent sense of smell as my pores pump thick salty sweat as abundantly as kernels in a popcorn machine. And because their ears are larger than elves', I massage my heart because it's thumping like a mad yoke.

I have a nosey in Joshua's bag of tricks in search of matches, oil, grenades, or I don't know—a living flame in a jar. And a bow and arrows would come in handy, too. Thankfully, I subtly collected weapons from all the Blocks I entered during my peace talks campaign, before I went somewhere between a bit mad and full-on off the deep end. As I search, one of the goblins must attack one of its more delicate neighbours, because Angoria's most renowned sewer rats are now literally tearing strips off one another. About a dozen goblins leap onto the cart and form an X with their limbs, protecting the cloth-covered contents.

I sit tight and consider my options: one, wait it out, and follow them from a safe distance in a few minutes, and kill them all at an opportune time; two, spring a trap on their fearless leader, Zj'hakim, when he departs to relieve himself, and then don his clothes, and masquerade as him; three, follow them until they unwittingly lead me off these hills and toward my destiny, and then do nothing pragmatic and let the world burn; or four, start an insurgence, and then just stand back and watch them all kill each other.

OMHD! How long has she been there?

My heart leaps with fright as I behold two great zooming yellow eyes staring at me, only a couple metres off. They're attached to the two feet short body of a pygmy, a goblin child. She's as ugly as the others in that she has the same marshy skin, elongated forehead, and thin strips for lips from which project warthog teeth and breath. Strange as it is to admit, there's something adorable about her, too: she has cute turtle cheeks, vibrantly curly eyelashes, and massive doe eyes too big for her face. She plays with a dog tail like it's a teddy and offers it to me to cuddle. Her smile is a rainbow. If she wasn't birthed by and for evil, I would honestly want to babysit her. As it stands, she represents the next generation of Angoria's oppressors. The enemies I swore to annihilate in Laxciila back when they were hypothetical, absent, voiceless shadows, for no other reason than because that is apparently my job.

This reveals the true sickness that lies within all living things. That this semi-cute demon is my enemy just because it's—*she's*—green. And I'm the Chosen One, the killer, the legitimate slayer, the one who has been given a pass to murder that I never asked for—the authorised Destroyer. I am the Mex Confetricus. Not in the way Mehkabikil led people to think, but I am. I am above the law. I am the law. I am better than everyone else simply because the Higher Orders kidnapped me from Earth and ordained it so. It makes sense now, the reason Joshua put so much pressure on me to kill mega-big spiders and random farmyard animals who scurried past us. It was all preparation for this. To know that when the moment came and I had to: that I could kill, that I could do what needed to be done. Because I am superior. And I have to make the hard choices, the deadly decisions, for the greater good.

No wonder he's a stone-cold, viper-tongued, brooding, nasty booze-hound. Being the Chosen One drove him mad.

But now that the moment is at hand, I don't know if I can kill her. She looks innocent... apart from the severed tail and the overall resemblance of wickedness and cruelty. But if I let her live, she will kill. It's in her nature. And she'll breed killers, and train those killers to kill, until she is killed.

She opens her mouth and yawns lengthily. And then she screams. It is a long scream, a harsh scream. I'm surprised the rocks do not cry out and shatter into mossy smithereens.

And Fetch thumps her jaw and slits her throat. I flee.

Drawn by her squeal, orcs climb the mountaintops and try to sniff me out, but I'm masked by their own repugnant odour. Keeping as close to

547

invisible as I can, I dash along the rock-toothed grassy terrain until I'm about twenty metres ahead of the wagon. I paste my back behind a large rock. My heart races. I can't assume none of their amber traffic light eyes saw me, so whatever I do next has to be done quickly.

I keep low and pull out a quiver. I draw out a handful of arrows, too, each with a resin-dipped tow just below the silver arrowhead, respectively. I've never used thermal weapons before, and I am acutely aware of the potential repercussions for giving away my position like this; but the last thing I want right now is to dance toe-to-toe with each one of these brutes in hand-to-hand combat.

*Let it fly… Let it burn… Let it ignite…*

I release the first arrow and it skirts along the grass and dies. *Flip. Focus.* I release the second arrow. It goes further but smashes into a big stone. That one was spotted for sure. Last chance. I readjust my position, take aim, envisage where I want the arrow to go. The wagon, the wagon, the wagon… I release the third arrow. Strike!

I fire another, then another. With each shot, the inferno gets higher and boogies with more Dionysian revelry amidst the tangible black sky. Some orcs are so devoted to protecting whatever's on the wagon that they burn trying to preserve it by pushing it to the grass. The screeches they unleash as they barbecue evoke no sympathy—as they'll evoke none from their tormentors in Sheol. A few singed or burning cretins have the cop-on to back away from the fiery wagon and run, and they form a serpentine red line that traces along the hills and shifts and bends and splinters into sizzling gashing lumps of soggy flesh and tin.

After the initial confusion and surprise has worn off, a few orcs and goblins begin to fire cocktail stick arrows back at me. I squat lowly, keeping my chin close to the ground, and crawl like a crab for cover under some shrubbery, then hold my breath for dear life. Huffs and puffs and *grrrs* alert me to the general whereabouts of their swordsmen. They're closing in on me. I might have an action-packed story to tell Joshua at our reunion, after all. It was naïve of me to think it wouldn't come to this. I whip open my sack of goodies and draw out two gold-handled swords.

Twelve creatures run past my rock before I strike the first one. His armour seems thin and weak, but it resists the force of my sword—though perhaps this has more to do with my unwillingness to mortally wound any of them. Why can't I get over that? I mean, he doesn't afford me the same luxury; and for a fat little guy, he packs a powerful punch, as my bust lip soon learns.

Yet, just then, something awakens inside of me. A lion! A mighty roaring king, intent on displaying to his pride his awesome strength and credentials! And, lost in infinitesimal hysteria and power-lusting craze, I spring from my den; then lash out at the poor devil, and he hurtles off the mount. I'm actually unsettled by how quickly whatever trace of benign benevolence I had left grows wings and takes flight, until only an excitement for battle remains, and more than this, an eagerness to initiate war.

A few of my foes back away. I pull Joshua's green coat out of the bag and throw it on in the space of two seconds. This thing is as strong as chainmail, as three of them figure out when they strike at me at once. I must look so threatening to them, all donned in Joshua's gear. I think his coat has gained greater notoriety among the orc community as a whole than the Chosen One. Well, that's about to change.

"I see my reputation precedes me. Good. Orcs, I am the Avenging Son. The Final Plague. Triumvir Supreme." They charge at me. Darn. I had five more of those planned.

One runs at me. I knife his hind legs, one of his only exposed areas. "The Ultimate Judgement." A second later, I poke another in the eye through his visor with a sword, and another in both eyes with both swords. One hulky brute armed with a chained mace and black metal shield thick as a small tree puts up a real fight, but I eventually damage his feet so badly he can hardly stand, let alone attack. "Achilles Made Manifest."

One hits my arm with a swipe of his toothy discoloured boomerang.

"Mmm," he groans and foams at the mouth, then licks some poor victim's blood clean off it. He laps his froggy tar tongue at me. Slitting the legs clean off everyone in my way, narrowly dodging their swipes as I go, I sprint over to Boomerang and hurl myself on top of him. What follows is a lot of tumbling, bruising, and near-neck-shattering jolts, but when I've got him alone, the claws come out: I *Tudan Zuki* him. *Age Zuki. Kagi Zuki. Mae Geri.* And all this, sandwiched between weapon-to-weapon warfare. Nothing works.

He withdraws something like a hurling stick from his back pocket and batters my cheek with it so fiercely, the wood snaps. I'm blinded for two seconds too many, in which time he grabs my right arm, and a newcomer (a peculiarly tall orc) grabs my other one. They prise the swords from my hands. They snap one and fling the other on a large flat stone just beyond my reach. Another goblin who leaps about like a toad for a while then hops behind me and cements me to the spot; his froglike digits keep my shoulders from moving. I try to wrestle free, but to no avail. Another goblin I call Cackle, for obvious reasons, bounces over on her tiptoes and manically dances to a tune only she can hear. When the song has run its course, she glides over, her feet moving in semicircles, and scrapes my face in a half-moon shape with her filthy inches-long talon. By the smell of it I can only guess where it's been. Then she reaches into her sackcloth skirt pocket and whips out a dagger.

I elbow Frog in the gut, as in the final moves of *Pi-Nan-San-Dan*, then grab him by the belt and thrust him in front of me. He gets a nasty poke in the belly, before erupting into a cannibalistic frenzy which culminates in him biting Cackle's breast. Most eerily, she's still cackling. With lightning quick movements, I break both their necks.

Then I step on the in-tact sword and it flips up. I grab the handle and spin just in time to parry a shower of arrowheads and an almost-fatal thrust from the tall one. He and I *clang-clang-clang* for a while whilst boomerangs whiz past our heads and arrows hail from above, but in the end, I slice his arms off, then his head. Well, kind of. It's not a clean cut, but the gurgling and name-calling cease. "Skylar, Orc-Gorger."

Actually, that's a good idea! And no sooner have I thought of it than I hear Skylar fly out of the bag and begin cutting down the archers from further off and causing mayhem all on its own.

I cartwheel over to his heavy thick shield (he dropped it or set it down at some indeterminate time amidst all the chaos) and throw it on my back. I do pretty well actually for someone who has never cartwheeled before. My hand only slips at the last second, and it's over some gooey mustard-smelling blood, so it's not really my fault. The shield is as big as me, which means so long as I keep my back to the archers, I'll be covered from their cocktail sticks—until Skylar gets to them. This just leaves

Boomerang and me.

Our duel is certainly not the fiercest, but it lasts longest. He's quite a skipper, so he is, incapable of staying put and just fighting me. After a couple minutes of this, frustration becomes me and though I'm not up to date on my demoniac anatomy studies, I kick whatever hangs between his legs and send it zooming like a rocket up to his stomach. His pupils dilate, his bestial mouth shrinks to a small hole, and he collapses. There's my answer. "Expert of Orcish Physiology." Boiling fluid like pea green soup oozes down his leg in streams.

I could do this all day. Slicing, dicing, and inflicting kinds of pain I'd never dream of back on Earth. Of course, I don't have to. I grab Skylar as it's whizzing past. The few remaining archers scram, as do the cretins who had just scaled down the mountainside. "The Final Cataclysmic Storm," I call back after them, though they probably don't hear me. Pity. I'm ready for another fight—eager, actually.

Then fear, conviction, or clarity slaps me hard—and warns sternly: *do not turn into Joshua.* We are similar in a lot of ways, aside from the notable physical attributes: we brood, we don't like to talk, we're emotionally inarticulate, we're both exceptionally skilled at what we do best, and we hate injustice. Who knows, maybe he was once as pacifistic as I am, but then just snapped after he got a taste for blood or the rush of adrenaline that accompanies slitting someone clean.

But I cannot give into the deathly indulgence. I cannot risk losing control. Not again. Not after Roop. Not that the Triune need to know...

Every engagement I have had with evil thus far has portrayed me in a poor light: I've been the prisoner of goblins, mercenaries, elves, arachnids, Gregory Saint Germaine—with an E at the end of Germaine. I have to show them that the kid gloves are off, that I am a real player in all this and not just some child being aimlessly buffeted from one bondage cell to another, so I clamber back up the mountain where the great and mighty campfire still burns brightly, dining on the wagon. Whatever was on it is gone now, but the path is littered with… jakers… eighty-odd foul corpses and half-dead demons. *Did Skylar and I really strike so many?*

Sleeves rolled up, I get my hands dirty, and drag all the vermin to the centre, where I arrange them in a large B. Then I set them all ablaze and, because I know they're watching, give the Triune a cheeky wink.

# 23

# MONGRELS

I try my best to honour Aurora's last request: to get off these endless mountains and find Joshua. Overall, I'm doing quite well with the first part until I lose my footing in a wood near a meadow, roll down a slope, and land in a heap of blood-spattered human lumps and deer meat. Several dozens of stags have had their scalps scythed and mauled and their antlers whipped. Some of their necks are crushed and limp; many have been pulled too far back and snapped like a cheap brightly coloured elastic band. Their skeletons are cagey like insect shells, their coats foamy, red, and blistered. There are sad black eyes everywhere.

Vomit stirs in the pit of my stomach, but I do not permit it to rise. I need every kilo of weight I can spare at this point. Like a drunk, I stumble over the foul-smelling butcher pit, mouth and nose covered with the neck of my shirt, dirtier than any carcass heaped beneath me, and saturated in body oils thick as margarine. My other hand shields my eyes from the thick black clouds of flies with their irritating chorus of buzzes. When I see cat-sized rats scoot over the sprawled expired meats at superhuman pace, I tiptoe ten times faster, and shake all over like a hypochondriac in a dystopian horror novel.

What could have done this? I soon get my answer.

From a pit beneath comes the howl of dogs. And down tumble tens of deer and cloven hooves like women's shoes as though into a sinkhole. And up claw the sniffing noses, pointed furry ears, and hungry eyes of hellhounds. Dozens of paws pounce and patter and squish down on the stag frames. As they scale from the pit to all-fours, some stop to feast with carnal relish, but they are in the minority. One gets its foot caught in a ribcage as though in a leg-hold trap. The "heh-heh-heh" of their dangling tongues and excited yelps sickens me, and the wet compulsive snap of their teeth heats my blood to boiling. The smell of rank musk and blood weakens my innards and sticks to my clothes like cigarette smoke. Snapping jaws of half-surfaced hounds nearly nip my boots, eyes taunting me with giddy evil mockery. But worst of all is the sound, clear as a bell, of my name on their tongues— "Chosen One!"

It's a rocky road, but I sprint like crazy to an enclosure of trees that separates the meadow from the field. I run as close to the irregular shaped barks as I can, grateful for whatever cover they provide. But the yips multiply: dozens, fifty, one hundred. I'll soon be overtaken unless I change dimensions. The only way left is up.

And comprehensible thoughts abandon me. I throw rationality to the wind. And I give in to the fictitious, the imaginary, and the hyper-real. I run with speed not even adrenaline can provide. I jump like I'm Spider-Man. I swing from sturdy boughs like I'm Tarzan. I no more than wince as the bark cuts my rough and calloused hands. I kick any mouth that comes near me, not caring if they somersault in reverse, or if their jawbones shatter or if their teeth sink into their tongues like ham. Good enough for them. At my core, only one natural instinct remains: survival.

I climb a tree, even though I've never climbed one so tall in my life, narrowly missing the gnashing mouths' exceptionally high jumps. When I can go no further, I look down at the predators. A few of them stand out, in particular: a black and brown mutt with beady pallid eyes, prominent dark eyebrows, and a mostly human mouth, but for much sharper canines; a tanned beast more fiend than animal with spindly legs, a massive head, and even larger jaws; a midget dressed as a punk rocker with a frog tongue too elongated to fit inside its trap; and a random man dressed as a dog who, in view of his crass displays of indecency, appears to forget the breed to which he actually belongs. (To each their own…). The onesie man aside, the other oddballs are Warpers, who smell like they've been fumigated in *Bolta*, disinfected of their free will and loyalty to Gregory Saint Germaine—with an E at the end of Germaine.

I've got a bow, some arrows, and see so little ground that I'm guaranteed to hit something. And why shouldn't I kill them? They're trying to kill me, and they'll see it through if they get the chance. They've already killed everyone in the pit, and they've probably used it as a dog bowl, toilet, and vile copulation bed.

My tree sways dramatically with the force of so many head-banging skulls. This makes taking aim more difficult, but not impossible. I miss my targets, but twelve are dead within a few short minutes. An arrow snaps one of Punk Dawg's front legs. He then tries to pull the arrow out with his teeth but cannot because his tongue keeps getting in the way. I snicker, then wait for the feeling of regret to come, or the thrill of the kill, or the tears—but I feel nothing. I'm just doing my job, and they, because they are my enemies, deserve it.

Well, congratulations, Resistance. It took me long enough, but I have unquestionably finally become your weapon: your emotionless machine, your do-what-must-be-done Chosen One. The Dark Lord of the Resistance. The Destroyer cultivated by your prophecies and fear. Next time I face the Triune, I will have no qualms ending them on the spot.

"I commend you, Triumvir. You had a good run," growls the dog with the eyebrows. "Few prisoners have succeeded in escaping the Triune, and fewer still have run as long and far as you have. But alas, this ends the only way it was ever going to. You should have stayed on the Earthen Star, little one."

"Rest assured, pet, I had little say in the matter." I have to say it more than once for him to hear over the yips, yelps, and barks of his company.

"Then what say you renege your Triumvir duties, Harker; however ambiguous they may be?" I'm not sure what he means by "Harker". Maybe it's a doggish dirty word. "Surrender yourself to Lord Lear and promise to return home instantly, and I'll call off these hounds."

Yeah. Because that promise worked out so well for Edgar and Skull. This mutt must think I'm pretty darn thick. I already know cross-dimensional transference is not within the Triune's power. "To a world where dogs do little more than sniff dirty grass and whine when abandoned by their owners? Oh, don't make me go back," I taunt.

"'Owners'?" He seems genuinely shocked, repulsed even, whereas the man with the flappy dog ears glued to his head looks most intrigued.

"Mm-hmm. And they eat food... from a packet."

"Take him down, boys," he orders, and throws his head to the side. The head-butting accelerates. It won't be long before this tree collapses.

"What's your name?" I call.

"Kenny," he responds.

"When I get down from this tree, Kenny, I'm going to kill you myself."

"What a bold sentiment—however misleading it may be. I'll make sure it's your epitaph!" He turns and walks away.

Since this trunk's on its last legs, I leap onto another giant broccoli. Then another. And another. From up here, I see the outline of a Maze entrance towering a couple thousand metres diagonally on my left. It's weird, but the place I should least want to be seems to offer me the most semblance of safety. Not long term, of course, but at least from my present predicament. But no sooner have I decided on my next destination than I feel a chill like evil is watching. I turn my head to the right and see a black cloud of smoke heading straight towards me like a fiery cannonball. Bursts of fire jet from black gloves and scorch the tails and paws of the perversities... *Mósandrirl? Sharmedes? Pyro?*

And as quickly as it debuted, it's gone, leaving only streaks of smoke in the sky, and a confused sea of sizzling dogs scurrying about madly on top of each other and into hedges. Soon the whole wood will be red and burning. I climb across branches and leap and sink my nails into bark for dear life, until finally I make it to a tree with no close neighbours. The fire chases after me and soon my tree is like a pole in a witch trial. I jump off before I'm smoked off. And I drop thirty feet.

There's a lot I could complain about. The landing. The dizziness. The gashes. The likelihood that I've broken, or at least sprained, something. The fact that half my face was torn off by prickly boughs during my descent. The pinching stones I landed on. The funny angle at which my leg is pointing.

But not right now. I'm not dead, and I have no time to behave as though I am. Lying down is for sleepers and corpses. I must make the best of this opportunity I've been afforded, not wait until fingers of smoke twiddle up my nostrils and my skin melts and bubbles.

I follow the trail that leads to the Maze opening I saw atop the trees. It takes a while before it comes into view, and when it does, what I witness before it spurs me to exasperate and to quicken the day of the Triune's eradication: the pitiable form of a quietly moaning, dying dryad.

Where did she come from? How did she escape her Block? Was she trying to make it through the Maze and on toward Loux Laxciila for the Meeting, or to Aarilyn the Wise Woman's city, Breathing Stone? Or was she running around aimlessly, and if so, how? Maybe she'd been taken captive by the Triune, as I've read is their custom, and was being led away to a brothel frequented by orcs, and escaped. I consider asking for her name, but it'll do no good: her root-like windpipe, grown outside the neck, is severely crushed and splintered.

Her smooth blue skin is losing colour. Some of her green scales and light brown wooden chips lie scattered on the grass. Purple blood spews from the holes in her face like she shaved carelessly and soaks her blonde fringe and long brown tresses. Her knees have been mauled off. One of her arms has died and discoloured. The other one flows freely at the elbow. A dress made of reeds covers her from the breasts to her thighs, and clumps of moss are everywhere. A purple bubble froths the corner of her purple mouth, and a purple ribbon trickles down her left cheek. Her eyes are dying flames.

A year ago, I would have walked on by. Prayed for her. Hoped for the best. Then went back to mourning my own troubles. But now, I own my zone and take responsibility for those in my plot, my sphere of influence, my inheritance. Even if I have no way of saving her.

Thus, I kneel beside her, stroke her hair, and smile.

"I'm Benjamin," I say, then break it down for her, syllable by syllable. She tries to formulate the sounds on her lips, but "Benjy" is all she can muster, and for once, I don't hate it.

Her eyes fixed on mine, she says, "Ada." It takes her ages to say this one thing.

I nod and say that's a beautiful name.

Then I point to one of her metallic green scales and tell her of a Saint Patrick's Day float that colour I designed, but never made. I nod at the cerulean skin beneath all the glittering scales and tell her I once watched a street artist slap paint that colour on a sheet of canvas until the blobs and splatters became a girl. He'll never make it big, but next to Munch and Botticelli, he's my favourite artist. I beam at the square azure scales that box her eyes, and whisper that's my favourite shade of my favourite colour.

I don't think she understands me. There's a look of fear in her eyes, either because she's dying, or because she thinks I'll speed it up. Who knows how far my haters' poison has spread? But I don't know what else to say. I'd introduce her to Jesus, but she's not human. I'd give her words of encouragement, but building others up is not how I was hardwired. I'd show her compassion, but what does that even look like? Armed with nothing else in my humanity arsenal, I sing my own rendition of the Irish national anthem that I'll resound moments before I burn Silas alive.

"I will avenge you," I gently whisper, as a light like a halo dawns on the horizon. Her wide hazel eyes flicker in confusion, then settle to an obscure stillness. It is not apparent if she sees anything or if she has indeed now discovered the secret of everything. The one thing I do know is, if it is true that the eyes are the windows to the soul, she feels no more fear. Her chest, having heaved and convulsed violently during the fourth verse, has quietened and relaxed to the pace of a slumbering child. Her once-contorted mouth arches into a smile. And she breathes her last.

Less than a minute later, a giant bear prowls into view; its fur tipped with silver and weighing easily a thousand bags of sugar. The plantigrade stands over three metres tall and takes a few steps forward with a lumber. It throws out its paws and ten curved claws, whips its ears backwards, and unleashes a mighty roar.

I take a breath, not knowing if this is a Hybrid who was born in goo in a chamber somewhere, or a created being, an isolated hunter out in the wild marking its territory or making a name for itself. Regardless, only one of us can be crowned king of this turf, and I predetermine it won't be him.

I don't know if the "Stay Still"-protocol for snakes applies, so I drop to the ground and with expert speed fire three arrows at its legs, two at its body, and one at its head. I fire another three arrows, but their destination obscurus is not worth the speculation. Then I dash for the Maze and root around inside my jacket pockets for my stake.

The beast drops to all fours, and hair brushing back in the light wind, zooms towards me like a cannonball, only onslaught on its mind. Its neck swings frantically and it *clack-clack-clack*s. Come on. Just a little further!

I'm so close to the entrance when the grizzly extends its arm and swipes five thick non-retractile cone claws through my jacket, shirt, and back. It scarcely misses my spinal cord. Agony and force drop me to my knees, but I turn to face the beast and bellow with everything I have got.

My fingers subtly scurry for the largest rock they can find as the monster's pitiless eyes hone in on my head. Going for the kill. I appreciate that. The simplicity. The frankness. The time-management. Too many people are alive today because their persecutors were too fixated on psychological torture rather than just manning up and doing the deed.

My fingers give my brain the head's up: they've grasped a rock. As its teeth move in to chomp, I forward-kick it on the nose. I shove the stone in its mouth, narrowly saving my fingers, and shatter some teeth. The sound makes my very cells cringe. And, knowing that there is no second chance at this, I sink my stake through the roof of its mouth, then jab it under the chin. And, before its limbs can retaliate, I leap into the great unknown of the nocturnal mouth of the Maze, nearly slipping over the blood that jumps from my back with each step.

The back of my shirt, jacket and trousers are soggy with blood. I had hoped it would clot already. Weakness pulls me under.

W.W.J.D.?

Good question: what would Joshua do?

I rummage through his bag and pull out a fire starter, a small ball that feels coarse like sandpaper. I peg it to the ground like he showed me once or twice, for he was never keen on lighting fires except for cooking or, on the coldest nights, preventing death by hypothermia. When the flames are alive and scorching, I remove the backpack, tear off my layers, and withdraw a short sword from my belt. With grave reluctance and an acute awareness of necessity, I heat the blade over the furnace.

Oh, how little I want to do this… I take a deep breath. Then another. And infinitely more. And with each breath, I want to do this even less... Obligatory moment of reconsideration... One... Two... Three... Then I reverse the countdown. I chicken out a few times and have to reheat the blade. I touch the torn folds of skin on my back one last time before possibly making a fatal mistake.

And all Faux-Angoria must hear me scream.

# 24

# NOTHIN' BUT MAMMALS

The banging in the walls was caused by the piping system resonating, I know that. But still, whenever it began and I was on my lonesome, I'd grab my gold-plated Turkish knife and tiptoe through every room, searching under every couch, table, and bed, ready to stick it in an intruder's gut.

And the floorboards didn't creak because someone broke in and inadvertently exposed themselves. It was just one plank of timber rubbing against another. Why then, when the house was deserted and I heard this infernal groan, did I always make a great deal of noise to warn intruders that my kip of a house was not primed for the taking? And why, at those times, did I slam the drawers shut while fixing myself a cup of tea? Was it all just to prove what I already knew? That I was alone? Or because I knew that I never really was? That somehow evil was always watching…?

And if the fridge-freezer and washing-machine always hummed gentle songs to each other when plugged in, why the apprehension when their conversation continued after everyone else had departed? Or worse— when the humming stopped? Why the sudden urge to switch on a show of meaningless chatter, a loud chirpy song, or to read aloud words as I typed them? Why are mundane, banal, irritating, or heartbreaking sounds so much more euphoric than silence? Is it because, as long as we can hear even the most screeching, scratching, or chattering disturbances, we know we aren't dead?

When the doors swung and I was in my house alone, why did I pretend I was chilled with a draft, or concerned with keeping the heat in, and consequently shut every door in the house? I knew no one was there to open—or walk through—them. Or did I, even then, know a deeper and more sinister truth: that we are never truly isolated—even when forced into the throes of isolation? That the prison of observation is ubiquitous? That the ultrasound that shows we've been conceived only widens in scope, scrutiny, and malevolence the older we get? And that safety is an illusion: that if they want us removed from the Chessboard badly enough, nothing will stop them, especially flaking wooden doors with cheap, thin, opaque glass panels?

Or when the neighbours' chats swam on the wind and in through my windows, why did I read chats on social media aloud that I wasn't even part of? Was it to show that a defender of the property was within range? That I was comfortable alone? Or to craft the illusion that there was somebody else with me—when that was the very thing that I didn't want to be true?

If I spoke about something, or read about it online, *ping-ping-ping-ping-ping-ping-ping-ping-ping-ping-ping-ping-ping-ping-ping* would go my H.B. with related advertisements. Some uniformed, coffee-drinking pod person out there was clearly always monitoring and listening in—and not just to 87's goings-on, but to all devices and homes. Why then do we speak "crazy conspiracy theorist" over our lives?

And if every house speaks and goes still; and every tooth-brusher sees faces in the mirror that are there one second and gone the next; and every child sees the demon within open their wardrobe door a crack; and every widow at home alone hears feet walking upstairs; and every person feels an unseen figure's breath on their nape; and every family wonder if, as they watch their shows, they are themselves being watched and livestreamed for someone else's entertainment, then who truly are the mad people?

The certifiably insane who get locked away in the White Room?

Or the ones still making excuses to uphold their autonomous, free agent, alone in the world delusion?

When did I wise up to behave so irrationally? When did we as a species learn to do this? What is it about the dark, the solitude, and the silence that disturbs us so? And how is it that we aren't overcome with such terror every second of the day that we don't curl beneath our beds in the foetal position and cry until we perish and escape it all? What craze overtakes us so forcibly that we fight with everything within us to keep our heads above the water, when that's exactly where all the monsters roam?

It's fear. It's *the* Fear. Faith that the enemy has the power to snuff us out like a flaming candle. Trust that the best-guarded secrets of our pasts will jump out and bite us where it hurts. The hope that the wickedness in our hearts will be met with unrelenting merciless retribution, because deep down, we know we deserve to be punished.

Take my current predicament, for example: exaggerated echoes bounce off all the walls and jutting stones every time my ghosts breathe: *"Don't say a word"*... *"Rise and shine little Luke. (Lucas Mucus)"*... *"SPYDER"*... *You and I are one and the same. We're brothers. We're twins"*... *"Reckoning"*... *"I came to rescue you"*... *"You look beautiful"*... *"I want you to die"* ... *"Please don't leave me in here! Not the White Room! I'll be good! I won't speak anymore!"* ... *"Princess"*...

How do the Triune do it? Poke into the criss-crossed, chicken-wire canals of my memories and pull out these snippets of conversations and one-liners? Well, the truth is, they can't. (Okay, the telepathic Silas can, but he isn't here. He's out there somewhere plotting how he's going to get his body back via carving me like a Christmas turkey). But in the pit of my gut, I know that I'm choosing to think on these things; that my ghosts aren't real, but rather, are figments of my imagination that I created because I'm bored and lonely. Then how are their voices externally projected?

It's fear, the one thing that connects the race of Men: whether an unborn baby in distress, a bullied child, a broken teenager, a going-nowhere adult, a going-somewhere-you're-not-going-to-like old person. It's fear—the opposite of faith, and the dread that what we know exists might also be real.

Consider this cave: haunting though it is—I mean, it's got the cave mouth, stalagmites, stalactites, the classic dripping water, the ghoulish "*woo-o-o-o-o-os*", the smelly skeletons lined up along the walls, naked but for brown tattered cloth—at the end of the day, it's just a cheap film set, comprised of the horror tropes that typically freak people out. Fear-inducing and unsettling, to be sure, but the entire world is inherently artificial. *Kudos* to your production team, Triune. The only thing missing is the rolling stone from that *Indiana Jones* movie.

It's all one great copy that lacks an original. A fully-functioning, breathing machine. An image that itself has eyes. Perception is king.

I dodge all the classic traps: flame-throwers, pits, upright needles, and swishing disc blades until I approach him, squatted next to a roaring, heatless, lilac fire; his owl brown eyes enlarged behind thick goggles, his ginormous shadow grinning on the stone wall behind him. His hair is sleek and combed, unlike the state of mine: dusty, white with dandruff, and overgrown like a bush. The little I see of his skin is browned and sandy, but clear and healthy, too. Over his watermelon tummy, he wears sackcloth and a heavy tan cloak. Jealously, I note that his arms and legs have more meat on them than my whole person, and when I see his finely clipped fingernails, I shamefully hide my long filthy ones deep in my pockets.

Three black narrow exits surround us. It probably makes most sense to take the tunnel that leads straight ahead since it looks the safest, but I'm too world-weary to trust appearances, so I'm against taking the obvious road. After a minute, I still have no immediate preferences, so I decide to just wait awhile for the lightbulb moment.

"Fetch," I nod. I know he's not really there, only a dozen metres from me. And even if he exists, I know he's not real. It's all some great mind trick, an optic illusion caused by dim lighting, shading, a hidden mirror, and the fluctuation in the stability of edges of the object—me—that is reflected in that mirror. … Or an over-active imagination.

"Fancy a beer?" He pulls one of out of nowhere and offers it to me. It smells sickly and sour like cat urine…

"I'd kill for a cup of tea."

"You would and all," he stands to his feet, nearly tipping over with the roundness of his belly, "were the wrong person to stand between you and the kettle." He laughs, and for the first time ever, I feel his breath on my face—soft, warm, and human—which is odd, since our relationship has always been exclusively visual and aural. (Of course, his "breath" is merely wind, a gentle breeze gushing down one of the tunnels. I mean, I'm not crazy).

"You can't be here. This isn't right. That'd be insane."

"That's rich, coming from the guy hunting down three undead old magical men," he retorts cuttingly, and mocks, "and who is destined to fight a rogue Laxciilian that goes by the name of a Bible hero. You ought to be more careful about using labels, Mister White Room." He gurgles a disgusting sound and tries to spit into the fire, but it splashes on my hand; the saliva and a splodge of meat he'd gotten caught in his teeth. I jump back.

I repeat myself, emphasising every syllable. He can be explained away easily enough: the saliva is actually water dripping from the ceiling, and the small ball of meat is probably plaque that came from my mouth. I haven't used a toothbrush in months. There could be a forest of cedars growing in my cavities and I wouldn't have a clue.

"Beej, shut up and let the scene play out," he snaps and, as if by mind-control, we in perfect harmony assume a sitting position. (Obviously, I'm looking in a mirror). And all of a sudden, he's the most congenial guy in the room; the perfect host. "Allow me to introduce you both. Benjamin, this is the Fear," he says, eyeing a lilac blaze with its violet and indigo flickers. "The Incident. SPYDER. The vivid dream of Pocket. The White Room with One Window. The bath. Every misgiving you had before, between and after those seminal moments with your *shamily*, your classmates, and strangers who automatically took a dislike to you. This is your fear in the flesh…ish. He usually appears a little more equine, but he's been split up and flung throughout this faux-land, and now he's, well, this. Take the leap. Say hello."

"We've met. And I'm not saying a word to that thing."

"Enter into what's entered you. It's the only way to conquer the Fear. Stare it in the face. Tell it what happened and what is to come. Prove that you're no longer its slave, held back by condemnation. Show it you're no longer afraid. That you're full of faith and pursuing purpose."

"I am not afraid," I hollowly prophesy, futilely hoping the authenticity of those words will manifest upon their utterance. "Of anything," I say even more weakly.

"If you're not afraid of the Fear, and you're not afraid of the past, and you're not afraid of tomorrow, then why did you try to kill yourself?"

I used to do that a lot. And not always in a bath. When I first decided to end it all, there was no bath. It had been pulled out—and half the floor tiles with it. One, two, three... fifty-eight, fifty-nine, sixty... I thought the citric seashell would do the trick. One, two, three... fifty-eight, fifty-nine, sixty... Since no one could see the shell I'd become. One, two, three... fifty-eight, fifty-nine, sixty... Sea... See... C... One, two, three... ABC... ABC 6-5-1-18 9-20-19-5-12-6... ABC 6-E-1-18 9-20-19-E-12-6... ABC F-5-A-R 9-T-19-5-12-F... ABC F-5-1-R I-T-S-5-L-6... ABC FEAR ITSELF.

"We're not doing this."

"Why?" In fairness to him, he genuinely looks like he cares, for once. Usually, he rams his motor-mouth in my eardrums and shoots people down with bazookas. I prefer that Fetch.

"You see the way you're looking at me right now? That's why we're not doing this."

"Is pity really such a bad thing?"

"Sympathy means you want to relate to my pain, leave me stuck, and keep me company. Compassion means you want to help. Pity means I'm lost. Nothing more than a tragic story. A never-ending train-wreck.

Beyond saving. Beyond hope. But I'm fine. I'll get by. I'm the Chosen One. I don't need pity. I don't need friends. And I definitely don't need to talk to an alter-ego superman my brain created out of loneliness!"

"If not for me, and others like me, you never would have survived. You didn't appreciate the efforts (isolated though they were) that people like me made to save you enough to remember them, so whenever hardship arises, you willingly choose death. Every. Single. Time. I kept you alive on Earth, and you thanked me by trying to off us! You were rescued from trolls and Zj'hakim by Mo-Mo, so you got captured by goblins. The mousey man with the lanky legs died for showing you kindness, yet you waited until *Aid* was upon you before you ran away. Joshua would have given his life for you, but you deserted him."

"That was an impossible situation. It was hectic. Anarchy." But that's no excuse. Leaving him was never far from my prerogative. He meant little more to me than a walking Google Maps. "Do you have a point?"

"Benjamin, it's just us. No one else is here, other than the Fear. Tell it how you feel. You cannot fool Fear. It knows you too well. It is intrinsically impossible for someone who cares as little for life as you to be the Chosen One. When will you end this Resistance-friendly masquerade and embrace your ultimate destiny as the Dark One? Because unless you accept that the darkness is as natural a part of you as back hair, toenails, and defecating, you're going to chase shame, paralysis and guilt until they kill you."

"I'm prolife. ... Don't *Pffft* at me. I'm a Christian. If anyone respects life, it's me." The sentiment sounds deluded even as the words leave my mouth.

"Don't say that like it means something. Fear is your god and pain is your sustenance. You rush to them as vigorously as a dog humps its owner's leg. You played with fire the second you sat down with Blondie and began tea-partying, in full knowledge that if she'd leaked her premonition to the wrong person, you'd have been done for. You only goaded the Elder Elf when he had an audience and could apprehend you for treason."

"You don't know what it's like being me. I was happy. Once. I laughed. Hysterically. I had friends. I joked among strangers. I told stories. I sang. I smiled in my sleep."

"And now you're wasting your life. On fear, pain, and death." Before I can object and thump his pretty face, he enquires about what happened with the bear. That's a good question. "*You had Skylar,* but it didn't even cross your mind to use it. And for goodness sakes, you fed it a stone with your writing hand!"

"Everything happened so fast. And it just appeared. I didn't know how fast it was!"

"It was a bear! You scored A1s—all the time! Surely your cop-on could have told you to... cop on."

"That sentence started off a lot better than it ended."

"You get the gist. Last question: what happened that night in the bath? The last time...?"

"My hand slipped. That's all."

"LIAR! What was your head doing under the water?" Would he just drop it already? I am seconds away from breaking his face. As though he can read my mind, he continues: "You have to face your demons sooner rather than later. It's the only way you're going to be powerful and clear-headed enough to destroy your enemies and replace the current establishment."

"I was trying to feel something! Alright? I never intended to die. I just... Gosh, (it sounds so stupid saying it out loud) I-I-I wanted to... d-d... I wanted to die, so I could be reborn... as someone *new*... someone *else*. Someone with a family who l-l-l—... had never let them down. Someone with friends. Someone without a past that made them feel unclean, like worms incessantly wriggling between their toes, and millipedes constantly crawling up and down their back... Dirty, filthy, evil... But I never meant to kill myself... permanently. Only until a phoenix feeling came, of endings and rebirth."

"That's sick."

"I AM TALKING! I murdered my best friend in cold blood. I picked up a rock and beat his skull with it. I stabbed him in the chest with a stake. And even as I buried him, he was reaching for life! And I got off scot-free. And I have had to live with that. Every day! And I was told never to talk about it. And that's not to mention the six days I spent in the White Room. And alone in that house. Every day. Every summer. Every holiday. Alone. Abandoned. Forgotten. Terrified that any day could be my last day, yet morbidly depressed that the end never came. And where the Hell were you? You, with your pompous superiority rhetoric? Well? Where were you? You're all talk, just that nasty voice in my head that reinforces my hatred of everyone. The sarcastic one, the mean one, the killer. But you know what? You're not superior. You're not better than me. In fact, you're the reason I can look at myself in the mirror and say, that with all my shortcomings and faults, I am a better version of myself than you could ever hope to be. So, you don't get to judge me. You don't get to speak into my life. And you don't get to offer me any advice other than the tunnel I should take to get the bloody well out of here!"

He must know I'm in no mood to play games, for he turns his head left and says, "It's that way." A direction I dislike in general, but from here it looks as though it poses only moderate difficulties. I step into the tunnel faster and with greater eagerness than is probably wise, Fetch yelling in the background, "You know, you could say 'Thank you'!"

And then, whether caused by fever, or an undiagnosed case of schizophrenia, bipolar disorder, severe depression, psychosis, or a brain tumour, every aspect of the hallucination fades: auditory, olfactory, and visual. And I am truly alone.

The corridors are lit by torches. (That's convenient and not scripted at all, I say sarcastically). The route he recommended treats me to three pits, a barricade of thistles and nettles and thorns, paths as thin as those found in Newgrange (getting the bag through is a struggle) and a sliding wall. Not too bad; more of an annoyance than anything. I was expecting spiders. Large spiders. That shoot venom. And even larger rats that talk and lash out with their whip tails and spindly wicked claws.

But, as I learn several hours later, I'm not entirely starved of company... When I come to a corner wall, inhuman shadows snarl, scrape, shove, and bite just around it. The bounce of the echoes up and down the tunnels suggests there are hundreds of beasts congregating there; though, when I'm brave enough to very carefully inch my eyes over the wall, there are only two bipedal dogs. They battle and mate to the tune of cats.

They look somewhat human because my brain's face-specific interpretation systems are working in overdrive to compensate for my loneliness. If there weren't monsters here, my visual processors would forge faces in the fiery torches, the stonework, or the cobwebs. This is the same way that doctors detect early signs of intellectual disabilities in newborns, for healthy babies instinctively look for facial recognition, particularly from their parents. On a cute note, this shows that no man is an island (good catch, John Donne) but also that our species is inherently relational, even if we spend the rest of our lives mauling each other in the fashion of these two uncivilised, mammalian primates. On that note:

One is a male. Clad more in scratches than in the filthy brown cloth that's supposed to cover his genitals; he resembles the hanging skeletons in this respect. Hair like a lion's mane bands his wrists and ankles. His head is all teeth: disfigured, overgrown, out-of-place, sharp. His neck draws forth from what's left of a wolverine's fleece that trails down his back. His dagger nails are the colour of stale vomit. His feet are about two and a half times longer and wider than mine and webbed like those of a duck. The skin has been pulled so tightly I could count his bones if I was stupid enough to get closer. I think I've seen him before in a nightmare, a long time ago.

The female is just as vicious, if not more. Her eyes are bumblebees, her thin streaked eyebrows smoking and crispy like burnt rashers. Her small angular nose is black; every other skin cell on her face is purple. Her hair is an assortment of long wine-brown fingers that move like worms and give her a look of cruel, intense mania. Hollow vines flap and flow from beneath her bear skin dress. She hop-hop-hop-hops, as though on hot irons, on her metre-long tiptoes because she's at least three heads shorter than the male. (Okay, so maybe the dog analogy was loose).

Both Hybrids ooze of sweat, sex, muck, and blood. They lick, eat and slice. After a while, she dies. No, actually, she doesn't die: she's bludgeoned to a pulp and, skull cracked and head drooping, has her heart ripped from her chest cavity. Just another day out in the wild.

And the very instant her cadaver *thud*s to the ground when he disposes of her, all ferociousness leaves the male. Pitiable and twisted though he is, he weeps: "Cat...in ... Cat...ir...in... Cath...rrrinn..." Listening to it is as sick as an ex turning up at a funeral and whining about how they never got to say goodbye or make amends. *You had your chance, hoe, and you blew it.*

Then the dead Hybrid shrivels or metamorphoses. The wine-coloured worm bush shortens and re-colours dark brown. Her snout becomes a big nose. Her exotic bumblebee eyes shrink and become brown, I think. Her bestial face reverts to an adorable one, aged no older than seventeen. And she is very human. I'm guessing her name was Kathryn.

So, what? The Triune is warping humans now? You poor saps just keep giving me reasons to kill you. I can't believe I came here as a pacifist. Joshua was right: there is no talking to these people. Just killing. The cycle never ends. The Tapestry never stops weaving. It can't. And if we take it off the loom, we're dead, and the rotten villains who outlive us will toast and *glug-glug-glug* our blood.

Then, with the speed with which someone flicks a switch, the remaining Hybrid stops sniffling with grief. His nose erects and his nostrils widen and pulsate. He's sniffing my scent.

OMHD, his eyes! In my attempt to avoid looking him in the face, I see the only remotely human part of him—his eyes. And I know them! And his image flashes into my mind, and I realise that he's the same boy Lear had imprisoned. I step out from behind the corner and circumspectly walk towards him. His name forms on my lips when suddenly he bowls me over giddily and claps his hands playfully. It is sick watching an inhuman feign humanity, let alone speak like us: "Enimin... En...jhnn... Ben...jim..."

"Benjamin," I help him out, and the longer I eye him, the better I recall Kenny, the leader of the mutts, saying they were after an escapee prisoner. In my ignorance, I assumed Kenny knew which runaway vagabond he was chasing after, though perhaps not.

The Hybrid hangs out his tongue like he's looking for a treat, and pats the ground, inviting me to sit beside him. I politely decline. It's as if he's forgotten Kathryn's dead the way he lifts her corpse and "Goochy-goochy-goos" her, before flinging her away like a ragdoll to make space for me. Alright then. I sit awkwardly, keeping my legs tucked tightly to my person, and my hands elbow-deep in Joshua's bag of tricks should I need at a second's notice to employ one. Having never been a good conversation starter, I skip the greetings and dive straight into the heavy stuff.

"What did they do to you?"

He points to himself. "Fay...duh... Fay...eld... Spear...mint... Fay...eld... kks... spare...ih...mint..." I assume he's saying "Failed experiment." Even if he isn't, I nod anyway, as over-enthusiastically as when one speaks to a non-native who struggles to string a sentence together and butchers the language of the land, but somehow comes out with an array of syllables that are overall semi-coherent. The Hybrid indicates to his half-eaten lady friend: "T' hulp... muh... breed..." I think of the vines that were beneath Hybrid-Kathryn's dress. Ew.

I don't want to accuse him of anything indecent because he looks temperamental, so I say cautiously, "Did it work?"

"No." He looks sad, and then makes a Ro-ro sound for a while. At first, I think he's barking or singing "Row, row, row you boat", but when I compile all his sounds together, I think he's saying that in the event of failure, he was programmed to kill her.

He noses at me curiously, which I find as disgusting as a pet eating off its owner's plate, and try to hide my disdain through further interrogation: "How did you escape?" I don't want him to know that I knew Lear had him but that saving him hadn't crossed my mind once, so I add, "The Resistance informed me that Lear had you." That's kind of true.

He says Silas found him in Lear's dungeon and let him go—just further proof that the Triune are not of one accord. I don't want to pry, but all it takes is a gentle prod for him to say:

"Mmmh... naught... Sch...oh...zen... On... Tt...Try...oon... ee... need... you..."

*"I'm not the Chosen One. The Triune need you."* "For what?"

"Ev... ree... theen..." *For example?* "Bawdeees... And... armeee..."

*"Bodies."* I knew that. "And I contribute to the building of their army, how?"

"Pow...ruh... in... da... blood..." So I keep hearing. "Hi... brrrd... Maxssss... ih... mussss..." The Hybrid Maximus. What Gregory Saint Germaine—with an E at the end of Germaine wanted to build, basically? An organic machine sufficiently powered to erase all Triumvirs!

He wants to elaborate. The struggle is real. But the beast takes over. And before me, I see whatever humanity the sadness of Kathryn's death awoke wear off, and the predatory curse surges through him again. And I tell my feral neighbour that it's not personal, and that for as little as it's worth, I am sorry. And before he can swipe me with those claws, I put my hands either side of his neck, and twist until it cracks. Now if he's anything like half the supernatural creatures featured on the H.B., he should be grand, and his neck should snap back into position in half an hour or so.

Then I run in a straight line that leads gradually uphill and out into open air. No sooner have I reached it than the white light of day blinds me, like I'm some subterranean nocturnal fiend. Vision returns to me little by little, and the first thing I make out is that I'm standing on a stony mountain littered with tufts of green grass.

And from above the mouth of the cave, a harsh familiar voice roars at me. I shield my eyes with my fingers like a thorn bush and squint through them. I see a coated figure jump from on-high and land metres before me with the precision of a feline. I try to speak, but I'm choking on fresh air. I didn't even think about how I survived this long without it. Like, was oxygen pumping through the walls while we lab rats scurried around in there?

But who cares what kept me breathing? The fact of the matter is: I still am. I survived. All on my own. Sure, I killed Bambi's mother which I will never speak of again. But who cares? I'm alive. I drop his bag, tear off his green coat and toss it to him, then cock my head.

"Hey, boss. Welcome to my graduation."

I run to him, ready to give him a bear-hug and apologise for being such a head-wrecker, judging him at every turn. I'll tell them that I get it now. That I understand why he's the way he is. He does what needs to be done in order to survive. And I know his name! Yes, I read his diary, and I know that crosses lines, but I needed to know who I had on my team. And I'll tell him that my name is Joshua too! And then I'll examine his reaction and see if it means anything more than that he and Nuala had a crush on one another.

My arms are seconds from closing in when he shrugs me off and retracts a step or two. There is a look of disgust in his eyes at finding me alive, and in his tone.

I pretend I'm unexcited to see him. That was no attempt to hug; I was stretching. I cough lightly. "How did you find me?"

"I know how you think."

"No one knows how I think. I'm personality-type INFJ, like Atticus Finch and Adolf Hitler, but other than that, nada."

"You drew attention to yourself. A lot."

"Well, I am the Chosen One. I insist on a certain amount of commotion."

"You entered dozens of villages and towns, even after I warned you not to. You got them all killed." My blood boils at this heart attack. I've been a homeless vagabond, sleeping in bushes and holes, wasting away, and here he is condemning me. Who does he think he is?

"I showed them more grace and compassion than they had received in three hundred years." Ugh! He's ruining the moment! It wasn't supposed to be like this!

"'Compassion', you say? I was unaware you were familiar with the concept. I figured you were just something of a Duchess; that it was all for show." What? I have never used that word around him. He lifts my journal out of his pocket and fires it at me.

"Did you read it?" I don't need to ask. I also don't need to reintroduce myself or tell him my connection to Nuala.

"You read mine, surely." My mouth hangs open, angry and dumb. He smirks. "Did you read something you found particularly illuminating?" His suggestion is obvious, and irksome.

"If you are referring to your poetry, then no. I am not so asexual that you explained to me any mechanics or operations that the wide array of perverse twenty-first-century H.B. channels may have overlooked. That said, I'd still stamp a PG-18 sticker on the front cover."

"Alright," he says.

Then I say "Okay."

He okay's.

And we leave it at that.

And then an overly stretched, ferocious-looking man making ghoulish noises appears in the mouth of the cave. He's hunchbacked under the weight of a long thick silver beard. I see only one large eye; the other's either covered by his hair or has been torn out. A short red robe, almost entirely faded of colour, circles his waist and reaches down to his knees. His face is deformed, and his bones are brittle. He leans on a walking stick. Shock prevents me from immediately offering him help. How long had he been down there, and what did he survive on?

He throws his stick at the Watcher. No. Wait. It's a spear!

I back-fist Joshua to the ground. The spear whizzes past where he had been. Instinctively I whip my stake from my jacket and boomerang it through Old Man's shoulder. He falls to his knees. My mentor gets to his feet, leaps behind Old Man, and wraps a chord around his throat.

"Oh, my gosh! He's an old man! What is your problem?"

"You said I was not a good man."

*Huh? When? Did I say that in the Savage Block?* Oh, please. He hasn't honestly been stewing over that all this time?!

On second thought: why shouldn't he have taken offence? I had never thought of it before now, not even when I read his journal, but maybe he has an inner self, too.

"Well, let me tell you something, General of Good"—oh, cringe! I did call myself that, didn't I?— "Good men do not win wars."

*Then why are you following me?* I'm too afraid to ask. Then he tests me; orders me to kill Old Man. He knows I won't. So he slits the geezer's throat in front of me and walks ahead.

When I am unmoved, frozen in fear, bitterness, and disappointment, he barks, "General, follow!" Behind these two words is so much mockery, hatred, and venom that I'm tempted to lie prostrate at his feet, kiss his boots, and beg to again be called princess.

# TEASER
# PARLAY

*Silas laughs evilly and stretches out his arms. Reality becomes a series of blocks. At this, Lear's eyes bulge and he vibrates with horror as though he's been tasered.*

*"Brother!" shouts Lear. "What are you doing, man? You will weaken the Collective!"*

*"Buying us the time we need to get the Stone!"*

*I sprint in Lear's direction. He's still shaken by Silas's carelessness. I whisper in his ear, "When you're strong again, and we're both alone, come find me. Let's talk."*

"I had begun to think you'd stood me up. A Triumvir could feel neglected," I say.

"Running the world, particularly after a seismic shift like the one Brother Silas caused, takes a lot out of even the best of us—especially when you are pretty much dead to begin with." Lear walks up from behind me, wine glass in hand—not that he can even drink, being a spirit. I'm not sure how he even holds it. Maybe he's controlling the metals in the wine. "Added to that, my servants keep betraying me. They sell out to the highest bidder: Resistance personnel; board members of the Triune's hand-selected External Affairs Committee; senselessly ambitious heads of departments; and factions who are convinced that Gideon will rise again and usurp us. It's a tough economy out there!"

"Preach it. I hear you."

"Not to mention the fact that you did not seem yourself for quite some time after that encounter. Whenever I looked into my crystal balls or

*Radharc* to leer into your activities, to put it frankly, you looked mad."

"So far as I know, there's a law against using the word 'leer' when that's your name."

"All of a sudden, I realise why. Consider it omitted from my vocabulary."

"What was up with that broadcast in the sky earlier tonight—the one with the stone slab? Forgive my ignorance, but I'm not sure I understood it."

"Ah, yes... Althrodùr! It used to reside in the Kingdom of Breathing Stone back in the day. Before the Maze, it was the traditional throne on which the Fates sat when they would come to Angoria. It symbolised the long-established customs of the Higher Orders: Good versus Evil; fairness, freedom, and fraternity; that we all had a preordained destiny to which we were enslaved; and that there's a castle in the sky for good kings and lords. But the Elohim have been significantly less active since my brothers and I created this world. I do not even believe they are still there. In taking the Ancient Stone, we declared that we have the power now—irrespective of lies you have been feeding the prisoners through your mind games!"

"The Stone the goblins and orcs were carrying on the wagon..."

"Yes," he says matter-of-factly. "The Resistance had hidden it away in a backwater community. None remain. The simians made sure of that. The footage is about a week old, but we're broadcasting it tomorrow in the skies. Mind games, and all that."

Speaking of mind games, as I look around, I see that we're standing on a blank canvas. I imagine us atop a cliff somewhere with golden deserts swimming as far as the horizon at sunset—and suddenly, that's exactly where we are.

Then the Statue of Liberty appears behind me. Her torch is an ice-cream cone. It drips all over me.

I do myself a favour and send her packing, because that was embarrassing. She travels by ferry. It becomes a spaceship and she's gone. Then the spaceship freezes and becomes a thousand-eyed arachnid; a spider who's watched every moment of my life up to this point yet seen nothing.

"I appreciate that this is probably one of the weirder trances you've been drafted into. I didn't realise just how much creative licence I actually had in these or how even stray subliminal thoughts can affect the visual. I'll try to focus better."

He glares at it with contempt. "Needless to say, Dark One, this is one conference call I never foresaw you making nor me answering."

"I told you we'd hook up and I keep my word so long as it suits me. And for some reason, you strike me as the most reasonable of my adversaries in my ever-expanding rogues gallery."

"I doubt Cillian Joshua Axebreaker is best pleased with this."

"That douche is never happy. He hasn't spoken to me in three days inclusive because, apparently, I hurt his precious snowflake feelings the day you and I last fought. So tonight I went against my better judgement and took advantage of Angoria's drinking age—fifteen's legal, right?—and I drank that stone-drunk rummy under the table. He won't interrupt us."

"And what do you wish to discuss?"

"A parlay."

"Let me save you the trouble of making offers I will laughingly decline."

"Lear—Can I call you 'Lear'? Hey, you've tried to kill me! I'm going to call you Lear—"

"I wanted you neutralised. I intend to kill you later."

I put my finger to my lip and shush him. "It has become very clear to me that you men don't know what you want. You see me as a threat to all life in Angoria, Silas sees me as the Saviour, and I don't have a bull's notion who the other one of you three is or what he hopes to get out of my death"—I really need to write that third guy's name down next time someone says it. "But, from one perceived villain to another, I think you and I could do wonderful things together."

"The Triune are not *Men*. We are more than you can possibly conceive!"

He's deflecting. Things between them must be more divided than I'd realised. Then I'll respond with a show of strength: "As am I."

"Oh, I know. That is why you fascinate me! I do not think you understand just how terminal and malignant you are to the Great Tapestry! Mósandrirl and Joshua never told you where you came from, did they?"

"Tell me," I say. He shakes his head. I press him a little more, but his lips are sealed. "Joshua mutters in his sleep. We're en-route to a mountain where dwarves and elves live in peace. We'll be there within a month. He's all yours."

Clearly, he doesn't take much convincing because he immediately turns to the setting sun on the horizon and the image changes to a cavern teeming with glowing blue-hued shards jutting from the rocks. Within the vastness of the cave appear the apparitions of a shadowy masked figure on the right; a stylised crowned eyeball with angel wings atop its eyelid on the left; a rhombus beneath them; and a fiery cruel face above them. Lear says they represent the Mex Confetricus, the Pretender, the Lady of Light, and Skylar. They are all joined in the centre by a cross of chains.

"Shall we speak freely?" he asks. His eyes are on me, but he nods to the vision.

"Cross my heart and hope to die."

He explains: "Contrary to popular belief, many Fates fell from grace long before Gideon. After the Void slipped into our realm, it seduced a number of their party into sin. Giving themselves over to evil entirely, the wicked Fates threatened to annihilate the World Above, and if successful, all life below. There was war in the heavenly realms for some time before the Dark Angels—as they became known—were finally stopped and permanently shut out of the Highest Place. This was to make the lives of Those Above simpler.

"But unperturbed, the Void then set its sights on the one you call Gideon. Persuaded by its offer of power, wealth, and immortality, Gideon became one with the Void and allied with the fallen Dark Angels to amass a terrible army. The lesser beings that walk the earth would come to mimic the foulness which had been demonstrated to them by their gods, and the world was lost to chaos.

"Meanwhile, a few pragmatic, but controversial, Fates hand-selected lesser beings from your world and Angoria to solve the problem—somehow that made sense to them! They lulled the Beast to Blue Crystal Cave."

"The first Dark Lord," I assume— "Gideon."

"Not only Gideon, but all the Dark Lords, even those who had not been born yet: the Leviathan, Warlord Kahn, the Imp whose name has been lost to time, Caligula, and—I bet my hat—you. The Fates bled Gideon to near-dryness and cursed his blood, and then infused it within each of the Dark Ones. There they determined that as it is with wizards, so shall it be with all magical creatures and creatures born of magic: that the power would be in the blood. The Prophet-Scribe, K'k'ko Zset documented this decision in the Book of Life, and it became so.

"The Darkness—you know it as the Void—violated these men and Great Animals in the cave until their every thought was wicked and their every hope of finding true happiness was lost. Then the Fates returned the Dark Ones to their respective timelines and set Gideon free. They loosed him upon the world to fulfil his cruel agenda—terror!

"The Fates also led the first Chosen One to Blue Crystal Cave, and not only the first Chosen One, but all Chosen Ones. What's more, they also summoned the First through Eleventh Age's Chosen Ones' replacements, for were one to fall, another could be called upon to fight the good fight. There they bound all the Chosen Ones with steel chains and imbued them with the blood of Gideon. The Darkness made sweet love to them as it warped and darkened their souls: their wills, minds, and emotions.

"And then, as quickly as it began, it was done. And the Fates returned the Chosen Ones to their respective timelines but sent forth the first Chosen One to kill Gideon. So it has always been: the Chosen One walks in darkness, ashamed of the light for it blinds him. He harms himself for he is dirty and unclean—and he knows it; an empty rat sent out to rid the world of filth by devouring its moral carcasses. He sleeps comfortably on a bed of bones. Loneliness brings him solace. He is in the world, but he is not of the world. He receives its hatred and returns its hatred to the vile things it is unequipped to confront. He overcomes evil with evil for the source of his power is evil, and he bullwhips evil until he is spent. He dies every day, finds life in the kill, and in the fullness of preordained time, he welcomes Death when Death cradles him in his multiple arms.

"When an Age reaches its end, the pernes and gyres rotate, leading the primordial energies that birthed the Chosen One who died—for all Chosen Ones die, within or with-out—to forge a new model, and a new Dark Lord. And the cycle begins afresh. The Tapestry never stops weaving.

"For finality is an illusion and immortality a curse. Life is sweet as strawberries, and it does Man's heart good to see the sun. Every day is a gift and should be appreciated so. But remember the days of darkness, for they are many, and when they come, they render all else meaningless. In the end, all that remains is Eternity, a long stretch of graveyard made of Time and tombstones. The Tapestry never stops weaving.

"At least, that is the lie. The truth is the Fates never intended for Angoria to outlive its Twelfth Age. No one wants to live forever, not really—not even the Creators—and was even such a thing permitted, annihilation would prove the inevitable climax. Thus, they decreed that the Chosen One and the Dark One would do battle one last time, now deceived by the enigmatic Pretender whose identity shall not be disclosed until the appointed time. He, too, was lured to Blue Crystal Cave and

589

imbued with the Darkness. And the Triumvirate will battle one last time where one will fall, one will die, and one will rise. Only then will the cycle be broken and the end come. Only when the optimum measurement of blood has been spilled will peace be made available—after all, love is sacrifice, and grace is death. Only then will the Tapestry stop weaving.

"There was one other who was lured to Blue Crystal Cave: a beautiful Elven maiden, blossoming and unspoiled. Already filled with light, for she had not known evil or bloodshed, the Fates drew forth her evanescent essence and harnessed its power within a diamond-shaped shard of the crystal star under which she was born. The Fates molested the virgin twelve times and dismembered her in twelve places to reflect the twelve molestations of Lady Angoria by the masculine threat, which in the Fates' tongue is 'Mex Confetricus', or 'Dark Lord'. In a crass dispersal, the Fates flung her remains throughout Angoria, and wherever the pieces of her person rested, there, it was foretold, an Age of Angoria would end. The last of her remains—her right foot—landed at The Gallows. Thus, that will be site of the last battle.

"Then the malevolent Fates who had initiated these abductions, murders, and cultivated the damned Dual Cycles and the climactic Triumvir Cycle were reprimanded by the Higher Orders and stripped of their bodies, for their unnatural spells lay outside the parameters delineated at the Angorian Convention of Acceptable Magical Practices at the dawn of the First Age, an agreement to which all magic-users are bound. The equine-featured Fear was one of those Fates; now it is but a wayward spirit. Most of its co-conspirators, however, have been locked away in deepest darkness.

"That is why you are here, Dark One. You are a means to an end— to *the* End! It is by no fault of your own. It is just your lot in life. But by killing you all, I prevent the unfolding of the prophecy and save the world. Your death by my hand will have nothing to do with personal grudges—only love for my world, disobedient, prone to rebellion, and suicidal, though it is."

"You baffle me, Lear. How could you feel anything other than contempt for the Angorians? The Laxciilians are selfish to the core and invent oppressions and enemies to justify leaving the rest of the world to perish. The poor sods who get help rebel against you. And the wisest among them can't tell the difference between heroes and foes—they're thick in the head! It is my earnest belief that the wilfully ignorant ought to be impoverished and exploited."

Lear laughs and says that under any other circumstances, we could probably have been friends. "Dark One, if it is not too impertinent of me to acknowledge, it is not only the captives who are peculiar—you are also a little off. You usually adapt to your role sooner than this. Your adjustment has been askew somehow."

"Maybe I'm not the Dark One," I smirk.

Lear thinks this is hilarious: "Oh please! Brother Silas could smell the sweet, citric fragrance of your inner animosity when he was still several countries away from Andronicus's jungle, despite believing that you were the goody. And from what my spies tell me, I suspect even Mósandrirl no longer believes you are the incorruptible saviour, and he is the best friend of humanity! Perhaps your black soul has a case of hypogonadism, or maybe hypopituitarism; that would explain why you are a lot shorter than your predecessors, and why you exercise such perverse masculinity. Or maybe you are just consuming too much soy!" he cackles, thinking himself hilarious.

591

"Speaking of perversions and consummation, was the hybridisation of those two kids really necessary? I mean, what is your teenage trauma?"

"Oh, you should concern yourself less with my trauma, and instead turn your attentions to Angoria's newest one, for the short time her people have remaining," he says more nastily. "I have long desired to create the ultimate beast to carry out my will in governing the Blocks—and ridding the world of its inferior races! The creative-destructive power in your blood can help me corporealise and is instrumental to my new creature's origination. Consider the Hybrids a mere prototype of better things to come!"

The Beast's blood has made every Dark Lord and Saviour for millennia, so it only makes sense that this para-scientist believes the Dark One's blood could form the ultimate warrior to enforce his utopia's rules.

"Let me guess: that's why you're holding the First Vampire in a cell?"

He nods, completely unsurprised that I know that.

"The Maze will soon witness the genesis of the Hybrid Maximus Contagion! A self-replicating warrior! A weapon of mass destruction! It will answer my every beck and call and fight all the battles I cannot be bothered with, but that my position demands are dealt with. I could liberate anyone I deem an ally from bondage. I could prevent wars from happening or win them before I reach the battlefield. I could see to it that my enemies' throats are slit without ever requiring a napkin to wipe away the blood—I do hate resorting to violence, you know. I could turn a town into a refugee camp in half an hour or eradicate a large cosmopolitan city in a day. All I need is to drain most of your blood, which I will."

"Yes, you will, because I permit it, for I believe you're fighting for what you think is best. All I ask is that you wait. You'll know when it's okay. I won't resist."

"How unlike every other archvillain of the Ages you are, in some ways! And yet, in other ways you are similar: you welcome death."

"Life's too short to want to live forever."

"And what do you want in return?"

"When it matters most, I want you to punch a hole in the belly of the brother or nephew you deem most dispensable."

"Your conditions are tame. I suspect you have not had a lot of practice in diplomacy. Understandable, of course—your teacher is best known for his rashness and aggression; not his wise word choice."

"One more thing: I need the Witch of Angoria. The Grin (or whatever you call him) is blackmailing me. Her head helps me keep mine."

"Everyone who is anyone in Angoria would pay a hefty price for the shrew, but surely I handed her to you already—not for his sake, mind you, but because I trusted that she would worm her way into your heart, and that you'd keep her safe. We never did not know you were in Loux Laxciila, and surely, so was she—hidden in plain sight! The Witch is a skin-shedding snake and so chronic a liar she convinces herself of her falsehoods! Undoubtedly, she is just as rotten to the core as the Dark Lord, hence, her incessant attraction to whoever holds the title. Deep cries out to deep, if you will. She always has her eyes on power, and she goes where the power is."

"You could have been released from your prison three hundred years ago had you just told the Grin where she was."

"I intentionally hid her away in the safest place in Angoria. She is the mother of my son—the Wizard of Time; a secret we had only ever shared with Mósandrirl until right now."

Mósandrirl once said that people suspected there were two Lears—if Lear Junior takes after this moron, I can see where the confusion set in.

"I'll keep your secret. No harm will come to him."

He nods in appreciation, and then looks at me curiously. "Are you sure you did not know her? She is charming, beautiful, and has high notions of herself. And though she often changes her name to conceal her identity from those who would burn her at the stake, it nearly always begins with an A." OMHD! NO WAY! "Now while I have no love for the slag these days, I feel bound to promises I have made her, and I require you to make a marvellously tempting offer if you want me to orchestrate her demise to save your oily skin—until you surrender yourself to me willingly."

They all flash before my mind: the evil Laxciilians; the kind but, I now suspect, deceptively secretive Elder Wizard; the vile Elder Elf; the horrid Alk'erion; the people who've rejected my help; the callous Joshua; and Aurora the Witch, apparently! And I consider the fate they all deserve...

"Alright. Let's get down to the nitty-gritty then; the real reason I called you here... You were right all along—for longer than I knew. I am the Harbinger of Darkness. During my months-long ruse in Laxciila, I systematically tore their Royal Family—and the entire Resistance—apart, finding them unworthy to inherit the earth. But after I've played my part in the Triumvirate Cycle, I believe you have what it takes to jumpstart a

Thirteenth Age; to manufacture a world I'd be proud of. You've already recreated space. With your son's help, surely you can rewrite time, as well. And screw any prophecy that tells you it's impossible. Hence, Liriondias, on behalf of the Resistance that I still bombastically represent, I've come to negotiate a surrender!"

## TO BE CONTINUED

# ABOUT THE AUTHOR

Brendan Thomas Marrett has been writing fiction since before he knew there was a difference between "their", "they're", and "there". After karate class, he would stare at the carpet and imagine each of its strands was an orc or dragon that needed to be bested by a miniature assemblage of heroes. The stories he wrote then, aged seven, prepared the foundation for the tales of Angoria.

The idea for Angoria, Gideon, and the Triune came to him one day in Madrid, where he went holidaying the morning after his debs. Between switching on a kettle and the water being boiled, the entire first arc of *The Triumvirate Saga* had been downloaded in his brain. The character of Benjamin promptly wrote himself, and the interconnected histories of the characters and worlds flowed organically thereafter.

Brendan is an E.S.L. teacher. He has a fiction addiction; sports a black belt in karate; digs superheroes; is obsessed with weapons; and has never encountered a problem that couldn't be solved over a nice cup of tea!

Follow him on Facebook, Twitter, Instagram, and YouTube, and catch the podcast he co-hosts, *From Dublin to Cleveland.*